Polygamy in Primetime

BRANDEIS SERIES ON GENDER, CULTURE, RELIGION, AND LAW

Series editors: Lisa Fishbayn Joffe and Sylvia Neil

This series focuses on the conflict between women's claims to gender equality and legal norms justified in terms of religious and cultural traditions. It seeks work that develops new theoretical tools for conceptualizing feminist projects for transforming the interpretation and justification of religious law, examines the interaction or application of civil law or remedies to gender issues in a religious context, and engages in analysis of conflicts over gender and culture/religion in a particular religious legal tradition, cultural community, or nation. Created under the auspices of the Hadassah-Brandeis Institute in conjunction with its Project on Gender, Culture, Religion, and the Law, this series emphasizes cross-cultural and interdisciplinary scholarship concerning Judaism, Islam, Christianity, and other religious traditions.

Polygamy in Primetime

MEDIA, GENDER, AND POLITICS IN MORMON FUNDAMENTALISM

Janet Bennion

BRANDEIS UNIVERSITY PRESS

Waltham, Massachusetts

Brandeis University Press
An imprint of University Press of New England
www.upne.com
© 2012 Brandeis University
All rights reserved
Manufactured in the United States of America
Designed by Vicki Kuskowski
Typeset in Fairfield by Copperline Book Services, Inc.

University Press of New England is a member of the Green Press Initiative.
The paper used in this book meets their minimum requirement for recycled paper.

For permission to reproduce any of the material in this book,
contact Permissions, University Press of New England, One Court Street,
Suite 250, Lebanon NH 03766; or visit www.upne.com

Portions of this work were previously published in somewhat different form, and are used by permission of the respective publishers:

"History, Culture, and Variability of Mormon Schismatic Groups" and "The Many Faces of Polygamy: An Analysis of the Variabiliy in Modern Mormon Fundamentalism in the Intermountain West," in *Modern Polygamy in the United States: Historical, Cultural, and Legal Issues Surrounding the Raid on the FLDS in Texas,* edited by Cardell Jacobson (New York: Oxford University Press, 2011), 101–124 and 163–184.

"Mormon Women in the 21st Century: A Critical Analysis of O'Dea's Work," in *Revisiting Thomas F. O'Dea's* The Mormons: *Contemporary Perspectives,* edited by Cardell K. Jacobson, John P. Hoffman, and Tim B. Heaton (Salt Lake City: University of Utah Press, 2008), 136–170.

Evaluating the Effects of Polygamy on Women and Children in Four North American Mormon Fundamentalist Groups (New York: Edwin Mellen Press, 2008).

Women of Principle: Female Networking in Contemporary Mormon Polygamy (Oxford: Oxford University Press, 1998).

Library of Congress Cataloging-in-Publication Data
Bennion, Janet, 1964–
Polygamy in primetime: media, gender, and politics in Mormon fundamentalism /
Janet Bennion.
        pages cm.—(Brandeis series on gender, culture, religion, and law)
Includes bibliographical references and index.
ISBN 978-1-61168-262-5 (cloth: alk. paper)—ISBN 978-1-61168-263-2
(pbk.: alk. paper)—ISBN 978-1-61168-296-0 (ebook)
1. Polygamy.   2. Mormon fundamentalism.   3. Mormon women—Social
conditions.   I. Title.
HQ994.B46 2012
306.84'230882893—dc23   2011049316

5 4 3 2 1

Contents

Preface

"Jill Mormon" Autoethnography

I sat watching Season 5 of HBO's *Big Love* with my husband the other night and began shouting at him, waving my arms about.

"What is it, my dear?" said my ever-calm, non-Mormon life companion.

I squawked that Barb, the first wife of Bill Henrickson, had just demanded the right to hold the priesthood alongside her husband and he had abruptly told her, "No way!"

"So?" replied my husband, not realizing that this was the worst thing he could have said to me. How could my Native American hubby understand the heart-wrenching battles I and other liberal Mormon women have fought? How could he understand my efforts to show the full picture of women's lives in Mormonism, as a fringe LDS, feminist anthropologist? Yet somehow, beautiful Barb, played by actress Jeanne Tripplehorn, understood me. I entered her world and, like "Barb," took Bill's refusal *very* personally, forgetting that the show is supposed to be fiction. It was an extreme, bizarre case of an anthropologist "going native" with a television personality.

How is it that this prime-time drama about polygamy could so perfectly depict the nature of the gender and political battles we face in Mormon Country? How could it portray the narratives of marginalization many of us experienced during the famous Purges of the 90s so accurately?[1] How could the writers, two gay men, generate, in five poignant seasons, the most blatant critique of the LDS Proclamation of the Family ever televised in the context of a program whose main tenet is that polygamy is "A-OK"?

Big Love has become a symbol to me, to my key informants who live in polygamy, and to the larger U.S. television public of the new American sexual revolution—a revolution that is focused on *alternative* marriage and family. This symbol provides a global display of the struggles of a fundamentalist minority to overcome marginalization at the hands of the monogamous mainstream. It has become a sublime witness of my twenty years as an ethnographer, during which I tried to analyze the variability in polygamous lifestyle and at the same time fight to decriminalize plural marriage.

I have been "blessed," as they say in Mormon culture, to have begun my fieldwork at a time of fundamentalist *glasnost,* when a few select journalists and scholars were allowed to visit polygamy compounds and towns. I was lucky to have selected such a complex and truly interesting topic (or did it select me?), one that paved the way for my status as a tenured full professor. Yet the costs of this research have been innumerable. I offended and alienated my church leadership, my friends and family, and my first husband (living with polygamists is *not* good for a healthy marriage!). I was sometimes at risk of arrest because of contempt of court charges for refusing to divulge the identity of my informants, who were, after all, guilty of third-degree felonies as well as other crimes (illegal arms possession, statutory rape, and so on). I may have put my daughters' emotional and physical well-being at risk, having carted them to and from fundamentalist households during my intense three-year field studies, during which I relied heavily on herbal home remedies rather than a doctor's care. I also risked the danger of compromising my ability to conduct research in certain groups by disobeying a patriarch's orders (I saved a child's life by taking her to the hospital against his wishes) and participating in courtship correspondence with two other wives (who believed that I might marry their husband, though I rebuffed their overtures). At one point, as a young doctoral researcher in my twenties, I felt myself truly going native, beginning to believe in the fundamentalist ideologies and customs. So I left the group for a season, fleeing to Oregon to meet with other hippy Mormon career moms, cut my long hair into a bob, and returned to find that my informants treated me with some disdain (only long-haired women can wash the feet of Christ when He returns).

I was hindered in my fieldwork because of my informants' deep-seated fears of arrest, so I could not use tape recorder or a notebook. I had to rely on my own memory to account for all that was said and done, translating these memory-scribbles into descriptive prose and coded patterns at the end of a long day. Was there bias in the decisions I made about which conversations to record and which I should leave out? Most definitely. Yet I tried to temper this emic bias by stepping back to see the larger picture of legal and political dynamics in the compound. I followed Pierre Bourdieu's guide on reflexive ethnography (having learned of this methodology when I taught at the University of California Santa Cruz among other postmodernists). I also mimicked Weber's process of interpretive ethnographic *verstehen.*[2] Yet all the while I recognized the dangers of ethno-methodological immersion as a potential risk in the scientific process. Could I have used any other methodology? As a feminist Mormon with polygamous ancestry, I entered my research with a deep-seated belief in feminine empowerment and a contempt for abusive male dominance. But what I failed to realize was that fundamentalist women offered a new breed of feminism that made perfect sense to them within a rigid patriarchal context. In short, it was because of my intimacy with the subjects and their cause that I was able to achieve naturalistic, situational accuracy in my data and a more complete knowledge about the intricacies of plural marriage.

My very first ethnographic research was conducted twenty years ago in one of the coldest places on earth, the Montana Bitterroot Mountains.[3] My goal was to complete my Portland State master's degree in anthropology on the subject of women's attraction to fundamentalism. I was drawn to the concept of economic communalism and was curious about the polygamous experiments of my own ancestors, who drove out the Ute Indians of the Wasatch Range in Utah to carve out a pioneer life for themselves and their many wives. In 1988, I wrote a formal letter to the elderly, gregarious prophet of the Allredites, Owen Allred, who inherited the post from his murdered brother Rulon, telling him about my relationship to George Q. Cannon to gain rapport with the old fellow. In a spirit of openness, Allred invited me to investigate the lifestyles of women in their remote polygamous colony in Pinesdale, Montana, ten miles northwest of Hamilton. The colony is tucked in the pines of the eastern slope of the Bitterroots, bordered on the south by the Salmon River. The only hitch in the plan was that he neglected to tell the priesthood leaders of my impending arrival in the steel-cold winter of 1989. When I showed up in the town in Pinesdale with my cranky, colicky eighteen-month infant; a carload of food supplies; my brand-new K-Pro word processor (top of the line!); and a pair of cross-country skis from the thrift store, there was some confusion as to what they should do with me. I was taken by one of the top patriarchs, Marvin Jessop, to meet his wife Sharon, who was recovering from a hysterectomy after having birthed thirteen children. She would "check me out" and determine whether I was worthy to be welcomed into the group. She was a practicing phrenologist, a feminist of sorts, and the first of his three wives. She felt the bumps on my head, prayed for a time, and pronounced me spiritually fit to enter the order, placing me with her sister wife, Marvin's third wife, "Mary Ann." Mary Ann's place was a bit crowded because she was caring for her own children plus Sharon's kids in the west wing of a modular-style three-bedroom duplex. That winter Mary Ann taught me how to survive in the Bitterroots. She showed me how to heat a house with an oil-barrel stove, grind wheat, shop on a budget, can fruit, bake a true Swedish pancake, and care for twelve children—all on about $76 a month. She wasn't alone in her efforts. Her co-wives and other women from the community all pitched in to provide her with wheat to grind and honey for oatmeal in the mornings, among other gifts. Dixie, the mayor's wife, traded honey for canned peaches, and June, the midwife, assisted in the births of her babies.

That first season of fieldwork led to two more decades of work. I published two ethnographies on polygamous lifestyles: one about the Allred Group of Montana entitled *Women of Principle: Female Networking in Contemporary Mormon Polygamy* (1998) and one about the LeBaron polygamous colony in Chihuahua, Mexico, entitled *Desert Patriarchy* (2004). I have also published articles on polygamy in 1992, 1996, 2007, 2008, and 2011.

Why Did I Choose Polygamy?

As a researcher, I am a strange bird. Like Barbara Myerhoff in *Number Our Days* (1978), I conduct reflexive autoethnographic analysis, searching for answers about human behavior among my own people. I have polygamous ancestry in three of my four grandparents' lines: the Bennions, the Cannons, and the Bensons. Yet I have not adopted the practice, nor do I ever intend to in my lifetime.[4] My Vermont-raised, skeptical, young adult daughters certainly do not see it as a possibility for their future.

As a product of pioneer stock, I was taught that my ancestors who crossed the Plains and helped build Zion were valiant, courageous Saints who handed down a legacy that I should be proud of. Yet where I was raised, in the insular Mormon community of Vernon, nestled between the lower Wasatch Range and the Sheeprock Mountains in western Utah, polygamy was actually banned. Though it was considered highly inappropriate, my great-grandfathers, Israel Bennion and George M. Cannon, both practiced it *after* the 1890 LDS manifesto prohibited it. We were taught in Sunday school that those who practiced the Principle of Celestial Marriage after this manifesto were surely sinners who had lost the true path to God and therefore should be excommunicated. If we should ever find apostate polygamists in our town we were to be "doctrinally distant" and steer clear of them socially. As orthodox, or mainstream, Mormons, we were taught that polygamy had a function in the nineteenth century, that it had been restored during a particular dispensation for a particular reason: to help populate Utah territory, build family kingdoms, take care of widows and unmarriageable women in the 1800s, and compensate for a skewed sex ratio in favor of girls. After Utah was adequately populated—with an average number of children six per family, which is actually about the same as monogamous fertility rates within the same population (Logue 1985)—Utah Mormons abandoned the practice, having "fulfilled" the law by the end of the nineteenth century.

In spite of the general abandonment of the practice, most Mormons today anticipate that in the heavens there is polygamy. They cannot ignore the teaching of Joseph Smith that plural marriage would be necessary for the greatest glories. LDS apostle Bruce R. McConkie said he looked to a time when polygamy would be practiced again (1991), reminding others that current church policy condones a form of spiritual polygamy in which a widower is sealed in the temple to a second woman for all time and eternity. Other Mormons, however, who felt that McConkie's statement was unofficial and inappropriate (such as my late colleague Eugene England, 1994), are quite embarrassed about polygamy. They wish it had never been "restored" by Joseph Smith, who, they say, must have had a momentary lapse in judgment when he took his first plural wife. Some try to diffuse the tension about polygamy with jokes, such as those told during the 2002 Utah Olympics ("in Utah you can always be a bride and never a bridesmaid") or the humor depicted in ads for Wasatch Beer's new ale ("Polygamy Porter: You Can't Just Have One!").

Like many others of pioneer stock, I have a rich history of polygamy, recorded in more detail in a recent volume (Bennion 2008). My great-great-grandfather, John Bennion (1820–1877), was one of Brigham Young's close associates and followers. He crossed the plains with his first wife, Esther Wainwright, arriving in Salt Lake in 1847, where he married two additional wives, Esther Ann Birch and Mary Turpin. He established the town of Taylorsville in southwest Salt Lake. Bennion and his wives produced twenty-seven children and have approximately 27,000 descendants (so far). Angus M. Cannon (1834–1915), another great-great-grandfather, was also a close advisor to Brigham Young. He served as the mayor of St. George and later as president of the Salt Lake Stake for twenty-eight years. (LDS "stakes" are like Catholic dioceses, composed of several congregations or "wards.") In 1903, many years after the prohibition of polygamy, Angus refused to give up his six wives and served a prison sentence for his beliefs. Angus's brother, George Q. Cannon, married five women and served as an apostle to four LDS prophets, one of whom was John Taylor, his uncle and close friend. When *Reynolds v. United States* banned polygamy in 1879, G. Q. Cannon stated that "our crime has been: we married women instead of seducing them; we reared children instead of destroying them; we desired to exclude from the land prostitution, bastardy and infanticide" (Cannon 1879, 79).[5] In 1888, after spending years as a fugitive, G. Q. Cannon was arrested and spent six months in a Utah prison.

On my Benson side, Ezra Taft Benson (1811–1869), my third great-great-grandparent in polygamy, was a member of the Quorum of the Twelve Apostles. Originally from Massachusetts, he married his first wife, Pam Andrus, and made money managing a hotel and investing in cotton. In 1840 he converted to Mormonism in Illinois, then followed the Saints to Missouri. He eventually married seven additional women who had thirty-five children.

This ancestry provided the initial catalyst for my analysis of variability in the experiences of women and children in plural marriages. Because of my unique inheritance as a fifth-generation Welsh Mormon and my extensive fieldwork among many of my own people, much of my research is native-based participant observation. I add my own lifelong observations and knowledge of ideology and genealogy to the many interviews I gathered using a reflexive approach. Part of this knowledge base comes from my role in the LDS Church, which included many callings and leadership positions, from Primary to Relief Society. It was in the belly of church activism that I was able to understand the basic ideology that guides both orthodoxy and fundamentalism. It was also there that I could see, at first hand, some of the challenges for young, divorced, single mothers that can lead to conversion to polygamy. My ethnographic *verstehen* was surely influenced later by my status as a "disaffected" Mormon woman and a product of several generations of "native Mormon intelligentsia."[6] In the mid-1990s, after a Church court disfellowshipped me, I began to challenge the efficacy of applying 1950s-era gender models of Mormon life, as Thomas O'Dea did in his sociological analysis (1957), to the vastly heterogeneous and culturally diverse Church body. Such an archaic model marginalizes and trivializes the lives of Mormons like myself and my polygamist subjects whose experiences do not mirror the goals of the 1950s behavioral charter.

For example, many Mormon women—and some men—are underrepresented in the typical sociological analysis as well as in official Church policy and structure. These include single women, unmarriageable women, single mothers, lesbian women, feminists, women of color, working/career women, female academics, "Jill" Mormons,[7] barren women, environmentalists, liberals, single fathers, female heads of households, gay men, and polygamous women. In Robert Merton's terms (1968), these ostracized individuals are innovative creators of new cultural means by which they can attain their ideal version of Mormonism. They redesign codes within the doctrine to meet changing socioeconomic demands, adopting meaningful careers, exploring alternative relationships, or incorporating a more gender humanistic approach to the plan of salvation.

Much like Nancy Scheper-Hughes in "Ire in Ireland" (2000), I am caught between my "emic" love for the culture and the need to occasionally point out its dysfunctions.[8] I must reconcile my responsibility to the fundamentalists, my fealty to my own ancestors, and my allegiance to the reader to provide an honest ethnography. Thus, in a sense my autoethnography constitutes yet another example of the strong Mormon predilection to examine family roots, even ones entailing "skeletons in the closet" that mainstream Mormons have tended to suppress in their ongoing efforts to achieve middle-class respectability in U.S. society.

The data presented in this volume are drawn from twenty years of anthropological fieldwork conducted in three environments: the Apostolic United Brethren (AUB; sometimes called the Allred Group) of the Bitterroot Mountains of Montana, the AUB and surrounding independent polygamists of the Salt Lake Valley of Utah (1998), and the LeBaron group of Galeana, Chihuahua, Mexico (2004). I have lived and worked with twenty-two extended polygamous families and interviewed more than 355 individuals about their conversion to the movement, their living arrangements, and their lifestyles. Thus, I draw upon my own history as a descendant of Mormon polygamy, on the ethnographic observations I made while living among the Allreds, and on scores of interviews and observations made over ten years of living in Zion and in the world of Babylon. I also include seventy to ninety hours of television dramas, news reports, and talk shows as well as Internet articles and polygamy websites as part of my dataset. All of these sources provide descriptive analysis of the way polygamy is viewed in the context of twenty-first-century popular culture. Like Lila Abu-Lughod, I believe in the need for Geertz's "thick description" of culture in popular media (1997). My description of the characters and events portrayed on shows such as *Big Love* and

Sister Wives is part of a new tradition in media ethnography that looks at how plural marriage is portrayed and how that portrayal affects the lives of polygamists, the larger mainstream populace, and laws relating to alternative sexuality and marriage.

Please note that although I use the term "polygamy" throughout this volume, I am referring to "polygyny," where one man is married, or mated to, several women. Polygamy is actually the umbrella term for multiple matings, or multiple spouses, that includes polyamory, polyfidelity, and polyandry, where one woman is married or mated to several men. Mormon fundamentalists, as a whole, dislike both "polygamy" and "polygyny," preferring "the Work," "the Principle," or "Celestial Marriage."

To maintain anonymity I have given aliases to nonpublic figures and have obscured the personalities and identifiable characteristics of individual informants. Private subjects are cloaked with fictional descriptions and some of the details of their lives have been collapsed and telescoped for the sake of brevity and camouflage. Their names will be set off by quotation marks the first time they appear. I have used the real names of public individuals if they are used on the Internet, in newspapers, or on television. These measures to protect anonymity do not compromise the representative nature of the events I describe or my descriptions of life in fundamentalism.

This volume is a comprehensive analysis of the variability in Mormon polygamy. I emphasize the need to separate the criminal abuses related to welfare fraud, underage marriage, and sexual coercion from the institution of polygamy per se and argue that we need to understand the implications of decriminalization for the future of polygamy and other creative family alternatives. At its core, this volume is concerned with exploring the impact of polygamy on women and children and the challenges that polygamy presents to society.

This book differs from my other publications in a few key ways. My 1998 and 2004 books were focused exclusively on the AUB Pinesdale and LeBaron Galeana orders in their respective mountain and desert environments. My 2008 publication, a response to the raid on the YFZ compound of the Fundamentalist Church of Jesus Christ of Latter-Day Saints in Eldorado, Texas, attempted to evaluate the factors that contribute to abuse and, conversely, to "wellness" in polygamy. The present book provides a more thorough review of literature relevant to polygamy in the social sciences, history, theology, law, media, and gender studies. It also includes new discourse on polygamy and the law. In short, the volume brings together topics that include media influence, legislative history, gender dynamics, the politics of kingdom building, polygamous sexuality, and the cultural context of crimes related to plural marriage under one cover, giving readers a more holistic view of the dynamics of polygamy than has ever before been published. I hope that it will have a calming influence in the confrontation between the media and fundamentalist Mormon communities.

In the introduction, I discuss why polygamy is a relevant focus in the twenty-first century and examine the efficacy of the practice in various Mormon fundamentalist movements. In Part 1, I describe and explain Mormon fundamentalism as a cultural phenomenon, providing a brief description of the history, ethnography, and ideology of fundamentalist Mormons for those who are new to this field.[9] In this section, I try to dispel the assumption in many media accounts that all polygamy is the same by providing a brief description of the four major movements, detailing the dispersion of schismatic groups from Salt Lake City into the insular desert and mountain hinterlands of Montana, Arizona, Texas, Mexico, and Canada. In Part 2, I address the question of how society has dealt with or reacted to polygamy and describe the role of media in portraying plural marriage as both the ultimate evil (as seen in prime-time news reports, newspaper headlines, and escape novels) and as the latest "cool" alternative to monogamy (as depicted on Internet websites, in the memoir of the Darger family [2011], and on the television programs *Big Love* and *Sister Wives*). I also review the legal, political, and criminal ramifications of plural marriage in the West, including a detailed history of anti-polygamy legislation and the current state policies of protecting fundamentalists through somewhat ambiguous "secular eye-winking." This section provides an evaluation of the pros and cons of campaigns to decriminalize and legalize polygamy, which are often promoted in conjunction with right-to-marry crusades of gays and lesbians. And finally, the conclusion examines polygamy's expanding scholarly audience and the rights of twenty-first-century poly families, addressing the question on the lips of any woman contemplating becoming a polygamist's wife, "is it right for me?"

Acknowledgments

I would like to thank the HBI Project on Gender, Culture, Religion, and the Law, which in 2010 hosted the highly successful conference "Polygamy, Polygyny, and Polyamory: Ethical and Legal Perspectives on Plural Marriage," inspiring the writing of this volume. I also acknowledge the gentle critique of my editor and colleague, Professor Alan Boye, the continual encouragement and support of my colleague, Phil Kilbride, as well as the contributions of political specialist Ari Wengroff and law professor Linda Smith. I am also grateful for my husband, John, and my two daughters, Liza and Frances, for their tolerance and support of my work. They can attest to the fact that I'm an angry bear when I'm working on a book, and it takes courage on their part to endure it all. Mostly, I am grateful to my students and to the members of the public who show an interest in alternative love and marriage. May this book be a reminder to them to foster respect for all cultures and to diligently search out the truth before placing judgment on a people's way of life.

Polygamy in Primetime

Introduction

Why Study Polygamy Now?

Debates about the social viability and human rights violations of contemporary fundamentalist Mormon communities have found their way into scholarly literature. The discourse about the protection of women and children are but the academic portion of a larger cultural awareness of and recent fascination with polygamy. During the spring of 2008, for example, two key events challenged our view of contemporary American family life. On April 3, authorities raided the Yearning for Zion (YFZ) Ranch in Eldorado, Texas, in what they described as the largest child-welfare operation in Texas history (Fahrenthold 2008). Six weeks later, on May 15, the California Supreme Court issued a historic decision in favor of same-sex marriage, a decision that potentially opened the door for the legalization (or at least the decriminalization) of other alternative forms of marriage.[1]

Two additional significant events related to alternative marriage occurred in 2010. One was the premier of the TLC channel's reality series *Sister Wives,* which joined HBO's fictional series *Big Love.* These two programs delivered drama sympathetic to polygamists to a combined audience of more than four million people each week. The other event was a trial in Canada in November 2010 to test the constitutionality of that nation's current polygamy laws as laid out in Section 293 of the Criminal Code. These events further fueled the discourse on the efficacy of alternative marriage and sexuality and have sent ripples of activity and interest throughout the American mainstream media and the academic community.

How do we begin to sort through the varied portraits of plural marriage provided by the news, talk shows, government and human rights agencies, and prime time television? Does plural marriage cause irreparable harm to women and children or is it a viable alternative for a small but legitimate cohort of men, women, and children? Since lesbian and gay marriage is now legal in

Massachusetts, Connecticut, Iowa, Vermont, Maine, and New Hampshire, should not plural marriage also be freed from persecution?

Few people had heard of the present-day Mormon polygamists before the Texas government raided the Yearning for Zion Ranch. As that story unfolded, Americans watched daily news reports on the removal of over 400 children from their mothers. I was flooded with requests for information about fundamentalist Mormonism from the media by e-mail and telephone. The most frequent question was about the women's hair and clothes. "Why do they wear that wave in their hair? What are those dresses made of?" The raid made for gripping television, but such drama can often obscure the facts. When the state of Texas removed the children, they put them directly into state protective services. Texas officials took cotton-swab DNA samples of children and mothers to determine parentage and placed them in a variety of mainstream "gentile" housing. This rash, traumatic measure was the largest government raid of children in the history of the United States.[2] SWAT teams armed with heavy artillery were brought in, though they found only thirty-three legal firearms at the YFZ Ranch.

The raid had been precipitated by phone calls to a domestic violence shelter, purportedly from a 16-year-old girl who claimed she was being sexually and physically abused on the ranch by her middle-aged husband. What lent credibility to the calls was that the residents of YFZ Ranch were disciples of the Fundamentalist Church of Jesus Christ of Latter-Day Saints (FLDS) and its "prophet," Warren Jeffs, who had been convicted in a Utah court in 2007 for officiating at the marriage of a fourteen-year-old girl to a church member. A Texas appeals court later found that state authorities had not met the burden of proof for the removal of the children from the YFZ Ranch, and most were returned to their families within two months.

Yet after interviewing teenagers who were pregnant or had children, Texas authorities began investigating how many underage girls might have been "sealed," or married, to older men who already had other wives. This search located twelve church members, including Warren Jeffs, who were married to underage girls. These men were indicted on charges ranging from bigamy to having sex with a minor.

Texas Child Protection Services placed the children removed from their parents during the siege in foster care, which has often been associated with abuse.[3] They ignored the history of failed raids of religious movements. In 1985, the governor of Vermont approved the removal of 112 children from the

Twelve Tribes commune in Island Pond after government officials became concerned that the children were being beaten. In 1953, authorities removed 236 children from their mothers in Short Creek, Utah/Arizona (Bradley 1990). And in 1956, Utah authorities seized seven children of Vera Black, an FLDS plural wife in Hildale, on grounds that her polygamous beliefs made her an unfit mother. Black was reunited with her children only after she agreed to renounce polygamy. In each of these cases, the U.S. Supreme Court ruled that the raid was unconstitutional.

When the state of Texas removed the children from their homes in Eldorado, it neglected to acknowledge the damaging cultural shock that FLDS children would experience in foster care and the outside world, which they had been taught to see as hostile, contaminating, and evil. They were trained to fear government and the outside world, where people watched cable TV and listened to hip-hop. In the end, Texas authorities admitted that the raid was focused not on individual cases of sex abuse, as it should have been, but on the entire FLDS culture (Fahrenthold 2008). By June, Texas Rangers had opened investigations of twenty alleged cases of abuse and fifty alleged cases of bigamy. After these investigations, leaders of the sect stated that they would no longer contract marriages that included underage girls.

Because of shows such as *Big Love* and *Sister Wives,* polygamy has become part of prime-time culture, no longer relegated to the hidden cultish confines of southern border towns and western desert wastelands. Although part of its recent notoriety has come from the stories of "escapees" such as Carolyn Jessop and Carmen Thompson, both victims of abusive marriages in the FLDS group, its current fame stems from the presence of "progressive" polygamists associated with the Allred Group, as portrayed by *Big Love*'s Bill Henrickson, *Love Times Three* polygamist Joe Darger (2011), and TLC's real-life "fame whore" Kody Brown (Murray 2011, 1). Who can resist these good-looking, charismatic personalities who want to open up their polygamous lifestyles to the world?

Big Love, which premiered in 2006, was the first television show to feature the contemporary Mormon fundamentalist polygamous lifestyle. In spite of the show's overemphasis on sex, a focus that often takes attention away from the real issues for women in fundamentalism, the series has the potential to awaken the mainstream to the realities of the lives of Mormon polygamous women. Bill, the protagonist, is a firm believer in decriminalizing plural marriage and encourages all polygamists to come out of the woodwork. He is even voted into public office as the first polygamist to become a state senator since 1905. Feminist viewers love the dynamic of the women of *Big Love,* who are always vying for a stronger voice, more autonomy, and more direct control of the resources. For example, in Season 5, Barb pushed the gender envelope by demanding the holy priesthood, reminding us of Sonya Johnson, who chained herself to the gates of the Salt Lake temple in the 1970s to fight for the Equal Rights Amendment.

Although primetime paints a positive picture of American polygamy, people are still concerned with what could go wrong. Besides the Eldorado raid, which directed our gaze at the possibility of coerced underage marriage, we remember the 2002 case of Elizabeth Smart, who was kidnapped from her bedroom and forced to have sex with her polygamist captor. We also recall the arrest and trial of FLDS prophet Warren Jeffs and his abuses against underage women, including a girl of fourteen, Elissa Wall, whom he forced to marry her nineteen-year-old cousin (Fremd 2006). Before that, polygamist Tom Green was convicted of marrying a thirteen-year old girl during the time period of the 2002 Olympics in Salt Lake City (Pomfret 2006).

In their efforts to investigate polygamous lifestyles and intervene in alleged cases of abuse, governments have always faced the challenge of violating religious rights, on the one hand, or ignoring potential abuse risks, on the other. Not surprisingly, many prominent Mormons, such as 2008 and 2012 presidential candidate Mitt Romney and former LDS prophet Gordon B. Hinckley, have expressed concern about the negative publicity polygamy can bring to mainstream Mormonism, which they fear could damage the LDS missionary effort. They demand that fundamentalists stop calling themselves "Mormon" and separate themselves completely from the history of the mainstream Church and from mainstream society.[4] This request for segregation increases prejudice against polygamy within the general public. It also reinforces the "don't ask, don't tell" strategies of local law enforcement officials that require polygamists to hide their lifestyle or face ostracism and imprisonment. The stance Mormon officials have taken toward fundamentalists ignores the common history, ideology, and culture of the two groups; forces polygamists to fade even more into the background, away from the evils of Babylon and government scrutiny; makes it harder for polygamists to solicit public support for their civil rights; and makes it easier for abusive polygamists to thrive in isolated, rural regions.

Most states in the Intermountain West have used the principle of mutual non-interference, where polygamists are allowed to live in peace, as long as they do not break additional laws, although the states of Utah and Arizona are initiating dialogue between law enforcement and sect leaders wherever possible (Dougherty 2003). Arizona's attorney general, Terry Goddard, has outlined a bold initiative aimed at cracking down on the abuse often associated with the practice of polygamy that includes generating discourse between group leaders and his office combined with active monitoring of at-risk individuals. This plan was recently tested with the Kody Brown case, the polygamist who agreed to go public with his family's plural lifestyle on *Sister Wives* in 2010. Facing prosecution by the police in his hometown of Lehi after the public revelation, Kody moved his family to Nevada at the end of the show's first season. This threat of prosecution violated the tacit understanding with the state attorney general that any prosecutions would be based on charges of abuse, not polygamy.

Canadians are also concerned with how to handle the polygamy issue. Late in 2010 the British Columbia government brought the issue to trial. The primary inquiry concerned Section 293 of the Canadian Criminal Code, which makes polygamy illegal. The trial is a test of this code to see if it still is necessary in this day and age of progressive social praxis and whether it is actually violating individuals' constitutional rights to live according to their beliefs. If the law is struck down, Canada would join other Western nations such as Britain in removing criminal sanctions from polygamy. Advocates of maintaining the ban on polygamy point to the abusive conditions at the FLDS branch located in Bountiful, British Columbia, headed by Winston Blackmore. Those of us who are familiar with the diversity within polygamy shake our heads in frustration that it is this group that is held up to the world for scrutiny rather than any of the many noncontroversial, female-affirming communities associated with the Allred Group or even progressive independent groups. Although many in the Blackmore community say they are contented, many others say they have experienced family stress, depression, jealousy, low self-esteem, and feelings of disempowerment. Children at Bountiful were said to have lower levels of socioeconomic status and reduced academic achievement compared to their peers. Of primary concern was the high percentage of teen mothers. In Bountiful there have been 833 births to 215 mothers and 142 fathers. Of those babies, 10 percent were born to girls aged eighteen or under. Other groups, such as the Allreds and LeBarons, have a lower birth rate and do not allow underage girls to marry at all. When young women do marry, it is with their full consent.

Whether there is harm or not, many inside the FLDS group agree that the criminalization of polygamy only serves to compound the problem. For example, one British Columbia mother of nine told the court that because of the polygamy law she can't see a marriage counselor. If she works outside the compound, she has to lie about her status or she'll be fired. Another young woman testified that she and her siblings have learned to lie to doctors, teachers, and officials so their father won't go to jail. A third woman bore witness that she has to spend money on lawyers and worry about child protection services taking away her children. If polygamy were legal, she could spend more time living her life openly like a normal person, without threat of prosecution.

Many feel the law is antiquated and doesn't take note of the variability in polygamous lifestyles. Other witnesses at the trial suggested that there are just as many problems with monogamous communities as there are in polygamous ones. For example, Tim Dickson, a lawyer who argued that the anti-polygamy law is unconstitutional, suggested that the high instance of teen pregnancy in Bountiful, B.C., may be linked to religion and isolation rather than to polygamy per se. He referred to a U.S. study that suggested that evangelicals and members of other highly religious groups tend to have higher rates of teen pregnancy than the general population (Keller 2011). Dickson indicated that other small religious towns in the same region have extremely high teen birth rates (such as Hazelton, where births to mothers under 20 account for 22 per cent of all live births).[5] Should these communities be criminalized as well?

One witness who had lived in polygamy in Utah acknowledged that some fundamentalist Mormon groups have unsavory practices, such as arranged marriages and teenage brides. Yet she believes that if polygamy is decriminalized, polygamous groups could be educated about incest, underage marriage, and sexual assault. Abuse could be dealt with more effectively than in the current situation, where polygamists facing prosecution are sent into hiding. To the surprise of many in the court, even Carolyn Jessop, author of the acclaimed *Escape,* a book about the abuse she experienced in a polygamous marriage, testified in favor of decriminalization.[6] Carolyn said that neither the courts nor the police are enforcing the polygamy law, so making it legal would increase the possibility that women and children living in polygamous structures could get help. Polygamy could be regulated as monogamy is regulated, giving people the right to be protected.

Inspired by recent events that put polygamy in the spotlight, Lisa Fishbayn

Joffe of Brandeis University organized a meeting in November 2010 of polygamy scholars from around the world to examine ethical and legal perspectives on plural marriage. The meeting was hosted by the HBI Project on Gender, Culture, Religion, and the Law. I met with scholars such as Martha Bailey of Queens University and Sarah Song of Berkeley who, like me, are advocating the repeal of criminal sanctions for plural marriage (Bailey 2010; Song 2010) and others, such as Maura Strassberg (2010) of the Drake Law School, who want to keep polygamy illegal. This conference highlighted the need to provide more data about polygamy to encourage the public as well as policy makers to be fully aware of the vast diversity of experiences in polygamy instead of accepting a uniform, typically negative and sensationalized depiction. The conference also inspired an openness to the possibility of viewing polygamy in a more pragmatic light that would discourage polyphobia, or cultural contempt for polygamy. In a Durkheimian sense, the spread of polyhate by the media, political rhetoric, or anti-polygamy websites identifies evil and labels it in order to create normalcy and solidarity for the mainstream. By marginalizing polygamists, we can reaffirm our values as monogamists, labeling ourselves more righteous or superior than the deviant group. The so-called deviants are seen as un-American and even threatening to the majority.

My role in the conference (as it is in this volume) was to dispel some of the media-driven ethnocentric myths about Mormonism and tap into the rich and varied experiences of polygamous women who are often marginalized in the mainstream. It is my hope that polygamy, like lesbigay marriage, can come out of the closet and into the full legal and political sunlight of public awareness. One myth that needs to be dispelled is that polygamy exists only in isolated cults. We now know that polygamy exists in both small towns and big cities and that it stretches beyond the Mormon-offshoot enclaves to non-Mormon Christian and Muslim immigrant communities. Another myth is that Mormon fundamentalist "cults" are oozing polygamists, as if it were a plague that could be contagious. Few people realize that only a small proportion of Mormon fundamentalists practice polygamy. Although some men in various sects are able to marry more than one wife, most males cannot do so because there is strict competition for wives. Most men within these movements are monogamous. Further, if we define polygamy loosely, as a sexual arrangement rather than a strictly marital one, we will find that it is much more common in mainstream America than in identifiable fundamentalist groups. The vast majority of so-called monogamists are not loyal to one spouse throughout their lifetime. Instead, they have multiple sexual partners, sometimes at the same time and sometimes sequentially, such as in serial monogamy, or polygyandry, where both males and females have multiple partners over time. One can thus see parallels between fundamentalism and mainstream monogamy in that they both contain monogamy with some polygamy, polyfidelity, or quasi-polygamy.

The difficulty for me, as a scholar, is to tease apart the stories that represent most polygamists' experiences from the sensational stories often found in the media. Whereas I have observed the many faces of polygamy, the press tends to see only the ugly one. Journalists seem compelled to paint fundamentalism with one brush that depicts the horrors of neglect, sexual abuse, and criminality. During the Eldorado raid, I even heard a report that labeled fundamentalists as the "Mormon mafia." I often get a flurry of calls from reporters in times of crisis, but I never do when things are going well. No one wants to read about a happy little polygamous, self-sustained community whose members lived contentedly off the grid, tucked in the mountains away from pollution, traffic, and technological overkill, although my data shows that such communities exist, such as in Pinesdale, Montana, or Eagle Mountain, Utah. I maintain that females in such communities tend to be attracted to Mormon fundamentalism because it provides them with the security of home, family, and friendships that they have not been able to find in the larger society, including within mainstream Mormonism. Many of the converts constitute the "disinherited" of mainstream Mormonism in that their socioeconomic and marital status left them on the periphery of a seemingly prosperous religious organization. Once they enter the Mormon fundamentalist movement, many women find economic and emotional security, often in fellowship with their sisters. However, other women do not have this experience, and it is the stories of these women that the mass media feeds upon.

Some readers may mistake my statements in favor of an open approach to polygamy as patriarchal and perhaps even misogynist. But I would ask How can we be feminists and not fight for the freedom of choice for *all* women, regardless of whether they are liberal or conservative, career women or stay-at-home mothers, agnostic or piously religious, living in monogamous relationships or polygamous ones? As long as the United States remains a highly stratified society socially, women, including those who are attracted to Mormon polygamy, will find "sanctuaries by which to cope with the vagaries of life under corporate capitalism" (Baer 2008, vi) and, I would add, with monogamy and the absence of fathers in households with children. Women in these unique communities may have opportunities for autonomy, friendship, and (sometimes) economic benefits. At the same time they may be constrained by rigid patriarchy, elite polygyny, and economic deprivation. This variability is further punctuated by differing gender dynamics in fundamentalist communities and the vagaries of federal and state laws. Thus, many factors contribute to both wellness and crisis in North American polygamy.

As an anthropologist who has studied Mormon fundamentalism since 1989, I find it strange that these unique, fully Mormon, women are often ignored in studies about LDS women.[7] They, perhaps like lesbians, single mothers, divorced women, and working mothers, do not easily fit within the descriptions of the LDS Proclamation of the Family (Hinckley 1995) and are often glorified by the orthodoxy as "dysfunctional." Yet they are part of the Mormon experience. Most fundamentalist converts come from the Mormon Church and continue to raise their children using Mormon doctrine and import policies and practices from the Relief Society and the priesthood. Most polygamists do not make the ten o'clock news because their lives are considered relatively boring and not newsworthy. Reporters who seek sensational stories of arrest, abuse, and radicalism overlook this everyday humdrum tranquility.

My effort to provide a glimpse of polygamous lifestyles will show the great variability of expression, not just those depicted in Jon Krakauer's *Under the Banner of Heaven* (2004) and in Carolyn Jessop's *Escape* (2007). All polygamy does not, as Oprah suggests, perpetuate third-world Taliban-type abuse (Llewellyn 2004), nor do all groups require that their women be treated like property, good only for breeding and child rearing. On the contrary, there are many examples of female autonomy, achievement, and contentment within a polygamous context. I follow columnist Rebecca Walsh's recent counsel (2008): as a native ethnographer, my task is to observe women's experiences in their cultural context, and as a feminist within that culture, my task is to defend other women's right to choose how they wish to make love, marry, and raise their families.

Review of the Literature on Contemporary Mormon Polygamy

Until recently, North American Mormon fundamentalist polygamy has been seriously examined by only a handful of scholars: social psychologist Irv Altman (1996) of the University of Utah, anthropologist Robin Fox (1993) of Rutgers, anthropologist Bill Jankowiak (1995) of the University of Nevada, anthropologist Phil Kilbride (1994) of Bryn Mawr, and myself, working as an anthropologist at Lyndon State College of Vermont (Bennion 1998–2011). The topic has recently begun to attract a much wider audience, including readers and researchers in the social sciences, history, theology, and law and the fields of gender studies, marriage and family studies, and media studies.

Altman was one of the first to explore contemporary polygamy. He focused on the complexity of relationships among a few key families in the Apostolic United Brethren, emphasizing how these families struggled to fit into a polygamous structure using Victorian psychological frameworks developed in a monogamous context. Jankowiak investigated the father-adoration concept in polygamous relationships in Colorado City (also known as Short Creek). Fox and Kilbride were both interested in showing the benefits polygamy offers in the context of the crises of American modernity; they emphasize how women choose alternative family forms as a way to cope with the socioeconomic obstacles they confront. These studies applaud the adaptive measures polygamists have taken to share resources and provide protection from the harsh realities of urban life. My research explores the unexpected ascendance of women in rigid patriarchal communities, especially how women gain autonomy and power during the prolonged absences of their husbands. I recorded the experiences of female converts in the Montana Allredite order (Bennion 1998) and found that many women are attracted to the commune because of the socioeconomic support it offers. They say they are fleeing a difficult life in the mainstream where their status as divorcees, single mothers, widows, and "unmarriageables" limits their access to good men and the economic and spiritual affirmation that comes from a community of worship.[8]

In my book *Women of Principle: Female Networking in Contemporary Mormon Polygamy* (1998), I concluded that some Mormon women experience more individual satisfaction within the dynamics of a polygamous family than they could in any other marital form. Kilbride's book *Plural Marriage for Our Time: A Reinvented Option* (1994) similarly states that plural marriage can help rebuild a strong sense of family for specific groups of Americans, especially in times of socioeconomic crisis. Another helpful study about the reality of U.S. marriages was conducted by my former classmate at the University of Utah, Steven Josephson, who studied co-wife conflict among a cohort of Mormons but also took an interest in marital practices in mainstream U.S. society. He suggested that our widely accepted practice of serial monogamy–marriage, childbearing, divorce, remarriage or repartnership, and subsequent childbearing—"is really just slow-motion polygyny" (quoted in Martin 2009). This is all separate from what Josephson called "polygyny in all but name" (ibid.), in which men in the contemporary Western world—where we explicitly condemn polygamy but pass no laws against men who take mistresses—secretly have two families or two long-term partners. Josephson wrote that our evolutionary software is designed for polygamy. In agreement with Josephson, Zeitzen maintains that the threat of polygamy—that is, the possibility that a present or future husband might take another wife—influences women's "perception and management of relationships, marriage, and family life" (Zetizen 2008, 170). It is thus wrong, on some level, to call any marriage truly monogamous because all marriages are potentially polygamous and both men and women organize their relationships on this assumption.

While studying the factors that draw convert women to these polygamous communities (1998), I concluded that the surprising success these groups had in recruiting women from the mainstream monogamous Mormon community could be attributed to the fact that plural marriage ultimately improved the situation of a considerable number of women who had experienced extreme social, economic, and/or emotional deprivation in the Mormon mainstream. Fundamentalist women converts who have been marginalized in the mainstream Mormon community are attracted by the opportunity to be married and raise their children within a strong, supportive network of sister-wives and other community women within the familiar and valued context of their religion. These networks are particularly advantageous for lower-class women, whose economic and educational opportunities increase in polygamous settings because they are sharing the burdens of homemaking and child-rearing with sister-wives. A woman's status in Mormon polygamous communities is determined by her husband's status in the religious hierarchy, and high-ranking men are most likely to be given permission to take on additional wives. Consequently, polygamy also makes it possible for marginalized women to quickly improve their social status and power by marrying powerful men in the community. Furthermore, despite the fact that in these poly communities women are formally subordinated to the sovereign authority of their husbands and the male clergy and cannot hold positions of religious or political power in the community, they do exercise considerable independent power. They can raise their children with minimal oversight by their husband, manage their household, and work in the all-important female support networks. Finally, Mormon fundamentalism balances the deprivations and difficulties of the lives of polygamous wives with a promise of an afterlife as "queens and priestesses."

Polygamy has also been offered as an alternative to divorce. In fact, it is my view that in certain instances, polygamy may in fact lead to greater stability in the marital relationship. This view is supported by the research of other scholars such as Anastasia Gage-Brandon, who did research on polygamous marriages in Nigeria in the late 1980s and early 1990s. She found that marriages involving two wives were the most stable unions and were much less likely to end in divorce than marriages involving more than two wives. Significantly, these unions were also less likely to lead to divorce than monogamous unions (Gage-Brandon 1992). In addition to these potential benefits, polygamy may enhance family life by providing more loving parents for children. Anthropologists William Jankowiak and Monique Diderich (2000) report that children raised in polygamy develop "sibling solidarity," the bonds developed between full and half-siblings relating to inclusive fitness, which is measured in terms of the survival and reproductive success of your own kin.

In my research, I have also found that polygamous women enjoy autonomy and freedoms associated with the multifaceted ties established between married women of the same patriarchal kingdoms. For example, women man united in opposition to a husband who "gets out of line." One woman I interviewed said that her husband was not spending enough time with her son and that he had also forgotten her birthday. The other wives joined her in boycotting the husband from their homes, barring him from access to food and sex for a week. In her review of anti-polygamy laws, Stephanie Forbes (2003) corroborates this feature of polygamous relationships, noting that women have a greater chance of halting or changing the behavior of males by expressing their dissatisfaction collectively. These women said that they also valued being surrounded by women in an environment where emotions are not suppressed, as they are with men, and that they can escape from the demands of their husband in ways that a monogamous woman cannot.

Polygamy allows women to cope with the imbalanced sex ratios often associated with war or inner-city violence. According to Debra Majeed of Beloit College, African American Muslims of the Chicago area are drawn to polygamist marriages to cope with the severe shortage of eligible, marriageable men (e.g., single, heterosexual, legitimately employed, living outside of prison walls, and free from drugs) within black America (Majeed 2010). Majeed states that because African Americans comprise the largest group of Muslims in the United States, they are likely candidates for polygamy. Further, the higher status routinely afforded married women has led some African American Muslim women to accept plural marriage to obtain resources and prestige. It is an irony that the educational and financial strides Black Muslim females have made in the last few decades have attracted them to the possibility of knowingly sharing their husbands. I say "irony" because these are strong, capable women who are actively seeking to marry into one of the most rigid forms of patriarchy, all in order to experience marriage and motherhood and to foster friendships with other Muslim women in the black community. Patricia Dixon-Spear of Georgia State University challenges us to rethink plural marriage as a vehicle for coping with the shortage of African American men and to foster a "womanist ethic of care for sisters" (2009).

I have observed the importance and vitality of this womanist ethic among co-wives, especially during the prolonged absences of husbands. Women develop a strong interdependence with each other and in doing so create a large repertoire of domestic and mechanical skills. "If one wife can't fix it, the other can," is a statement I heard repeatedly. By contrast, monogamous women do not experience this type of shared skill set, especially if they are isolated from their friends, sisters, or community networks. Similarly, the South African women Anderson studied in 2000 perceived relationships with co-wives as an important source of economic support, companionship, and assistance with child care. Because South Africa has such a long tribal history of polygamous marriages, these marriages are protected by law. In fact, Jacob Zuma, South Africa's president since 2009, has three wives.[9] One South African man, forty-four-year-old municipal officer Milton Mbhele, wedded four woman at the same time, saving money and time, bringing the total number to five wives. His first wife, Thobile Vilakazi, was with her husband for 12 years before the new marriages. The wives planned to live separately, with their husband rotating between them. According to Judith Stacey and Tey Meadow (2009), the South African legal stipulation simply requires that first wives give their written consent to the husband's marriage to a subsequent wife and that the husband prove that he has the financial means to care for an additional wife.[10] Malaysia also regulates polygamy. There, a state representative is requesting that local legislators and magistrates marry needy single mothers in order to protect the growing number of marginalized women from poverty (Malaysian Insider 2009).

A Status of Women Canada report (Campbell et al. 2005) expressed reservations about imposing criminal sanctions on plural unions. Martha Bailey, one of the Queens University law professors who contributed to the report, sought to decriminalize polygamy but to retain the criminal sanctions on the harms associated with polygamy (Bailey 2007). Bailey argues that in order to cope with an ever-changing marital environment, North America needs to decriminalize polygamy, as so many other western democracies have done. (For more details, see Chapter 6.) She also points out that when polygamy is criminalized, female victims of abuse may be less likely to report their status because they are afraid of being charged or that they will jeopardize the welfare of their entire family with the threat of criminal charges. In this way, prohibition, which is designed to protect women from abuse, arguably in fact puts them at greater risk (Bailey 2010).

While many studies, including my own, have documented the value of the female solidarity networks developed within polygamous relationships (Leis 1974), others have identified the potential for competition among co-wives (Strassberg 2010). As Angela Campbell (2005) noted in the study conducted by Status of Women Canada:

> It is impossible to reduce the literature on this topic to a general, blanket statement in regard to the social aspects of polygamous life for women: polygamy is neither entirely "good" not is it entirely "bad" for women. . . . On some levels, the social structure of a polygamous family might forge a sense of support and even "sisterhood" among the wives. At the same time, polygamous women, although possibly collaborative on occasion, are likely to compete with one another in different circumstances. (3)

Madhavan's (2002) study of polygamous women in Mali offers a reconciliation of these inconsistencies. Rather than finding that cooperation and competition are inherent in polygamous relationships, Madhavan concludes that collaboration or competition among co-wives depends on the sociocultural context that frames the polygamous family. Similarly, I have found that factors such as living arrangements, family size, the availability of resources, and how controlling the husband is as the head of the family will determine whether women pursue cooperation or competition. Irwin Altman and Joseph

Ginat (1996) are emphatic in their finding that close personal relationships are inseparable from other social contexts.

Despite the many positive and successful examples of polygamy I have encountered in my research, not all polygamists are contented, productive, and positive. One of the primary justifications for the continued prohibition of polygamy is the sexual, physical, and emotional abuse many women who have escaped from polygamy have documented. According to Maura Strassberg (2010), an advocate of criminalization, polygamy is abusive to both teenage girls and adult women. She believes that since it also promotes anti-government sentiments and a polity structure that fosters men's control of women, it should remain a criminal offense.

While investigating evidence of abuse among the LeBaron Group (Bennion 2004) and the Allred Group (Bennion 2007), I discerned five conditions that, when combined with polygamy, may produce a greater risk of abuse and human rights violations. These factors mirror some of the factors identified in a report completed for the Department of Justice of Canada (Cook and Kelly 2006). They are: the absence and low parental investment of the father, an isolated rural environment or circumscription (the inability to leave a group because of geographical barriers), the absence of a strong female network, overcrowding in the household, and male supremacist ideology. It is important to note, however, that these factors are not by any means limited to or unique to polygamous family structures.

In 2006, I published an article that detailed the results of a study I conducted in Utah Valley on abuse within polygamous communities. I found that 95 percent of the abuse cases occurred in a rural environment. In the study, I described six cases of arrests of perpetrators from polygamous groups and examined the factors that contributed to the abuse. Three men were arrested for sexually abusing their daughters, two were incarcerated for marrying child brides, and one was arrested for beating his children. In all six cases, I found the following conditions: a rural environment, frequent absence of the father from the home, lack of a female network, isolated locations with natural geographical barriers to escape, overcrowded households, and the presence of "father worship," as defined by Jankowiak (1995). Combined with the adoration of the father was a strict code that required the obedience of all children and wives. The punishment for breaking this code was known as the blood atonement, a physical whipping or cutting of the skin to atone for the sins against the father. In my view, correlation between abuse and isolation is twofold: abusers deliberately choose remote places in order to maintain control over their victims without being observed; and women in such isolated locations are unable to leave the community easily. I believe that this correlation offers strong evidence against finding a necessary causal connection between polygamy and abuse. Instead, it is my belief that forcing polygamous families to the fringes of society facilitates instances of abuse taking place outside the watchful eye of law enforcement. This concern was also raised by Campbell in the Status of Women Canada report. She found that criminalization of polygamy in Canada leads to families "often practicing polygamy clandestinely and inconspicuously" (Campbell 2005, 6), creating the potential for loss of perspective and abuse within the group. When women are isolated, the need for a strong female support network becomes increasingly significant. My research indicates that when this network is present, it may be more difficult for abuse to go unnoticed, as community members are more likely to be engaged in and aware of daily events in the lives of their peers. In addition, strong female networks facilitate the sharing and efficient use of resources, which in turn creates more leisure time for women and thus, arguably, more contentment. These networks also provide women with a protective emotional and financial safety net that reduces the need for women to rely exclusively on their husbands for these resources. It is also important to note that the correlation between isolation and abuse is not limited to polygamous family relationships. Examples of abuse within monogamous relationships related to isolation have been found in northern Maine, the state with the highest rate of sexual abuse in the United States, and the remote areas of Midwestern states. And, as was discussed at the 2010 Canadian trial, small towns are prone to high teen birth rates (Keller 2011).

Other factors that contribute to instances of abuse are the interrelated issues of absent fathers and economic deprivation. As Randy Thornhill and Craig Palmer note in their book *A Natural History of Rape* (2000), most male perpetrators are raised in poverty and then use sexual force to gain access to women with good genes. In my study of Utah Valley perpetrators, abusers came from households with lower incomes, where the offender was either unemployed or underemployed. Families in these households lived substantially below the official U.S. poverty level of $17,000 a year for a family of four, but this was due primarily to the professional choices made by the male heads of the families where abuse occurred and was not a product of polygamy itself.

When women have a way to support themselves financially, they are more likely to be in a position to leave an abusive relationship.

My analysis of abuse cases led me to believe that a thorough investigation of polygamy must be made to clarify whether only a few miscreants are guilty of abuse or all polygamous families contain abuse. If it is shown that significant numbers of families are at risk, this study would then become part of a larger theoretical discourse on predominant factors of abuse and would challenge White and Burton's famous study on conditions of polygamy (1988). Investigations should also be made about the degree to which monogamy contributes to low levels of female satisfaction and high rates of physical and/or sexual abuse of children.

Male dominance is often associated with abusive conditions. In some conditions, women in polygamous households can find satisfaction and self-actualization when the husband is open to female decision-making and autonomy and is willing to use a more feminist approach to family structures and policies. In many homes, however, I have discovered cases where women were alienated, were subject to verbal abuse and ridicule, and were subordinate to their husband. The husbands in these households insisted on restricting the ability of females to travel, pursue an education, or even go to a hospital for medical care. In my view, this treatment of women was not a factor of polygamy itself but was rather a manifestation of the husbands' extreme fundamentalist beliefs. These men abused their priesthood powers and presented themselves as the sole guardians of the family's spiritual welfare.

Studies of polygamous Muslim households have also linked abuse and unequal treatment to extreme patriarchal beliefs. In Dena Hassouneh-Phillips's study of U.S. Muslim women who were victims of abuse, the majority of participants reported that their husbands' "misuse" of polygamy rather than polygamy itself constituted the abuse and that this abuse occurred when their husbands "strayed from Islamic dictates in their pursuit of other wives" (Hassouneh-Phillips 2001, 741). Similarly, the majority of participants expressed a belief that the unjust treatment of wives, not polygamy itself, was abusive and emotionally destructive to women. Studies conducted by other scholars have further discredited the notion that gender inequality is inherently linked to polygamous practice. In 1999, Kanazawa and Still used computer-generated models with data from a large number of countries to test competing hypotheses derived from two theories of polygamy (male compromise theory and female choice theory). The authors concluded that the negative correlation between polygamy and women's status might in fact be spurious and attributable to an antecedent variable in the analysis (Kanazawa and Still 1999). This then offers a potential solution to the empirical "puzzle" of why there appears to be a negative correlation between polygamy and women's status across societies.

A study by Alean Al-Krenawi (2006) raises important questions about wife order, differential treatment, and mental stability. He sought to compare how satisfied "senior wives" (the first wives in polygamous marriages) and women in monogamous marriages were in the West Bank, Palestine. In a sample of 309 women, 187 from polygamous and 122 from monogamous families, Al-Krenawi found significant differences between Palestinian senior wives and wives in monogamous marriages with regard to family functioning, marital satisfaction, self-esteem and life satisfaction. Many of the mental health symptoms were different for these two groups of women. Particularly noteworthy were somatization, depression, hostility, psychotic behavior, and the GSI—Global Severity Index (an index of a patient's distress). Though the senior wives approved of polygamy over monogamy, they expressed more psychological problems than their monogamous counterparts.

The issue of female conversion to fundamentalism is often neglected in the literature. In my research, female converts were drawn to the security of a home, a family, and friendships. For men, there is the obvious appeal of a variety of sexual partners and the possibility of lust as a reason to marry plural wives. However, most men I interviewed provided evidence that they were drawn to polygamy for political and religious reasons: to gain a family kingdom and a calling as a high priest of that kingdom. These are the reasons for conversion among men and women in their 30s and 40s, yet there is a growing number of college-aged Mormons who are also drawn to the "mysteries," particularly from Brigham Young University. These younger adults are bored with the "milk" they get in the LDS experience, often associated with what they call a shallow social emphasis. They hunger for the "meat" they find in fundamentalism, by which they mean the deeper doctrinal and spiritual dialogue associated with the mysteries of the Gospel and the *Journal of Discourses*.[11] Michael Quinn (1993) writes that some converts, such as Roy Potter, a Mormon who joined fundamentalism in 1979, were angered over the changes the Mormon Church made to original doctrine and for being censured by the LDS Brethren. Although Quinn mentions that "few current Mormon fundamentalists have ever been baptized members of the LDS

Church" (ibid., 251), I found that within the Allred Group most converts came directly from mainstream Mormonism, at an average rate of about 25 to 30 convert families annually during the period of my study. The exception to the pattern of conversion into fundamentalism, according to Jankowiak (2008), is among members of the FLDS, who are generally born into the group. Quinn points out that most converts are not interested in polygamy but in a purer version of Mormonism. Fundamentalist groups do not actively pursue these converts, but converts are drawn to sect leaders and writers such as Ogden Kraut and Fred Collier. Many converts find that the AUB most closely resembles the LDS experience yet also provides the doctrinal discourse they seek. Fewer converts seek to join the more restrictive and separatist FLDS group because it is geographically remote from jobs and cities and the clothing and behavioral rules are not appealing. Likewise, the Davis County Corporation does not attract converts because it requires new families to fully submit to the Kingston family rule. Because of extraordinarily high natural birth rates, most groups don't need to solicit new members, especially more male converts. All who convert to fundamentalism are required to show allegiance to the original Mormon doctrines that were preached by Joseph Smith and Brigham Young.

The ever-growing literature on polygamy demonstrates both the advantages and disadvantages of polygamous marital forms. It provides a wide array of data on the economic, psychosocial, and religious significance of polygamy for the well-being of women and children. While some households have been described as places where women and children experience abuse and belittlement, others appear to generate a healthy, emotionally stable environment. It is my intention to further investigate the impact of polygamy on the men, women, and children within polygamous households and its impact on society as a whole.

In summary, many recent events, such as the raid on the FLDS community, the Canadian struggle to decide whether or not to ban polygamy, the spreading legalization of same-sex marriage, and prime-time shows that depict the day-to-day workings of polygamy have all provided fodder for the academic analysis of alternative marriage and family life. Where do we go from here? In order to truly understand the nature of Mormon fundamentalism, we must look into the past and analyze its ethnographic roots. Then we can assess how media and the law play a role in molding the new face of polygamy.

PART ONE

A Mormon Polygamy Primer

What Is It?

This section tells the story of how Mormon polygamy was founded and how fundamentalists refused to let their Principle go, even after two series of manifestos declaring it no longer a church doctrine. The deep-seated beliefs of fundamentalists are described, including a section on the "mysteries," underscoring the three most vital areas of ideology: plural marriage, the law of consecration, and the united order. This section then provides a brief ethnography of how polygamists live out their lives, emphasizing gender dynamics and the politics of kingdom building.

The History of the Principle

Polygamy in North America is practiced by as few as 38,000 or as many as 60,000 individuals, depending on which data you read (Quinn 1993; Van Wagoner 1986; Bennion 1998; Daynes 2001; Wilde et al. 2010). Mormon fundamentalists are those who subscribe to a brand of Mormon theology founded by Joseph Smith that includes polygamy, traditional gender roles, and religious communalism. About 75 percent of these polygamists come from the three largest movements—the AUB, the FLDS, and the Kingston Clan. The remainder come from the small LeBaron community in Mexico and unaffiliated polygamists spread throughout the western United States who are known as "independents."[1] These schismatic sects and individuals are dedicated to an Abrahamic kingdom-building paradigm that leads to the ultimate goal of entering the celestial presence of Elohim, the Father.

Although many mainstream Mormons seek to distance themselves from the practice, polygamy first arose in the Mormon context in 1831 when Joseph Smith Jr., founder of the Mormon Church, also known as the Church of Jesus Christ of Latter-day Saints, claimed to have a revelation that it was his duty to restore plural marriage to the earth (despite the fact that Africans and Asians had been practicing it for millennia). Smith, who married at least thirty-three women and had children with thirteen of them, claimed that he had been given the authority to practice "celestial marriage" from the same source that commanded Abraham to take his handmaid, Hagar, to bed in order to produce a righteous seed and glorious progeny. Smith, like others of his era in western New York, was caught up in the "American dream of perpetual social progress, believing in a unique theology made up of an eternal monopoly of resources (including women) by males and whole congeries of gods" (Young 1954, 29).[2] Smith described a vision he had of God and Christ together in a grove of trees in which Christ told him that he would be instrumental in restoring the true gospel. In 1830, Smith organized a Protestant- and Puritan-based religion based on his visions and his translation of the Book of Mormon, a record engraved on golden plates of a people who inhabited the

Americas before the time of Christ. He believed in restoring the Old and New Testament traditions of baptism, covenants and ordinances, washings and anointings, prophets, plural marriage, temple rituals, and priesthoods, practices that were common in many Protestant movements of his era.

Although Smith disclosed the Principle of Plural Marriage in 1843, it was practiced for several years after that in secret in Nauvoo, Illinois. After Smith was assassinated by an anti-Mormon mob, Brigham Young led believers on an epic 1,300-mile journey west to the Salt Lake Basin of present-day Utah. In 1852, Young publicly revealed the polygamy covenant and the notion that a man's righteousness before God would be measured by the size of his family. Young, hesitant at first, eventually overcame his timidity and married fifty-five wives. He had fifty-seven children by nineteen of the wives he slept with. In its heyday in Utah territory, however, polygamy was practiced by only about 15 percent to 20 percent of LDS adults, mostly among the leadership (Quinn 1993). Although plural marriage was practiced openly in the Utah Territory, it wasn't until 1876 that it became an official religious tenet that was included in the Doctrine and Covenants.

From 1862 to 1887, the U.S. government condemned polygamy and passed a series of laws that denied the rights of polygamists and their wives and were intended to weaken the Mormon Church. As a result of anti-polygamy legislation, many advocates of plural marriage began an exodus to Mexico in 1885 to avoid prosecution. There, they created a small handful of colonies, three of which are still intact today. In 1890, because of threats from the federal government, LDS president Wilson Woodruff issued a manifesto prohibiting polygamy. Woodruff claimed to have had a revelation that the church should abandon plural marriage, as that law had been "fulfilled." In a historical context, one can see the tremendous pressure from both within and outside the Church to make some concessions to the federal government. It had taken away valuable assets and imprisoned several hundred members. The Church was threatened with destruction. Thus, the "revelation" served two purposes: it facilitated the process of gaining statehood and increased the potential in the United States and abroad to win more converts who had refused to be baptized because of the practice. According to Leonard Arrington, government and church leaders entered an agreement prior to the issuing of the manifesto: in exchange for the Mormons' abandonment of plural marriage, the United Order, and the Mormon political party, Utah would be granted statehood (Arrington 1961, 31–32).

Interestingly, many members of the LDS Church, including my own Cannon and Bennion ancestors and President Woodruff himself (Kraut 1989), continued to obtain wives long after the 1890 manifesto prohibited it. In 1904, to address the continued practice of contracting plural marriage, Joseph F. Smith issued a manifesto that was designed to eradicate polygamy once and for all. Fundamentalist Mormons believe that both manifestos were used to manipulate the holy covenants for political gain (Willie Jessop, quoted in Anderson 2010, 40); they believe that God had secretly transferred the power to continue polygamy to John Taylor (third prophet of the church) through a revelation in 1886. This revelation was the defining narrative for fundamentalists and led to their separation from the mainstream church (Driggs 2005). Taylor claimed that while he was hiding in John Woolley's home in Centerville, Utah, he spent a whole night with Joseph Smith, who commanded him to continue the practice of polygamy. John Woolley's son, Lorin, a bodyguard to the prophet, was present during a clandestine meeting on September 27th in the Woolley household. At this meeting John Taylor ordained George Q. Cannon, John W. Woolley, Samuel Bateman, Charles Wilkins, and Lorin Woolley as "sub rosa" priests and gave them the authority to perform plural marriages. John Woolley was first given the keys to the patriarchal order, or priesthood keys. He subsequently passed them to Lorin, who was later excommunicated by the LDS Church for "pernicious falsehood."

From 1928 to 1934, Lorin C. Woolley led a group called the Council of Seven, also known as the Council of Friends. This group was comprised of Lorin Woolley, John Y. Barlow, Leslie Broadbent, Charles Zitting, Joseph Musser, LeGrand Woolley, and Louis Kelsch. Woolley claimed that the council was the true priesthood authority on earth and had previously existed, in secret, in Nauvoo, Illinois. This underground movement reinforced some of the early doctrines of Brigham Young such as communalism, the Adam-God belief,[3] and plural marriage. Leaders of the movement claimed that the LDS Church had lost its authority to gain direct revelation from God when it discontinued the holy principle of plural marriage during the Woodruff presidency.

Although the Council of Friends started in Salt Lake, it moved its order to the town of Short Creek on the Utah-Arizona border in order to avoid prosecution. Short Creek set the stage for the first attempt to create a United Order or Effort, to help organize properties and manage lands. The location, surrounded by majestic red rock buttes and tiny fertile creek beds, was consecrated by Brigham Young, who said it would be the "head not the tail" of the Church.[4] For a decade it was the gathering place for many members of the LDS Church who wanted to keep polygamy alive. The members of the Council of Friends were generally in agreement about how to run the underground priesthood movement, and the population of adherents to Mormon fundamentalism began to grow, mostly through natural increase and the immigration of disgruntled members of the Mormon Church who wanted to live the "old ways." In 1935, the LDS Church asked Short Creek members to support the presidency of the church and sign an oath denouncing plural marriage. This request was not well received with twenty-one members, who refused to sign and were subsequently excommunicated. Several members were jailed for bigamy.[5]

Coinciding with the organization of Short Creek was the development of a fundamentalist movement in Colonia Juarez in northern Mexico. Benjamin Johnson, a member of the Council of Fifty (a new world government orchestrated in Brigham Young's time), claimed to have obtained the priesthood keys from Young. He, in turn, gave them to his great-nephew, Alma "Dayer" LeBaron. Dayer later established Colonia LeBaron, located 80 miles southeast of Colonia Juarez in Galeana, as a refuge for those who wanted to practice plural marriage. Meanwhile, back in Short Creek, the council leadership shifted from Lorin C. Woolley, who died in 1934, to J. Leslie Broadbent, who led until his death in 1935. John Y. Barlow then took over as prophet from 1935 to 1949, after which Joseph Musser controlled the priesthood council. Musser and L. Broadbent wrote the *Supplement to the New and Everlasting Covenant of Marriage* (1934), which established three degrees of priesthood leadership: 1) the true priesthood made up of high priests, anciently known as the Sanhedrin, or power of God on earth; 2) the Kingdom of God, the channel through which the power and authority of God functions in managing the earth and "inhabitants thereof in things political"; and 3) the Church of Jesus Christ (the LDS Church), which has only ecclesiastical jurisdiction over its members. The first category, according to Musser, was comprised of the fundamentalist key holders, himself and other members of the council. The second category referred to the large body of general members, who were in service to the key holders. The third referred to the mainstream orthodox church, which no longer had direct authority to do God's work but still provided a valuable stepping-stone to the next top levels.

In 1944, during Barlow's leadership, the U.S. government raided Short

Creek and the Salt Lake City polygamists, putting fifteen men and nine women in the Utah State Prison. There was another raid in Short Creek on July 26, 1953. After this raid, thirty-one men and nine women were arrested and 263 children were taken from their homes and put into state custody. Of the 236 children, 150 were not allowed to return to their parents for more than two years. Other parents never regained custody of their children.[6] Prior to the raid, the Short Creek priesthood council had begun to split apart, fulfilling a prophecy by John Woolley many years before that "a generation yet unborn, along with some of the men who are living here now, are going to establish groups . . . [and] . . . would contend among each other, that they would divide, that they would subdivide and they would be in great contention" (quoted in Kraut 1989, 22). After Joseph Musser had a stroke in 1949, he called his physician, Rulon C. Allred, to be his second elder. This put Allred in a strong position to take over Musser's post when he died. In 1951, Musser recovered enough to join Richard Jessop in voting Rulon in as patriarch of the priesthood council. Musser's decision was vetoed by most of the council, who were absent during the appointment of Rulon, inspiring contentions and different interpretations over who would be the "one mighty and strong." This bickering split the original movement. Rulon Allred led one faction and Louis Kelsch headed the other.[7] Leroy S. Johnson and Charles Zitting, who were loyal to Kelsch, remained in Short Creek, where they created the official Fundamentalist Church of Jesus Christ of Latter-day Saints, while Musser, Jessop, and Allred began work to start a new movement, which eventually became known as the Apostolic United Brethren. This latter group created a new council in 1952 made up of E. Jenson, John Butchereit, Lyman Jessop, Owen Allred, Marvin Allred, and Joseph Thompson. Although this split led to major changes in the expression of Mormon fundamentalism, all contemporary groups whose origins lie in the original Short Creek movement share common threads of kinship, marriage, and core beliefs.

The Fundamentalist Church of Jesus Christ of Latter-day Saints (FLDS)

The FLDS Church is the largest Mormon fundamentalist polygamist group. Its approximately 10,000 members live in the headquarters of Hildale, Utah, and Colorado City, Arizona. Sagebrush, piñon pines, and juniper trees grow abundantly in the two towns. Irrigated farm fields and walled compounds

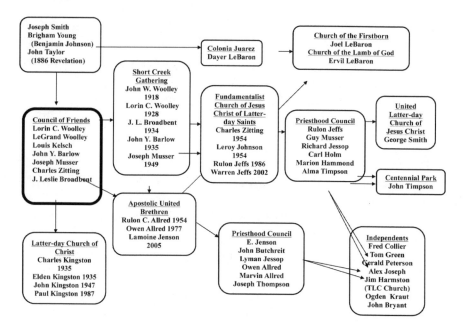

Figure 1. Contemporary Mormon groups with origins in the Short Creek movement.

prevent those from the outside world from entering. Since 2004, there has been a movement to shift the headquarters to the Yearning for Zion Ranch located six miles northeast of Eldorado, Texas. The ranch compound consists of about twenty-five two-story log cabin–style homes and a number of workshops and factories, all of which is scattered over 1,700 acres. At the center sits a gleaming white stone temple, created out of "hardscrapple" rocky terrain (Anderson 2010). The FLDS Church also has a long-standing colony in Bountiful, British Columbia, which is currently under scrutiny for its practice of marrying underage girls to older men. Bountiful was founded in the 1950s and now has about 1,000 people. Other branches are located in Colorado and South Dakota.

The land and houses occupied by the FLDS Church on the Utah-Arizona border are owned by the United Effort Plan (UEP), a collective controlled by FLDS Church leaders that owns most of the property and businesses of members. In 2005, the attorney general of Utah filed a lawsuit and seized the holdings of the UEP for the current residents of Colorado City and Hildale. A court order froze the assets of the UEP, which was worth $100 million at the time, pending a resolution of the lawsuit. The group thrives on land deals, various in-house industries, and machine shops that sell airplane components to the government, which is quite strange given the fact that their bigamist practices are considered a Class C felony (Kaye 2008). From 1998 to 2007, the community received more than $1.7 million from the government for airplane equipment. FLDS members are central to the economy of Colorado City. For example, when Warren Jeffs recommended that FLDS Church members pull their children out of public schools, the number of students in the Colorado City Unified School District declined from more than 1,200 to around 250.

Like the other groups that split off from the original Council of Friends, the FLDS Church has been led by a succession of prophets who believe themselves to be the "one mighty and strong." The first leader of the FLDS Church, John Y. Barlow, led the community at Short Creek until his death in 1949. He was succeeded by Joseph White Musser. The core group in Short Creek rejected Musser's appointee, Rulon Allred; instead, they followed Louis Kelsch and Charles Zitting. In 1954, Charles Zitting died and Leroy S. Johnson took his place. Johnson renamed Short Creek as Colorado City. Also in the 1950s, Harold and Ray Blackmore of the FLDS group aligned themselves with Canadian polygamists and began a colony near Creston, British Columbia.

For thirty years, the rather avuncular LeRoy Johnson led the FLDS. Johnson relied on a group of high priests to guide the church. In 1986, Johnson died and was succeeded by Rulon Jeffs, who assumed the position of "prophet," a title his predecessors never used. Under Rulon, the FLDS gained a reputation for rigid patriarchal control. The prophet was considered the firm ruler of the group; he arranged marriages of young girls to older men and expelled those who dissented. Some dissenters, such as Marion Hammond and Alma and John Timpson, left the community and built a new group in nearby Centennial Park, Arizona, calling themselves The Work. This offshoot group has about 1,500 members who still practice a form of arranged marriage, but dress in slightly more contemporary clothing and live in large mansions paid for by members of Centennial Park, not the larger FLDS group. Another sect that now lives in Salt Lake City split from the Centennial Park and FLDS sects around 2002. This group, which calls itself the Nielsen/Naylor group, has around 200 members.

In the 1990s, Rulon Jeffs began having a series of strokes. Within this time frame, Winston Blackmore, who had been serving in Canada as the Bishop of Bountiful for the FLDS Church, was excommunicated by Rulon in an apparent power struggle. This led to a split within the community in Bountiful, and an estimated 700 FLDS members left the church to follow Blackmore. In 1990, a group of women fled the various polygamous sects, an action that initiated a series of investigations into polygamy in Colorado City and Bountiful.

When Rulon died in September 2002, he had twenty-two wives and more than sixty children. After burying his father, Warren Jeffs assumed the role of the prophet. He married several of his father's wives and then proceeded to wed many more women, including eight of Merril Jessop's daughters, which tied the two families together. The current estimate is that Warren has around sixty to eighty wives (including one who was under age at the time of the marriage). Although many FLDS men have multiple wives, the number of wives of those closest to the prophet can reach into the double digits. Carolyn Jessop, Merril Jessop's former fourth wife, left the household in 2003 with her eight children. She went on to write a best-selling book called *Escape* that described FLDS polygamist wives as unhappy, trapped women (Anderson 2010, 2). However, Carolyn's daughter has returned to the group and has said that her mother was delusional. A church document called the Bishop's Record that was seized during the Texas raid in April 2008 shows that one of Warren's lieutenants, Wendell Nielsen, claims twenty-one wives.

FLDS members are rigidly patriarchal, more so than other groups. They believe that a man must have plural wives in order to attain highest form of salvation. It is generally believed in the church that a man should have a minimum of three wives to fulfill this requirement. According to one academic observer, they have achieved this goal. Each FLDS man has an average of 3.5 wives and an average of eight children per wife (Altman and Ginat 1996). Because of its focus on underage marriage and its emphasis on wife quotas, the FLDS has often been associated with abuse. The church's practice of hoarding young women and marrying them to older males inevitably leads to shortages of brides. As a result, the church has been linked to child marriages, incest, and child abuse.[8] Abuses also occur against boys and men. For example, after Warren Jeffs purchased land in Colorado and Texas he began excommunicating males in the church. In the case of the "lost boys," 400 young men left or were forced from the community and ended up fending for themselves on the streets of Las Vegas, Salt Lake City, and St. George, Utah. Dan Fischer, a former member of the FLDS, has worked with 300 such young men, a few of whom were as young as thirteen when he began working with them, over the past seven years. The reason he gives for this expulsion verifies my 1994 findings that a "successful" polygamous group must somehow expel its males to limit competition for the small pool of marriageable young women. As Dan puts it, "If you have men marrying 20, 30, up to 80 or more women, then it comes down to biology and simple math that there will be a lot of other men who aren't going to get wives. The church says it's kicking these boys out for being disruptive influences (such as for listening to rock and roll), but if you'll notice, they rarely kick out girls" (quoted in Anderson 2010, 56).

In order to organize the larger surplus of women left behind when hundreds of men were excommunicated, Rulon and Warren Jeffs restored an early Brigham Young policy called the "law of placement," which transfers the wives and children of a church member to another man. Traditionally, this was done upon the death of a patriarch so that his widows might be cared for or to rescue a woman from an abusive relationship. Warren Jeffs has used this kind of wife reassignment as a weapon against anyone who threatens his "one man rule." Under this rule, young women are assigned to much older husbands by revelation from God to the leader of the church, who is regarded as a prophet. The prophet elects to take and give wives to and from men according to their worthiness.

The formal FLDS gender code requires that wives be subordinate to their husbands and wear their hair long. Women avoid makeup, pants, or any skirt above the knees. Men wear plain clothing, usually a long-sleeved collared shirt and full-length pants. Men and women are forbidden to have any tattoos or body piercings. Women and girls usually wear monochromatic homemade long-sleeved "prairie dresses" with hems between ankle and mid-calf. They wear long stockings or trousers underneath and usually keep their hair braided in back with a Gibson wave in front. Some FLDS women speak in favor of such rigid strictures that set their roles in stone as mothers and wives of Zion. In contrast, others such as Carolyn Jessop and Carmen Thompson felt trapped and abused in such a male supremacist framework and left the group as soon as they were able. More escapee literature is written by ex-FLDS women than any other group. FLDS women are rarely granted a divorce, and if they are awarded a release from a marriage, the prophet quickly assigns them to another man.

The FLDS branches are invariably isolated from the outside world, and members scrutinize each other's behavior closely. Members began questioning Warren's motives in 2004 when he started to take other men's wives and oust their husbands from the church. On January 10, 2004, Colorado City mayor

Dan Barlow and about twenty other men were excommunicated and stripped of their wives and children (who were reassigned to other men) and the right to live in the town. Because of Warren Jeffs' powerful position and the potential of increasing their status, many women agreed with this arrangement and stood by Jeffs. Some had little choice in the matter. He also alienated many members when he ordered a group of teenagers to spy on people and search their homes for evidence of sin and dissent. This alienation of wives from husbands and the excommunications caused about fifty families to leave the group. The exiles reentered mainstream Mormonism, fled to the AUB, and/or converted into the Centennial Park group. Warren's diary, which was seized during the Texas raid, reveals a man who was obsessed with control. He micromanaged all decisions in each household within each family. He decided who married whom and which economic stewardship each man would have and who would be kicked out. Warren said that God guided his actions, even to the point of telling him to monitor sun-tanning activities at the local salon. Warren also required people to avoid wearing red (that color belonged to Jesus, he said) and to keep their hair long so they could bathe the feet of Christ when he comes again. He also forbade people to use the word "fun."

The FLDS has recently been depicted by *National Geographic* as "an isolated cult whose members, worn down by rigid social control, display a disturbing fealty to one man, the prophet Warren Jeffs" (Anderson 2010, 3). In 2005, an Arizona grand jury convicted Warren Jeffs of child sex abuse, and in Utah two civil suits were brought against him for expelling young men and for sexually abusing a nephew. That same year, a Utah court transferred control of the trust that oversees much of the land in Hildale, Utah, and Colorado City from the FLDS leadership to a state-appointed fiduciary. Warren escaped to Canada to avoid arrest and was later apprehended by authorities in Nevada. In October 2005, a Colorado deputy who pulled Seth Jeffs over for erratic driving at 3 a.m. found incriminating evidence against Warren Jeffs in the form of $140,000 cash and letters intended for delivery to the prophet on the run. After being a fugitive for a few years, Warren was arrested near Mesquite, Nevada, with computers, disguises, and $50,000 in cash in his possession. After spending over a year on the lam to avoid legal issues in Utah—and earning a spot on the FBI's Ten Most Wanted list—Warren was caught was sentenced to life plus twenty years in 2011 for sexually assaulting a twenty-three-year-old and a fourteen-year-old girl. An audio recording bore witness to the sexual assault of the twelve-year old, which instructed other child brides how to please Jeffs sexually. Jeffs instructed the girls that when they please him, they are pleasing God, atoning for the sins of the community. Evidence showed that Jeffs often raped young women in his home, indoctrinating them to hold each other down during the "heavenly" sessions of sexual assault, as shown in a videotape. Jeffs' nephew and niece testified that he raped them as small children, threatening them to keep the "godly" assaults secret or risk their salvation. DNA evidence showed that Jeffs had fathered a child with a fifteen-year-old girl. Eleven other church members are awaiting trial in Texas, including Jeffs' heir apparent, Merril Jessop, who was indicted for performing the marriage of Jeffs to an underage girl. When other lawsuits were brought against Jessop relating to his misuse of United Effort funds, the state government seized FLDS assets, including land and homes in Bountiful, Utah. Though his attorneys made a statement that Warren Jeffs had resigned as president of the church upon his conviction, FLDS members still call him their prophet. It is unclear whether the leader is William E. Jessop, a former first counselor, or Merril Jessop, the bishop of the Eldorado branch.

Warren Jeffs wasn't the only one who was arrested for illegal activities in the FLDS movement. In 2003, FLDS police officer Rodney Holm was convicted of unlawful sexual conduct with a sixteen- or seventeen-year-old and one count of bigamy for his marriage to and impregnation of plural wife Ruth Stubbs. In 2005, eight FLDS men were also indicted for sexual contact with minors. All of them turned themselves in to police in Kingman, Arizona, within days of the indictment. Brent Jeffs filed suit accusing three of his uncles, including Warren Jeffs, of sexually assaulting him when he was a child.

Although all Mormon fundamentalist groups practice some welfare fraud, which members call "bleeding the beast," the FLDS has had the greatest impact on this practice. There is also some evidence to show that FLDS leaders have encouraged their flock to take advantage of government assistance in the form of welfare programs and the WIC Program. Since the government recognizes only one woman as the legal wife of a man, the rest of his wives are considered single mothers and are eligible to receive government assistance. The more wives and children one has, the more welfare checks and food stamps one can receive. In 2003, more than $6 million dollars in public funds were channeled into the community of Colorado City, Arizona, alone. Since members feel that the federal government is corrupt, they believe that it isn't cheating to take from it in the form of food stamps, welfare checks, and free health care.

The FLDS share other controversial beliefs. For example, because FLDS members believe that blacks are associated with Cain and the devil, they fiercely condemn interracial relationships. In his church sermons, Warren uses Brigham Young's nineteenth-century teaching of "blood atonement," which states that certain serious sins, such as murder, can be atoned for only by the sinner's death.

There are biological issues as well. The FLDS also have the world's highest incidence of fumarase deficiency, an extremely rare genetic condition. Geneticists attribute this to the prevalence of cousin marriage between descendants of two of the town's founders, Joseph Smith Jessop and John Yeates Barlow. It causes encephalopathy, severe mental retardation, unusual facial features, brain malformation, and epileptic seizures (Dougherty 2005).

In March 2011, William Jeffs replaced Warren Jeffs as prophet. William Jeffs is actually William Edson Jessop, the son of Kathy Jessop and Alma A. Timpson, an apostle of the Centennial Park group. In 2007, Warren Jeffs reportedly said that William had received an apostolic calling and ordination. According to one FLDS informant, the group is in a state of political upheaval and no one is sure who the true leader will be (e-mail interview, 2011).

Apostolic United Brethren (AUB)

The Apostolic United Brethren (AUB, or Allred Group), informally known as The Work, The Priesthood, or The Group, has approximately 8,000 members throughout the world. I have estimated that from 1990 to 1996, an average of six mainstream LDS families converted to the Allred Group each month. Of course this figure was offset by relatively high attrition rates, mostly disgruntled males who left the system (Bennion 1998). This short-term conversion frenzy decreased around 2000. The official headquarters is in Bluffdale, Utah, where the AUB has a chapel/cultural hall, an endowment house, a school, archives, and a sports field. Although there is an Allred compound of houses for family members, most of members live in medium-sized split-level homes in the Bluffdale/Draper area. Those who have done well in business or enjoy favorable stewardships (more lucrative economic callings) have "McMansions" of 3,000–4,000 square feet to accommodate all their wives and children, such as those you'll see in the Eagle Mountain branch (near Cedar Fort, Utah). The church operates at least three private schools, but many families home school or send their children to public or public charter schools. The AUB has other branches in Santaquin, Utah (Rocky Ridge); Eagle Mountain, Utah (Harvest Haven); Cedar City, Lehi, and Granite, Utah; Pinesdale, Montana; Lovell, Wyoming; Mesa, Arizona; Humansville, Missouri; and Ozumba, Mexico, where it has a temple with around 700 followers. More AUB members live in Germany, the Netherlands, and England.[9]

Upon Joseph Musser's death in 1954, Dr. Rulon C. Allred was named the contested prophet (Allred 1981). As an orthodox Mormon, Allred had originally sought to discipline polygamists who were furthering the work of the devil, often referring to the "strayings" of his father, Byron Harvey Allred. However, when Rulon began studying "the mysteries," he found that he agreed with his father, who had secretly married many wives. He tried to convince his wife, Katherine, a staunch Mormon, to adopt polygamy and told his family that he had seen a vision of Christ asking him to comply with the "fulness." In 1940, Katherine left him and he was excommunicated from the LDS Church. However, he always maintained that Harold B. Lee was God's prophet and that he held the priesthood keys in a limited sense, without polygamy or true priesthood authority. He did not see the fundamentalist effort as being *above* the church but parallel to it, something that provided the missing ingredient of pure celestial marriage.

Because of Rulon's teachings, the AUB believes that the early leaders of the polygamy movement — George Q. Cannon, John Woolley, and the other three witnesses to Taylor's decree — used the priesthood keys to take up the Lord's work and make sure that the celestial covenant and law of consecration were kept alive. When Rulon took up the mantle he made it clear that not everyone could (or should) participate in the holy principle of polygamy and that even in the church there would be many who are not capable of the highest glory. In other words, although all leaders are polygamists, many Allredites do not practice polygamy, although they still believe in a time when they will be given the holy opportunity to take a plural wife, be it in this life or the next.

By 1959, the AUB had grown to 1,000 members with the help of Joseph Lyman Jessop, Joseph Thompson, and other converts, who met covertly in the Bluffdale home of Owen Allred, Rulon's brother.[10] The ranch was located in the Bitterroot Mountains of western Montana in an area that was later incorporated as Pinesdale in 1983. In 1960, Rulon Allred bought the 640 acres of ranch land for $42,500, and by 1973 more than 400 fundamentalists called it home. When I was there, from 1989 to 1993, there was a school/church complex, a library, a cattle operation, a machine shop, and the vestiges of a dairy operation. I counted approximately 60–70 married men (patriarchs) with around 140–150 wives (around 2.8 each, on average) and 720 children. The Jessops (Marvin and Morris) and their eldest sons were the leaders of Pinesdale, along with less powerful members of the priesthood council. In 2000, a series of forest fires drove out some members, but many stayed behind. Pinesdale residents often sell morel mushrooms locally.

Throughout the 1960s, the Allred Group membership expanded significantly in Pinesdale and the Salt Lake region, primarily through new converts and plentiful births. Converts interested in building their own family kingdoms were drawn to the AUB and were given permission to marry plural wives. These ceremonies were always performed by members of the priesthood council. They were conducted in homes, in the endowment house, in the church building, or even on a hillside or meadow. When possible, they would be conducted at a sacred altar constructed in a makeshift or symbolic way wherever the marriage took place so that the marriage would be sealed for all eternity. By 1970, the number of AUB members was close to 2,500. In 1973, to make room for the growing church, Rulon directed that a small group relocate to Cedar City, Utah. By 2003, the new group had twenty-two families and a small school. In 1971, Rulon also approved the purchase of 225 acres between Santaquin and Mona in Utah, on the hillside known as Rocky Ridge.

Rulon Allred's priesthood council was made up of ten members. The composition of the council evolved continuously. In the 1970s the council included Rulon, Owen Allred, George Scott, Ormand Lavery, Marvin Jessop and his brother Morris Jessop, Lamoine Jensen, George Maycock, John Ray, and Bill Baird. Over the years, Rulon replaced members who died, who were excommunicated (as in the case of John Ray), or who apostatized. Rulon kept his two brothers, Owen and Marvin, close at hand, bestowing upon them favorable stewardships and granting them permission to marry several wives each.

In 1977, Rulon was killed by a female assassin sent by Ervil LeBaron[11] and his brother Owen took the helm. Owen led the group for twenty-eight years, a period when the AUB expanded its membership and entered into a time of collaboration with the press, academia, and the Utah attorney general's office. The AUB is the fundamentalist sect most similar to the LDS Church, and among the Mormon groups it has the most converts directly drawn from the mainstream Mormon community. Like the mainstream Latter-day Saints, they have developmental programs for males and females of all ages, explained below. The bishop is the leader of each branch, but AUB councilmen live in each branch to provide priesthood authority. They are known to use some religious and educational material published by the LDS Church in their sermons and for Sunday school lessons. The AUB's members also tend to integrate with surrounding Mormon communities, much more so than other Mormon fundamentalists, like the FLDS or LeBarons, which tend toward isolation. This can largely be attributed Owen's desire to work with local law enforcement officials, especially to end rumors of arranged marriages with underage girls. Allred believed that transparency was an important factor in his efforts to show the non-Mormon community that the AUB and its members were not a threat.

The structure of the AUB's priesthood organization duplicates that of other groups and the original LDS Church design. The church is headed by a president of the priesthood. Next in authority is a priesthood council (of which the president is a part). Below the priesthood council are presidents of the Seventy, the Seventy quorum members (high-ranking priesthood leaders), high priests, elders, members of the Aaronic Priesthood, the Relief Society (a women's group), Sunday schools, and young men and women's groups, Boy Scouts, and the children's primary groups (which may be different according to region). Present at the local level are bishops, representatives of the priesthood council, and patriarchs. The general sacrament meeting (which is open to the public) and Sunday school meetings (as well as many private family Sunday schools) take place on Sundays, as do meetings for all male priesthood holders. The Relief Society and young women's, primary, and scouting groups meet during the week. Dances, firesides, musical events, plays, and classes are often held at meetinghouses.

Although the Allred women have had their share of abuse, especially during the John Ray years of the 1970s, the rates of abuse are no greater than what you would expect to find in the mainstream monogamist communities of the United States.[12] According to the sheriff of Ravali County, the rate of abuse in Pinedale is far less than in most towns in the region (personal interview, 2008). AUB members consider child and spousal abuse and incest to be serious sins. Members who perpetrate such crimes are excommunicated, and victims are encouraged to report the incidents to the police. In addition, it is my feeling that the AUB is more progressive and law-abiding than other groups. Its members pay their taxes, seem to dress like everyone else for the most part, send their kids to public school, and even have a Boy Scout troop. However, there are some flies in the AUB ointment, such as the ex-Allredite man who recently was arrested for raping twin sisters in Humansville, Missouri. There is also evidence of money laundering and some welfare fraud.[13] According to one former member, attorney John Llewellyn, plural wives are sent into nearby Hamilton to apply for welfare as single mothers, and they take this money directly to the priesthood Brethren. In my own research in 1993, I heard of welfare misuse in 25 percent of my sample of fifteen extended families. They looked on it much the same way that the FLDS wives did, as "creative financing" that was taking from the federal government, a corrupt entity. Another issue is the problem of racism. Like the FLDS and other fundamentalists, the AUB believes that blacks should never have been given the priesthood. In the 1990s, when it was discovered that Richard Kunz, a Caucasian-looking man who had been ordained to the priesthood, had African ancestry, he was released and ostracized.

Yet to its credit, under the leadership of Owen Allred, the AUB provided a template for female autonomy. In 2001, Owen Allred spoke publicly about accusations that polygamists in Utah were guilty of promoting marriages of underage teenagers. He stated: "We are not opposed to laws preventing parents or anyone else using force or intimidation to get a girl to marry against her will before she is of the age of eighteen" (Adams 2001, 2).[14] Government officials and law enforcement agencies applauded his clear stance. Owen also provided sound advice about the equal treatment of wives in plural marriages. He said that a man should "never discuss private problems between him and a wife with another wife," and should never "allow privileges to one wife that he does not allow to the other wives" (ibid.). However, on one occasion he said that some of women's duties were limited. While his own finances were handled by a woman (Donna Baird), in a bizarre statement he said: "The minute a man turns over the finances to his wife and lets her handle the checking account [and] lets her keep track of the bookkeeping, he is lamed. . . . No woman should ever handle the finances in a celestial family. This must be solely the responsibility of the man, the head of the family" (quoted in Hales 2008a, 2).

In 2004, the priesthood leadership was comprised of Owen Allred, Lamoine Jensen, Ron Allred, Dave Watson, Lyn Thompson, Shem Jessop, Harry Bonell, Sam Allred, Marvin Jessop, and Morris Jessop. In 2005, Owen Allred died at the age of ninety-one, after appointing Lamoine Jensen to be his successor, passing up more senior council members. Recently Lamoine developed intestinal cancer; knowledge of this has caused some commotion in the group. Lamoine has focused on Harry Bannell for the presidency, although Morris and Marvin Jessop have seniority and may be vying for the position, especially since they disagree with many of Lamoine's policies. Dave Watson is also a prime candidate. According to several former members of the Allred Group, Jensen is much more rigidly patriarchal in his organization of the Work than Owen was (Bennion 2008).

Latter-day Church of Christ (the Kingstons)

The Latter-day Church of Christ, also known as the Kingston Clan, The Order, The Davis County Cooperative, and The Co-op Society, has around 3,500 members. They are led by their prophet, Paul E. Kingston. The church is based in Salt Lake City but has a branch in Davis County and settlements scattered along the Wasatch Front in Utah.

To trace their history, we must go back to the early 1920s, when Charles W. Kingston struck up a friendship with Lorin C. Woolley, J. Leslie Broadbent, and Joseph Musser in Short Creek, all men who had been excommunicated from the LDS Church. When L. Broadbent died in 1935, a succession dispute between Charles Kingston and John Y. Barlow ended with the Kingston family leaving Short Creek. The Kingstons believed that Elden Kingston, Charles W. Kingston's son, had been set apart as Broadbent's second elder and rightful successor. Elden, who settled in Davis County, claimed that an angel visited him in a cave near Bountiful, Utah, and directed him to build up a society based on the United Order. In 1941, Elden formed the Davis County Cooperative Society, which sought to establish the Golden Rule among the Saints, do away with war and bloodshed, create a self-sustaining community, establish brotherly love among all men, and operate a thriving economic enterprise. Though Elden was still tied to Joseph Musser—he even sent missionaries down to Short Creek—his son, John Ortell Kingston, broke away from Musser's influence in the 1950s. John Musser diligently pursued financial wealth and sought to expand the group. He eventually relinquished his title as the "one mighty and strong" in 1987 to his son Paul Elden Kingston, the current prophet.[15] In 2011, the group had about 1,500 members and held about $150 million in mining, gambling, and various other investments. Their assets include a 300-acre dairy farm in Davis County; a cattle ranch and coal mine in Emery County; a 3,200-acre farm and 1,200 acres in Idaho; a discount store; a grocery store; restaurant supply company with outlets in in Tucson, Phoenix, Denver, Las Vegas, Boise, Portland, and Los Angeles; and the United Bank.

The Kingstons are the most secretive of all polygamy groups. They used armed guards outside their Sunday meetings and ban visitors. They are known for the large number of underage marriages they perform, the highest number of incestuous marriages, and the highest natural birth rate of any of the fundamentalist Mormon groups. Girls are often married soon after their first menarche in order to increase the possible number of children they can have over their lifetimes. The priesthood leaders determine who these girls will marry, most often assigning them to the most powerful pureblood patriarchs. This activity meshes nicely with their goal of kingdom building and making sure their bloodlines are pure.

Like the other groups discussed in this chapter, the Kingstons practice polygamy. Girls and young women are married to patriarchs who have consanguineal and affinal ties to the Kingston extended family. This ensures a holy progeny for each kingdom builder/patriarch. The Kingstons claim that their bloodlines can be traced all the way back to Jesus Christ himself. Elden believed that his divine birthright gave him Godlike powers as well as "unlimited health, knowledge, intelligence, sympathy, tolerance, realization, ambition, courage, patience, vitality, forgiveness, perseverance, energy, obedience, joy, satisfaction, cleanliness, beauty, confidence, determination and independence, which cause my personality to penetrate and influence all of God's creations" (Kingston 1947, 1). The logic used to "purify" the Kingston family genetically was said to have developed at the Kingston Dairy in Woods Cross, where J. Ortell experimented with cattle breeding. This theory encourages incest to perfect the bloodline and protect it from outside contamination. There are many examples of inbreeding in the Kingston Clan. Jason Ortell Kingston was married to Andrea Johnson, his half-sister. Jeremy Ortell Kingston was married to LuAnn Kingston, both his first cousin and his aunt. And David O. Kingston married his fifteen-year-old niece, Mary Ann Kingston.

The Kingstons differ from other groups in their extreme emphasis on blood hierarchy. For example, Elden taught that he held all the priesthood keys, which put him at the center of all things. Other members would be bound to him just as if he were God. This hierarchical order was called the Law of Satisfaction. This law places immense importance on honoring all participants who have been assigned low numbers. These individuals are higher in the hierarchy, similar to the biblical kinship nomenclature (or the

Sudanese system). Such numbering systems are designed to organize large patrilineal clans into quick, recognizable units for distributing resources and calculating tribute obligations. Elden adopted this biblical template, stating that "each individual . . . no matter what authority, standing, or station he is in, is responsible to the one above him in exactly the same way as if that individual was the Savior himself. . . . We must look at the one above us in the same light as we look at the Savior" (Kingston 1947, 1). The Kingstons designate their priesthood nomenclature through the title of "brother #1," "brother #2," and "brother #3." Their children are also numbered, since there are so many. Everything is seen as a hierarchy of numbers. For example, if a priesthood bearer is known as #27, his first wife will be #127 and his first male child is #1271 and the first female child #1272. His second wife would be #227 and her children would be #2271, #2472, and so on; girls are assigned even numbers and boys are assigned odd numbers. The Kingston church holds that every child is a priceless blessing, and members believe in the values of family, industry, education, and self-sufficiency. Children are allowed to attend public school and some go on to attend college, which enables them to give more fully back to the father church once they are gainfully employed. The church recently established a private school, which almost all of the children now attend.

In the early days of the church, the Kingston men wore blue coverall-type suits tied with strings and the women and girls wore plain blue dresses. Blue was seen as symbolic of the Kingston renunciation of worldly goods. The outer clothing contained no pockets for possessions, and many members wore no hats or shoes. Since those times they've adopted a rather 1950s style of dress. Men wear white business attire with skinny ties or bolo ties, and women wear modest home-made long-sleeved dresses with hemlines at the ankle. Long hair is preferred for women. The Kingstons believed in a more stringent version of the Mormon Word of Wisdom (Doctrine and Covenants, 89). They believe that some foods like squash or radishes are to be consumed on certain days as the primary food and that other foods should be avoided.

In 1987, when J. Ortell died, he had twenty-five wives and dozens of children. Honoring his father's Law of Satisfaction, he had given all his seven sons from his first wife the highest positions of financial and religious power. They were awarded the most wives and were given the power to determine how the group would be run. These sons claimed to come from genetically superior ancestry, which gave them an advantage over all others. They used this power to convince much younger women (some as young as fourteen) to join their bloodline. This ensured that other men were not eligible for wives and had to become servants to the pureblood lines. Although I have no evidence, I assume that many of these rogue males were ostracized through the same vehicle of alienation and excommunication that FLDS prophet Warren Jeffs used.

Paul E. Kingston, who is now in his sixties, has followed in his uncle Elden's footsteps. He sanctions inbreeding and marriages to child brides. He is a certified public accountant and attorney with forty wives and an unknown number of children. He believes that plural marriage allows a man to achieve glory through as many wives and children as possible. He encourages his wives to restrict lactation to only a few months so they will be ready to conceive again shortly after childbirth. It is estimated that some of his wives have sixteen children, which would give him somewhere in the neighborhood of 300 children (Tracy 2001). He was an achiever in his youth as student body president of South High, Boys State representative, and a law student. But in spite of his many accomplishments, Paul likes to remain secretive and isolated. His cousin Carl, on the other hand, is constantly in the public light as the group's primary legal counsel. Carl has several wives and thirty children and has been kept quite busy representing Kingston relatives in a handful of newsworthy incidents. For example, he represented his cousin John Daniel Kingston, Paul's brother, who was accused of beating his sixteen-year-old daughter, Mary Ann, when she fled the group. She was the fifteenth wife of her uncle, David Kingston. John Kingston served seven months in jail and David was convicted of incest and sentenced to four years in prison. John was also involved in a custody battle with one of his wives, Heidi Mattingly Foster, during which he had problems remembering the names of his children. In 1987, Carl Kingston gave his sixteen-year-old daughter to his cousin, David, in a Bountiful wedding. The groom already had two wives. Jeremy Ortell Kingston, Paul's nephew, also defended by Carl, was convicted for his marriage to fifteen-year-old LuAnn, his first cousin. In 2000, she attempted to leave the group with her children. She was taught that if you were not married by seventeen, you were considered an old maid in the Kingston clan (Janofsky 2003). Carl also defended his uncle, J. Ortell Kingston, the former prophet of the group, in 1983, when he was sued for welfare fraud. Interestingly, at a time when the group had assets of $70 million, J. Ortell's four wives, at his encouragement, posed as single mothers and collected public assistance for a decade. He repaid the state $250,000 in welfare compensation and the case against him was dropped. In spite of the wealth of the group, some families live in extreme poverty and must go on welfare or scrounge for their food and clothing. It was reported that the homes of lower-ranking wives are often rundown and had peeling paint and broken windows (Janofsky 2003).

Though they often make the headlines, the Kingstons do not believe in bringing attention to themselves. They harbor a deep distrust of hospitals, the media, and government agencies. For example, when the wife of Jason Kingston (who was his half-sister) developed preeclampsia during her pregnancy, Jason and his brother Paul waited to take her to the hospital until the last minute because it would disclose the incestuous relationship. She died during a C-section (Moore-Emmett 2004).

The Church of the Firstborn of the "Fulness" of Times (The LeBarons)

The Church of the Firstborn was established in 1955 as a sanctuary in the Mexican desert, away from the sinners and corruption of the modern world (Bennion 2004; LeBaron 1981). The church has had a tumultuous history, primarily due to severe mental illnesses associated with the LeBaron gene pool. But today it is a peaceful agrarian community of a few hundred members. The group is hidden in the Chihuahua Desert in the small town of Galeana, thirty-five miles south of Casas Grandes. I conducted fieldwork there in the summer of 1999 with a few students from Utah Valley University, staying with the family of Brent LeBaron and his three wives (Bennion 2004). The LeBarons have branches in Los Molinos, Baja California; San Diego, California; and parts of Central America. In addition, several hundred members are scattered around the Salt Lake Valley.

On entering the Colonia LeBaron ranch, you first see a tiny roadside grocery store stocked with soda, tortillas, car oil, and toilet paper. Then comes a series of innocuous *muralla* adobe homes, a few cottonwoods, and small fields and gardens. Once you turn west into town, the compounds become visible. These are large, five- or six-acre plots with two or three homes and several sheds and lawns, surrounded on all sides with large cottonwoods, elms, and fruit trees. Most of the roads in LeBaron are dirt (except for El Centro, which is now blacktop), and most of the homes are of whitewashed adobe brick or cinder blocks with decorative trim, a chimney, or window dressing to provide a distinctive style. Occasionally, usually outside town, you see larger, more modern homes.

Colonia LeBaron has orchards, fields, and a community church/schoolhouse. It is located in a flattened desert basin next to mountains. Natural feed for cattle and horses is scarce. The community relies heavily on the strength of the family farm and on seasonal migratory work for U.S. farmers and construction companies. This work centers primarily in the orchard and drywall businesses but also includes selling pine nuts and fireworks and doing contract construction work. The LeBarons tap into the traditional Mormon ideology of the work ethic, self-reliance, and right-wing patriotism. Most members will tell you they despise taxes and government interference. Their parenting style is strongly authoritarian, applying the "old pioneer tradition" of physical discipline coupled with strict religious training.

LeBaron males experience a more strenuous rite of passage than do the females, just as in the neighboring Mormon town, Colonia Juarez. Rather than go on a mission for the church, however, the LeBaron males leave their homes and accompany their fathers and uncles to learn the drywall business in various U.S. cities. Some boys go up to Utah on their own, hitchhiking and working for a year or two. They return with grins on their faces and new American trucks, clothes, and "worldly" ideas about life. This experience gives them prestige and money, but it also means that they have lost some of the purity they had before they left; they have been "touched by Babylon."

Although interracial marriage is more common in LeBaron than in the FLDS group, Latino converts and *mestizo* offspring are sometimes required to show allegiance to white polygynous patriarchs and deference to pureblood families. Further, although education is bilingual, English is the dominant tongue, and all religious books and teachings are in English, not Spanish. As in other fundamentalist groups, a nonsecular education that includes prayer and Mormon ideology dominates the education system. But many LeBaron families do not require their children to go to school; they do not want their children getting Babylon in their system from public secular schools. The average education level among residents of LeBaron is fifth or sixth grade.

Although the LeBaron family once lived in Colonia Juarez, an LDS town thirty miles west of Casas Grandes that was set up in the 1880s to be a haven for polygamists, they are no longer welcome there. Colonia Juarez folk view Colonia LeBaron as the "bastard child" of Mormonism, a rebellious offshoot of Zion hidden away on the east side of the sierras where few will find them.

Bruce R. McConkie, a member of the Quorum of the Twelve of the Mormon Church, cautioned good Mormons to avoid the LeBaron "cult":

> The most effective response, when slinking dogs bark greedily at the great caravan-of-the-kingdom as it rolls unalterably towards its ultimate celestial destination, is to maintain a dignified and discreet silence. A few jackals and coyotes on the horizon are of no particular concern to the great army of the Lord as it marches triumphantly under the banner of the great King . . . but the worth of souls is great, and if even one member of the church should be wounded or destroyed by the bite of a rabid dog, such would be an eternal tragedy. (McConkie 1961, 1–2)

McConkie further warned the saints of Colonia Juarez and Colonia Dublan that most of the LeBarons have been excommunicated from the correct church and that there is reason to "question the moral status and personal integrity of all who advocate the present practice of adulterous relationships under the guise of plural marriage" (ibid., 43–44). An apostle visiting a church leader in Juarez said, "The only ones in the world we have to fear are those boys in your own back yards" (LeBaron 1981, 128).

In 1944, the LeBarons were excommunicated for teaching and practicing plural marriage. Alma "Dayer" LeBaron left Colonia Juarez to escape persecution from the local Mormon congregation, leaving behind a thriving orchard business. He and his family drove south from Casas until they reached Colonia LeBaron, where Dayer announced, "This is where we are to settle" (LeBaron 1981, 107). The group initially settled near the black hills in the *ejido* of Galeana, between the towns of Galeana and San Buenaventura, in a single adobe dwelling with a dirt floor and a dirt roof. Under the Mexican law of possession, Dayer acquired several 50-acre farms in the El Valle region.

The LeBarons began building their paradise by digging a proper well and clearing the land of mesquite and sagebrush (Bennion 2004). When it rained, they irrigated using a canal that brought water from the floodplains and rivulets. They cleared more land for gardens, orchards, and homesteads and planted fruit and nut trees near the irrigation ditches. Joel and Verlan, Dayer's boys, drove their cattle from Colonia Juarez to the new ranch site, and soon the entire family was growing corn, beans, chilies, and cotton. Hearing of their move, friends of the LeBarons, including the Charles Cox, Henry Covington, and Floyd Spencer families, came down from Utah to help establish the community.

To supplement their meager diets, the settlers hunted deer in the nearby sierras and rabbits, ducks, and cranes that were drawn to the cornfields. In the early days, they lived in makeshift tents and lean-tos whipped around by the desert winds and rainstorms. Each year, the LeBarons added new projects to the ranch. They raised goats, cattle, and fowl, and they planted new wheat and alfalfa crops. They built adobe homes until they had enough money to build homes of wood and rock. Although the ranch was called by many names, including Matortiz, Parcelas LeBaron, and Seccion LeBaron, it eventually became known as Colonia LeBaron, the settlement created by the LeBaron clan.

When Joseph Musser died, Dayer LeBaron aligned himself with Rulon Allred. The Allreds and LeBarons intermarried and lived together peacefully for ten years in the Chihuahua Desert. In the early 1950s, however, they fell into disagreement about who should be the prophet. In 1955, before establishing his church, Joel LeBaron claimed to have seen heavenly messengers while he was praying in the sierras west of LeBaron: "They talked to me as plain as you and I are talking together. I now know the exact pattern to be used in setting the house of God in order" (LeBaron 1981, 125). Joel said that he had received the mantle of the priesthood from his father. Later that year, he received a revelation from Christ that he should build a new church. In September, Joel and his brothers went to Salt Lake City to set up their religion. He named his brother Floren as first counselor in the First Presidency and his brother Ross as head patriarch. At this time, Joel saw a vision of Jesus, Abraham, Moses, Elijah, and Joseph Smith Jr., who confirmed his status as prophet. Joel said his priesthood line of authority came from his father Alma, who had been ordained by Alma's grandfather Benjamin F. Johnson, who had received the priesthood from Joseph Smith (Bennion 2004). Upon their return from Salt Lake, Joel's father, Alma Dayer LeBaron, and his younger brother, Ervil, became the fourth and fifth members of the new church. This news perturbed the leadership of the AUB and the orthodox Mormon Church of Dublan, both of which Joel and many of his family were still official members. In 1956, Joel was summoned to a hearing in the Dublan First Ward and charged with apostasy, and after a lengthy church court, he was excommunicated.

Joel's followers have described him as kind, meek, gentle, humble, and Christlike (Bennion 2004). Joel taught that Christ had tried to institutionalize the Kingdom of God on earth by establishing the royal laws of obedience but was not successful because the political world was too corrupt. He explained that Joseph Smith had taken up the mantle from Christ to build the kingdom, establishing the economic order of God (the United Order) and plural marriage as the most holy forms of celestial unity. But the earth's people were not ready to accept such powerful laws of liberty and truth, and they murdered Joseph and his brother Hyrum in the Carthage, Illinois, jail. So it was up to Joel, the next in line, to establish the Kingdom of God outside the United States in the Chihuahua Desert. Joel made it clear that he was establishing one kingdom for all people — Catholics, fundamentalists, Mormons, and Protestants. This was different from the Mormon concept of three kingdoms (Celestial, Terrestrial, and Telestial). He summoned all true saints of God's kingdom to leave the United States and other "nations of Babylon" and gather in the Mexican wilderness, where the kingdom would be built anew under his divine leadership. The bloodlines of new converts would be fused with Joel's own royal blood. He called himself the Firstborn (Lebaron 1981).

Joel quickly converted many family members and neighbors, and he sent out missionaries to California, Texas, and Mexico City to spread his message. He converted hundreds of people to his new church, including Mormon missionaries from France and staunch members of the Mormon leadership in Dublan. The Church of the Firstborn grew quickly and established colonies in San Diego and Baja, Mexico (Los Molinos). While most Anglo-Mormons converted because they believed that Joel's interpretation of Mormon scripture was the most correct, many Hispanic members sought out the young church because it promised economic equality, farmland, and the opportunity for plural marriage, which locals were already practicing informally.

New members were asked to consecrate all their properties and assets to the church in order to be "worthy to have their names written in the book of the law of God" (LeBaron 1981, 166). They were asked to increase their stewardship (private industry) so they could give 10 percent of any surplus to the poor and help build up Zion. In addition, they contributed labor to build a communal school, a laundry facility, and a kitchen. Each of these projects was overseen by Ervil LeBaron and was intended to eradicate the evils of both wealth and poverty. Unfortunately, the early church experienced serious financial problems that included bankruptcies, indebtedness, and extreme poverty. The LeBaron brothers, including Joel and Verlan, lost thousands of the community's dollars in one ill-fated project after another — a cheese factory, a lumber industry, and a cattle herd all ended in disaster. In fact, this legacy of doomed ventures still plagues the LeBarons; many sons, including Brent, my informant, pour funds into visionary projects, only to lose most of their profits the next year.

Joel's teaching followed the Mormon scriptures closely, stressing above all the Ten Commandments and Christ's law of love. "The inherent essence of Deity is that He does not or will not vary from that law" was a framing statement of the new ideology. These royal laws of God would be maintained by force if necessary, Joel said, and physical penalties for disobedience included death for treason, murder, and adultery. The laws were designed to "preserve the inalienable rights of mankind" and create "a peaceful harmonious kingdom for all peoples" (LeBaron 1981, 179). In 1955, Ervil published *Priesthood Expounded,* the foundational text for the new church. In it, Ervil explained how his insights were far superior to those of the LDS Church. He stated:

> If we LeBaron brothers are so fortunate as to be able to explain these things correctly, in this time of confusion and turmoil, when all others of our time have utterly failed to do it, then let every man and woman sit in silence and put their hands on their mouths, recognize where the authority is, and cease to speak evil of the servants of God. (LeBaron 1955, 2:42)

Ervil described three grand orders of priesthood. This was part of a new revelation about Mormonism that had never been taught before. The first order includes the prophet who represents the Melchizedek Priesthood, which leads all other levels and coordinates all organizations. These are the Right of the Firstborn, whose authority is traced directly back to Abraham himself and then through the lines of Christ to Joel LeBaron. The second line is the patriarchal role associated with Aaron, the brother of Moses. This line holds the keys of blessings, works for the dead, and is designed for apostleship. It also presides over the administration of church duties. The third line relates to the role of bishop, who holds the keys of temporal blessings. *Priesthood Expounded* contained ideas that were new to Mormonism, such as the concept that Brigham Young did not hold the same authority as Joseph Smith—that he was a Joshua to Joseph Smith's Moses (LeBaron 1955). Ervil believed that Brigham Young was subordinate to Joseph Smith in spiritual things yet superior to him in political government, just as he, Ervil, was subordinate to Joel LeBaron in some things yet superior to him in others.

As the Grand Head of the priesthood, a "Firstborn," Joel considered himself the true representative of Christ on earth. He had been called by God to organize God's children in three distinct areas: spiritual, economic, and civil. He placed his brother Ervil, as patriarch, in the role of spiritual leader with the task of ensuring that individuals were living up to their moral codes. Many members say that Ervil took his mandate too far by controlling their assets and inflicting pain (even death) on those whom he felt had disobeyed the laws. Joel did not fully explain the economic and civil leadership positions; these callings were charged with vaguely maintaining the right to life and liberty and with educating and organizing the people to be in compliance with the law of liberty.

Joel explained that the community would advance through three levels if it was to achieve full unity of purpose. First, through God's civil law, the hierarchy of priesthood leadership would be established and all members would be made to obey their rule. The Grand Head of the priesthood, Joel, would stand at the pinnacle of authority, supported by two councilmen, who were supported by the Quorum of the Twelve Apostles. The successor to the Grand Head would be, as it is in the Mormon Church, the president of the Twelve Apostles (who happened to be Joel's brother Verlan). The second level of law, according to Joel's revelations, is the law of love, which is above and beyond the civil level. Only a select group can reach this level—those capable of the greatest love and compassion. The law of love requires each person to love his neighbor unconditionally. The third, and highest, level, the law of perfect "pure" sacrifice, offers the most far-reaching benefits. This law requires that individuals prove themselves to God by giving up their own lives to the cause. At the very least, it requires individuals to willingly relinquish the right to live out their own dreams so that others may benefit.

In addition to Joel's contributions, the LeBaron formal religious structure, much like the Allred structure, centers on three main principles of the Joseph Smith gospel: celestial marriage, kingdom building, and the law of consecration (the United Order). Intrinsic in all of these principles is the bedrock of priesthood power—a power that is recognized as being directly from God. It gives a man ultimate control over his wives and children and over Gentiles. LeBaron members generally believe that men rule and women and children obey; women are under a strict obligation never to say no to their husbands' demands. In broader terms, the priesthood is seen as the power of God used by both male and female for the perpetuation of a righteous seed. Men receive this privilege through the "laying on of hands" by high-ranking members of the priesthood, just as Christ ordained his disciples 2,000 years ago. Ideally, in the process of ordination, the father is in charge of his own son's progress. In LeBaron, however, it can be either the father or the bishop who appoints young men to their priesthood offices, depending on how maverick or independent the father is.

The LeBaron priesthood generally authorized all marriages, granted economic stewardships, approved all policy changes, and called deviants on the carpet whenever necessary. The priesthood had financial control over dozens of projects and industries under the incorporated heading of the Church of the Firstborn. The LeBarons, unlike most of the other groups, engaged in active proselytizing. They focused on drawing people from the other groups but also gained a foothold among the Hispanic peoples of Mexico, who already practiced informal polygamy in many regions.[16]

While Joel was considered to be a natural leader of the group, many described Ervil as narcissistic, crafty, and uncontrollable. Verlan's autobiography depicted him as insane (1981). At 240 pounds on a frame of six foot four inches, Ervil was also intimidating. By 1962, Ervil had succeeded in becoming the Presiding Patriarch, the second in command under Joel, at which time he introduced the doctrine of the "Civil Law," which allowed LeBaron priesthood leaders to use force to establish principles of the church. As early as 1967, Ervil was teaching that he, not Joel, was the "one mighty and strong." When Joel heard about this, he and his "general authorities" denounced and discredited Ervil's ideas, and he released him as second in command. This angered Ervil. By 1970, he proclaimed that since he was the only man who could put the kingdom in order, he would do it even if it meant using bloodshed. In August 1972, Ervil formed a rival church called the Church of the Lamb of God. He preached that since he was the real prophet, all others were fakes and should be put to death, including his brother, Joel. On August 20, 1972, Joel LeBaron was shot in the head by Dan Jordan, one of Ervil's followers. Verlan, Joel's other brother, became the new prophet, but he was also killed in an automobile "accident" in 1981, presumably by one of Ervil's followers.

Other Groups and Independents

In addition to the FLDS, the AUB, the Kingstons, and the LeBarons, there is the small sect known as the ULDC (United Latter-day Church of Jesus Christ), whose early leaders were George Woolley Smith, Heber Gerald Smith, and Steven H. Tucker. George W. Smith claimed that his status as holder of the keys of priesthood came directly from his grandfather, John Woolley. (The same story is told of Joel LeBaron.) He joined other underground polygamists in Short Creek, then moved his group to Nebraska. He and his twelve wives moved in several different directions: a few in California, a handful in Wyoming, and the rest in northern Utah. After his death, Smith was succeeded by his son Heber. Another small group of about 100 to 160 members is the Righteous Branch of the Church of Jesus Christ of Latter-day Saints, led by Gerald Peterson, who at one time was a member of the AUB. Peterson founded this new church based on a vision of an angel who gave him the priesthood keys after Rulon C. Allred died. This group mirrors much of the liberal philosophy of the AUB and has branches in Utah and Nevada.

Another independent, Jim Harmston, is not affiliated with any group. He is known for drawing women from other polygamist movements to his fold. His church, called the True and Living Church of Jesus Christ of Saints of the Last Days (TLC), was founded in Manti, Utah, 130 miles south of Salt Lake, with about 400 people. Harmston and his wife sought to restore their new church before the Second Coming of Christ (Johns 1996). Harmston said he was confirmed in the Melchizedek priesthood by Enoch, Noah, Abraham, and Moses, by the laying on of hands. He preached plural marriage, consecration, and "mortal probations," which relates to reincarnation. Jim also taught his flock that he was the reincarnation of Joseph Smith and that he could beam himself to various planets in the night.

Harmston governed his church through the Quorum of the Twelve, a group of a dozen men who have forty wives among them. Many of their wives are well educated, with college degrees. In fact one polygamist's wife was a reporter for the *Chicago Tribune* who fell in love with the lifestyle and stayed. Local Sanpete County officials state that the polygamists are peaceful, law-abiding citizens who work hard and are honest. By 2004, Harmston had married twenty-one women, two of whom were mother and daughter. In 2006, however, he lost membership when members failed to see Jesus and the world did not end as he had predicted. Harmston was also accused of racketeering and fraud. By 2008, Jim was down to eight wives, and many of the other members of the Quorum, such as Randy Maudsley, Jeff Hanks, and Bart Maelstrom, had lost their wives and children, typically by apostasy. Member simply went back to the mainstream LDS church or the Allred Group whence they came. These three men left the group, one with a nervous breakdown.

In the 1980s, other breakoff fundamentalists inhabited limestone caverns in Missouri, where they created an underground structure to house their homes, a church, workshops, and a temple. I was told by polygamy historian Anne Wilde that the leaders of this group believe in their prophet is the re-born Christ and that his three councilors are Peter, Paul, and James. They await Millennium in Adam-ondi-Ahman, which according to the orthodox Mormons is located in Independence, Missouri. This site is also, inciden-tally, the headquarters of the Community of Christ, formerly the Reorganized Church of Jesus Christ of Latter Day Saints. Many unaffiliated independent polygamists live or lived in and around Utah, Arizona, Montana, Oregon, Canada and Mexico, such as Tom Green, Roy Potter, Addam Swapp, Fred Collier, Ogden Kraut, John Singer, John Bryant, Alex Joseph (deceased), and Ron and Dan Lafferty. These polygamists do not want to defer to any prophet or priesthood leadership but seek to build their autonomous family kingdoms and live freely, sometimes directly within the Mormon orthodox community, as depicted accurately on HBO's *Big Love*. Each of these independent men sees himself as the prophet, seer, and revelator of his own family/church.

Some independents, such as the Lafferty brothers and Addam Swapp, are serving prison terms for various crimes. Ron and Dan Lafferty murdered Brenda and Erica Lafferty, their sister-in-law and her daughter, stating that God had ordered them to do so. John Singer's crime was trying to home school his children without government interference. He died in an FBI-led shootout in 1979. Both Ogden Kraut and Fred Collier are famous as authors of Mormon fundamentalist doctrine and philosophy. Another independent, Bob Simons, had a vision that told him to preach plural marriage to American Indians, known as Lamanites to Mormons. He lived on a ranch near Grants-ville, Utah, with his two wives until he was killed by Ervil LeBaron in 1975.

Two other groups have come to light in recent years. The Church of the Firstborn of the General Assembly of Heaven started in 2004 in Magna, Utah, when prophet Terrill Dalton claimed that he had received a revelation in which Jesus called him the Holy Ghost and commanded him to start a new church. The small family/church fled Utah for Idaho and then to Montana due to charges of sex abuse. Dalton claims that his members were persecuted by federal agents after Dalton's threat to assassinate President Barack Obama, former president George Bush, and LDS president Thomas Monson. Another group from Humansville, Missouri, affiliated with the AUB, is under investigation for the statutory rape of two young women. I am told by insiders that this branch of the AUB is currently being disbanded.

NON-MORMON FUNDAMENTALISM

Not all polygamists are associated with Mormonism. In Circleville, Utah, Steve Butt and his three wives and five children live in a renovated church house (Wolfson 1999). They call themselves Christian polygamists who believe in continuing the legacy left by Abraham. Ten years ago, as a monogamist, he worked, ironically, as a "cult exit" counselor in Maine, helping young people who had been abused in a nontraditional religious movement to find treatment. One of his patients became his second wife, and they moved to Utah. Their church, which is headquartered in Utah, is called the Be Free Patriarchal Christian Church. It ministers online to about 1,000 people in the United States. They hope to convert Mormon polygamists and proselytize among other Christian churches throughout Utah and California. Each of Steve's wives has her own bedroom. He rotates whom he sleeps with each night, starting with his first wife, Diane, fifty-one, who has two children; then moving the next night to his second wife, Merry-Ann, forty-four; and then to his third wife, Dawn, thirty-five, who has three children. Butt doesn't want to be confused with the FLDS group that practices sex abuse. He says that his lifestyle is not about oppressing women, it is about liberating them. The father is designed to be the strong patriarchal leader, he states, but that doesn't mean that the wives are slaves. The husband provides "headship" so the women can fulfill their potential. The women say they love the lifestyle because they are in charge of their own activities in the home. They teach the children in the kitchen/dining hall, share the mothering and housework, and enjoy each other's company as sisters.

Dave Harmon founded another non-Mormon church called the Liberated Christians in Arizona for people who wanted to come out of the closet and practice both Christianity and polygamy (Wolfson 1999). Once they see the biblical basis of polygamy, they lose their guilt over their "plural" tendencies. Harmon insists that people should be ashamed of celibacy instead of feeling guilty for loving more than one person. There is no biblical basis for being single, he claims; it is against God's law and can lead to prostate blockage and female sexual dysfunction. The Bible, through its focus on concubines and multiple wives, admonishes men to have a lot of sex, Harmon teaches

(Harmon 1997). A growing number of both non-Mormon and Mormon polygamists are finding support on national polygamy weblogs. For example, Martin
(last name undisclosed) and his two wives, Karen and Lisa, are founders of
the Polygamy Now blog. Their family represents a clear departure from what
they call the "brainwashed childbride scenario" commonly associated with
the Kingstons and FLDS. Martin, fifty-nine, has a bachelor's degree in Asian
culture from Brown University and a degree in the anthropology of dance
from UCLA. He is also a musician, a Vietnam veteran, a lecturer, an author,
an interpreter, and a computer programmer. He has lived and worked in Japan,
Taiwan, Vietnam, Germany, and Sweden, and currently writes for Microsoft.
His first wife, Karen, sixty-two, is a retired advanced-placement, bilingual,
biology teacher. She has one daughter who is handicapped, and two sons.
Karen has been a ballet dancer, a house contractor, and a jewelry designer. She
has a master's degree in biology. His second wife, Lisa, forty-seven, is a piano
teacher, a Reiki master, and a health educator. She has two sons.

Another poly-focus group is the Unitarian Universalists for Polyamory
Awareness (UUPA), which promotes "the philosophy and practice of loving
or relating intimately to more than one other person at a time with honesty
and integrity" (UUPA 2011, 1). The UUPA advocates for "any form of family structure, whether monogamous or multi-partner, which is characterized
by free and responsible choice, mutual consent of all involved, and sincere
adherence to personal philosophical values" (ibid.). Unlike Mormon fundamentalists, polyamorists do not live in separatist communities and may not
necessarily cohabit with more than one mate. Interestingly, because of their
rather loose affiliations with multiple spouses, they are less likely to attract
prosecution under anti-bigamy statutes than are Mormon fundamentalists
who are married in a religious ceremony.

In summary, one can see from this review of the historical roots of Mormon fundamentalism that polygamists have a great deal in common with
mainstream Mormons. Generally speaking, the Mormon polygamists are
peace-loving, honest, hard-working, and agrarian. They are a bit Victorian in
their gender roles and have a very strong belief in nineteenth-century Mormon doctrine. Obviously there is dispute over priesthood authority among
Mormons and Mormon fundamentalists, and there is a significant debate
about present-day revelation (which the mainstream church subscribes to)
versus the concept that the "gospel never changeth" (which fundamentalists
believe). Yet both types of Mormonism share many of the same early doc-

trines and values, they share ancestors who crossed the plains with Brigham Young, and they eat the same foods, read the same scriptures, and live in much the same way. This being the case, it would be unfair to lump all polygamists in the same category as Dan and Ron Lafferty, Warren Jeffs, or Ervil LeBaron, just as it would be incorrect to label all Mormons in the same category as Arthur Gary Bishop, Gary Gilmore, and Mark Hofmann (a serial killer), who were members of the LDS Church.

It is my hope that this chapter has provided valuable historical and cultural data to social workers, government officials, and media representatives and will prevent future cross-cultural misunderstandings that can lead to violence and sieges. It also has the potential to prevent overt prejudice against alternative marriage forms. Once people understand the full history, culture, and variability in lifestyles of fundamentalists, they can form better ideas about the impact of polygamy on women and children.

2

Further Light and Knowledge

Ideology and Culture

> For it is necessary in the ushering in of the dispensation
> of the fulness[1] of times . . . that a whole and complete and
> perfect union, and welding together of dispensations, and
> keys, and powers, and glories should take place.
>
> —DOCTRINE AND COVENANTS 128:18, 21

My first glimpse of polygamy twenty years ago presented a stark contrast to what I had read in the newspapers and what I had heard in my own orthodox Mormon congregation in Vernon, Utah. The women of the AUB branch of the Montana Bitterroots were not brainwashed victims of a cult led by "thugs, rapists, and lawbreakers" (Perkins 2003, 1). Here was a group of men and women who were struggling to feed and clothe their families and worship their God in their own way without interference. They entered plural marriage, seeking to revive an ancient and complex family form that is practiced by at least one-third of the world's cultures (Driggs 2011; Altman 1996) and as much as 85 percent of human groups (Murdock 1967).[2] I had expected to find rampant child sexual molestations and beaten and cloistered women reminiscent of some of the depictions of women's lives in Afghanistan during the Taliban rule. Instead I found feminism, female autonomy, and widespread sharing. I found a subculture of people living in unique poly relationships with their own set of challenges and quirky, often contradictory, features such as food storage, herbalism, midwifery, Goddesshood, Jell-o salads, and *Mother Earth News* coinciding with beliefs in blood atonement, NRA advocacy, libertarianism, home schooling, gospel "mysteries," the Savior on Mt. Zion, the Holy Priesthood, and the sisterhood. The essential survival ingredient for these polygamists was the ability to drop personal idiosyncrasies and stubborn pride and open themselves up completely to absolute sharing and reciprocity. The women developed a fierce interdependence with each other in the face of cold weather and frequent absences of their husbands doing construction work and priesthood business in Utah, Oregon, and Mexico. Surprisingly, many of them experienced autonomy by forming efficient female economic and spiritual networks that included a Montessori school program, a wheat-grinding mill, a fruit cannery, and a dairy—all operated by the Relief Society, an auxiliary project led by women that was designed to help fulfill the needs of the community. This matrifocal network provided these women with shared childcare that enabled them to pursue an education or a career outside the community. It offered them relief in companionship and solidarity when they were abandoned by their husbands.

Their husbands, on the other hand, seemed less content than their wives—always scurrying around from wife to wife, community to community, job to job, like vagabonds in search of themselves. How could they remember all those birthdays and anniversaries? I would often see Marvin, an Allred man, sitting alone in his Ford pickup right in front of one of his houses, asleep or reading. He was not anxious to enter a house where scores of kids and wives would make demands of him. I observed, that first winter, how hard the life can be on young men as well (something you never read about in the newspapers) who compete for their father's affections and stewardships with dozens of other brothers. They are also at risk for being expelled from the community when the population of men increases beyond capacity, as in the case of the FLDS group under the leadership of Warren Jeffs.[3]

The beliefs that give rise to such lifestyles are identical to mainstream Mormon ideology in many respects: the concept of the evolution of God; the belief in the atonement and resurrection; the use of core scriptures such as the Bible, the Book of Mormon, the Doctrine and Covenants, and the Pearl of Great Price; the belief in a patrilineally established kingdom of heaven; the belief in the three degrees of glory; the Word of Wisdom (which encourages wholesome eating and the avoidance of alcohol and tobacco); and links to common pioneer ancestors who crossed the plains with Brigham Young. They also believe in various Mormon "Talmud"[4] rules such as avoiding Coca-Cola, bargain-hunting, and mastering gardening. As in the LDS Church, fundamentalism is based on patriarchy; only men can hold the priesthood. Women and children learn to respect and obey their spiritual male "head." And the male (often elderly) prophet is the conduit for direct revelation from God. Male-directed families are built upon the promise that they will become heavenly kingdoms in the hereafter. As in Mormon orthodoxy, one's religion is one's lifestyle, not something to be observed in church once a week but an everyday practice that puts faith into action through "good works." One difference in Sunday activities, however, is that while the LDS meet in churches for three-hour meetings, polygamists meet for one hour in their meeting houses or even in their own homes for services, during which the father leads the sermon, administers the sacrament, and reads from the scriptures and the mother or eldest daughter leads in the singing. As do orthodox Mormons, they believe in modesty, hard work, eternal families, and community service. They require baptism by immersion with confirmation by the laying on of hands and temple endowment sealings to unite people for all eternity.[5]

To summarize the differences of fundamentalists from the mainstream church, polygamist Ogden Kraut (1983) lists several key issues: the practice of polygamy, the practice of missionary work, beliefs about the priesthood, the adoption of the United Order, belief in the concept of the gathering of Israel, belief in the Adam-God theory, adoption of the concept of the "one mighty and strong," development of the concept of Zion, beliefs about blacks and the priesthood, and belief about the kingdom of God. Fundamentalists also differ in their association of the "fulness of times" with plural marriage and their belief that one must acquire wives through the Law of Sarah to attain the highest glories of the Celestial Kingdom.[6] They also believe that the gospel is unchanging; accordingly, if God told Joseph Smith to practice polygamy, it should be practiced today and always. In other words, truth is a knowledge of "things as they are, and as they were, and as they are to come" (Doctrine and Covenants 93:24). Smith also stated that if "any man preach any other gospel than that which I have preached, he shall be cursed" (Smith 1838, 327) and that God "set the ordinances to be the same forever and ever" (ibid., 168).

Endowment rites, fundamentalists feel, should therefore not be altered, as they were in 1927, when LDS apostle Stephen Richards renounced the Adam-God doctrine and removed its associated symbols from the priesthood garment (Richards 1932), and in the 1990s, when LDS prophet Ezra T. Benson reformed the ceremony to allow women to have a direct pathway to God rather than having to go through their husbands or fathers.[7] The latter change also removed the punishment symbols and gestures used to illustrate what might befall one if the sacred rites were divulged, not unlike those used by the Masons. The LDS Church also altered the rite that brings Saints into God's presence and shortened and modernized the holy garment. Fundamentalists believe that the rites and symbols that were lost should be reinstated and that women must go through their Saviors on Mt. Zion in their pathway to God. They also maintain that the exact words in sacred ceremony, the ones used in Joseph Smith's day when priesthood blessings were conferred, should be used in the modern day, spoken in nineteenth-century verse.

Fundamentalists also reject the 1978 revelation given to President Kimball that allowed blacks to enter the priesthood (Doctrine and Covenants, Declaration 2). They believe that God told Joseph Smith that "negroids" are marked by the blood of Cain[8] and would defile the priesthood and the temples. The FLDS removed a Polynesian from their midst, stating that he was too dark, and they frown on interracial marriages of any kind. Warren Jeffs contended that blacks "are low in their habits, wild and seemingly deprived of nearly all the blessings of the intelligence that is generally bestowed upon mankind."[9] The AUB and LeBarons are also against blacks but allow mixed alliances with both Hispanics and Polynesians. Nevertheless, the AUB removed Richard Kunz (an individual who is phenotypic white and genotypic black) from his position on the priesthood council.

Another difference between the LDS Church and fundamentalism is that offshoots believe that God's law is intended to surpass man's laws. Although welfare fraud, bigamy, the collection of illegal armaments, or certain types of home schooling may be against the civil law, they are means of following the higher mandate of providing for large numbers of children (Hales 2006). It should be noted that some polygamist communities, such as Pinesdale, Montana, work very closely with law enforcement and are law abiding. They register any sex offenders and excommunicate any criminals.

Fundamentalists also feel that missionary work should be conducted as Joseph Smith commanded it, without "purse or scrip," meaning without financial support. They also disagree with the mainstream church's identification of Independence, Missouri, as the "one place" for the gathering of Zion. This location is also known as Adam-ondi-Ahman, or the former Garden of Eden.[10] Most fundamentalists feel that Zion is located in the Rocky Mountains, where the Savior will one day return.[11]

The Mysteries

Mormon fundamentalists, like mainstream LDS, are asked by God to consider themselves as Adam or Eve, a concept embedded in the endowment ceremony. They all serve a probationary period on earth until they may return to the presence of the Father. During this probation they must, like Adam, pursue "further light and knowledge"[12] and seek messengers who can guide them in receiving the keys that can unlock the power of the priesthood and remove the veil that borders earthly life and the Celestial Kingdom.

For the apocalyptic fundamentalists, portents and signs abound and every symbol and text has sublime meaning. Many of these signs direct the millenarianist to go above and beyond orthodoxy and to strive to be among the truly blessed who live in the society of the Gods (Michael also known as Adam, Jesus, and Joseph) and embrace the "mysteries of the kingdom" (Doctrine and Covenants 63:23; 76:1−7). But not all can understand the mysteries; the truly righteous must have the "eyes to see and ears to hear" the truth about the fulness of the gospel. Many fundamentalists see their modern prophet (Jeffs, Allred, Kingston, and so on) as the source of divine revelation, but independents often claim that they themselves hold the "sacred secret" of direct man-to-God revelation (Doctrine and Covenants commentary, 141). That is the lure of fundamentalism—that you can be your own prophet, seer, and king.

When I was taught the "mysteries," I was cautioned that the faint of heart or common member should not attempt to understand them because they would seem absurd or irrational if spoken without spiritual understanding (I was also asked to rely on my "Savior on Mt. Zion" to interpret the mysteries, which was impossible as my father was dead and my husband was an apostate). I was told that only God understands the far-reaching consequences of the doctrines he reveals to his Chosen, if they are spiritually ready and willing to understand them. Without such understanding, polygamy could be viewed as absurd.

The "mysteries" include divine steps to test the validity of revelations and true prophets. One involves making the calling and election sure (Young 1867) so that the Chosen will have the right to converse with the dead beyond the veil and gain personal revelations from God. Another step is to humble yourself in the true order of prayer, a method that was used by Adam; those who follow this practice wear temple garments, kneel, and pray with upraised hands of praise and supplication, crying, "Oh God, hear the words of my mouth." Just as Joseph Smith was given the divine ordinances and doctrines, so too can any man who seeks with the appropriate priesthood authority, who honors the covenants, and who hungers and thirsts for the knowledge. Saints who devote themselves to righteousness and receive higher ordinances of exaltation become members of the "church of the firstborn," an inner circle of faithful saints who practice the fulness and who will be joint heirs with Christ in receiving all that the Father has (McConkie 1991, 139–140). They will be sealed by "the holy spirit of promise," will become kings and Gods in the making, and will take part in the first resurrection. This will enable them to live on Mt. Zion with God in the company of angels in the Celestial Kingdom (Doctrine and Covenants 76:50–70). Members of the firstborn may be asked to break the law of the land for the higher law, perhaps even commit murder, as Book of Mormon prophet Nephi was commanded to kill the evil one, Laban. It is through this process that "just men will be made perfect" and be given the gifts of kingdoms and principalities in new worlds beyond the limits of their imaginations.

Besides the "mysteries" the most valued fundamentalist principles that were abandoned by the LDS Church are polygamy, the Adam-God doctrine, and the Law of Consecration. When these principles are intact, the order of heaven correlates four different gospel-oriented elements in a workable system: social, political, spiritual, and economic. The social element of the heavenly order is polygamy, the political element is the kingdom of God or the government of God, the spiritual element is the priesthood as the conduit for revelation, and the economic element is the United Order.

PLURAL MARRIAGE

Polygamy, also known as Celestial Marriage, is considered an essential ordinance that was created before the foundation of the world. Mormons who look to the Bible as a precedent for plural marriage find several examples of prophets who required their wives to allow them sexual access to another female to further the work of God. There is the prime example of Abraham mating with Hagar, his wife Sarah's handmaid, in order to bring his first son, Ishmael, into the world. There is also the case of Solomon's use of 800 concubines to fulfill the need to spread the seed of Israel far and wide in the empire-building process. In this practice, Solomon followed the example of his forefather, Moses, who had at least two wives. Finally, there is Jacob, who had at least four wives and worked fourteen years of bride service for his second wife Rachel, only to find out that she was barren. It is not really clear whether it was Jacob or Rachel who came up with the idea of recruiting Bilhah, Rachel's handmaid, as a "surrogate." In the end, this handmaid served her purpose of increasing Jacob's seed as part of the Abrahamic covenant.

And when Rachel saw that she bare Jacob no children, Rachel envied her sister, and said unto Jacob, Give me children, or else I die. And Jacob's anger was kindled against Rachel; and he said, Am I in God's stead, who hath withheld from thee the fruit of the womb? And she said, Behold my maid Bilhah, go in unto her, and she shall bear upon my knees, that I may also have children by her. (Genesis 30:1–3)

A further scriptural rationale for polygamy is found in Jacob 2:24–30, which states that the Lord commanded men to have one wife, unless he wishes them to "raise up seed unto him," a process that requires the plurality of wives to increase offspring in preparation for the Last Days. Yet another scripture that is often quoted from the fundamentalist pulpit is Doctrine and Covenants 132: "Abraham received concubines, and they bore him children; and it was accounted unto him for righteousness . . . and if he have ten virgins given unto him by this law, he cannot commit adultery, for they belong to him . . . for they are given unto him to multiply and replenish the earth according to my commandment" (37, 62–63).

Fundamentalists believe that polygamy is a requirement for exaltation[13] and is the supreme kingdom-building tool, one that brings more spirit children into this existence than is possible through monogamy. For example, AUB patriarch Joseph Lyman Jessop had three wives—Winnie, Beth, and Leota—who collectively had 39 children, 273 grandchildren, and approximately 950 great-great-grandchildren, all of whom deferred to their apical ancestor as Lord and Ruler (Bennion 1998). A second example of increasing the family kingdom is the case of Verlan LeBaron and his ten wives, one of whom, Irene Spencer, had 13 children and 120 grandchildren. Multiply that by ten to get the full picture of his progeny, a number that ranges from 70 to 130 children and from 600 to 1,000 grandchildren.

Fundamentalists also believe that polygamy, or "the Principle," is an answer to the evils of modern society. Those "evils" include single motherhood and widespread divorce. When a man is limited to only one wife, some women will have the choice of marrying a worldly, carnal man or remaining unwed. If men were eternally limited to only one wife each, some women would never have the opportunity for exaltation. Fundamentalists quote Isaiah 4:1, which states that "in that day seven women shall take hold of one man, saying, we will eat our own bread, and wear our own apparel: only let us be called by thy name, to take away our reproach," meaning that for every righteous man there are at least seven righteous women (which is about the ratio you will find in today's mainstream Mormon temples). This prediction articulates the fundamentalist belief that wars and famines will destroy many men in the near future, upsetting the sex ratio. Women will be so numerous that it will be common to see many righteous women (usually sisters who have been raised by a righteous patriarch) clinging to one righteous man.

This ratio was confirmed by Mosiah Hancock (a colleague of Joseph Smith), who had a vision about pre-existence in which there was a grand Romanic arena with Christ preaching in front of a great throng comprised of all the souls not yet born to earth. He laid out his plan of salvation and gave the floor over to Satan, who successfully lured away one-third of the congregation to his plan, all of whom happened to be male. This male-to-female ratio of those who remained with Christ was exactly one male to seven women. Each male was attached to several good women who followed Christ. This vision paved the way for contemporary plural marriage: one good (alpha), priesthood-bearing male married to several righteous handmaids of the Lord (Bennion 1998). According to Gordon, author of *The Mormon Question* (2001), plural marriage under proper regulations is considered by fundamentalists to be "an institution holy, just, virtuous, pure, and, in the estimation of God, abundantly calculated to bless, preserve, and multiply a nation" (91). The Saints offered "eugenically focused" claims that the children of polygamous marriages are physically superior because of their connection to the blood-lines of Christ himself and their parents' engagement in a celestial form of matrimony sanctioned, and practiced by, both God and Christ (Gordon 2001; Bennion 2008). Location is also key in identifying the Chosen. LDS apostle and former prophet George Albert Smith wrote that the Mormon polygamous society known as Zion is the most blessed group on earth, designed to prevail against all hardships and promote freedoms and privileges for its members. This proclamation has become a creed for contemporary fundamentalists:

> Of all men upon the face of the earth, we are the most favoured; we have the fullness of the everlasting Gospel, the keys of revelation and exaltation, the privilege of making our own rules and regulations, and are not opposed by anybody. No king, prince, potentate, or dominion, has rightful authority to crush and oppress us. We breathe the free air, we have the best looking men and the handsomest women, and if they envy us our position, well they may, for they are a poor, narrow-

minded, pinch-backed race of men, who chain themselves down to the law of monogamy, and live all their days under the dominion of one wife. (Smith 1856, 291)

Some fundamentalists feel that they should join their blood with the blood of Lamanites (American Indians or Latin Americans) so that they can purify the bloodlines of these groups by making them whiter (a belief similar to the underlying ideology of the British eugenics program in Australia depicted in the film *The Rabbit-Proof Fence*). They refer to Joseph Smith's 1831 revelation directed to his male followers doing missionary work among a Native tribe: "For it is my will, that in time, ye should take unto you wives of the Lamanites and Nephites, that their posterity may become white, delightsome and Just, for even now their females are more virtuous than the gentiles" (374–376).

Plural marriage is considered to be a matter of faith and "principle," a practice ordained by God for the direct salvation of mankind. In the early Mormon Church only the most important "elite" families practiced it (Quinn 1993), and today those that have many wives have higher prestige in their respective groups than monogamists. Any suffering or inconvenience women experience in polygamy is considered a necessary requirement to attain an eternal reward that surpasses any other prize: a kingdom of her own where she reigns as queen. Every sacrifice yields good fruit, and women, if they remain pure, will be considered wives and children of the holy covenant. Women believe they will inherit a prized place in heaven for their efforts to live the "eternal round," which is a metaphor for becoming the perfect Mormon family by living through the challenges of life each day, a process in which they are polished like diamonds. The women feel they will be worthy of the greatest glories in the kingdom. Polygamy is also said to wash away the filth of the "daughters of Zion," as recorded in Isaiah 4:4. Many suggest that if polygamy were adopted throughout the United States, prostitution would be eliminated. To fundamentalist Mormons, polygamy is the catch-all solution for prostitution, infidelity, homosexuality, spinsterhood, childlessness, and various types of sexual sin (Bradley 1990).

Brigham Young enthusiastically complied with the law of celestial plural marriage, teaching that "this is the reason why the doctrine of plurality of wives was revealed, that the noble spirits which are waiting for tabernacles might be brought forth" (Young 1869, 197). Fundamentalists believe that God himself had many wives, two of whom are well known: Eve and Lilith. They believe that Christ was married to Mary Magdalene and to her co-wife and blood sister, Martha. A joke among Mormon fundamentalists is that you can find a Mary and Martha in every polygamous household. Mary is the favorite (typically the first) wife who wields the power, bosses around her co-wives, and gets the best housing. Martha is the dishwasher, diaper-changer, stay-at-home wife who lives in the attic or the basement of the first wife's home.[14]

Interestingly, one Allred member told me that without the religious foundation for polygamy, men would seek wives only to feed their voracious and unchecked libido. Polygamy is certainly not followed for the money either, as many incur enormous debt to provide housing for additional wives and children (Bennion 2008). As I was told in many interviews with members, it is *faith* that propels them toward what is, in the end, a very challenging way of life. Mormon apostle Orson Pratt recognized the difficulties of living the Principle back in 1853, so he devised a set of twenty-seven guidelines for people wishing to enter the Celestial Kingdom (see Appendix A for the full transcript).

The nature of polygamous relationships requires one to emotionally cope with the dichotomy of dyadic relations between a husband and wife *and* communal relations in that same family among the husband, wives, and numerous children (Altman 1996). As one FLDS women writes, the hardest part about polygamy is to "keep a balance of who you are as an individual soul, where your balance is, in and of yourself, and in the family relationship and your balance in your service to the community and the world" (Sloan 2011, 2). Altman, a social psychologist who wrote about the vast complexity of relationships within polygamy, stated that no single statement is adequate to describe the intricacy and diversity of the lives of fundamentalist polygamists. On the community level, individuals struggle to balance their loyalties and devotions to the individual family (husband/wives/children) and yet remain true to the larger community as a whole, as an eternal round, as the covenant, or as "all parts of the body of Christ" (Bennion 1998). The covenant provides continuity and solidarity to members by reminding them of their united deference to Elohim and the promises made in righteousness that bind them together as a holy community. Another psychological challenge is an outgrowth of dealing with the contradictory relations between converts and established, born-in members of the community. On the one hand is the convert's desire to build his own kingdom and marry many wives, on the other is the established leader's desire to control all economic and priesthood resources, thus limiting the extent to which others can share in the abundance of community resources. To help them deal with such complexities, fundamentalists are promised that the Lord will send "one mighty and strong . . . to set in order the house of God," a priesthood leader who will righteously manage property and the contracting of plural unions (Doctrine and Covenants 85:7).

THE ADAM-GOD DOCTRINE

Directly related to the concept of plural marriage is the evolution-of-God philosophy. Mormons believe that all worthy members of the Church can one day become Gods. Fundamentalists explain this man-God philosophy through the Adam-God doctrine, taught by Brigham Young, which states that Adam (also known as Michael) is actually God the Father (Elohim), who first entered a designated Garden of Eden created by the previous Father as Adam, a human man with wives, living his earthly life. He then went through a grand sacrifice, just as Christ did, and became the Exalted One and finally became the new God, taking his office as the Father. Further, when Mary conceived Jesus, he was also the begotten son of the Father-Adam (Young 1852, 51). Young saw polygamy as a vehicle for the God-making process, a practice "dedicated by the Gods for the perpetuation of life and birth of earths" (Musser 1944, 102). Men are promised that they may become God, as God himself was once a man. Thus, men become Gods and have spirit children who will worship and pray to them in the same way as people now worship and pray to Elohim. Men learn how to become gods on earth, inheriting the same powers, glories, and exaltations that God experienced in his respective station.

THE LAW OF CONSECRATION

The United Order was a nineteenth-century program to administer the Law of Consecration, a form of voluntary communalism designed to attain near-egalitarian conditions whereby all incomes were equal, everyone was self-sufficient, and there was no poverty. In 1831 Joseph Smith received a revelation that members should donate their land and money to the church (Doctrine and Covenants 48). All Mormon fundamentalist groups use some form of economic communalism, variously called the United Effort, the Cooperative, or the Order, in adherence to original LDS concepts of the Law of Consecration, which requires that every family donate their surpluses (tithes, goods, assets) to the bishop's storehouse (or bank). This bank contains investments, cash, building supplies, foodstuffs, and so on. These resources are distributed to those in need by the Brethren, as the priesthood leadership is called. This economic order combines with celestial marriage to form a union of the spiritual with the temporal (Young 1864), functioning to utilize the abilities of everyone: the weak and the poor, male and female alike. Because the family is the basic unit of society, the Order must function at this level, requiring that each member be made a "steward" over a certain entity or enterprise, such as a building project, a honey-collection service, a water access plant, or the children that one bears. The concept of the order that is significant for co-wife relations is that individual stewardships rely heavily on unity and "oneness" to assure that in the afterlife, a man, his wives, and their children will all live together and work smoothly together without duplication of tasks as "one great" family in a common household (Young 1867).

Although the concept never fully succeeded during Brigham Young's time, fundamentalists attempt to follow its redistribution practice today. Their efforts to establish true communalism fall short due to a variety of problems that include inequities, exploitation, and favoritism. Yet in some environments, such as at Pinesdale, I observed that their version of the United Order resembles the Israeli *moshav* in promoting individual industry while maintaining a communally protected economy. Each man is given an economic stewardship, such as a dairy, an orchard, or a construction business. Those that have close ties with the Brethren and "blood families" are the ones to get the most lucrative stewardships, which is why this system often alienates younger, "rogue" males. The wives are also given stewardships such as working in accounting, textiles, teaching, childcare, and food preparation. The FLDS uses the United Effort Plan (UEP, worth $100 million), whereas the AUB uses the United Order; both organizations control and redistribute property and businesses in the form of stewardships (Goodwyn, Berkes, and Walters 2005). The AUB may suffer financially over the next few years because they lost a civil law suit filed by Virginia Hill that, along with interest, will cost them nearly $7,000,000 plus 2.41 percent interest (*Hill v. Allred,* 2010). This judgment may require them to sell one of their more remote orders in the next four to five years, which will put the Montana order at risk for either bankruptcy or dismantling. This same misuse of donated funds occurred in Warren Jeffs' group, which led to the seizure of properties by the state of Utah.

New members in both groups are typically asked to consecrate all their properties and assets to the order to be "worthy to have their names written in the book of the law of God" (LeBaron 1981, 166) and improve their stewardships (private and community industries). Further, men and boys are expected to be "kings in the making" who will take up the mantles of religious priesthood leadership, economic stewardship, and absolute purity. This responsibility often makes it much harder for males to thrive and become content in fundamentalism than for female converts, who aren't required to donate and are not competing for prestigious stewardships.

Community labor is a significant resource in this plan. As in Amish or Hutterite communities, work parties of male and female members gather on Saturdays to construct houses and buildings, work on the water line, harvest crops, or drive cattle. There are also focus groups of men and women for clean-up projects, youth fund-raising drives, and crisis prevention. Women are especially active in creating work parties to stitch quilts, can fruit, sew bedding, teach children, shop for bulk foods and household goods, and do general repair work on rugs, appliances, and plumbing. This informal network is done outside priesthood callings and is run only by the women to meet their needs.[15] Occupations in polygamy vary a great deal; the AUB and the FLDS tend to concentrate on construction work and fabricating machine parts, while the Kingstons focus on industry and law. The LeBarons are farmers, drywall laborers, and sellers of goods such as fireworks and herbal remedies. In a study of converts to the Allred Group (1998, 65), I found that 69 percent had a high school diploma and of that number 35 percent were employed in blue-collar work. Smaller proportions were engaged in manufacturing (12 percent) and white-collar employment (20 percent).

According to Brigham Young University scholars Tim Heaton and Cardell Jacobson (2011), the economic demographics of the FLDS Hildale–Colorado City population in 2000 is quite unusual when compared with the demographics of the state of Utah. For example, one-third of the population is living below the poverty line, and many families rely on public assistance. This is due to a high fertility rate, a skewed sex ratio, lack of financial opportunities in the region, and patriarchal ideology. First, the natural birth rate of Hildale-Colorado City is twice that of Utah; 62 percent of the population was under 18 and the average household is 7.8 people. Although the sex ratio slightly favors males, there is a shortage of adult men (88 men for every 100 women) and elderly men (56 men for every 100 women). This skewed ratio is due to the cumulative effect of selective recruitment of women, alienation of men, and labor migration (Heaton and Jacobson 2011). Further, educational attainment in 2000 is quite low in FLDS; only 71 percent finished high school. Although farming and ranching provides labor-intensive jobs for some boys and men, most males migrated to other locales for work in a variety of white- and blue-collar professions, primarily in the construction sector. Most females do not work for pay, instead contributing to social production in the form of child care, food processing, cooking, cleaning, gardening, and home maintenance.

Overall, it is difficult to discern where the money in polygamist groups comes from. Obviously, a 10 percent mandatory tithe donation feeds the community pot to take care of emergencies and church projects. There is also the initial donation of any surplus assets at the time of conversion (in the case of the AUB and the LeBaron group). For example, one member who converted in the mid-1980s donated a small offering of $5,000 at the time of his conversion. At present, he and his two wives and nine children live in a nice, priesthood-built four-bedroom home with no mortgage. In 1989–1990, he and his second wife brought in a combined income of $65,000 (after taxes and tithing), enough to provide the family with food, clothing, and health care. On the other hand, some families give large donations and then are left with meager living arrangements that are based entirely on their relationship with the high-ranking families (Bennion 1991, 1998).

Many fundamentalists use food stamps and are given housing assistance to make ends meet, especially in the Kingston and FLDS groups. Some families get $50,000–60,000 a year in public welfare benefits, since polygamist wives are classified as single mothers. Because they have so many children, many of these women are awarded roughly $1,200 in cash and food each month. At the same time, these communal groups are designed to be self-sufficient by raising their own crops and livestock and making their own textiles; the homes are built by the community, eliminating mortgages or rental payments. They also use alternative energy technologies to reduce utility costs. Both the FLDS and the AUB own construction companies worth millions of dollars, and the Kingstons have dozens of companies that provide favored economic stewardships for most of their men. The FLDS is awarded lucrative government military and civil contracts that provide millions of dollars for the group. Polygamists are successful in winning public works contracts because they make extremely low bids. They are able to do this because their internal labor force does not require the high wages that a non-Mormon competitor would have to factor in when preparing a bid for a government contract.

Yet where do individual polygamous families get their money? How do the husbands provide food, shelter, and clothing for three or more wives and their children? In the FLDS group, half the work force is engaged in white-collar (business, professional) jobs and about half in blue-collar (manual labor, manufacturing) occupations. Jobs in agriculture and construction are the most popular blue-collar occupations (Heaton and Jacobson 2011). In addition, a small fraction of members of fundamentalist groups over the age of sixteen is in the civilian labor force. Although the mean family income is 37 percent lower than in the state of Utah as a whole, some families do quite well, making over $100,000 per year. Thus, there is high inequality in some fundamentalist communities. Isolation and lower education rates limit job opportunities for the majority of males, who do manual work when they can get it. In contrast, the few men given favorable stewardships based on their political alliances with the prophet and his counselors make quite a good living. In the AUB, besides construction, many men and women work as civil servants, teachers, nurses, social workers, and accountants or own their own businesses in a wide array of industries such as auto parts, advertising, and engineering. Many independents such as Rod Williams and Alex Joseph use their wives' salaries from work in the fields of law, business, commerce, and teaching to increase the family's income.

Fundamentalist men's jobs include teaching elementary school (Dee Jessop) and providing counseling for immigrants (Rod Williams). Randy Maudsley of the TLC works in computer programming; his neighbor John Harper is a building contractor. Their neighbor Doug Jordan is an artist, and his neighbor Bart Malstrom owns a factory that produces homeopathic remedies. Other polygamists such as Jeff Hanks are chiropractors or naturopaths. Some, like Clyde Stoker of Pinesdale, are auto parts salesmen. Ron Bierer owns and operates a hardware store, while Glen Allred manages a cattle ranch. Women also vary in their skills and professions. I lived with a woman who was a certified public accountant; her sister-wives stayed home to care for the children. June Jessop is a midwife; her neighbor and sister-in-law, "Mary Ann," teaches school. Sharon Jessop and "Emily" Williams are both administrators in their family businesses. Alex Joseph's wives work in a variety of professions: doctor, lawyer, teacher, and businesswoman. Mary Batchelor is a legal secretary and the co-director of Principle Voices; her friend Anne Wilde is a historian and author. In the FLDS group, women primarily spend their time working in gardens, sewing dresses, quilting, preparing food, and caring for children.

A side effect of the belief in communalism and polygamy is a psychological predisposition toward anti-government sentiment, distrust of "Babylon" (the outside modern world), and an attraction to isolation (Bennion 2004). These positions are likely outgrowths of the threat of arrest and the prejudice of orthodox Mormons living in the same communities. The isolationist mentality is also designed to remove the true Saints from the temptations and corruptions of the Gentile world. Many groups choose nonsecular education for their children and do not require women to take jobs outside the community so that the community can achieve distance from evil. In the LeBaron movement, for example, polygamists often speak of their heavy reliance on isolation and on freedom from oppressive government as major components of their conversion. They seek liberty to follow a religious code without interference, yet they also pride themselves in being good citizens of the United States. Joseph Smith, who was raised in an era of utopian experimentalism, believed that the Saints could live in an insular, collaborative bubble where everything was shared and no outside forces could penetrate their peaceful Zionesque community. In the LeBaron and FLDS communities, men work in the fields and with livestock and women work in the home, just as it was in the old days. Children are raised in a "wholesome environment free of television and junk food and social pressures" (Anderson 2010, 3). Fundamentalists live this insular lifestyle in many rural locations: the underground utopia outside Independence, Missouri; Bob Foster's red rock cavern community in San Juan County, Utah; and the Pinesdale Allred commune, tucked in the hidden benches of the Bitterroot Range of Montana. These hidden, isolated compounds serve to keep children and women safe but also shield families from "gawking Gentiles," as non-Mormons are known (Anderson 2010). It is in these remote places that Zion is built, but these remote places can also foster abuse, economic deprivation, and the absence of fathers, as I show later in this volume.

Some groups thrive in rural environments, such as in Big Water, Utah, where Alex Joseph and his wives lived as libertarians and convinced the other members of the town to abolish all town property taxes. Joseph's successor as mayor, Willy Marshall, was an openly gay man who likewise labeled himself as a self-reliant, anti-government libertarian. The polygamists in Pinesdale, Montana, are also libertarian; they intend to vote for Ron Paul and his Campaign for Liberty in the 2012 presidential election.[16] They pride themselves on their ethic of freedom and independence; they have one of the lowest tax rates in the nation because they believe in taking care of their own roads, buildings, water systems, and law enforcement. Many members of both of these communities subscribe to *Mother Earth News* and *Home Power* so they can learn better ways to live "off the grid" instead of relying on expensive water, oil, and electricity. In fact, many polygamists oppose the war in Iraq, which they believe to have been initiated by an overreliance on foreign oil. They favor alternative energy to heat their homes and subsistence strategies such as greenhouse horticulture, herbalism, bee keeping, hunting, and grinding their own wheat. One family had installed a windmill, solar panels, and a thermal heating (radiant floor) system twenty-five years before they became popular. Members of these communities also typically heat with an oil-barrel wood stove and drink well water. Some even live in caves, using the natural coolness and heat from the rocks to cool them in summers and warm them in winters. They also store foodstuffs and household products such as toilet paper, whole grains, wood, water, and canned fruit.

In short, most fundamentalist Mormons believe that Armageddon is at hand and that they must prepare for a dire future in which only the "Chosen People" will survive massive unemployment, electrical blackouts, oil shortages, warfare, earthquakes, and many other calamities until Christ returns. Through this fear of a bleak future they have become adherents of solar and wind power, hydro-energy sources, and sustainable living. However, since the 1970s, more polygamists have sought work in the larger industrialized regions, meshing more with mainstream lifestyles. This is particularly true of the Allred group. Thus, fundamentalists experience a duality between nineteenth-century values and modernity. They are drawn to new technology, modern dress, and relatively progressive ideas about gender roles. They want to steer clear of Babylon, yet they rely heavily on her materialist culture. This duality is seen in the most isolationist group of all, the FLDS. Despite their old-fashioned dress, many FLDS adults now have cell phones and favor late-model SUVs. Although televisions are now banished, church members tend to be highly computer literate and sell products that range from soap to dresses on the Internet. The latest fad within the community is having laser surgery (Anderson 2010).

Housing

Zionism and isolationist ideologies often produce peculiar living arrangements. Like Rappaport (1971), I observed architecture and housing design in order to find cultural meanings related to ideology, economy, politics, and gender. Polygamist structures ran the gamut from dyadic dwellings for each wife to communal configurations with five or six wives living under one roof with a separate bedroom for each wife. Most families use slightly modified existing conventional architecture (split-level homes or modular prefabs) with a full basement to accommodate second wives (Bennion 1991b, 1998). Jim Harmston, prophet of the True and Living Church, renovated a bed and breakfast in Manti, Utah, for his eight-wife family. It has eleven bedrooms and five bathrooms with a communal kitchen/living area. Steve Butt of Circleville remodeled an old LDS church for his three wives and six children. The church's massive kitchen remained the same, but the wives' bedrooms were rebuilt from existing Sunday school classrooms. The pews and "chapel" area are used for family meetings and entertainment centers. The AUB and FLDS often use the "separate but equal" design that features personal entrances and parlors for each wife, which allows the women to have more independence from each other and greet visitors without being under the continual scrutiny of other wives.

Less common but much more practical for polygamy are the homes of 3,500–7,000 square feet such as Rocky Baker's home in Utah Valley, which has ten bedrooms, seven bathrooms, two kitchens, a school, two nurseries, and two laundries. These creative McMansions are a part of a new subculture of bourgeois polygamists (Williams 1997). The homes are designed in variety of intricate shapes—quadra, octagonal, and plus-sign (Bennion 1998). The simple quadra structure is a three-story conventional rectangle with separate bedrooms and bathrooms for three to four wives and a large central dining/ family room on the first or main floor. This was the style Grant Bierer of Pinesdale used for his three wives, but I have also seen it in Colonia LeBaron and Bluffdale. The first wife typically lives on the same level as the communal rooms as a sign of her higher status and convenience. Her master bedroom suite is typically bigger than the others and has easy access to the electrical, water, and heat utilities, the kitchen, and the TV room/living room. One of her co-wives lives in a small basement apartment and another in an attic loft on the third floor, while two co-wives share a kind of duplex arrangement on the second floor. Of course, this rectangular design can be modified, as in the case of the Bierer and Williams families, where each of the three wives had her own floor with its own kitchen, bathrooms, bedrooms, and living room. In the case of the Bierers, the first wife designed the basement in an open style in

Santa Fe–style pastels with adobe features. The second wife, who shared her floor with a communal dining/living room, decorated her bedroom/parlor/bath in a Victorian style with high-post bed sets, white walls, and chintz furnishings. The third wife had the top floor, which also hosted the husband's den. She designed her rooms with simple, Mormon features of mismatched furniture, family portraits, and framed embroidered scriptures on the walls. Each wife had her own kitchenette and additional bedrooms for her children.

The plus-sign configuration accommodates four wives in each of the four outside squares; the living/dining room is in the middle. This style has no area just for the husband. Likewise, the octagonal style provides four modular units on the periphery and a centralized family room. Between each modular unit are accordion-style rooms where children's bedrooms are located. Wives with more children living at home will expand the number of bedrooms on each side of them, taking space that is not used by the other wives.

Brigham Young, who had fifty-five wives and fifty-seven children, set a precedent for building polygamist-style mansions in his efficiently designed Lion House in Salt Lake City. This huge home had twenty gables that accommodated twenty bedrooms. To reduce jealousies, Young created a private hall to his office for one of his favorite wives. According to Ray Timpson, who specializes in fundamentalist homes, the secret to building a polygamist home is in knowing how to expand the architecture. Timpson grew up with sixty-five siblings in a 12,000-square-foot home. Rocky Baker, who built his home himself, had to accommodate his wife, Marion, and her nine children and his second wife, Gigi, and her four children plus his mom and dad. Since Marion and Gigi get along well, they were willing to share a common prayer room, school room, and entertainment center, but they each needed their own kitchens and bed and bath suites. It is vital that each wife prepare food for her own children and for the visiting husband in order to define her unique dyadic relationship to her husband, yet the co-wives must also have an area of sharing to underscore their attempts to have the plural family live as a family kingdom (Bennion 1998; Williams 1997).

The largest mansion for polygamists in the West is a 35,000-square-foot house shaped like a three-pronged wagon wheel in southern Utah. Two blades are bedrooms and the third includes a bedroom suite, the husband's den, a library, and a Jacuzzi. In the center of the blades is the communal kitchen. In total this house has thirty-one bedrooms and thirty-seven bathrooms for the husband's ten wives and twenty-eight children. The wives do housework such as child care, cooking, yard work, and cleaning, on a rotating schedule. This plural manor also has an elaborate wine cellar filled with premium wines. The owner has twelve wives and a private jet (Jankowiak 2008).

In Colorado City, the houses are all communally owned by the priesthood council and are in various stages of construction. This is true in Pinesdale, Montana, as well. There is always the need to expand as more wives and children are added to the family. Some of the homes look like motels. Some families live in trailers. Fundamentalists typically leave some homes with tar paper or insulation showing in order to reduce property taxes. The priesthood owns the land and provides the construction so there is no mortgage to pay. By contrast, in places such as Centennial Park, Rocky Ridge, and the new highly popular Eagle Mountain community in Cedar Fort, families take out loans to build their huge mansions of 8,000–12,000 square feet. These latter communities do not belong to the FLDS group but are offshoots of the larger orders. They tend to blend in with mainstream U.S. society more than other groups and are willing to do business with non-Mormon banks.

These larger homes reflect the notion of the "eternal round" where all members are committed to the salvation of the whole family. The home must accommodate an intricate division of labor and must be able to expand to accommodate new children as they are born. It also must provide space for schooling, strict child rearing, and the unique personalities of each wife. Providing equal beauty and space for each wife can be extremely expensive. One husband told me that he acquired a debt of $200,000 when he renovated his home to suit the requests of his three wives. Sometimes, however, the architecture exhibits inequality among co-wives, such as cases where a first wife gets the main floor and subsequent wives get a tiny attic or a damp basement or even a separate small trailer in the backyard. One first wife has the spacious top floor of her big home (which offers great views) and a separate entrance, giving the impression that she is truly the queen. Further, although some structures allow for freedom for the male to move about and access his wives and resources, many homes I've witnessed are designed for the women at the expense of the man. He roams like a vagabond, going from room to room, from home to home, without a space of his own.

Brady Williams of Rocky Ridge built a big home for his three wives using the separate-but-equal philosophy (Williams 1997). The house had three 2,000-square-foot compartments with an entrance for each wife. Much like the home Kody Brown built for his wives, here were simply three of everything:

kitchens, furnaces, TV sets, and master bedrooms. The three women shared a laundry and a family room, but everything else was separate. Williams recently left the AUB and moved his family out of Rocky Ridge to accommodate a more independent religious philosophy and the addition of two more wives. During the summer of 2008, I visited Brady's father, Rod Williams, and his three wives, "Ann," "Rosa," and "Emily," in Washington. Their home is located in the middle of a huge cedar forest near the coast on the Olympic Peninsula. Eight years ago, when Rod and his family left the AUB, he found the five-acre property with a large 5,000-square-foot home to be ideal. It was isolated, it was located in a small town, yet it was only half an hour from a Wal-Mart. He renovated the garage to be a full apartment for his second wife, Rosa, and her five children, installing a kitchen, three bedrooms, a bathroom, and a living room with a woodstove. Rosa's style is simple, clean, and earthy. The second floor of the home belongs to Emily, the third wife, and her three children. It has a kitchen with a wraparound counter, a living room, two bathrooms, a laundry room, and three bedrooms. Her style, which is more luxurious, features cranberry-colored walls and exotic furniture. The top floor belongs to Ann, the first wife. It is decorated in a traditional Mormon style of soft pastel colors and Victorian furniture. It has a master bedroom, a living room, a kitchen, a bathroom, and one spare bedroom for Ann's crafts and sewing. Ann is in her sixties and has less need for extra bedrooms as all her children are grown. Outside is a large vegetable garden, a chicken coop, and a woodshop. In all, the house has nine bedrooms, five bathrooms, and three kitchens and living rooms. Rod figured that it would have been less expensive for him to build a brand-new home than to spend so much money to renovate each floor to adapt to the decorating styles of each wife. Since the wives did not want a common living room and kitchen, the contractors had to tear down walls to provide for new kitchens, each of which has its own style of cupboards and fixtures.

Many fundamentalists hide their lifestyle, fearing that they will lose their jobs or be excommunicated from the LDS Church. Those that are a part of groups have some support, but they are still open to scrutiny from government or the media. This is why many polygamists live in the country, away from the public eye. Some, such as Bob Foster and his three wives, hide their dwellings underground or in caves. For instance, one compound in Missouri has a temple, a church, a school, workshops, bedrooms, kitchens, and recreation rooms, all built underground in a limestone mine. The Fosters blasted into sandstone near Canyonlands National Park in Utah. The three wives each have private houses built in caves. A central 4,000-square-foot cave is used as a communal meeting area.

Another way to hide a polygamous lifestyle is to spread families in different homes, towns, and even states to minimize suspicion. This is common among the Allred Group. Each of the wives after the first wife uses her maiden name to avoid scrutiny. For example, in Marvin Jessop's family, each of his wives live in different dwellings: one lives in a two-story home, another lives in a duplex, and another in a split-level home. Many of the wives do their shopping separately in nearby Hamilton, where one wife does the bulk buying for the week for herself and her co-wives. Above all, fundamentalists are advised to avoid outsiders and children are taught to refrain from talking about *all* their brothers and sisters. The children are also told not to refer to their father as "Dad," because if three twelve-year-old, blue-eyed towheads all clamor around their father at the Wal-Mart, heads will turn. Second and third wives are told not to socialize with their husband's business associates and their wives. And finally, while at college, students from polygamous families do not disclose their background to friends or teachers and they rarely accept dates.

Once separated from Babylon, or the evil outside world, fundamentalists are free to express their culture. They commonly home school their children, at least during the formative years (preschool through sixth grade). Public high school is an option for grades nine and above. In Pinesdale, children go to the Corvallis High School and are readily accepted by the larger community. In Colorado City/Hildale, children have the option to attend the Hildale High School, but many young women are married during their junior or senior years and drop out. In the Eldorado branch, there is no public school; the sect provides secular vocational schooling in its compound.

Other Culture Traits

Another way polygamists culturally distinguish themselves is through uniquely polygamist apparel and hairstyles. Women in the FLDS group are required to have long hair that is braided in the back with a Gibson-girl, hair-sprayed wave in front (the bigger the wave, the more righteous the woman). They are modest and wear "Easter egg–hued" (Anderson 2010, 1) prairie dresses with long skirts and puffy sleeves. Under the skirts they wear trousers or thick stockings and modest boots or shoes. The clothing of AUB women reflects a continuum—often paralleling mainstream Mormonism—from a modest pioneer style (gingham or calico patterns) to polyester pants and T-shirts. The hairstyles vary, from long hair done up in a bun or put in a barrette in the back to modern curled short hair. In Pinesdale, clothing typically reflects the old farm-family style of Montana with practical garb for work and modest clothing for church. Members of Harmston's TLC congregation also wear modern machine-produced styles, rejecting the plain, old-time, home-made dresses. In most groups, long hair for women is considered more virtuous than short hair; it is to be used to wash the feet of Christ in the Millennium.[17] Fundamentalist men of both groups typically have short 1950s-style haircuts and wear clean white shirts with narrow bolo ties. Occasionally, in Pinesdale, I would see men wearing beards, in imitation of the Brigham Young, nineteenth-century frontiersmen look. The men wear conservative work clothes or old-fashioned 1950s-style western dress shirts and pants, typically nice Wrangler jeans.

Despite these generalizations, polygamous families adopt a range of clothing styles. I observed a bizarre variation of "poly" dress at Yankee Reservoir near Cedar Breaks, Utah. An FLDS family comprised of two men, their five wives, and seven kids arrived in two brand-new Chevrolet minivans for a pleasant afternoon of fishing. Three of the women were wearing pastel pioneer dresses. One was standing up to her knees in water to fish, clad in a dress in a unique camouflage pattern with long puffy sleeves and a tucked-up skirt. While the women fished and gutted the catches, the men relaxed and talked in the shade. On another occasion, I spotted an Allred family I knew shopping in Spanish Fork, Utah. The patriarch was around forty-five, and his five wives varied in age from thirty-five to eighteen. Their dress was modern, with brand-name shoes and fancy colors, yet it was still quite modest (dresses for the girls and women and nice jeans and button-up shirts for the men and boys). The women's hair was long but done up in creative braids and buns, not the typical Gibson-girl wave seen on news reports. A final example of dress comes from a family of an independent businessman, his two wives, and five of their thirteen children who live near Seattle. The man and his first wife were in their sixties, both dressed in modern L.L. Bean shorts and oxford-style shirts, whereas the younger wife, who was in her thirties, was dressed in a more conservative-style skirt and long-sleeved blouse and had a braid trailing down her back. She looked nearly identical to Nicki, Bill Henrickson's second "born-in" wife on the television program *Big Love*.

Music and dancing is another distinguishing feature of fundamentalist life. I enjoyed several hours of guitar playing and singing of old Hank Williams songs at the Brent LeBaron household. During family home evenings in the Allred group, everyone joins in to sing hymns and folk songs, play the piano, and occasionally dance in the Tennessee tap or western swing styles. On Sundays at church the congregation sings the Mormon Protestant-based spirituals from the old black hymnal, reflecting the early pioneer music styles. Often they use their cultural halls on Saturday nights for in-house bands (typically bluegrass or western), which play easy-to-dance-to reels and fox trots. Musical talent in youth is applauded and encouraged and every household has at least one piano.

Food and feasting is also extremely important to Mormon fundamentalists. Some jokingly refer to food as sexual foreplay,[18] as the sacrament after a sermon, or as the glue that binds established families to new converts. The food is best defined as typical Mormon fare, which includes Jell-o salads, brownies, home-canned pickles, zucchini bread, and funeral potatoes (i.e., one package of frozen hash browns, one can of cream of mushroom soup, and grated cheddar cheese, baked for an hour at 375 degrees). Frog-eye salad, another specialty, is made with orzo or acini de pepe pasta, non-dairy whipped topping, and marshmallows with fruit and coconut. Cowboy specials (ground beef, pasta, and cheese) and boxed cake mixes are common fare. Sour cream and butter are used plentifully in everything, and ranch dressing is a staple. In Pinesdale, at various households, my daughters and I ate many meat and potato meals with ethnic variations such as Swedish pancakes at Mary Ann's and Niçoise salad at the Stokers. Another household was famous for casseroles. Most meals were accompanied by a rich dessert of chocolate pudding, chocolate chip cookies, or lemon meringue pie. Few families ate a fully organic diet; none were vegetarian.

Each family has at least two years' supply of food. Rice, whole wheat, freeze-dried onions, and potato flakes are stored in five-gallon plastic buckets. Shelves are filled with toilet paper and bottled water for times of crisis. Each wife is expert at bottling peaches, pears, and cherries and is continually shopping for bulk canned goods such as beans and corn. Yet not all polygamist wives are attracted to this old-fashioned, Mormon-pioneer model of domesticity. I have visited some women who live for Chinese take-out food and shop at Costco in the ready-to-serve aisle. These women balk at the idea of slaving for hours to prepare a single Sunday dinner.

In summary, although fundamentalists have certain core beliefs and patterned behaviors, it is folly to assume that all men and women experience the same brand of polygamy. We would not expect all monogamists to conform to one behavioral standard. If travelers to the West observe closely rather than rely on the tabloids for facts, they cannot help but see the richness and diversity of polygamist's lives. Obviously, not all pictures of plural marriage are positive, but very few outsiders actually see positive depictions of plural life when they are right in plain view. For example, in Salt Lake City, an interested and open-minded observer might see a cluster of four wives visiting Temple Square or the mall, looking as if they came right out of the nineteenth century what with their braided hair, hand-sewn frocks, and black-laced boots. One might see them discuss the high prices with amazement and gaze skeptically at the corrupted world of Babylon on south State Street. By contrast, most observers wouldn't notice another type of polygamist: a husband with his several wives living in the suburbs in Draper, each wife with her own home or apartment, blending completely into the fabric of mainstream Mormon society. This suburban fundamentalist family will dress and act much the same as their neighbors: the wives attend college and pursue careers alongside their husbands, and the kids play soccer in the neighborhood park. It is difficult to measure how many of these families exist or whether they are truly content. What we can know through conversion data (Bennion 1998) is that people are still drawn to these groups (10–15 families a month) and that more women express contentment (65 percent) than dissatisfaction (22 percent).[19] In an analysis of longevity and "staying power," I observed that more than 72 percent of those who were disgruntled with the system were male, which suggests, ironically, that males are less content with fundamentalism than females (ibid., 132).

In short, ideology informs a variety of cultural expressions about lifestyle, including architecture, clothing, music, and food. The next section views how fundamentalist beliefs provide a charter for gender roles, sexuality, and marriage.

3

Gender Dynamics and Sexuality

As the characters on the television program *Big Love* illustrate, many of the battles of fundamentalist women are the battles of Mormon women in general. Two scripts for Mormon gender roles are found in Thomas O'Dea's seminal sociological work (1957) and its LDS General Authority corollary, "The Family: A Proclamation to the World," which orthodox Saints use as a guide to obtaining perfection (Hinckley 1995). Both works provide an inadequate and incomplete portrait of women's lives and potential; they omit significant groups of women in the United States, including working women, single women, single mothers, lesbians, and polygamists. The modern-day Church's reliance on these archaic models of womanhood further misrepresents the socioeconomic and cultural realities of most of its female members. After all, women are at least 50 percent of congregations, or in the case of polygamist communities, 65–70 percent. Further, most of the world's approximately six million Mormon women[1] are not living within a traditional family unit.[2] For example, Mormon divorce rates are only *slightly* lower than the national average for women who attend the LDS temple and those that do not, those that are active Mormons and those that are inactive, individuals (Judd 1999). In addition, more Mormon women than men choose divorce, seek therapy, and take anti-depressants (Ponder 2003).[3] Finally, there is a growing ennui and dissatisfaction among young Mormon women, as seen in the negative membership retention rates in Utah (Heaton and Holman 1994).

To O'Dea's credit, he recognized the essential dichotomy of Mormon life—self-actualized individualism versus patriarchal totalitarianism. Yet he did not apply this dialectic to the experience of women. It is not his fault entirely. He, like many scholars of the era, was more keenly aware of the male world and the influence on culture that came from male efforts and vision: a system where men were in the forefront as political and religious actors and women remained in the background as dutifully supportive "auxiliaries" of the larger patriarchal structure. Paradoxically, O'Dea genuinely felt that women in Mormon society were equal to men, while at the same time he underscored the basic inequities that women face within that society: "the father is the head . . . the legislator, the judge, the governor" of the family and "women are dependent upon men and marriage for exaltation and are subordinate to men on this earth" (1957, 249–250).

According to Anne Firor Scott (1986), Mormons believe in separate spheres for men and women, but this separation is more stringent in ideology than in everyday life. Men are responsible for all public life and in private life they are expected to rule their families. Yet the Mormon condition requires women to be in charge when men are away on church business. They have to earn their own keep and take care of the home. More is expected of Mormon women than of almost any other women in the country, but at the same time they are to obey priesthood authority; this goes unquestioned. The end result is a paradoxical empowerment for women that is ignored in many respects by their men, who are under the illusion that they have sole power over their family kingdoms.

O'Dea, like many scholars of the 1950s, was unaware of any gender paradoxes; he was blind to the complexity and diversity of female experience and the changing nature of women's roles in the contemporary world.[4] He failed to incorporate the hidden half of LDS cultural life—women's daily regimen, their work in the public realm, their spiritual and emotional needs, and their unique perspectives as Mormon women. He chose to describe the entire female experience in one paragraph of his monograph (O'Dea 1957, 182). He dismissed gender-based contradictions or tensions within Mormonism as epiphenomenal or "unimportant," suggesting that in the area of equity "no difficulties arise" (ibid., 249). This mirrors the sentiment of current LDS prophet Gordon B. Hinckley in the *Boston Globe*: "I haven't found any complaint among our women. I'm sure there are a few, a handful somewhere who may be disaffected for one reason or another, but I've never seen any evidence of it" (quoted in Black and Hanks 2000:1).

For Mormon fundamentalist polygamists, O'Dea's work and the Hinckley-supported LDS Proclamation presents a challenge. It depicts an idealistic, Victorian view of men and women who are married in the temple and provide a home for the children who are waiting to join them. Men and women are created in the image of God and are expected to follow in his footsteps, marry as he did, and raise his children in a monogamous, loving home.[5] Although polygamists embrace Victorian sexuality, contract marriages in the official endowment ceremony, and give all their attention to raising their children in a loving home, they do not see monogamy as the ideal. They also are not always interested in seeing the man as the sole breadwinner. Many fundamentalist women provide money for the household while they are also active in social production: raising a garden, processing food, caring for children, fixing the faucets, and milking the cows, as is the case of the Stoker family of Pinesdale. According to early apostle John A. Widstoe, "the place of woman in the Church is to walk beside the man, not in front of him nor behind him. In the Church there is full equality between man and woman" (Widstoe 1939, 83). Polygamous Mormon women were among the first in the nation to fight for voting rights, sponsor co-education, publish their own magazine that fostered female autonomy, adopt leadership callings, serve in the Senate, and participate, at least in the early church, in healing and religious ceremonies.[6]

Further, in the days of the early Saints, women actually held the priesthood and were active in temple work and worship as well as in domestic economy.[7] This is not surprising; Joseph Smith was surrounded by individualistic, feminist leaders during his formative years. His grandmother, Lucy Mack, organized religious communes for the poor (Anderson 2001); and in the western New York, where he grew up, Anna Lee, a self-proclaimed incarnation of the Godhead, established a Shaker colony only thirty miles from Palmyra, and former Quaker Jemima Wilkinson founded the Society of Universal Friends (O'Dea 1957, 15). Joseph's enigmatic first wife, Emma, was a scribe of the Book of Mormon and was president of the Relief Society, and his fourteenth wife, Eliza R. Snow, formulated early Mormon doctrine and was a poet and an administrator of the Relief Society.

Because of the disjunction between the more liberating teachings of the early Church and modern patriarchal dogma, the true role of Mormon polygamous women is difficult to assess (Beck 1994). On the one hand, women are depicted in the national media as depressed, subordinated housewives who are subject to the authority of their patriarch husbands and geriatric male leaders. On the other hand, they are seen as empowered, contented wives and mothers who have jurisdiction over their families and experience joy and autonomy. The latter category, according to Radke (2004), includes women who embrace their roles as mothers and daughters of God who have rare opportunities to advance spiritually, intellectually, and socially. As Brigham Young University law professor Cheryl Preston put it, "Am I less of a feminist because I am deeply religious and devoted to this traditional, conservative organized religion?" (2004, 12).

Yet even Mormon women who consider themselves feminists, academics, and orthodox often speak of the contradictory messages presented to them in Mormonism: how do Mormon women maintain their "autonomy and agency in the context of institutionalized patriarchy and then how do they make sense of church prescriptions on male authority both within the family and in the church hierarchy?" (Beaman 2001, 2). In addition, "Why do women disproportionately invest in an institution that systematically devalues them?" (Ozorak 1996, 17). Cornwall asks, "How are women simultaneously 'present and silent' in religious traditions, and what social processes maintain their presence and silence?" (1994, 240).

It is my observation that many polygamous women reach a level of autonomy and female collaboration that their monogamous counterparts do not experience, attributable in part to the forced interdependence that is required of them during the prolonged absences of their husbands. Also, the strength of the frontier lifestyle some Mormon women still follow enables them to tap into the nineteenth-century feminism of Emma Smith, the first source of Mormon female empowerment.

Gender Dynamics among Mormon Fundamentalists

According to gender scholar Michael Kimmel (2008), the two tasks of any gender study are to explain difference and inequality. We often hear about how men and women are different, but how is that difference mapped out on the rich and varied terrain of polygamy? Further, how do Mormon fundamentalists construct gender? The answers to these questions are as complex as polygamist relationships themselves. In some poly families, for example, an interplanetary analysis of gender ("men are from Mars, women from Venus") is appropriate: boys and girls are segregated and male priesthood authority reigns supreme over the subjugated females, such as one finds in the Eldon Kingston or Warren Jeffs families. These families adhere to strict anatomical and biblical notions of maleness and femaleness and universal scripts for male supremacy (kingship) and female subordination (subjects to the king). Right-wing social moralists like James Dobson argue that dichotomous scripts solve the problem of the modern confusion of sex roles and promote balance and efficiency (Dobson 1991). Inevitably, the girls in such groups are encouraged to marry young. First their fathers and then their husbands are their Saviors on Mt. Zion. Alternatively, some poly families adhere to a model of gender equity emphasizing the overlapping of tasks and individual autonomy (Hubbard

1990). In these polygamist families, the men either stay in the background or are on an equal footing with their wives, who make all the tough decisions about budgeting, workload, education, and family life. Examples of this model are the women associated with Kody Brown, Joe Darger, or Alex Joseph. These girls and women are outspoken, highly independent, and well educated.

And what of fundamentalist men? Rarely do we hear news reports or read studies of the difficulties men experience in Mormon fundamentalism. Are they happy and contented? What is the nature of their gendered difference? Are they mistreated? As the FLDS profile indicates, some males are actually more unhappy, and potentially more abused, than their female counterparts. As DoriAnn, an FLDS woman stated, "Polygamist husbands have it roughest of all" (quoted in Sloan 2011, 1). She feels that men are frustrated with their roles as fathers and husbands and with trying to juggle many relationships and provide for so many people. She has watched her own husband become angry about all the expectations of him. "It's probably the ugliest job in the whole situation," she says (ibid., 2).

In my observations, males have enormous responsibilities that stretch their energy, finances, and time sometimes beyond endurance, especially if they are required to donate any profits and assets to the Brethren. In addition, males who do not compete well for wives and resources are often exploited by pureblood elders and other established members. They are sometimes forced to leave their homes and families by priesthood mandate. Boys suffer from the absence of fathers, and this challenges their ability to find solid role models and affection. Girls do not suffer in the same way, as they have the continual presence of numerous mothers around them to bond with and gain affirmation from.

In general, the gender constructs of most fundamentalists are best described as being segregated based on religious and economic function. Men and boys are expected to be "kings in the making" who will take up the mantles of religious priesthood leadership and economic stewardship and become heads of household. The fathers are the conduits for God's law in the family; they are in charge of everyone's spiritual development. Some groups (FLDS, Kingston) require that a man have three or more wives to enter the kingdom (seven is a "quorum"), whereas others (current LeBaron, AUB) suggest that some men are not meant to be polygamists and should serve as monogamists.

Some groups, like the Kingston and Colorado City (FLDS) sects, sanction the marriage of girls as young as thirteen to fifteen (Fremd 2006; Dougherty

2003). In some cases, the young woman is in favor of the marriage because it will raise her prestige in the group; in other cases, as with Carolyn Jessop and Elissa Wall, the marriages are contracted against the bride's will (Jessop and Palmer 2007; Wall and Pulitzer 2008). For this reason, the FLDS loses more women than men[8] to apostasy (the formal rejection of the sect by a member). In the AUB, it is the opposite: more men than women seek to leave. One convert study shows that of 1,024 individuals (597 females, 427 males) who converted from 1953 to 1993, more than 35 percent (360 individuals) left the group. Of that 35 percent, more than 72 percent (250 individuals) were male (Bennion 1998, 132).

Jeff's FLDS Texas branch has been portrayed by media and scholars alike as a particularly patricentric sect that exerts enormous control over wives and children (Jankowiak 1995). Many women are isolated, financially dependent, and uneducated; they are married off in their young teenage years as "Stepford wives on the prairie" (Walsh 2008, 1).[9] FLDS and Kingston women experience more gender inequality than women in other groups. Their men typically preside over at least three to four wives and twenty to forty children. By contrast, in the Allred Group each man has fewer wives on average and women have the right to marry whom they choose, work outside the sect in the mainstream in a field of their choice, and dress the way they wish. Since the 1980s, following Owen Allred's lead, many independents have prohibited marriages of young women under eighteen. Despite a few notorious cases of abuse, the AUB is currently considered by the U.S. attorney general's office to be one of the more gender-progressive groups because it cooperates with the government and gives women choices about marriage, careers, education, and full releases (divorces) from unfavorable marriages (Dethman and Dillon-Kinkead 2005). Because females have these choices, the AUB's 35 percent divorce rate is much higher than in other Mormon fundamentalist groups (Bennion 1998). If anything, the AUB treats women much better than it does young men who are born in and male converts, who struggle for power and financial gain against great odds. Women are taken into the group swiftly, without effort on their part. They experience very little competition with others for husbands; they are free to choose single or married men for their companions, and their choices are respected. They also aren't asked to contribute wealth when they convert. Many are encouraged to marry high-status men; women who choose to do so are integrated into the group easily.

The formal roles of AUB women, however, are hidden, particularly in terms of fundamentalist doctrine and political authority. Officially, women are formally relegated to auxiliary programs and the domestic sphere. They cannot hold the priesthood, which is the power of God on earth, and they cannot attain Godhood on their own without their husband. It is often said that a man will resurrect his wives in the hereafter, not the other way around. Yet, as I shall show in Chapter 4, a handful of women exert enormous influence in the group. For example, for decades Dauna Baird was the managing force behind the AUB prophet's actions. Any who is worthy and is married to a high-ranking holder of the Melchizedek Priesthood may serve as his proxy for financial and political decisions. For example, it was not branch leader Marvin Jessop but his first wife, Sharon, who was called upon to "test" me when I entered the AUB for research. In Alex Joseph's household, his wife, Elizabeth, a lawyer, was the spokesperson for their large family to the media and in public gatherings. Fundamentalist women believe that God is an exalted man and that if women are worthy, they can become Goddesses of their own worlds.

Ideally, fundamentalist women are expected to bear and raise a "righteous seed" for their husband's kingdom. Expectant mothers are tabernacles who are anxiously waiting for their spirit children. Women often speak of dreams they've had where their future children appear to them and beg them to open up the gates of heaven that lead to earth through their wombs (Bennion 1998). Because of this heavy emphasis on childbearing, women who are barren or have fewer children are stigmatized.[10] For example, in a family of three wives in the Bluffdale, Utah, area, the third wife has three children, whereas her co-wives have six each. Her blood sisters and stepsisters in the larger group each have a dozen children. There is a subtle slighting of the wife with only three children whenever she is introduced to company. In spite of the fact that the third wife is running her family's business, she knows she is not living up to her potential in the group because of her small family.

In addition to raising up a "seed," women are to be spiritual leaders in their household, second in command to their husbands. In 1854, LDS Apostle Parley P. Pratt established the following Rules of Conduct that are considered to be appropriate guidelines for polygamists today:

1. Men should be leaders and counselors to women and children and rule with wisdom.
2. Men should have good judgment in their selection of women for

their kingdoms; fancy pretty women with no talents are like the dew-drops which glitter for a moment in the sun, dazzle the eye, and vanish. Men should look for kind and amiable dispositions; for modesty and industry; for virtue and honesty; for cleanliness in apparel and household; for cheerfulness, patience, and stability; and genuine spiritual righteousness.

3. Men should call their wives and children together frequently and instruct them in their duties to God and to themselves. Men should pray with them often and teach them to invite the Holy Spirit in their midst.

4. A woman should unite herself in marriage with a man, submitting herself wholly to his counsel and letting him govern as the head. She should not rebel against the divine patriarchal order of family government to protect against condemnation.

5. Each mother should correct her own child and see that they don't dispute and quarrel. The husband should see that each mother maintains a wise and proper discipline over her children, especially when young; it is his duty to see that all children are obedient.

6. Let husbands, wives, sons, and daughters, continually realize that their relationships do not end with this earth life, but will continue in eternity. "Every qualification and disposition, therefore, which will render them happy here, should be nourished, cherished, enlarged and perfected, that their union may be indissoluble, and their happiness secured both for this world and for that which is to come." (Pratt 1854, 107)

Joseph Smith taught that the appropriate role of husbands and wives is that of ruler and subject, respectively (Musser 1944, 1948). Husbands must be instructional and dominating, and wives must be obedient and respectful. Further requirements for women are summarized in Genesis 3:16: "Thy desire shall be to thy husband, and he shall rule over thee." Women should "respect and revere themselves, as holy vessels, destined to sustain and magnify the eternal and sacred relationship of wife and mother." A wife is the "ornament and glory of man; to share with him a never fading crown, and an eternally increasing dominion" (Musser 1948, 134). Musser also wrote that a man "shall fight the physical battles in protection of his loved ones, and bring into the home the necessaries of life." The wife "adorns the home, conserves the larder and renders the habitation an earthly heaven where love, peace, affection, gratitude, and oneness shall abound, she the queen and he the king" (ibid.). These ideological scripts are not always translated into reality, as in the case of Rod Williams's family, whose youngest wife, Nora, runs the family business and is outspoken and "in charge," or in the case of Elizabeth Joseph of Big Water, who was a breadwinner and spokesperson to the media instead of her husband, who did not like to be in the public eye. By contrast, one FLDS woman, DoriAnn, states her duties in this manner, mirroring nineteenth-century paradigms:

> A woman's duty is to turn herself in when she is ready for marriage and pray for a knowledge of who will be willing to receive her place in this man's family, then place herself under his mind and will for her life and take directions in all things. A man's duty and faith requires him to take whomever he is given and honor and regard her by having children with her and providing emotionally, spiritually and physically for her and all of his other family members equally in all things. (Sloan 2011, 2)

While men are allowed to have many wives, women may not have many husbands. This restriction is absolute, and it is true of even the most progressive of fundamentalists. Polygamy, fundamentalists believe, is God's way and nature's way. As polygamist Bart Malstrom states, "Men have the urge to have more than one woman and woman have the urge to have more than one child. That's the difference of our God-given roles" (quoted in Laytner 2008, 2). Another Manti polygamist stated that men and women should not have the same roles; God intended that they follow nature, where the male leads and the females follow. Families are better off, they say, with a mother in the home, taking care of her children. The hierarchy is set in stone: the husband obeys God, the wife obeys the husband, and the kids obey the parents. As Rod Williams remarked, "I was destined to be a polygamist; I can't imagine being anything else . . . it is my nature" (Bennion 2008, 3).

Why would a woman be drawn to such a patriarchal lifestyle given the patriarchal rigidity? According to Mormon scholar Rex Cooper (1990), women who are attracted to fundamentalism often face serious obstacles in the mainstream Mormon Church. Single women, single mothers, divorced and widowed women, and unmarriageable women are often socially and economically deprived of the resources available to the rest of the membership. Women who convert are typically drawn to polygamy to find a husband, bear children, and access priesthood resources tied to their salvation. Women in polygamous relationships are baptized and integrated into an already established network. During my AUB/Allred research, I learned that the female converts came from the LDS Church. The majority, 68 percent, spoke to me of being stigmatized for the reasons that Cooper lists: lack of husband or abandonment issues. In some cases, women had been ostracized in their home wards for being unable to fulfill their roles as described in the Proclamation (Hinckley 1995). They were drawn to plural marriage — despite the fact that polygamists' views of God were different from mainstream Mormon beliefs, in spite of the male dominance that is typical of polygamous households, the illegality of polygamous marriages, and the focus of polygamous groups on communal sharing — often as a last resort, because their social situation didn't match the mainstream reality of monogamy.[11] In the analysis of conversion histories, I discovered that after entering the groups, convert women experienced upward social and economic mobility (at least temporarily). The greatest mobility occurred among single educated women in their thirties who entered the group and married into the priesthood hierarchy. This increased their employment advancement and access to economic stewardships from 26 percent to 43 percent of the total number of financial callings in the branch (Bennion 1998, 66).

One could thus argue that the options for some disenfranchised women in the mainstream Mormon world are relatively few; they are tunneled toward polygamy as their only viable choice. Once within the group, they are often instantly incorporated into a family as a third or fourth wife and have access to their husband's sperm, his priesthood powers, and the valuable economic and emotional network established by his wives. They were suddenly given affirmation and told that they were queens in the making, as opposed to being called "spinsters and single moms" in their old wards in the LDS Church. Their children, if they had any, were promised a home in an already established family kingdom with several "aunts" to help meet their needs.

Some Mormon women experience more individual satisfaction within the dynamics of a polygamous family than they would in any other marital form, which may partially account for the extremely high rate of female conversion (Bennion 1996, 1998). Advocates of polygamy, such as Anne Wilde, say that it can be seen as a "viable alternative lifestyle between consenting adults" (quoted in Lee 2006). Anthropologist Phil Kilbride states that plural marriage can help rebuild a strong sense of family for specific groups of Americans, especially in times of socioeconomic crisis (1994). He suggests that we ask ourselves whether monogamy is perfect. Many monogamous women suffer under the thumb of a dominant man with no one nearby to help them. At least polygamous women have their co-wives to talk to and potentially protect them from a tyrannical husband. This coincides with one plural wife's opinion that most people want to outlaw polygamy yet treat adultery and divorce as commonplace. Some feel that America is all about polygamy—"It's just that they do it one person at a time—serial polygamists" (Wagner 2008, 2).[12]

According to Blake (1996), the sex ratio in America is skewed in favor of women, especially in the 1980s and 1990s. Among people aged forty-five, there were 200 single women for every 100 available men. She thinks a return to plural marriage could be the best alternative to divorce because it would provide husbands for women, fathers for children, and an end to loneliness. Samuel Chapman, a supporter of polygamy, agrees, stating that the surplus of women in the U.S. population creates competition for good men, which requires men to strive to show their best traits. Women then select the best men instead of settling for leftovers (Gray 2001). As Randy Maudsley has stated reinforcing one method of dealing with these skewed sex ratios, if a man is in love with two women, he should just marry them both (20/20 1997).

Polygamist Elizabeth Joseph writes that if polygamy didn't exist, "the modern American career woman would have invented it. Because, despite its reputation, polygamy is the one lifestyle that offers an independent woman a real chance to 'have it all'" (1997, 1). Elizabeth, who worked as a journalist, relied on her co-wives to help her with child care and meal preparation. She called it a "free-market approach to marriage" that allowed her to pick the best man available, regardless of his marital status. Her husband's other wives actually enhanced her marriage to her husband. Alex, she said, had vast experience as a good husband long before he married her so he was skilled; he didn't need to be trained like most husbands do. When Elizabeth became a lawyer, she introduced her beautiful and talented secretary, Belinda, to her husband. He married Belinda shortly afterward, uniting the two women as friends and wives. Elizabeth's family, the Alex Joseph clan of Big Water, Utah, has been widely popularized in the media. When I met Elizabeth Joseph at the gay-polygamy forum at the Salt Lake library, I found her to be very strong and outspoken. Ted Mikels's documentary *Alex Joseph and His Wives* describes how Alex, a former policeman, became a polygamist in the Allred Group, eventually taking on twelve wives (ironically, from non-Mormon families). He and his wives started their own town in Big Water and introduced libertarian ideals to all new citizens (Mikels 1976).

In addition to seeing polygamy as a viable alternative to monogamy, many fundamentalist women are empowered in their roles as mothers of Zion. This concept is related to the notion of Republican motherhood that was used widely in the Mormon movement for women's suffrage in the late nineteenth and early twentieth centuries, directed by outspoken polygamous women such as state senator and doctor Martha Hughes Cannon (Hanks 1992). The ideas of Republican motherhood benefited pioneer women in the private and public realms of life. For example, in the early days of the LDS Church, Brigham Young encouraged women not only to become "mothers in Zion" but also to advance their careers in business and politics: "Women are useful, not only to sweep houses . . . but they should stand behind the counter, study law or physics, or become good bookkeepers. . . . All this enlarges their sphere of usefulness for the benefit of society at large" (Young 1869, 61). Elizabeth Joseph, Alex Joseph's plural wife, agrees with Brigham Young. She says that plural marriage is empowering for women. "It provides me the environment and opportunity to maximize my female potential without all the tradeoffs and compromises that attend monogamy" (Joseph 1997, 2). Another advocate of legalizing polygamy writes that plural marriage frees women to pursue a career and increases the overall value of women in society (Gray 2001).

Of particular importance is the ability of women to increase their status with the number of children they bear for their family kingdoms. Marvin Jessop's first wife, who bore thirteen children, for example, is considered a "queen among women." June Jessop, a naturopath and midwife trained by Dr. Rulon C. Allred, served as midwife at the birth of most of her community's children. She also enjoys enormous prestige and delegates tasks to men and women alike. Mary, the wife of the mayor, is another example of empower-ment. She was once married to one of the AUB councilmen and found him to be emotionally disturbed. She demanded to have a better husband, and the priesthood gave her the choice among all the men. She chose a wealthy man, the mayor, who had two kind and gentle wives. She is known for her ability to speak her mind and provide her children with protection. She is a feminist in every sense of the word. In addition, there is Emily, a business-woman with a bachelor's degree who runs the family's operations, which earn hundreds of thousands in income. She is an independent second wife (that is, she is no longer pledged to any group), and she enjoys "top dog" status as the family's primary breadwinner. Rarely does anyone in the family, including her husband, disagree with her decisions. Finally, Dauna Baird, the administrative director of the AUB, should be acknowledged here. For many decades, Dauna has overseen the financial and religious organization of the sect under the leadership of Owen Allred. I have never met a tougher lady. She is the check and balance of the group, reminding councilmen and members alike when they are in the wrong or in need of her fine-tuned adjustment to their moral characters.

In spite of potential obstacles to fundamentalism, many polygamist women find ironic power through a unique doctrinal interpretation of the gospel. When men speak of their kingdom, women often refer to themselves as royalty, sitting on thrones and ruling over their families as promised in Doctrine and Covenants 75:5. Apostle George Q. Cannon emphasized women's divine calling:

> A great glory is bestowed on woman, for she is permitted to bring forth the souls of men. You have the opportunity of training children who shall bear the holy priesthood, and go forth and magnify it in the mist of the earth. . . . God has reposed in them great power; if they wield that power for good it will be productive of peace and happiness and exaltation to them. (Cannon 1867, 338)

Some fundamentalist women claim to have had a unique revelation that was not given to men about their future children. These spirit children appear to them in dreams before they are conceived, requesting entrance into this world. Since women often control the sexual rotation schedules, they can control the number of children born into their families, making it possible for them to open the gates of heaven to new souls through their wombs. Women also speak of the nature of the sisterhood, which allows them to spiritually and temporally endure the hardships of this world. Learning to share is a heavenly art that is meant for the greatest of souls. Men, they say, are weak and cannot collaborate well with other men, so it is up to women to rise to the task. When I asked women why they can't have more than one husband, one woman told me, "Ha! Men could never deal with having to sexually share a woman with another man; they aren't capable of getting beyond their own inflated egos" (e-mail correspondence, 2008).

Fundamentalist women also experience relative power associated with the religious and political callings. For example, in the period 1989 to 1993, of 110

individuals (75 males, 35 females) men and women shared the same proportion of administrative callings (Bennion 1998, 60). Although some of these
callings ranked higher than others, this suggests that women are actively involved in the leadership of the community. There was, however, a significant
difference in the area of "spiritual" resources; that is, access to priesthood
power and the right to administer Melchezedek blessings; 7 percent of the
women and 40 percent of the men hold these powers (ibid.). The women were
typically the wives of the prophet or councilmen or rose to these spiritual
positions through birthright. Yet 54 percent of the women of the community
under study had access to the sacred ordinances and rites associated with the
endowment house, which only 34 percent of the men had.

Women use the blueprint of Jesus' wives—Mary and Martha—to help
guide them. In Mormon tradition, the two sisters loved each other and when
they married the Savior, they became an eternal round. Martha, focused on
home and hearth, offered unique gifts to the family with her cooking and
caregiving. Mary, who was more active in the public realm, provided support and counsel to her husband in his dealings with the community. She
worked in the marketplace, in the square, in politics. Each of the two sisters,
who were each devoted to their callings, their families, and their husband,
was the perfect complement to each other. That is what is sought among
sister-wives—the missing ingredient in their lives, the opposite characteristic
that will "complete" the other. So if one wife is an introvert, she will be drawn
to a woman who is an extravert so that her children will learn social skills and
public speaking. She, in turn, will teach her co-wife's children spirituality and
quiet contemplation.

Mother Eve is another symbol from which fundamentalist women derive
meaning. Eve is the supreme example of righteousness. Adam held the priesthood and Eve was the "mother of all living"; they were a team. So now each
wife, following Eve's example, joins with her husband, who walks in Adam's
footsteps, to populate and raise a righteous seed for the kingdom of heaven.
Every wife should be a check-and-balance on her husband's activities, to ensure he honors his priesthood. In fundamentalist doctrine, if a man is un-
worthy of more wives, his first wife shall stand as witness against him. In this
instance, a wife acts as a "spokesperson" for God to rebuke a man who may
seek wives for carnal or lustful purposes (Kraut 1983). Eve also represents the
life of a senior wife; she shared her role with Lilith, Adam's other wife, in a
way that promoted solidarity and cohesion.

Fundamentalists, like some Mormon liberals, speak of a Goddess, a heavenly Mother who was married to the Father, Elohim. This concept allows women to feel divinely linked to a female being who is a wife and mother like themselves and gives women the charter to be sovereign mothers to their own families. Women are willing to suffer for a good cause in order to help their children be lifted up with them to highest celestial glories, just as Eve suffered when she was forced to leave the Garden of Eden; just as Mary Magdalene suffered at the cross when gazing on her husband's wounds. In addition to being queens and goddesses in the next life, there are joys to be experienced while still on earth. Many polygamist women cultivate lasting friendships with other women in the community and see polygamy as a conscious life choice that expands their circle of happiness beyond themselves and their children. This is the same type of unity and empowerment Iranian women experienced in their informal women's network in the village of Deh Koh (Friedl 1989) and the Ijaw women of West Africa experienced in groups made up of non-kin co-wives that foster solidarity and friendship within the context of their husband's patrilineage (Leis 1974).

Within the Allred Group, many women described their ability to gain access to healing powers and feminist ideologies that the mainstream church abandoned long ago, such as using the priesthood to bless one's child and praying to Heavenly Mother (Bennion 1998). Eliza R. Snow is often spoken of by polygamists as a role model and saint in this respect. Eliza introduced the concept of a Heavenly Mother in the hymn "O My Father," which strongly suggests that a God the Mother exists in the heavens. Later, Bruce R. McConkie validated this belief stating that "implicit in the Christian verity that all men are the spirit children of an Eternal Father is the usually unspoken truth that they are also the offspring of an Eternal Mother" (McConkie 1991, 467). This mother figure emphasizes the role of Mormon women as daughters of a Goddess who have the potential to attain divinity. It also provides a blueprint for women to use the priesthood power to bless others, such as children, as Emma Smith did upon occasion, or even animals, as Mary Fielding Smith did when laid her hands on the head of her ox and healed it while crossing the plains.

Because of the communalism of fundamentalist Mormon groups, many women are able to tap into a large economic and emotional network to care for the needs of their growing families. Women also explained that they had control of the reproductive schedule (i.e., the sleeping arrangements of their husband) and the budgeting for their family. They would often say to me that they felt sorry for monogamous women who were with their husbands all the time. Within polygamy, and with the help of co-wives, they argued, one could gain respite from their husband and pursue an education or a career. During my time with the Allreds, the group sponsored a series of workshops for women about self-esteem and "divine potential," taught by Vance Allred, an educator, a writer, and the son of Owen Allred. The goal of these workshops was to help women discover self-confidence derived from fulfillment at home and in the community and to promote respect for others throughout the church (Allred 1993).

Anthropologist Lionel Tiger (1969) argued that in prehistoric time, males were the only ones who could adequately form bonds to impact the development of culture because of their need to cooperate during hunting. Nancy Chodorow (1978) discounted this theory with her discovery that mother-daughter bonds are the most enduring, powerful connections in a child's life and that because of those early attachments, women are trained to rely heavily on interpersonal relationships and friendships with other women. Sally Slocum (1975) also wrote about the strong possibility that the female-centered group was the first family structure among hominids and that vital evolutionary advances were made by females in groups, not males in groups. In agreement with Chodorow and Slocum, Africanist Nancy Leis (1974) showed that the polygamous wives of the Ijaw tribe of West Africa enjoy autonomy and freedoms associated with the huge female economic network established between married women of the patrilineage. The same phenomenon occurs among fundamentalist women in the Intermountain West. These women form very strong bonds with other females who are also raised in "the Work." They spend most of their day with a large network of other girls and women and a comparatively small amount of time with males. They also do not have to undergo a harsh "time of proving," or rite of passage, that young males endure in polygamy, so fewer young females are alienated or marginalized. Therefore, fewer adult females are likely to leave the group. This was substantiated by my research in Pinesdale, Montana, where only 5 percent of women opted to leave the group, whereas 27–30 percent of the men who converted eventually became apostates or were forced out.

"I know it must seem strange to outsiders," says Joyce Broadbent, a forty-four-year-old FLDS member, "but from my experience, sisterwives usually get along very well. Oh sure, you might be closer to one than another, or someone might get on your nerves occasionally, but that's true in any family. I've never felt any rivalry or jealousy at all" (quoted in Anderson 2010, 4). Joyce said she was thrilled to welcome Marcia, her husband's second wife, to the family. Marcia, who left an unhappy marriage in the 1980s, is also Joyce's biological sister. "I knew my husband was a good man," Joyce explains with a smile as she sits with Marcia and their husband, Heber. "I wanted my sister to have a chance at the same kind of happiness I had" (ibid.).

In conversion interviews, many women said that they enjoy having respite from the continual presence of their husband through an agreed-upon rotation schedule that recognizes each wife's individual desires and needs. "Who hasn't heard the tired housewife wishing she could hire a replacement for a day? What housewife doesn't occasionally want to escape her husband and children?" wrote polygamy advocate Christen Gray (2001). In polygamy, stated one wife, there is never "pressure to satisfy their husband because another wife is always available" (Laytner 2008, 3). These women also praised their ability to created a unified front when their husband gets out of line. In Saudi Arabia, a man was actually beaten by his two wives — part of his nose was cut off — when he threatened to take a third wife without their consent (Reuters 2007). These women were unified in their opposition to a system they objected to that had been created by men.

Strong, enduring friendships are forged in such unifying arrangements. For example, one polygamous woman remarked, "I have lots of companions, lots of friends, and lots of children. There's never a dull moment" (CTV 2005, 1). Another woman wrote, "the women in my family are friends; you don't share two decades of experience and a man, without those friendships becoming very special" (Joseph 1997, 2). Acker (2005) found that for American housewives, relationships with other women in the domestic sphere were central in structuring their lives and providing a source of empowerment. These networks were sources of support, affection, resistance commitment, and obligation. Further, network theorists suggest that women with multiple economic and friendship ties and with other women in the community are more empowered and political active than isolated women (Bennion 1991a, 2008). While women are naturally trained to socialize and make connections for survival and friendship, women who strategically link themselves to those who have access to valued resources will fare better than those who simply make ties via proximity. For example, in the AUB, Dauna Baird is married to a councilman, is related to the former prophet, and is sister-in-law to those with valued economic stewardships related to construction work. Her blood lines are pure, her affinal ties are secure, and she is in a position to ask for material items for herself and her family at any time. Likewise, in the town of Bountiful, British Columbia, Jane, the former first wife of Winston Blackmore, had network ties with almost everyone in the town. Because she was senior wife to twenty other wives, she had an advantage in negotiating budgeting and rotation schedules. She was also sister to the bishop and a product of five generations of fundamentalist polygamy. Her calling as midwife also connected her strongly to most households, and her skills as a naturopath made her invaluable to the community.

Another advantage of a female network is the collective socialization of children. In polygamous families, children are raised by multiple spouses, so there will always be at least one adult available for them at all times. In contrast, many dual-income families in mainstream U.S. society struggle to provide care for children six years and older during the "latchkey" period of 2:45 p.m. to 6 p.m. The multiple parenting arrangement within polygamy can lead to a collaborative mentality. As one young woman in Bountiful said, "Polygamy is a team of players that care about each other" (CVT 2005, 1). For example, when a biological mother dies, her co-wife, with whom the child is familiar and already loves as "another mom," can easily make the transition to primary caregiver. In addition, to compensate for their husband's absence, many wives give extra care and attention to their children and develop especially close friendships with them. "Polly," a Centennial Park teacher, argues that children in polygamous households are not brainwashed but are very successful, well-educated individuals (Wagner 2008). Polly's daughter, Lorine, thirty, a plural wife, is widely traveled and has a double major in business management and English literature. Her other daughter, Bethany, twenty-one, also a polygamist with a college degree, runs a graphic design business out of her home. And her son, Joseph, nineteen, is a freshman in college.

Polygamous women voice satisfaction in the Law of Sarah ceremony that links women to each other with their consent by covenant for eternity. Ideally, the first wife agrees to link the second wife not only to her husband but also to herself, in this life and the next. Through this eternal bond, women are encouraged to work together economically, socially, and spiritually and, in some rare cases, sexually (that is, in scheduling the rotation of their husband's nightly visits). These bonds are sometimes enhanced when women court other women as future co-wives. They are crucial during the prolonged absences of their husbands and create a strong interdependence that forces women to learn a large repertoire of domestic and mechanical skills such as dry-walling, fishing, plowing, and herding cattle. Few monogamous women experience this same, intense, training.

One of the best examples of the female network occurred in the Clyde Stoker family of Pinesdale, Montana, where four women—all skilled in different areas—worked together for the benefit of the whole family. For example, one wife was skilled as a nurse and worked part-time at a nearby hospital. Another woman with training in child development was a key figure in the care of the family's twenty-four children. A third wife, who had training in elementary education, helped at the local Montessori school. The fourth, an excellent cook, stayed home to help the second wife with the children. The Stokers exemplify the process of economic networking that Singh and Morey (1987) referred to in their study of 100 polygamous households in Burkina Faso. They estimated the value of economic contributions of wives to the home. Their results showed that the number of wives in the household significantly determines the wife's output in home production. Further, a mother's time in home production tends to increase as the number of children under the age of four increases. In short, polygamy has the potential for increasing household productivity in homes with numerous co-wives—*if*, that is, all the wives in that household are collaborative by nature.

Yet another example of female solidarity is Brent LeBaron's family in Colonia LeBaron near Galeana, Mexico. Brent, the son of Verlan and Irene LeBaron, constructed homes with his own hands for each of his wives and their twenty-two children. Together, they raise a variety of crops. They also raise cattle and operate a dry-walling business in the Midwest. LeBaron and his sons work in the United States and send money home to his three wives, who form a tight-knit survival group during his absence. Now, through the use of cell phones, the women can communicate with each other throughout the day about their work, from shopping in Casas Grandes to canning peaches. They take turns providing child care, teaching at the local school, and watching the livestock. They live only a few miles apart and are able to share tasks easily. All three wives married Brent of their own volition and feel free to move across the border as they wish. At present, the small colony lives peacefully in the foothills of sierras, ignored by mainstream society. Brent and his wives expressed worry that renegade FLDS members from Texas will flood their area, bringing with them ideas about forced marriage, pedophilia, and restrictive patriarchy. In 2002, when an FLDS outsider named Orson Black arrived with his underage brides, he was promptly kicked out of town (Corchadeo 2008).

Another prime example of female economic networking may be seen in the Alex Joseph family of Big Water, Utah. Alex Joseph first joined the Mormon Church in 1955 and then the Allredite fold in 1960, convincing three Missoula female students, none of whom were connected to Mormonism, to marry him. He left the Allreds to build the community of Big Water in 1983, where he organized the Confederate Nations of Israel (Quinn 1998). Although Alex fashioned a career as a writer, salesman, scholar, and manager, his wives were lawyers, accountants, businesswomen, and teachers. They provided the vast bulk of resources for the family's needs, yet they also had time to earn college degrees, bear and raise children, and build careers.

Yet another family that has experienced relative success in female networking is the Ariel Hammon family from Centennial Park, an offshoot of the FLDS (Phillips and Diaz 2007). Hammon is thirty-two and his first wife, Helen, is thirty. This is one of the rare "peer" marriages in fundamentalism.[13] Hammon and Helen have seven children. His second wife, Lisa, who is twenty, has two children. They all live in a cramped 1,400-square-foot cottage that was provided by the community. Though both of Ariel's wives were "given" to him by priesthood authority, Lisa and Helen have built a strong friendship committing to work together for the good of the family.

The Jessops of Pinesdale represent another case where women enjoy friendship and solidarity during the long absences of their husband, who is a councilman. The first wife, Sharon, who was born into a polygamist family of forty-five members, lives in a separate home. The second wife, "Mary Ann," shares a large duplex with her birth sister, located only a few houses down the road from Sharon. The third wife, "Mona," died of cancer some years ago, leaving a few children to be cared for among the wives, primarily by Sharon. Since their husband is always traveling to Mexico and Salt Lake City on priesthood business, the wives rally together in emergencies and to generally help support each other. For example, during Sharon's hysterectomy, she divided her thirteen children among the remaining two wives. Mary Ann took over Sharon's work at the office while she was recovering and Sharon helped Mary Ann by caring for her children while she worked at the school library. In this way, they formed a natural interdependence during their husband's absence that has enabled them to cope with the death of a co-wife, a serious illness, and the child care needs of a working mother.

"Tina," of the Allred Group, represents many experiences of convert women who find solace in sister wife relationships. Tina experienced a period of alienation from her husband. During this trying time, she was warmed by the friendship she had forged with her co-wife, Joyce, a friendship that developed into physical love. Tina had previously married a gay LDS, and when she left him, she found fundamentalism. She and her children attended the Allred meetings and felt that they were treated like a long-lost family. Joyce's husband, a high-ranking councilman, began to show fatherly concern for the welfare of Tina's children, at Mary's prompting. Tina's son began to be included in activities with the councilman's sons, and his daughters began taking exceptional care of her little girl. Joyce and her co-wives were kind to Tina and shared their knowledge of the scriptures and the gospel and spoke with her about the merits of their husband, who was an apostle of God. They had received a personal revelation with the accompanying "burning in the bosom" of their testimony that Tina and her children belonged in their family.

Tina said that she made every effort to be absolutely honest in her conversion process. "I prayed exactly as instructed and fasted, I anticipated a vision of some magnitude, and, yes, I finally got the testimony I was seeking," she said. Mary and her co-wives sang praises to the Lord for Tina, the new addition to the family. They were so anxious, honoring, and flattering, saying how much they loved and honored her. They prepared her to be a new "queen in their husband's beehive." No time was wasted in their preparations for her marriage to their husband. Everything was planned and done for her. She and her children were rebaptized, and Tina became the newest wife of an apostle of God.

Tina found that her best friend in the world and the only person who understood her needs was her sister wife Joyce. During the delivery of Tina's subsequent children, Joyce was there to hold her hand and comfort her, and Tina did the same for Joyce when she gave birth. The two wives were several years younger than the other wives and found that they were much happier living and working with each other than with the larger family. Their husband did not spend much time with them because they were removed from the other wives, who were higher ranked, and so they spent most of their time with each other, letting their children play and sleep together as if they were full brothers and sisters. Tina and Joyce coped with economic and emotional hardship in each other's love and devotion. "Joyce and I grew to love each other. We shared a mutual contempt for our husband and for his lack of attention and help. We often held each other in our suffering to comfort each other. We would lie naked and a fire ignited and we loved each other. We continued to love, comfort and nourish each other" (author's field notes, 1994). Tina said that for a long time their husband did not visit, nor did they expect him; that no longer mattered. They considered the intimate, sexual relationship they shared to be the action of "two desperate souls" hungering for a sense of love and acceptance. This was their special sisterhood.[14]

While many polygamous women find access to valued resources and are quite content, other fundamentalist women are dissatisfied because of abuse, abandonment, poverty, or jealousy issues. This is true for many disenfranchised fundamentalist males, who suffer extreme challenges to their access to priesthood authority and economic stewardships. Polygamy is, after all, a patriarchal marriage form associated with strict competition among men for scarce resources and the formal control of women and children by a powerful elite hierarchy.

One source of women's powerlessness is elite polygyny, a term coined by Musisi (1991), defined as a method of maintaining reproductive and productive control by a handful of powerful, blood-related patriarchs. This device effectively alienates younger rogue males, such as Robert Blackmore of Creston, while placing the control of all marriageable or fertile women in the clan into the hands of the elite, such as Winston Blackmore of Bountiful. This process includes a mechanism of wife capture (or in the fundamentalist case, conversion) that ensures a continual flow of fecund women into the community.[15] Along with controlling access to women, patriarchs must control financial stewardships, which are placed in the hands of the reigning brethren (e.g., top pureblood families such as the Jessops, the Allreds, or the LeBarons). These stewardships are further funded through the contributions of new converts through the Law of Consecration. All members give total control to the prophet and the brethren to make decisions on their behalf, including where they will live, how much money they earn, what clothes they will wear, how they will worship, and whom they can marry. The elite brethren, because of their access to valued resources, use polygamy to build strategic multiple alliances and maintain control over land, buildings, and manufacturing.

For this control to be upheld, some heads of families are given favorable stewardships in order to keep them from rebelling; these men are also used as officers to protect the rights and properties of the Priesthood Council.

Rogue males who cannot gain favored stewardships and wives either agree to work for the alpha males as "servants on Mt. Zion" or they must be disenfranchised through excommunication. In addition, women and children must not be allowed to easily leave the group because they are the "resources" of the family kingdom. They represent the glory and magnificence of the corporate lineages and therefore are cloistered from the outside world. To achieve this segregation, the brethren use home schooling and choose an isolated rural location with natural borders.

A further way to circumscribe women is to forbid them to get a driver's license or accept any outside job that might tempt them to leave the group. As Posner writes, many polygamists impose a hierarchical business arrangement upon their wives to better control them and to save money and time. Polygamy may actually reduce the freedom that wives in a polygamous marriage have by using those wives as laborers managed by a husband who does very little actual work (1992).

A final tactic is to strip a rebelling woman of her children should she decide to apostatize. When women try to leave a group, custody tends to favor the biological father and the pureblood kingdom. Disengaging is a serious task and is often too threatening for women because they risk their economic status and their salvation. Many are told that they will lose their children to the group or to the dominant family kingdom to which they are aligned if they leave. These threats are grounded in real cases where children have been kidnapped from their mothers by the fundamentalist leadership and elite families. Women are also told that they will not survive economically on the outside, which is often true; women are financially dependent on the polygamist order for their basic needs. Some are told that they will be damned and tossed out of their family kingdom and/or that their skin will turn dark like Cain's.

Many fundamentalists believe that everyone must be linked to his/her Savior on Mt. Zion, the representative patriarch in the heavenly family kingdom. Sometimes this can be a woman's father, but in most cases it is her husband, who can open up the gates of the Celestial Kingdom and let her in. This "Savior" is vital to her salvation, so her connection to him must be kept intact, even in situations of abuse or domination. Associated with this concept is the title of "husband, king, and priest," which is often associated with a patriarch's power over his subjects, as in the case of Jim Harmston, who married his stepdaughter Rachel. He wrote her a letter threatening to send her to a fiery death in hell if she refused to sleep with him (Borger 2005). His letter read: "Rachel, the facts are, whether you want to believe or not, the end is coming and judgment will be executed in severity, especially for those who have broken their covenants . . . for certain I will deal with you in the future eternity" (ibid., 1). Harmston used his power as king to coerce her into intercourse. Rachel claimed that she couldn't refuse him because he was the prophet of God. From the pulpit, Harmston struck fear in the hearts of many of his young wives, saying that "if any wife disobeyed [him] [he] would send her to hell for a thousand years" (ibid.).

Negative consequences that affect women and children within elite polygyny include the sexual abuse of children, the marriage of underage girls, financial abuse (such as extracting obedience in exchange for food and shelter), wife rape and battery, megalomania or narcissism, blood atonement, and the alienation of teenage males. Men can also experience abusive conditions through competition for valued resources and the threat of excommunication by the Priesthood Brethren. Alienated men who have these experiences often leave the group and experience depression, drug abuse, or alcoholism. Another issue related to male alienation is insufficient father-son contact and the resulting impact on the development of the son's masculine identity. Males are more likely to be separated, segregated, and marginalized at puberty, a situation that is directly tied to the fierce competition over scarce wives between fathers, uncles, sons, and nephews (Kitahara 1976). Elite polygyny can also breed competition between wives for the right to the husband's wealth and for stewardships for their sons. Patriarchs can also treat wives unequally as a way to rid themselves of unwanted wives and to make way for younger, more fertile wives (Hassouneh-Phillips 2001).

Warren Jeffs' group is a perfect example of elite polygyny. Jeffs successfully controlled all aspects of people's lives. In a 1998 sermon, he preached to a group of young women that men hold the priesthood, not women. The worst thing to happen to a woman, according to Warren, is for her to become educated and desire everything. Such a woman will "seek to rule over her husband." Warren's words sound like a 1950s marriage manual: a woman should wake up each morning yearning to please her husband, "rejoicing in his will towards you." In his sermon, he quoted Brigham Young: "The very nature of women in their desires shall be to their husband. . . . Completely submit where he shall rule over you. . . . True womanhood is attained through Priesthood" (quoted in Adams 2007, 1). These are all phrases designed to teach women to mute their own voices and desires and submit to the will of men. In this thinking, if all actions and thoughts are "centered in him," then the men will be better able to control the women and the financial resources. In his diary, Warren wrote about how he reassigned the wives of three men, including his brother David, because God had shown him that they "couldn't exalt their ladies, had lost the confidence of God." One of his brother's wives had difficulty accepting the news and could barely bring herself to kiss her new husband. "She showed a great spirit of resistance, yet she went through with it," Warren's recorded. "She needs to learn to submit to Priesthood" (Adams 2007:1).

According to ex-FLDS member Benjamin Bistline (2004), Rulon and Warren Jeffs both enforced a one-man tyrannical rule that was a foundation for elite polygyny. Bistline saw how older men competed with other older men for wives. He noted that plural wives were expected to apply for welfare as single moms so the brethren didn't have to provide for the expenses of extra wives.[16] He wrote that young men and boys were ostracized repeatedly to the point of being driven out of their homes so that the elite men could gain access to their family kingdoms. And he saw residents forced to obey the prophet out of fear for their salvation.

Men in extreme control of others' lives are in a position to oust any undesirables with trumped-up charges of abuse or neglect. The ousting of rogue males is common in polygamous communities in Africa and the Middle East. Interestingly, some leaders gather males who are rejected or alienated from their patrilineage in part due to competition for wives and resources. This is what Osama bin Laden did; he "harnesse[d] the chaos of young men," bringing them together in a political cause that would bring them prestige (Tiger 2001, 1). In African patrilineal societies there is also high sex segregation accompanied by internal competition for excellence that alienates males.[17] Men and women are separated by strict and "draconian moral codes" (ibid.). If they complete their rite of passage, young men must then compete with polygamous males for the right to marry. Those who cannot must choose celibacy or are marginalized by married men. This produces a need for emotional and economic unity among fellow rogues.

A similar pattern is present in Mormon fundamentalism, which may account for the many offshoots, satellite movements, and independents in the Intermountain West, such as Centennial Park, Harmston's True Living Church, or Blackmore's Bountiful Rebellion. In each case, the males who were alienated by the tyranny of a prophet in a larger group left that group and formed a new brotherhood. The new brotherhood is often made up of other rogue or marginalized males, who, in turn, alienate and dominate others.

Ironically, rogue males from the mainstream LDS church are also likely to convert to any of the four larger fundamentalist groups, as these groups promise each male a kingdom of his own.[18] Men who are drawn to polygamy are typically not satisfied with their callings and stewardships in the larger church. They may have been disfellowshipped, or reprimanded by a bishop or priesthood leader for any number of offenses. The disenfranchised men's anger builds up and they soon become attracted to restored doctrine, which they often find in the *Journal of Discourses.* The next step is conversion to one of the four fundamentalist groups, typically the AUB. Once there, the young men, brimming with energy and religious zeal, turn over all of their financial assets. Within a few months they find that they must defer to a different set of brethren who will dictate where they live, whom they will marry, and where they will work. Often this sequence of events is enough to turn new male converts away.

Another example of the alienation of males occurred in 1992, when Lamoine Jensen of the AUB excommunicated two councilors, George May-cock and Joseph Thompson, who posed a threat to his ascension to prophet. He charged them both, without sufficient evidence, with sexual abuse. Like-wise, Warren Jeffs of the FLDS is famous for ridding himself of anyone who threatens his ability to rule absolutely. Winston Blackmore, once a trusted colleague, was excommunicated because he was "getting too big for this britches" in Bountiful, British Columbia. Winston Blackmore himself alien-ated many of his own male kin, including his nephew Robert Blackmore, whose father owned much of the land in and around Bountiful. Jeffs also threw out Dan Barlow, a former mayor of Colorado City, in 2004, even though Dan's father, John Y. Barlow, had helped found the group in the 1930s. Jeffs also excommunicated Barlow's son and eighteen other men, taking away their homes, wives, and children. Barlow still doesn't know why he and the others, who all held influential positions in the community, were excommunicated (Anthony 2008).

Often polygamist priesthood leaders present themselves as infallible and Godlike. Because of their high priesthood status, they may feel that it is okay to lie and cheat because it is a means to an end. It may be possible for them to rationalize stealing another man's wife if their priesthood is of a higher status than that man's. A leader's calling and election are "made sure," as described in chapter 2, therefore he cannot sin. Controlling a man's exaltation by limited his access to priesthood authority and power is a familiar tactic used in elite polygyny. There is also the act of "spiritual assassination," where you curse your enemies with prayers. Jim Harmston achieved this by propelling his enemies symbolically into space with his hands through a sort of pantomime. Ervil LeBaron actually murdered his enemies.

In addition to delineating advantages and disadvantages for men and women entering polygamy, we must also look at differences among women. Those who have grown up in the system, or are "born in," differ in their experience and level of commitment from convert women, who come in directly from the orthodox LDS world. The convert women who are most attracted to the AUB achieve mobility, career advancement, and college education, and have greater decision-making powers in the home and community. Converts are educated in the secular world, where women's rights, feminism, and women's self-actualization are not only allowed, they are expected.[19] All of these advantages are accessed in the mainstream LDS church and larger urban environment, *before* women convert to fundamentalism, By contrast, the "born-in," or native, women—like "Mary Ann" Jessop or Irene Spencer—have been raised with the father-adoration perspective. They have been trained to never dispute a man's visions and desires, even when the man is abusive or domineering. Born-in women follow the calling of obedience—or, as Warren Jeffs taught, "a woman's desires should be to her husband"—and are often annoyed when their convert co-wives don't comply fully with this command (Adams 2007, 2). Born-in women are also more often sequestered in the home and community because they do not have driver's licenses or permission to work outside the boundaries of the sect. But since they are raised to distrust the outside world, they may not see this as a burden. In contrast, convert women, having lived with Wal-Mart, grocery stores, public schools, and the Internet, find it very difficult to cut off their ties to modernity. They have driver's licenses and they yearn to travel and expand the boundaries of their home and community.

According to Bonnie, a convert polygamist wife in the AUB, groups such as the FLDS who restrict their women "need to be stopped" (Pomfret 2006, 3). She prefers the freedoms she enjoys in the mainstream, in spite of the fact that she has lost three jobs because of discrimination. She, her co-wife, and her husband and children live in a suburban subdivision of fifty homes in the

Rocky Ridge order. She said she was attracted to the idea of bonding with women as well as with her husband. She was best friends with her first wife before they brought her into the family.

From a patriarchal standpoint, it is much easier to control born-in women because they are uneducated and are accustomed to polygamous ways. Often the mantra "keep sweet" is used to guide women into roles that are associated with the domestic realm and steer them clear of politics and controversy. According to Bledsoe and colleagues (2000), African polygamous women who are educated often raise issues of equity and individuality and have high expectations about their own mobility and autonomy, whereas African polygamous women who are lower class and are not educated are more apt to agree to share resources and remain in the community. Patriarchs thus are able to "sustain the costs of polygamy and of high fertility . . . by marginalizing low status women" (ibid., 117).

In defense of born-in women however, role fulfillment and dedication to family can allow women to be contented to remain in traditional, nineteenth-century gender roles. The promise that their role as handmaid to their husband's kingdom will facilitate their rise to queenly status keeps them satisfied, particularly because their role as mother is highly esteemed by others. In fact, like Dauna Baird and Sharon Jessop of the AUB, high-status women can be seen as sovereigns with great influence over others, even their husbands and other members of the council. According to one FLDS born-in wife, people should respect women's religious rights to rear their children in a safe, isolated community, away from the corruption and evils of the outside world. This is how she was raised and this is how she will raise her children (FLDS Women Speak 2008).

Interestingly, convert and born-in women of the Allred Group have virtually the same rates of access to employment and valued stewardships. In a sample of 75 working women, 13 percent of convert and 10.5 percent of born-ins were able to access lucrative callings (Bennion 1998, 70). The two groups of women are also similar in their access to spiritual resources (endowments, priesthood power, and callings). Out of the 53 percent who were linked favorably to spiritual positions and callings, born-ins have a small advantage over converts (30 percent and 23 percent, respectively; ibid., 60).

Converts and born-in women choose or are forced to marry at different ages. It is assumed, of course, that the younger a woman is, the less choice she has in the matter of marriage because she is considered vulnerable. However, one can also suggest that a young born-in woman may be better prepared for her marriage because she comes from a society that emphasizes marriage and motherhood to the exclusion of all other roles for women. Altman and Ginat (1996) found that 55 percent of the plural wives in their study (which included both FLDS and Allred members) were between fifteen and nineteen years old at marriage and 16 percent were between twenty and twenty-four years of age. They also noted that thirteen of the fifty-one wives studied were either widowed or divorced and that the average age of this group was thirty-three at the time of plural marriage. Altman and Ginat found that 58 percent of the wives they studied (thirty-four of fifty-nine) were born or raised in polygamy, while 42 percent (twenty-five of fifty-nine) were converts. In my study, 54 percent of the adult convert women who chose polygamy were single women between the ages of twenty-eight and forty-five, 15 percent were widowed or divorced, and 11 percent were already married and came with their husbands when they converted. Assuming that the widowed, divorced, and married women in my study were probably older than twenty-two , this means that the majority of converts are more mature and have more varied life experience than young adult women raised in polygamous communities and families. However, these mature and deliberate converts are likely a minority of plural wives.

Mormon fundamentalist polygamy is possible only because of the large number of women who are available as plural wives. These women come to their young adulthood in a community in which a significant proportion of young men are unavailable for marriage, due both to the priesthood's control of marriage and the large-scale defection of young men from fundamentalist communities. It is impossible to say whether these young women would become disillusioned with monogamy and mainstream life, because many of them may not have a real opportunity to explore those possibilities. Convert plural wives, however, seem less surprised by mainstream realities. This may be because many have already had a crisis of faith because their lack of success at monogamous marriage was in conflict with mainstream Mormon religious beliefs and because they had experienced loneliness and deprivation. They do not come into polygamy with misplaced monogamous fantasies. The reality of plural life is often better for them than the reality of failed monogamy they have already experienced. A shared husband is better than no husband at all; a part-time husband of any kind is easier to tolerate than a bad full-time husband; and a community of sister-wives who provide economic, social, and emotional support may be the greatest reward of all. In addition, converts have the opportunity to live their faith through polygamy in a way they simply could not make happen through monogamy. For convert women, fundamentalism as a way of life that they manipulate to meet their own needs.

A third category of polygamous women are independents; these women do not belong to any established Mormon group. Like converts, these women tend to be highly educated, independent-minded, and modern, and they blend into mainstream U.S. society with greater ease than born-in sister-wives. Examples of this type are Mary Batchelor, Anne Wilde, and Elizabeth Joseph. Independent women dress and act like typical orthodox Mormons, and some even attend the Mormon Church as part of the regular member-ship, disguising themselves as single. One "born in" woman, seventh daughter to a council member, left the group she was raised in with her husband and co-wives to live out her life in another state as an independent fundamental-ist. She is now the manager of the family business, working outside the home. She shares child care with her two co-wives. She said she would never go back to her life in the group because it would mean sacrificing many freedoms she now enjoys: her career, her autonomy, and removal from the continual scrutiny of others.

In sum, the gender dynamic in fundamentalism is grounded in a dichot-omy of experiences among women. On the one hand, 65 percent of the AUB women in my conversion study (Bennion 1998) and the majority of women I interviewed and who produce blogs about polygamy claimed that they have access to relative power and are contented. These women said they had ac-cess to valued resources and freedom to pursue their religious, economic, and social interests without constraint. They have friends, security, and autonomy. They are not overworked and feel that they are fulfilling their ideological goals in their roles of wife, mother, and queen. On the other hand, 22 percent of the women in my 1998 study said they felt marginalized and alienated by poverty and abuse, had no means of escape, and were stuck in a male su-premacist environment over which they had no control. They complained of being isolated from outside help in a world filled with rules that restrict free-doms rather than facilitate joys and privileges. Certainly there are women in the gray area between these two extremes who experience varying degrees of satisfaction and discontent, but for my analysis it is more helpful to examine the two poles: satisfied and dissatisfied. Women who are satisfied are those who have stepped out of the mainstream where they were less contented and converted to fundamentalism, which offers opportunities that are attractive to them. As converts, they carefully choose a spouse, explore the steward-ships that will accompany their marriage, and find collaborative ways to fulfill their responsibilities as mothers. They are drawn to the concept of having children and raising them in the supportive environment of co-wives and the other women of the community. They also are attracted to the potential of increasing their skill levels in the domestic or public arenas without having to put their children in mainstream day care facilities that would be culturally alien. The dissatisfied woman, by contrast, has limited choices. She may have been raised in a group where teens are obliged to marry and bear children before their junior year in high school. Perhaps she was placed with an elderly man who cannot please her sexually or emotionally and cannot provide for her financially yet who restricts her ability to gain an education and become economically sufficient. The discontented women may also face challenges from co-wives who resent her youth or "freshness" in the family. They may see her as competition for their husband's attentions. Co-wives may resent her children as well, as their husband may spend more time with them. Above all, impoverished, overcrowded conditions where men rule with an iron fist are difficult for both convert and born-in women, especially if they were raised with expectations of female autonomy.

Family and Kinship

Within the structure of the polygamist family a complex set of relationships exists. If a man marries several wives and they each have a handful of chil-dren, how do these children relate to each other and to their multiple parents? Further, how do fathers find time and energy for their many children and still remember their wives' birthdays and anniversaries? How do wives deal with each other in the act of mothering the family's children?

Mormon family and descent patterns are complex because they extend lineally from parent to child, laterally through multiple spousal relationships, and temporally as they reach into eternity, a belief that is commonly ex-pressed in the often-repeated maxim that "families are forever." But because men are so often absent from their homes, women must manage the house-hold and raise their children while they are surrounded by other mother-child units. The family unit can be loosely defined as a partially matrifocal post-marital residence pattern within a patrilineal descent system. Although the female-centered household is not fully matrifocal (the husband is in residence a portion of the time), during the husband's absence the tendency is for the co-wives to rule the roost.[20]

Within this matri-centric model, members reckon their placement in the family kingdom based on their relationship to either their father's side or their husband's side, depending on who is considered their Savior on Mt. Zion. This earthly template will then be replicated in the heavens, where male-dominated kingdoms will rule over subjects comprised of their wives, their descendants, and their adoptees. To avoid arrest and stigmatization, only the first wives and their progeny are able to take on the husband's name; the subsequent wives keep their maiden name. However, all wives and their children belong to his kingdom. Typically, the priesthood council provides the land and pays for home construction so technically the living arrangements are neither patrilocal or matrilocal. The husband determines where the wife and children will live, but most of the time the children live with their mothers only. In some cases, households are linked to the husband or wife's relationship to a high-ranking councilmen or a pureblood family. For example, one convert man lived in a home built by his second wife's father, who was a councilman. In another case, one man and his three wives moved to the Granite ranch, where a new stewardship was created for them. This is an example of a neolocal postmarital residence. In any event, once the household is established, the women take over the details of management and spend their lives working and raising their children in that home, while the man travels to and from his various homes.

The prevalent marriage form in Mormon fundamentalism is actually monogamy; only about 30–40 percent of Mormon men practice plural marriage (Bennion 2008). As it was in nineteenth-century polygamy, only 15 percent of the men in today's groups are able to have more than two wives, and 20 percent have just two wives (Quinn 1998; Bennion 1998). The remaining 65 percent are either single or are married to only one woman. Many unmarried or monogamous men eventually leave fundamentalist Mormon groups and blend back into the mainstream. The FLDS belief that polygamy is crucial to entering heaven puts enormous strain on young men, who must be awarded wives at the prophet's discretion; those who are not chosen to marry plurally are pushed out so the polygamous elite will have access to more potential brides. For example, Rulon Jeffs of the FLDS married anywhere from twenty-two-to seventy-four wives, and his son Warren currently has sixty wives (Goodwyn, Berkes, and Walters 2005). This excess of wives means there are not enough brides for young men and is directly related to the excommunication of this group of men for trivial offenses such as dating or listening to rock music (McDonough 2004). In 2004, to further reduce the competition for wives within the FLDS and to rid the community of rebellious "rogue" males, Dan Barlow and twenty other men were exiled and stripped of their wives and children, who were reassigned to other men.

Alternatively, the AUB allows monogamy. As Dee Jessop, the principal of Pines Academy, recently said in an interview: "We can't all have multiple wives; in fact, most Pinesdale kids grow up to be monogamists" (Montana's News Station 2008). The group also favors laws that punish anyone who uses intimidation or force to get a girl to marry against her will, and they believe that all brides must be at least eighteen years old. The AUB also gives women the full right to denounce a partner and be released from a husband for any reason. She then, ideally, has the right to pick a man who is more righteous and more financially stable than her last one was.

In my research, I did see polygamous households with child brides, households where husbands abused and battered wives, households where fathers practiced incest, and households where children were neglected. But these households are the minority. William Clyde (2004), an independent fundamentalist who maintained the ModernPolygamy.org website, suggested the following counsel, written especially to men considering adoption of the polygamous lifestyle:

1. Don't father more children than you can support.
2. Keep your family together in one household to foster financial, spiritual, and social networking among wives.
3. If you are not great in monogamous relationships, you will be horrible in polygamous relationships; the problems will be compounded.
4. Don't go into it for the sex. This won't work as all of the wives will be menstruating, lactating, or pregnant at the same time. In addition, that motive causes jealousy among the wives.
5. Don't violate women's rights; don't treat them like chattel or property.
6. Don't assume you can rule over your wives; treat them as equals.
7. Don't marry underage women, and limit the number of wives you marry.

These recommendations are remarkably similar to the current South African mandate for plural living (Stacey and Meadow 2009).

SEXUALITY

In spite of its prevalence in fundamentalism, monogamy is seen as a lesser sexual law. Monogamy is said to alienate women and restrict men and to put women in their graves as the "victims of the sexual over-indulgence of their husbands" (Musser 1948, 182). Because of Musser's teachings and the Puritanical modesty that is associated with the Mormon culture in general, most fundamentalists do not overtly celebrate sexuality, which is sometimes considered a necessary evil—a force men must learn to control and from which pregnant, lactating, and menstruating women must be protected. Because women's most important role is motherhood, a task associated with celestial rewards and kingdoms of glory, barrenness is seen as a reproach—God's curse on the woman and her husband. Part of a woman's prestige is intrinsically tied to her fecundity and willingness to produce and raise many children. Charles Zitting once told Rulon Allred that because the purpose of "the Principle" (polygamy) is to produce children, sexual intercourse between conception and the child's weaning is forbidden; a man who looks upon his wife with lust during this period is damned (Bradley 1990). Zitting wrote: "The sexual relation, properly employed, rather than reflecting mortal weaknesses and being immodest, lewd, course, vulgar, or indelicate, and something to blush over, would be elevated to a higher plane and become a divine principle dedicated by the Gods for the perpetuation of life and birth of earths" (quoted in ibid., 105).

Joseph Smith's behavior is considered the ultimate charter for sexuality among fundamentalists. Yet his sexual story exhibits both ascetic and sexual libertarian attributes, often confusing modern-day followers. His example to others has produced a continuum of sexual mores, from the stoic sex for the purpose of procreation associated with the AUB to the Viagra-popping sexual indulgences found in Jim Harmston's True and Living Church of Jesus Christ of Saints of the Last Days (*Big Love*'s Bill Henrickson is an apt example). Joseph Smith, setting the precedent, sealed himself to thirty-three women (Compton 1997), some of whom were "spiritual wives" only, not sexual partners. Many more were covenanted to him after his death. Eleven of these women were quite young, from fourteen to twenty years old. Eight were around the same age as he, from thirty to forty years old, and three were in their fifties. As one finds in Islam, Smith's polygamy was designed to care for all needy women, especially old and unmarriageable females. However, Smith also married teenage wives (ten of the thirty-three were under twenty), suggesting that there was an element of sexual attraction in his motivations for plural marriage, especially in light of the commandment to multiply and replenish the earth with spirit children. Sexual appeal and fertility thus appear to have both been compelling reasons for Smith to select adolescent wives.

Although the Community of Christ Church (RLDS) claims that Joseph Smith never had sex with his plural wives, the memoirs of Emma Smith and her co-wives Eliza, Melissa, Louisa, and Emily strongly suggest that he did have sexual congress with his plural wives (Compton 1997).[21] Smith fathered children by his plural wives, even those he shared with other men. He provided a template for polygyny *and* polyandry in early Mormondom and was sexually linked to women who were already married to other men, for example, Sylvia Sessions, who was sealed to Smith and married to her husband, Mr. Lyon (ibid.). Current polygamists such as Jim Harmston of the True and Living Church and Warren Jeffs of the FLDS have followed his example and have shared married wives with other men. Harmston loaned his wives to his councilors to strengthen their bonds and Jeffs ordered the excommunication of at least twenty-one men, giving their wives to other men in marriage.

Since Joseph Smith saw sex as essential to his relationship with at least thirteen of his plural wives, some of today's polygamists feel that sex is a requirement for reaching eternal glory. Jim Harmston, for example, believes that when his wives have sex with him it is like taking the sacrament. According to one of his wives, he believes that when a person reaches orgasm it is like witnessing the Holy Spirit and that this should occur as often as possible (Borger 2005).

But contrary to what many monogamists often think, Harmston's brand of sexuality is an anomaly. For that matter, Smith's template (which includes polyandry) is practiced by only a small percentage of the polygamist population. For most fundamentalists, polygamy is not a way to live out a sexual fantasy practiced by "lustful old men" (Compton 1997, 2).[22] The general rule is that there simply isn't the time or energy for men to become polygamous "playboys." Many fundamentalists are Puritanical prudes who view sex as necessary for procreation. These men view it quite practically, considering the workload and extra expense of dealing with the emotional fallout associated with sex with numerous women. Many men hesitate to take on another wife but are cajoled into doing so by wives who desire to live the "fulness."

"The responsibility is every day, twenty-four hours a day. It never goes away," stated Randy Maudsley, who is married to two wives and lives in

Manti, Utah (20/20 1997). According to Maudsley, budgeting time for sex is tricky. Some men spend one night with each wife and rotate. Others spend three nights with each wife and then switch. And some sleep with whomever they feel like, without a schedule. In many cases the wives organize the scheduling, telling their husbands, "Tonight is Jane's birthday, so you should sleep with her." Having constant access to sex is often very difficult for a man. If a woman is having her menstrual period or has a lot of work or emotional issues to contend with, she will not want to be with her husband. It can also be very tiring for the man to deal with the problems of three to five women in one day, as is aptly depicted on *Big Love*. If one wife gets a headache, they may all get headaches. If one wife complains about finances, they may all complain. In addition, because of menstrual synchrony, women in close proximity to each tend to ovulate at the same time, which creates challenges for men who want continual sex. If one wife is menstruating, pregnant, or lactating, and the wives live near each other, then all of the wives may be in the same condition. In fundamentalist society, sex is prohibited during these times. A woman can easily control the number of children if she wants to, and because she shares a husband with other women, she will actually have more difficulty conceiving than if she was monogamous and had exclusive rights to sex during her conception window, a week after her period. Polygamy also creates interruptions in conception opportunities. A husband may be with another wife or on priesthood business out of town during a wife's "window," so the birth interval is often at least twenty-two to twenty-eight months rather than the intervals of fourteen to twenty months seen in some mainstream Mormon or Hutterite monogamous settings. Social psychologist Irwin Altman (1996) observed that men looking for love, sex, and romance in polygamy will be sorely disappointed: "For men . . . any sexual motives must surely pall after a while, as the day-to-day pressures of plural family life cumulate; the financial burdens, the needs of large families, family tensions and conflicts, and so on. . . . Plural family life is not especially 'romantic' for men" (439).

Some polygamists advise couples to keep their sex lives very private to prevent jealousy and upsets. In this model, each marriage is separate and isolated. Each wife should not know what the love-making sessions of the other wives are like. Yet polygamous wives like to share their love-making stories and laugh about them; this brings them closer as friends. It is rare to see a man who invites all his wives to bed with him at the same time because this could ruin family harmony and trust. Another threat to a healthy and stable family environment is when a man marries both a mother and her daughter. In the TLC group, for example, the prophet, Jim Harmston, married a woman named Pauline Strong, who is now sixty. He also married her daughter, Rachel, who is now twenty-one. Pauline originally met and then married Jim as his third wife when Rachael was eleven years old. At seventeen, Rachel married a young member of the TLC but then divorced him to marry Jim, who is forty-three years her senior. Jim made all the sleeping arrangements for his wives and spent more time with some wives than with others, which fostered jealousy and awkwardness. It was particularly awkward for Pauline and Rachel to sleep with the same man, and in 2006 they both left the group. In the AUB, another mother-daughter set married the same man, a convert. This union actually lasted for ten years, but the mother eventually left the group. The daughter still lives with her husband, their six children, and his three other wives and children in a large home in the Bitterroot Mountains of Montana.

Although some fundamentalists view sexuality as potentially evil and something that should be discussed with caution and only in extreme privacy, fertility issues are everyone's business. It seems that most people know a great deal about each family's procreative activities because the standard is for most women in their childbearing years to have a child every eighteen months. Thus, if two years go by without a pregnancy, lactation, or a baby on the hip, then it is assumed that the woman must be barren or her husband is not fulfilling his duties. Enhancing fertility is a priority in kingdom building. Joe Jessop, the brother of interim FLDS leader Merril Jessop, has achieved his goals well beyond any expectation. He has 46 children and 239 grandchildren. It is not uncommon to meet FLDS women who have given birth to ten, twelve, and sixteen children. (Joyce Broadbent is the mother of eleven; Dorothy Emma Jessop has thirteen.)[23] As a result, it's easy to see why this corner of the American West is experiencing a population explosion. The 400 or so babies delivered in the Hildale, Utah, health clinic every year have resulted in a median age for the community of just under 14, in contrast with a median age of 36.6 for the entire United States. Because so many in the community trace their lineage to a handful of the pioneering families, the same few names — Barlows, Jessops, and Jeffs — crop up over and over in Hildale and Colorado City, suggesting a murkier side to this fecundity. Doctors in the Hildale area say a severe mental disease caused by a recessive gene has become more prevalent in the community due to interbreeding within these key pureblood lines.

Anthropologists have long studied fertility issues among polygamists, at first postulating that plural marriage would exponentially increase overall fertility in the community. This is true when fertility is examined from the perspective of the male genitor, or patriarch. But a study of polygyny by Steve Josephson (2002) showed that polygamy rarely benefits individual *female* fertility. Josephson compared the fertility of monogamous and polygamous women and found that in most societies monogamous women had higher fertility rates than plural women. In the 9 percent of societies where polygamous women had higher fertility, they may have had lower reproductive success. Josephson's analysis of nineteenth-century polygamy shows that several factors reduce an individual woman's fertility, including marrying at an older age, marrying older men, and conflict between co-wives. Sterility did not explain the reduced number of children among polygamous women, nor is there evidence of a "dilution effect" from sharing a husband. According to Josephson, women chose plural marriage because the increased fertility resulting from their husband's relationship with many women offset their relatively low individual fertility. My research on the Pinesdale women confirmed that women in that community are at risk of lower fertility than if they were monogamous (Bennion 1998). My analysis added one factor that Josephson may have overlooked: menstrual synchrony. If all of a man's wives are menstruating, lactating, or pregnant because of their proximity to one another, that limits the degree to which the husband can have access them sexually. Since men are limited in the amount of time they can spend with each wife (especially if the wives are in different states), they cannot always have access to all of their wives when they are not menstruating or lactating. Men often endure a lengthy rotation schedule in which they see individual wives once every three to five days if they live in the same town and once every two weeks to two months if they live in separate states.

Although courtship rituals vary among fundamentalists, the period of courtship is typically quite short, lasting from a few weeks to six months at the most. The range of marital prospects is wider and richer for unmarried women than it is for men. This is because most of the older women are already married unless they have been recently widowed or divorced, but every man above the age of eighteen, whether he is married or not, is eligible for marriage. All marriages must be sanctioned by God through the approval of a matchmaker from within the high-ranking members of the priesthood; this matchmaker is thus always a man. One woman told me her twenty-nine-year-old son, who was already married to two women, was about to embark on a new prospect. First he had to gain the approval of the matchmaker, who then spoke to the father of the woman, who then spoke of the match to the woman herself, as it is ultimately her choice whether the match will be sealed. All of this must take place before a man declares his intentions to a girl or a woman. The procedure for the bride-to-be, however, is much quicker and more efficient from the point of view of many of the women with whom I spoke. One simply gets to know another man's wife extremely well, in the process finding some commonality or bond. The wife then strongly recommends to her husband and the priesthood council that the girl or woman whom she has been "courting" be sealed to her husband for "all eternity." In this way, the bonds between women are often stronger than the bonds between a wife and her husband. For the men who choose women, it is paramount that potential wives have a vibrant testimony of the gospel and that they be fertile so they can produce many children for their husband's kingdom. Of course, sometimes men marry widows and older women beyond childbearing years, but this is a different kind of marriage, a ritual that is often referred to as a proxy marriage in which the new husband is a substitute for the women's former husband. When women choose men, it seems that romance is secondary to the primary criterion of finding a man who is "strong in his priesthoods," one who is a good father and a good husband and who provides ample economic and spiritual bounty for his wives.

In the sample of women and men with whom I spoke, women often seem to form more effective bonds with each other than they do with their male spouses. I found that in general, women tended to court and marry men with whom their sisters or other female relatives (cousins, aunts, nieces) were already involved. In one sample of co-wife kinship ties, chosen randomly from one patriarch's progeny, I found that a majority (60 percent) of cases were examples of sororal polygyny marriage; other cases showed some kind of co-wife kinship relationship such as niece and aunt and cousin and cousin. In other words, by far the most common form of marriage in my sample was that of one man marrying two or more sisters, and/or one man marrying the niece, aunt, or first cousin of another wife (Bennion 1991a). This fact of co-wife kinship is significant in the larger picture of religious life among members of Mormon fundamentalist groups. It not only reinforces crucial female bonding within polygamous marriage; it also satisfies the doctrinal requirement that wives become "one flesh," joined spiritually and physically through their covenants to God and their husband. This ceremony joins a woman not only to her husband but also to her sister wife.

For some groups, the average age for young women at marriage is sixteen or seventeen, for others it is in the early twenties, depending on which wife is being brought into the family at what time. For the most part, a man marries his first wife when she is nineteen or so; when the husband marries his second wife when he is fifteen to twenty years older, around age forty, the second wife is also in her late teens. His third wife is also quite young, from age nineteen to thirty, but by that point the husband is in his fifties. Thus, courtship practices determine both the age of a woman at her first marriage and the intervals between ages of spouses. Not all polygamous men marry at the intervals I described above. For example, Rod Williams, Bart Maelstrom, and Steve Butt each married subsequent wives in their thirties. In rare instances, women in their forties and fifties are brought in as "spiritual wives" for protection against spinsterhood and widowhood or to foster political ties between high-ranking families.

In my convert analysis, although I found that 33 percent of the women had married in their teen years (seventeen to nineteen), a surprisingly large number of women married between thirty and forty years old (27 percent), which suggests that older single women, widows, and divorced women in the mainstream church can find a husband in fundamentalism rather easily. In some groups, for example the FLDS, dating is prohibited. As DoriAnn states, "It's not even an option in our community. You try to stay away from that no matter what. It is something that's discouraged. Even in marriage, it's a distant friendship because you see each other once in a blue moon because of all the responsibilities and your limited time with the man" (quoted in Sloan 2011, 2). In other groups, for example the AUB, it is not uncommon for the woman to propose to the man, as in Kody and Christine Brown's case.

Courtship often lasts only a few weeks to six months. Marriage decisions can be made for religious reasons or can be made on the basis of private and personal considerations, depending on the situation and the group. Ideally, such decisions are made by consulting priesthood authorities. In some groups the Priesthood Council exerts great influence on the distribution of wives, while in other sects the women do the selecting without objection from the priesthood. In the AUB, there is often a matchmaker, typically either the prophet or one of the councilmen who have the reputation for knowing everyone so well that he has a good idea about who will be well suited. The prophet's first wife (or, in the case of Owen Allred, his administrative assistant, Dauna Baird) typically is the one to advise him about whom to select in the match. In one case, a girl with a promiscuous tendency was connected to an established man with two other wives so the women could tame her. In another case, when one woman was unhappy and sought a more ambitious match, the council gave her husband a young, teenage bride, which freed the older woman to marry another man. In the FLDS sect, the prophet determines by revelation who will marry whom. Often this results in young teenage girls being eternally covenanted to much older men. Another practice that is associated with the FLDS is the mandate that wives are to be subordinate to their husbands, using the "law of placing," where a young girl is assigned to a husband by revelation from God to the prophet, who then elects to take and give wives to and from men he deems worthy, often his own kin.

In other sects and among independents, it is the first or second wife who will court a new wife for her husband. I experienced this brand of courtship myself in three separate instances. In Colonia LeBaron, one of Verlan's sons asked me to consider marriage, but it was his second wife, Elizabeth, who wrote me "love letters." In Pinesdale, a woman took me to a restaurant in Hamilton to determine whether I was wifely material. She said she was attracted to the fact that I was college-educated, which meant that I could earn a good salary. It also helped that I was related to George Q. Cannon and that I was personable and a good listener. In the third instance, a polygamist I had known for years confessed that his third wife had always wanted me as their fourth wife because we had struck up a good rapport and were close in age. We would both have been converts from the Mormon Church, which is what she desperately needed in a co-wife; she was surrounded with born-in women every day.

Another example of co-wife courtship is found in the "Mason" family of Pinesdale, Montana. When a bright Brigham Young University graduate, "Bill" Mason, began to ask questions about the "mysteries," he was referred to a friend of a friend in his AUB group. He and his wife "Jill" began attending cottage meetings and soon converted to the group. Jill then told her best friend, a BYU student, about the "Work" and sought to convert her. She promised her that her husband would love her forever and that they could bear and raise their children together as lifelong companions, eventually growing old together. After "Yvonne's" conversion and the subsequent endowment ceremony where Jill gripped Yvonne's hand in the sacred way and then placed it in her husband's hand, Jill knew she would be tied to her BYU girlfriend for eternity, as friend, sister, and wife. She told me, "Yvonne and I were roommates at BYU. When she wrote me about the lack of good men down in Provo, I told her to come on up to Montana and I'd hook her up to my husband." Although Jill and Yvonne both live in Pinesdale, Bill spends his time traveling between Montana and Utah to visit his other wives and to take care of priesthood business as one of the ten AUB councilors. In all, Jill and Yvonne see their husband only six months of the year, an arrangement that has fostered a strong emotional and economic bond between the two women.

In some marriages, women seek to bring their sisters into the family, since they already know them well and, in many cases, are worried that their husbands will bring in someone they can't trust or control. There is also the advantage in sororal polygamy of knowing that your sister will be cared for by a loving man and that you can raise your children together as both cousins and half-siblings. DoriAnn of the FLDS, for example, was encouraged by her sister to marry her husband after DoriAnn divorced another man. Dori-Ann had several kids to care for and no job; it made sense for her to join her sister's family. Likewise, Mabel Finlayson Allred married her sister Melba's husband Rulon C Allred, becoming his third wife. Melba was her twin sister. They lived together long after their husband's death and were not parted until Melba died in 1998. Although they occasionally fought and had sisterly jealousies, they were devoted to one another. Two other women, Irene and Charlotte, were sisters to Rulon Allred. They eventually followed him to Mexico and met and married Rulon's friend, Verlan LeBaron. To this day, both sisters live in Galeana near their children, grandchildren, and great-grandchildren. Another example of sororal polygamy is Brenda and Carlene Tibbetts of Colorado, who both married Michael Comb. In this case, however, the sisters are not on good terms, and Brenda eventually sued her sister and their husband for her piece of the Honeycomb Industry profits.

Although it seems incongruous in the context of plural marriage, I found that many men are reluctant to take on plural wives. It is the wives who aggressively seek female companionship. Bonnie, a first wife from Rocky Ridge, says that it is usually the women who are the biggest advocates of polygamy and the men who are the shy ones. Further, as polygamy expert Mencken writes, most objections to polygamy do not come from women, as most who are linked to a good "alpha" male are content. Mencken wrote that "women prefer half or quarter of a good man to whole of a third rate man" (Mencken 1918, 1). One FLDS woman said she was glad to marry an older man because "there are only a few good men out there and if you don't share your good man with a sister wife, she'll have to marry a jerk" (West 2008, 1).

The formal procedure for a married man who wants to court a single girl is to approach his wives and ask their opinions and then talk to the match-maker/councilman. This follows the Law of Sarah. (Abraham's first wife Sarah, brought her handmaid, Hagar, to her husband for mating purposes, placing his hand in her hand.) Once the first wife agrees, the parents of the young woman are approached, and finally the girl herself is notified. In the FLDS group, she is strongly urged to comply, whereas in the AUB she is free to say no if the match is unsatisfying. A young woman who wants to court a married man can approach him directly or talk to his wives, if she likes them. The husband obtains priesthood approval, and then her parents are notified. In some cases, contrary to the Law of Sarah, a man will whisk off a young woman to marry her on the sly and then convince the brethren that he had a revelation about her. If the man is a member of the Priesthood Council, he needs no justification for his actions. He has the priesthood keys, and this gives him the right to marry whomever he wishes. Most commonly, a man will become attracted to a woman, usually someone much younger, and will try desperately to convince his wife that she is perfect for their family. This is what John Baker did in 2005, when he told his wife, Ronnie, that he wanted to take a plural wife. The woman he selected was Ronnie's best friend, and Ronnie was dead set against it. Everyone in the community told her she was defying God's wishes, but she refused to comply, so John moved out and left her and her eleven children. Fundamentalists believe that a man has the right to give up wives who don't cooperate and obey. So John Baker married Ronnie's friend and then he married another woman, all without Ronnie's consent.

Although some polygamists are attracted to young, giddy schoolgirls, Bart Malstrom of the TLC, who is married to five women with fourteen children, says he is attracted to mature, informed wives. Two of his wives went to college and one is a nurse. These wives entered the marriage with their eyes wide open, seeking polygamy as much as Bart did. Pam, his first wife, is in her late thirties and has six children so far. Wendy, who grew up in polygamy, is Bart's second wife. She approached Pam about wanting to join her family. Laura, wife number three, is forty-one; Monique, twenty-seven, is the fourth wife. And finally, Monique's baby sister, Nicole, twenty-two, is the fifth wife. All of the wives have their own separate living arrangements but work together. They take turns in order of their marriage to Bart; each wife has two nights with him. The wives don't wait in anxious anticipation for their night; it usually sneaks up on them because they are so busy. In Bart's case, the wives helped in the decision to bring in new brides; each decision was based on a full family consensus.

Marriage ceremonies take place in an unpublicized spot chosen by the priesthood. I was never told specifically where these weddings occur, as they are sacred. The location seems to be less important than the authority of the man who blesses the marriage. During the ceremony the husband is presented with the new wife by the latest wife in what is known as the "holy grip," a form of a handshake that is sacred to the group. The new wife's hand is placed in the husband's hand by his other wife as a symbol of the Law of Sarah. Though the senior wife (or latest wife, as the case may be) may not have full choice about whom her husband ultimately chooses to marry (although it is more often the case that she herself has arranged the marriage), in the ceremony, she *gives* him the new wife—a gesture of commitment to the bride and to the principle of plural marriage. All the other wives then place their hands on top of the wedding couples' clasp, and are all sealed together for eternity. Thus, not only is the husband sealed to the new wife, but each wife is "married" to her as well. During the ceremony, certain "oaths and covenants" are made by a husband and his wives. These oaths involve several promises to obey the laws of the gospel, the law of consecration, and the law of chastity. They require the wives to pledge strict obedience to their husbands and to promise to work together and love each other; the husband must promise to lead his wives in righteousness. The sealing that unites the parties in this manner is called "the Holy Spirit of Promise" and assures that the covenants that are made are strong and true. The husband and his wives wear the priesthood garment in this ceremony, a white, full-length undergarment bearing images of priesthood power and covenants that symbolize the covenants the parties have made to each other and to God.

Once married, it is assumed that the groom will care for the bride and that his wives will befriend the new wife. Thomas Aquinas once said that the virtue of polygamy was that it ensures that there is always a husband for every woman (quoted in Posner 1992). Polygamist Joanne Hanks of Manti agrees; she believes that men are naturally drawn to love more than one woman at a time and that women are naturally drawn to share the domestic realm with other women. She suggests that when choosing a new wife, it is important to select someone with the same beliefs. A woman should propose to a man if she wants; likewise a man, regardless if he is married, should first talk it over with his wife or wives and initiate contact. Hanks was jealous at first when her husband brought in a seventeen-year-old girl to the house to gain her approval. She felt defensive and angry, but she is fine with it now. Jeff spends two days with Joanne, two days with the other wife, and two days by himself.

In Mormon polygamy, the emotional bonds between the dyad (one man and one woman) are reduced so that the husband is free to devote his energies to religion, politics, and economics. This means that women must build strong friendships with their co-wives and children and learn to avoid emotional or financial dependence on a man. In this way, ironically, women in polygamous marriages learn independence and autonomy. This weakening of intimacy in the male-female dyad may also become a fault. Polygamy can dilute what Aquinas called "companionate marriage" (Posner 1992, 255). It can also give wives an incentive to have affairs or to strike up a relationship with another wife, behavior that does not cohere with Mormon values but may be seen as a viable option when the husband is absent for a long time (Bennion 1998).[24] Because the polygamist is dividing his time between so many projects, so many wives, so many homes, one wife might feel lonely or deprived. Further, if the husband is tyrannical and insensitive to her needs, the relationship could become abusive. It is also possible that the age of a wife could have an impact on her ability to achieve equality and satisfaction in a polygamous household. Older men may see younger women as naturally subordinate and inferior, and younger women may see older men as father figures who are not to be disobeyed. In addition, the more wives a man has, the more likely it is that he will use a hierarchical structure in managing his home; egalitarian-style households may be too costly in terms of his time and money.

The Rod Williams family has achieved companionate, egalitarian plural marriage — a rarity indeed. Rod Williams, a former Secret Service agent, converted to the AUB around 1985. He and his wife (Ann), who met and married in Washington state, were members of the mainstream LDS Church and then became attracted to the values of the Bluffdale fundamentalist congregation. These values ranged from belief in the necessity of food storage to antigovernment sentiments and an automatic mistrust of the modern "wicked" world. Rod, who wanted to expand his family kingdom, knew that such an expansion would be easier in the AUB than within the LDS Church. After Rod and Ann had lived for a few years in their split-level home in Bluffdale, Utah, Rosa, a thirty-year-old, strong-willed, educated Hispanic woman, began to attend AUB meetings. At some point, she approached Rod about joining his family. Rosa, who had served in the military for six years, wanted to settle down, have children, and be a part of a strong family kingdom. She liked Rod's laissez-faire style of governance, which gave her freedom to pursue her career and express her outspoken personality without rebuke. Furthermore, she got along well with Ann, a nurturing and loving woman who she knew would help take care of her children while she attended school. Rosa married Rod, as his second wife.

Rod had a thriving immigrant rescue business, and after a few years he became close to a few members of the council. He began taking trips with the AUB to the Holy Land, where he met his third wife, Emily, seventeen, who was a born-in daughter of a respected councilman.

When I met the three wives in their suburban home in Draper, Utah, I was reminded of my own Mormon sisters. The women were busy with dinner, getting their many children bathed for Sunday school, and gossiping about shopping purchases and new members of the ward. They shared common goals and tasks. They were Relief Society presidents and soccer moms who chauffeured their kids around in their "Mormon Assault Vehicles" to music lessons and day camp. They hosted chaotic, often jubilant, Family Home Evening events on Monday nights. They even had approximately the same number of children as my sisters, as well—five each. But in Rod's wives' case, the work was rotated among the wives rather than put on the shoulders of one wife, a consensual arrangement that allowed Emily to get her business degree and Rosa to get her master's degree in sociology. In the family's rotation schedule, Rod visited Ann one night, Rosa the next, and Emily the third night, so that he slept with each woman every third or fourth day. After a few years, Ann began working as an administrative secretary, Rosa began working as a social worker, and Emily and Rod ran the family business. For all the years they were in Draper, the family relied on Ann's health insurance, which covered herself, Rod, and all the children but not Rosa or Emily.

After Rod had been in the group for twelve years, he became disillusioned with the AUB, recognizing, as some converts do, that his access to high priesthood powers and kingdom-building resources was dependent on his ability to forge strong ties with the brethren. Rod offended the hierarchy with his accusations against them for money laundering and was soon expelled for alleged heresy. He and his wives were ostracized. His adult children, however, were allowed to stay in the group as long as they would follow Owen Allred and disassociate themselves from their father, which many of them did for a time. Rod, his wives, and his underage children became independents. The family still believed in plural marriage but was no longer tied to the AUB. Rod became part of an investigation of money laundering within the AUB, along with another former Allredite, the "iconoclastic muckraker" John Llewellyn. For nearly a decade, Rod has assisted Virginia Hill in her attempt to regain several million dollars the AUB stole from her. Needless to say, the AUB leadership has great contempt for Rod and his family, which is why the Williams family eventually left the Utah area.

Rod now lives in the Pacific Northwest in a 5,000-square-foot home in the woods. His second wife, Rosa, recently left the family after discovering that she was a lesbian. Rod won custody of their children. Rod and his three wives produced a relatively small polygamist family: thirteen children, forty grandchildren, and eleven great-grandchildren so far. He has left fundamentalism entirely and has nothing to do with Mormonism, stating he is now in a "consensual sexual relationship" with his two wives. Having separated polygamy from any religious associations, he believes that he is uniquely designed to live with and love more than one woman, which he believes is his right. His two wives agree with this assessment.

After twenty years of observing polygamous families within the Allred sect, I have made several generalizations about co-wife relationships.

- Co-wives are commonly related to each other by blood (sister, cousin, niece, aunt, etc.).
- Women have the final choice about whom they will marry, and more often than not, these unions depend upon the new wife's previous liaisons between women, not men.
- Marriages that are least likely to end in separation or divorce are those in which strong bonds form among co-wives.
- There is a strong correlation between female bonding and sororal polygyny.

There are exceptions, of course, to this very general line of deductive observations. Yet these patterns do seem to be the norm in most of the polygamous "patriarchies," or large extended families with which I lived and studied. In future studies of co-wife relationships, I hope to provide qualitative data based on a sample representative of the entire sect, not just a branch of the sect, which is the case here.

DIVORCE

Some families experience divorce and remarriage or even adoption when a co-wife or patriarch dies. When one wife dies, her co-wives take over her children's care and the care of her husband, as they are already married to him. Most groups implement the levirate form of marriage when a man dies, however. This type of marriage requires the brother of the deceased man to take over the care of his wives and children, as is done in most patrilineal tribes.

Divorce, although difficult and traumatic, has often been linked to increases in female power and status (Hendrix et al. 1995). Studies show that when divorce is available and prevalent, women gain more independence in and out of marriage and more equality with males. In fundamentalism, therefore, using rates of divorce as a measure of general equality, the AUB, the True Living Church, and various independent polygamists have more gender equality than do the FLDS or Kingston groups. In 1994, the AUB divorce rate in the Bluffdale and Pinesdale branches combined was approximately 40 percent, just 10 percent lower than the national average (Bennion 1998). The increase in the number of releases in the AUB was often related to the dissatisfaction women had with their current husbands and the desire to "marry up," rather than leave the group. Mary, a member of the AUB, had elevated hypergamy, where individuals marry above their status, to an art form. She was unsatisfied with her first and second husbands and used the Brigham Young mandate that allowed an unsatisfied woman to marry the next man with greater priesthoods (Young 1869).

Ironically, fundamentalists defend polygamy as an alternative to the high rates of divorce, adultery, and prostitution in mainstream society. Yet divorce is a reality in polygamous communities. One study found that the marriage of one man to four wives is the primary cause of divorce in Saudi Arabia because the husband treats the wives unequally (BBC News 2001). This is true in the AUB and FLDS as well. Divorce affects polygamists in a variety of complex ways. When one wife gets a release from her husband, she also must release herself from the eternal bonds she has forged with her co-wives, which can be more devastating than the failure of her marriage to her husband (Bennion 1996). For example, when Mary Batchelor's sister-wife divorced her husband, she told me that even though it was not officially *her* divorce, she still felt devastated when her co-wife left. Mary's heart was broken because she loved this woman and felt that they had been sealed together as a family for eternity through the celestial marriage covenant. And the breakdown of the marital relationship between the sister-wife and her husband did not transfer to the relationship between the two women; they still cared for each other. But because of the awkwardness of divorce, Mary had to say goodbye to their friendship. She also spoke of the confusion and trauma her children experienced when they lost their siblings and their other mom, and her own feelings of loss when she had to say farewell to her co-wife's children, whom she thought of as her own offspring.

When Rosa left the Rod Williams family to join a lesbian union after having lived in polygamy for twenty years with five of her own children and eight of her co-wives' children (Bennion 2008),[25] the family was drawn into a custody battle in court over Rosa's three minor children, who were still living at home. Rosa claimed that she was a victim of polygamy and should be given the children because polygamy is a felony. The county judge evaluated the longevity of care in the home by the patriarch, Rod, and the other two wives, Ann and Emily, and ruled that the children should stay in their current home with Rod as the primary caregiver. The judge's rationale was that it was in the best interest of the children to keep them in a familiar, consistent environment. Since the children have always been raised in polygamy with a cluster of adult women to care for them, a father who is always present, and many half-siblings, the judge felt that removing them to a more isolating household with just their mother was not in their best interest. The judge dismissed the notion that polygamy alone was enough to give Rosa custody since she had full knowledge of her actions at age thirty when she entered into the relationship and had stayed in that polygamous setting for twenty years.[26]

The unseen difficulty in this divorce scenario is the hurt left behind between co-wives after the judge's decision was made. Ann told me that she could handle the fact that Rod and Rosa could not live together; she understood the roots of their differences many years ago. But she and Emily had been best friends with Rosa for twenty years, and when Rosa left Rod, she also severed her relationship with them. Ann and Emily felt that this was cruel and unfair. The three women had shared thousands of hours of caring for children and household and years of emotional exchanges that were deep and meaningful. They had actually spent more time with each other than they did with the husband, and Ann and Emily mourned the loss of Rosa's presence in the home and in their lives, especially because they would now be taking care of her children without her around. Despite the prevalence of polygamy around the world, I have found nothing in the literature about the pain co-wives experience when one of them divorces the husband. Nor have I read anything about how child care is handled when a man and one of his wives part ways. Ann, who is approaching retirement, would normally be thinking about condos on golf courses and trips to Bermuda with her husband, but now because of the divorce she will continue to care for her "ex-co-wife's" children until they leave the house in their twenties or thirties. She won't be an empty nester until the last of all her co-wives' kids are out the door in fifteen years.

Mass divorces are an interesting phenomenon in polygamy. For example, in the FLDS group, Warren Jeffs issued the "release" of twenty-one men from their wives at one time, reassigning their wives to other patriarchs. These women were told to end relationships with their husbands of many years, and in some cases, they had to say good-bye to co-wives who remained behind with these husbands. In most cases, all the wives of the disowned men were "given" to one new husband, so they were able to maintain their eternal bonds and co-wife network with little upset. They could continue to raise their children and run a household together as sister-wives. They would have a different husband, but their routine and daily life would change very little. The FLDS also "released" or excommunicated a large number of young unmarried men and boys. Certainly this is not a divorce, but some of the same feelings of loss and alienation occurred. Relationships were severed, friendships were torn apart. A side issue of this release of members is that the parents could face criminal charges for abandoning their underage boys.

Divorce is not always an option. Women find it difficult to leave fundamentalist Mormonism for several reasons. First, plural wives tend to have many children. In a recent study of twenty-seven polygamous families, 78.3 percent of wives had four or more children, 43.3 percent had seven or more children and 18.3 percent had eleven or more children. Plural wives may be practically unable to leave the support system, which includes the assistance of sister wives and older children in making a subsistence lifestyle work. How will she grow and preserve food, make clothing, find household supplies, and find a child care provider so that she can undertake paid work? In addition, she may miss the financial support of the group in terms of free housing and collaborative labor. If women leave polygamy, they may lose their homes and lose the chance of eternal "exaltation" as a queen in their family kingdom. For women whose dissatisfaction with polygamy does not result in a loss of faith altogether, the eternal consequences of rejecting plural marriage may be too much to risk despite the difficulty of their earthly home and marriage.

Another factor that keeps women from leaving is the fear of losing their children. Mormon fundamentalism views children as belonging to the husband's patrilineal kingdom. A woman who maintains her adherence to fundamentalist religious beliefs might choose to leave even if she believes that doing so will result in her damnation. But she would not view herself as having a right to take her children. Alternatively, this belief may prevent women from leaving if their husbands have enough control over resources or psychological control to convince them that they cannot make it in the outside world. From a legal point of view, these women could easily win custody of their children, as there is no legal husband and the father's name is not listed on the birth certificate, if there is one. In addition, the mother will most likely have been the primary parent. However, if the child was born at home with no birth certificate, the mother may feel insecure and unable to leave. She may not know about her legal rights and may not have money or access to a lawyer. Her husband may also have the backing of the financially endowed brethren, who will pay for his lawyer, but not hers. Women who are victims of abuse or who are experiencing dissatisfaction in their marriage also fear being on their own as single mothers without enough money to make ends meet. They fear the stigma of divorce and how the custody battle will affect their children. But polygamous women also fear losing their relationships with their sister wives and their role as surrogate mothers to these wives' children.

LESBIANISM: IN THE HEAVENS ARE WOMEN GAY?

Although the research on this topic is inconclusive at best, sometimes abuse in a marriage, whether it is monogamous or polygamous, can lead a woman to the love of another woman (Austin 2008). I have interviewed several woman who have "confessed" their relationships with co-wives or women they met outside polygamy. Whether these tendencies arose independent of the polygamous environment or are simply part of these women's gender identity (Money and Ehrhardt 1996), I have not determined. Yet their relationships raised enough questions about the study of love between women in the context of plural marriage to merit further investigation.

Let's assume for a moment that the poly mindset is conducive to lesbianism. In polygamy a woman is surrounded continually by numerous women, twenty-four hours a day, seven days a week, all year round. Further, female-female love can often spring from a lack of love for the husband because he is much older or simply because of the prolonged absences of a husband. Such was the case of "Tina," who did not choose this kind of love initially but was driven to it because of a growing love for her sister-wife in the context of husband neglect. It may also be called for in order to train younger women in the art of marriage, as is the case in Lesotho, Africa (Gay 1986).

In spite of the existence of sexual love between women within polygamous Mormon groups, the formal ideology is firmly against such behavior. There is no mention of the existence of emotional and sexual bonds between women in any LDS literature or in O'Dea's seminal work (1957), though these bonds were written about in early church magazines, were discussed in public, and were often encouraged by nineteenth- and early twentieth-century church officials (Quinn 1996). In the contemporary Mormon world, lesbians attend church, take their children to Primary, a religion program to teach gospel lessons, and pose as single mothers and single women who seek to be part of the church community while maintaining a secret life with a female partner. Lesbians are more able to live this dual existence than their gay counterparts, as the stigma against male homosexuality is quite severe in the church. Church beliefs associated homosexuality with the sin of sodomy, which is considered to be second only to murder in terms of magnitude of sin. In addition, church members and members of fundamentalist groups associate homosexuality with the taint of HIV. Bisexual and lesbian women can float among the membership more easily than gay men. Their activities are less institutionalized and less visible than those of males — that is, unless they express their sexuality so vocally and overtly that bishops and stake presidents are compelled to excommunicate them.

Being lesbian in the modern-day church means that one is going against nature and God. Mormon doctrine clearly states that saints should obey a single gender standard, that of heterosexual male or heterosexual female, which was constructed in the preexistence and shall follow individuals throughout their eternal destinies. From a biological viewpoint, however, gender identity exists on a vast continuum and cannot always easily be separated into two distinct arenas of "male" and "female" (Kinsey, Pomeroy, and Martin 1948). Furthermore, homosexuality has been linked to differential cell size in the hypothalamus (LeVay 1991). There is also abundant cross-cultural data that suggests that lesbianism is often adopted as a natural progression toward a stronger heterosexual marriage (Blackwood 1993; Gay 1986).

The official LDS position on lesbianism is that it is a distinct category of sin; those who are guilty must confess their homoeroticism, but they also must confess to engaging in sex before marriage, a separate offense. In other words, if homosexuals can abstain from sex, their membership will remain intact. Otherwise, they must go through a repentance process. To aid in this process, the brethren provide Mormon counseling services that includes a protocol of treatment for the pathology. Often even LDS psychologists see it as an illness, or as "immoral," and seek to alter sexual behaviors by adopting "reparative therapy" (Bingham and Potts 1993). Rarely are empirical biological data employed in the analysis and treatment of clients in LDS social services.

The Mormon discourse on lesbianism is often guided by ecclesiastical generalizations about promiscuity and Western notions of dysfunction and mental illness (Carrier 1980). Such statements have little relationship to the actual lives of women. According to R. D. Bingham and R. W. Potts, the information provided about homosexuality is founded on stereotypes that distance lesbian Mormons from the rest of the fold. The unstated assumption is that all humans are created as heterosexual and therefore "anyone who is lesbian, *chooses* to be lesbian of their own capricious volition, going against the grain of nature. They must be confused or deceived by other lesbians, then, for them to stray off of the heterosexual path so easily, being recruited or cajoled by the dark side. Some are counseled to [pursue] men to curtail their lesbian urges" (Bingham and Potts 1993, 4). Furthermore, since there are no biblical accounts of lesbianism, it is considered to be unnatural, especially given the emphasis on God's commandment to reproduce offspring (Oaks 1995). D. Michael Quinn shines a refreshing light on the subject of Mormon lesbianism in his study of nineteenth- and twentieth-century polygamist women. He explains that same-sex sexual relationships were not uncommon in the early history of the church. For example, in 1837 Mary Fielding Smith commented that "some of the Sisters were engaged in conversing in tongues their countenances beaming with joy, clasped each other's hands and kissed in the most affectionate manner" (quoted in Quinn 1996, 91). The nature of women's relationships was often obscured. For example, in the 1830s, a Mormon girl in her twenties who was enrolled at Amherst, wrote to her girlfriend, "If I could sleep with you one night, [I] think we should not be very sleepy . . . At least I could converse all night and have nothing but a comma between the sentences, now and then" (quoted in ibid.).

Quinn refers to such intimacy between Mormon women as "female homoeroticism," citing an 1856 reference to an LDS woman who was recorded as "trying to seduce a young girl." The word "lesbian" was written in an 1870 Mormon diary, and the phrase "women lovers" appeared in the magazine *Women's Exponent* in 1873. In his study Quinn discovered that Mormon women have expressed their love for each other since the days of the early pioneers and continued to do so in the form of a lesbian and gay club that was organized in 1891 by Katherine Young Schweitzer, granddaughter of Brigham Young.

He writes that near the turn of the century, relationships between women within the LDS community were often celebrated or encouraged. For example, "Mormon suffragist Emmeline Wells publicly praised the same-sex relationship of Francis Willard, President of the national Women's Christian Temperance Union" (Quinn 1996, 424–425). And in 1912, an LDS magazine published a poem by devout Mormon Kate Thomas about her female lover (ibid).

Lesbian polygamous women have a double stigma: as fundamentalists they believe in Victorian sex roles and see homosexuality as akin to murder. When the lover is a co-wife, they are not only betraying their husbands but also the other co-wives because they are limiting the expression of their love to one individual. It is clear that they can *never* come out of the closet and still remain a member of the fold, so they often develop a form of "sisterhood" in which they keep their sexual activities behind locked doors and never speak of it in front of others. It would be considered the grievous sin if they were found out. They would be excommunicated and risk losing their children. These women who remain in the group must adapt to the occasional sexual union with their husbands so that he won't suspect or won't be upset. The husband is the women's Savior on Mt. Zion, after all.

This chapter has examined the varied and complex patterns of gender roles, sexuality, and family life in Mormon fundamentalism. Many polygamists find it very difficult to duplicate the dyadic relationship of the model Victorian monogamy offers in the context of a polygamous extended family. They must operate within a framework that contributes to competition among co-wives, overcrowding due to rapid growth, and male dominance over women. But many fundamentalists are remarkably flexible and adaptable to the needs of their expanding families, in spite of the fact that their role models for appropriate living come from the nineteenth century. Others, such as the wives of Alex Joseph, are inventing new models to accommodate their love of career and love of family, creating space and opportunities for women that monogamy does not provide.

4

Of Covenants and Kings

The Politics of Polygamy

The religiopolitical and economic hierarchy in Mormon fundamentalist polygamy rests on the concepts of the Adam-God doctrine, the Abrahamic covenant, and the United Order. When the prophet Joseph Smith established the United Order in 1831, he assumed that members would consecrate all possessions and sacrifice time to the cause, and that in doing so, they would fit seamlessly and perfectly into the fabric of priesthood hierarchy. Smith's concept of the kingdom of God was very much like Israelite theocratic hierarchy, where God is at the head; man, empowered with the holy priesthood, is on the next level; and women and children are at the bottom (Cooper 1990). The Old Testament kingdom of God was a political power that governed the house of Israel. Fundamentalists believe that this political power was restored to earth by Joseph Smith and is now under their jurisdiction. Consider the diagram of early apostle Orson Hyde's schema of the order and unity of the kingdom of God (Figure 2).

Imagine God, the eternal Father (Elohim, or Adam/Michael), sitting at the head in the form of a sun-crowned King of Kings and Lord of Lords. At the top of the pyramid are the various rays, where reside a king and a priest unto God, bearing rule, authority, and dominion under the Father. The rays branch out to represent the progeny and scope of the kingdoms, in all sizes, an infinite variety to suit all grades of merit and ability: "they have been chosen, ordained, and anointed kings and priests to reign as such in the resurrection of the just" (Millennial Star 9:23, 1847). Many converts are drawn to fundamentalism because it promises men the freedom and keys to begin building a kingdom.

The kingdoms, which were designed by Joseph Smith and interpreted by Orson Hyde, created polygamous extended families that operate as a cluster of sealing networks, organized around each man who has been anointed head priest. Each kingdom is semi-autonomous and traces it bloodlines back to Joseph Smith, who was considered a direct descendant of Christ and a mem-

ber of the House of Judah.[1] The kinship-
ordered nature of network links, which are
based on eternal covenantal sealings, make
these kingdoms an effective basis for group
solidarity during raids and legal problems
with the larger society. The sealing network
is essentially independent of the ecclesiastical hierarchy; this network created a new
structure of religious organization by fus-
ing the concept of distributed authority
with that of kinship association. A sealed
member can be assured of salvation and
will, ideally, be taken care of in this earthly
existence as well.

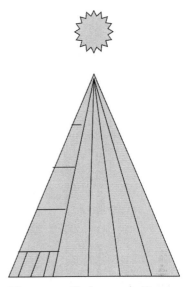

Figure 2. Early apostle Orson
Hyde's schema of the order and
unity of the kingdom of God.

Thus, Adam-God is the ultimate king of
kings at the top of the pyramid and represents the potential of men to become Gods
themselves. Under him and his wives is a
direct link to Jesus Christ and his progeny and then to the earthly head of
priesthood, the prophet—Warren Jeffs, Lamoine Jensen, or Paul Kingston,
as the case may be. Under these divinely appointed prophets are the council
members (or Quorum of Apostles), their wives and children, and then their
appointees or adoptees. Finally, near the bottom are the new converts and
rogue born-in males with little power to access valued resources, who are
considered to be servants to their council members in the afterlife. Below
this line of lower-status males are their wives and children. Barren women
and unmarried males rank quite low in this hierarchy and often leave the
group for better opportunities or become surrogate mothers to the children
of others. The wives of the leading elite are ranked above wives of common
priesthood holders; and within families, it is common for husbands to have
favorites (often first wives) who are ranked above other wives. Children are
likewise ranked according to which of the wives they were born to and their
ability to be linked to a favored stewardship.

Both female and male members can improve their status by marrying
well and accessing a valued stewardship. Women have more choice in the
selection of priesthood-ranked individuals, as they can marry a man who is
already married. Male converts and born-in monogamists must compete for

good wives and a favored stewardship. While some men improve their rank by marrying into pureblood families, most try to align themselves with power in other ways, such as through doctrinal sagacity or through large donations and good investments. In any case, the council tries to regulate the advancement of members of its group. For example, the council matchmaker advises men when and whom to marry, thus controlling their ability to advance in the kingdom-building process. The council also lends support to sons of high-ranking men through primogeniture. In my convert study (Bennion 1998), I found that the distribution of wives was skewed in favor of established men; 23 percent of established men had three or more wives, but only 8 percent of convert men had that many wives.

Kingdom Building

The kingdom of heaven is made up of the following socioeconomic, political, and spiritual divisions. Each man, his wives, and their children make up one "kingdom," in which each king ideally operates in perfect harmony and cooperation with his sovereignties (wives). The wives must also be able to work perfectly with one another as they will be occupying the same kingdom. Though each wife has power and control over her own children, she is obliged to share and communicate with her sister wife's realm, as they are bound together with "the Holy Seal of Promise," just as they are bound and wedded to their husband, the king.

The family kingdom ideal is a perfect order, wherein all families are equal under the direction of the prophet and his councilmen and all wives are equal under the direction of the priesthood head, or husband. These parallel structures should operate like a wheel, where the hub is the priesthood authority, the agent of God, and the spokes are the wives, or members, each intrinsically connected both to the hub and to each other. The wheel functions properly when all spokes are straight and strong, tightly sealed to the hub. Others have described the hub by comparing it to the "fulness of the Gospel." The rim, in this metaphor, refers to the congregation itself: the social, economic, and spiritual polity. The spokes are individual covenants that run through the priesthood council to the hub of the gospel. Christ's body is another metaphor that reaffirms fundamentalist values. Each member of the body is a leg, or an organ, or a cell, and all are operating parts of the divine form. This is much like the Hindu belief in the Absolute, where a drop of water (one human) blends with the ocean of God. When even the smallest cell deviates from the correct principles of the Gospel, the body suffers or becomes ill. So if someone is seen as a sinner, the treatment is often amputation (disinheritance or disenfranchisement), a blood atonement (physical punishment), or expulsion (excommunication) to allow the rest of the body to heal. Further, this metaphor provides members with the knowledge that they are, or can be, direct descendants of Christ and therefore also of the House of Israel, individuals who are filled with the actual genetic components of the ancients. According to fundamentalists, this metaphor stresses that one must be loyal and work collaboratively within the family and within the community of Christ by honoring and deferring to one's priesthood elder or senior, as stated in the *Teachings of the Prophet Joseph Smith*: "No matter from whom a man or woman receives a calling, ordination, or appointment, he or she is always accountable to the living man who presides over and administers the gospel ordinances on this side of the veil" (Smith 1838, 3).

Family kingdom building can strengthen a man's priesthood power by extending the saving power (through his role as Savior on Mt. Zion) to a new wife, to her children, and even to his affines (the husband's in-laws). It is common to see a senior-ranking apostle or councilman "seal unto his kingdom" the families of all wives, adoptees, and even associates. These adoptions may or may not be formally ratified in the group, but fundamentalists believe that they exist in the heavens, thus fortifying the family kingdom with large numbers of subjects. Further, a patriarch can be sealed to a woman for eternity by proxy for a man who is absent, deceased, or apostate. This sealing action will then strengthen the eternal relationship between the men to whom this wife was sealed for eternity, and the children born to this woman will have the option of becoming the covenant children of the new husband.

Through plural marriage, baptism, grafting, and adoption, these kingdoms increase exponentially. Early Mormon apostle Orson Spencer (1847) wrote that the union of families will form a solid phalanx against the intrusion of discord and the spirit of alienation from God. The righteous will be bound together as an eternal bundle by the ties of adoption and kindred. This unity is needed to "endure the shock which society must receive in the last dispensation" (12). Fundamentalists take this prophecy to heart and believe that they are now living in the Last Days before the Second Coming when Christ will reign on earth for a thousand years and all truth will be revealed.

The concept of the Abrahamic covenant is directly related to kingdom building. This covenant provides a genealogical template that organizes relationships based on patrilineal descent in a line from Abraham to contemporary members. It also facilitates the integration of rules, conventions, and teachings in family and community life, thus reinforcing political control of individual behavior. It was Abraham who first promised God that he would obey all the commandments and innumerable laws and codes of the Kingdom. In exchange, God promised Abraham that he would be rewarded with progeny whose numbers surpassed the number of grains of sands in the seas and a rich land where he could cultivate bounty for his vast offspring. The covenants individual fundamentalists make connect them to the community, and leaders, in turn, can use these covenants as a tool to control the individual based on the promises they have made to God and the priesthood brethren. The Book of Mormon promises each man that he will have the power of all the heavens to build his family kingdom on earth through his covenants: "Behold, I give unto you the power that whatsoever you shall seal on earth shall be sealed in heaven, and whatsoever ye shall loose on earth shall be loosed in heaven, and thus shall ye have power among this people" (Helaman 10:7).

Established polygamists who have a direct line to Abraham, Christ, and Joseph Smith are seen as genetically and spiritually "pure" and are typically identified as direct descendants of the House of Ephraim. Allred councilman Joseph Thompson once told me that he could trace his line directly back to Christ. Male fundamentalist converts are told that they will be able to find access to this holy line through their baptism, through which they will be grafted onto a stronger line. They enter the group with great aspirations of fulfilling the promise Joseph Smith made that they will become kings in their own right and not operate underneath any other patriarch's thumb save that of the prophet. This promise is made only to male priesthood bearers; women are formally subject to their husbands. Men seek to live up to Smith's proclamation that gave them the supreme right to rule over their families (including wives), as paraphrased by Thompson: "I have become your father, and I am your priest, your head, your prophet, your apostle, and your revelator, and from no other man can you receive revelation, neither now nor in eternity" (interview with Thompson, 1993).

The Priesthood Council of each fundamentalist group is made up of many "purebloods" who believe themselves to be chosen by God to lead enormous family kingdoms. Within each council there is a hierarchy that fluctuates depending on the current fission/fusion status of the larger group. The prophet, of course, has the highest ranking, and his councilmen are closely associated with this power. Proximity to a prophet increases a man's rank in the council. If the prophet is aging, however, as Owen Allred has in the last decade, it is wise to align oneself to the next most powerful candidate, such as Lamoine Jensen in the case of the AUB or Merril Jessop in the case of the FLDS while Warren Jeffs is in prison.[2] Each councilman is the patriarch of a large, powerful dynasty and serves as the intermediary who maintains control throughout the ranks of other established and convert families. Each baptized member is under the direction of the Priesthood Council. New members can progress to higher levels of authority and prestige by marrying into a pureblood dynasty or by being appointed by a council member to a prestigious calling. When women marry a member of a prominent dynasty or have numerous children for him to adopt, they can also gain a measure of formal prestige and, more importantly, security. Individual members side with the council kingdom that they aspire to join, aligning themselves with that particular councilman/God. When a councilman dies or is removed, comes a new spot becomes available on the council hierarchy. Those who are not grafted onto a rising kingdom will not be as likely to rise to power in their group or to mobilize sympathy during a crisis. The Priesthood Council authorizes all marriages, grants stewardships, approves policy changes, and calls deviants to task whenever necessary. They have financial control over dozens of projects and industries under the incorporated headings of "United Order," "United Effort Plan," or "Davis Corporation."

I use graph theory (Hage and Harary 1991) to show how important it is to align oneself to a good kingdom in the conversion process (see Figure 3). The graph illustrates three dominant family kingdoms in the AUB: the Allreds, the Jessops, and the Thompsons during the early 1990s.

Each kingdom is represented by a model of a rooted tree. Two convert kingdoms are also shown — the Judds and the Williams kingdoms. The trees for these two groups illustrate the relative weakness of new families in the kingdom-building process. Those with the most branches are the most powerful because they have multiple links with other vital kingdoms and individuals. The convert kingdoms have very few links and privileges in the sect. These graphs show connections among council members and their links to other, potentially valuable individuals, such as the senior wife of the prophet, a lucrative stewardship, or a son-in-law who is also the eldest son of a top councilman. Adopted and born-in members of a kingdom are expected to

Councilmen Kingdoms

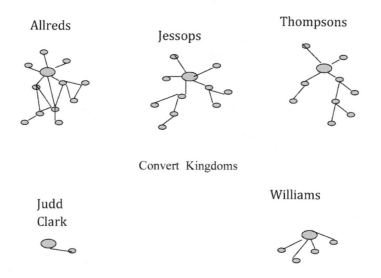

Figure 3. Tree graph of three dominant family kingdoms in the AUB in the early 1990s: Allreds, Jessops, and Thompsons.

treat each other as family and obey the council's instructions and advice. If the convert's parents are dead, he or she can be adopted into the family king-dom of a sealed couple. Each person must be sealed to a man who will accept the gospel on earth and in the spirit world. Women who marry high-ranking members save their own family through the sealing. Most fundamentalists believe a woman who marries a councilman or prophet transmits blessings and salvation from these men to her relatives, both living and dead. Some-times the ritual sealing is abandoned for a more informal mutual agreement to share in another's exaltation, where a lesser individual is raised up when sealed to a person of higher status. A woman can also be sealed to a patri-arch through her mother's side if she cannot find a worthy patriarch on her father's side. These marriage sealings are a way to establish a link between a high-ranking apostle and the men to whom the women are civilly married, extending the saving power that centers in the prophet and council.

Inheritance rights and access to financial stewardships are associated with a specific political hierarchical order. First, Mormons believe that the spirits of humans are descended from Gods and thus have rights to kingdoms in the heavens. Second, they believe that in the Pre-Existence, humanity was organized into lineages based on patrilineality and that these relationships will continue in the afterlife. Third, they believe that in the days of Adam's mortality, a patriarchal order was established that gave Adam everlasting supervision over all his posterity as king and ruler. Finally, they believe that this patriarchal structure is eternal; it never dies out. The genetics of salvation, based on adherence to bloodlines, provide the sect with strong group identity but are also the cause of conflict. Members are bound together by blood and adoption as a royal seed of royal blood. But some, who are predestined to be servants of the kings (purebloods), feel that their place in the hierarchy is limiting and unreasonable. Through adoptive sealings, fundamentalists can link promising converts to prominent council members with whom they have no formal blood ties. This involves being attached to another man's kingdom, sealed to him for eternity. In the Harmston's group (TLC), Jim achieved the expansion of his own kingdom by adopting new male converts. He then established spiritual wifery,[3] just as Smith did in the nineteenth century, by sleeping with their wives. This bonded him to these men through reproductive and priesthood ties. When a man marries a woman sealed to another man, their offspring typically go to the originally sealed man unless the second man is powerful.[4]

Figure 4 represents the conversions of members of the LDS church to membership in a fundamentalist Mormon sect and the progression of males and females into a generic family principality, I call, heuristically, the "Smith" kingdom. Note how women have fewer obstacles, overall, in their attempts to reach the goal than men do. "Kingdom," the goal, represents the stable, secure environment that is associated with longevity and obtaining spiritual and socioeconomic resources. Most men have less direct routes to kingdom building because they compete with the elite brethren for wives and stewardships. This process is very costly for convert males, who must donate money and other assets and promise allegiances. In contrast, female convert and born-in women have a much more direct route to the goal. In the first part of the process, those who eventually convert feel some kind of tension or strain in the mainstream. For men, the discomfort is sometimes about a lack of access to significant political and religious leadership roles. They simply do not feel they are "Gods in the making" when they are so removed from the role of prophets, seers, and revelators associated with the LDS, a church that has 10 million members. They feel puny in their kingdom-building process and are attracted to the mysteries and the promise of becoming kings in their own right, lords over their families, conduits of direct revelation. For women this first stage is often a problem of logistics and socioeconomic strain. Many cannot find a "good man" or are widowed or abandoned or unmarriageable. Most women who eventually convert want an escape from their marginalized placement in the orthodox Mormon Church. Both men and women are drawn to self-reliance, prophecy, immortality and exaltation; they seek early Mormon ideologies to help them cope with the losses they have experienced.

The second phase in kingdom building is the acceptance of fundamentalist ideological tenets—the Law of Celestial Marriage, the Law of Sarah, the Law of Consecration, and so on. These laws are constructed and implemented primarily by the male elite clergy, who contract marriages, appoint stewardships, and administer blessings. This phase creates tensions for newly converted males who were originally drawn to fundamentalism to find autonomy and power as kingdom builders in Zion. While the ideal portrays the male as the total sovereign of his family kingdom, in reality he finds himself in a position of subordination to elite priesthood holders. At this point in the process, some convert males are weeded out if they do not donate the time, energy, and finances to the cause that the elite require. Women go through no such screening process; they are swiftly incorporated into new callings as mothers, teachers, and wives. Single convert women are quickly married to established males, and married convert women are incorporated into female networks. If their husbands are seen as ineligible for kingdom building, these women are grafted onto more powerful family kingdoms. In other words, the system is simply not designed to house large numbers of male patriarchs; only so many men can achieve the roles of king and magistrate. The system is designed to produce numerous queens and auxiliaries (supportive structures who serve the royalty) who are encouraged to participate without being "culled" out of any phase.

After studying 142 communities, White and Burton (1988) presented a model of polygyny that mirrors Mormon kingdom building. They hypothesized that the incidence of plural marriage is a function of household economics, the presence or absence of male-centered kin groups, warfare, and environmental factors. They found that men's marriage rules are determined by fraternal interest groups and warfare. Of most significance is their emphasis on conditions that must be met if a polygamist community is to thrive: there must be a way to draw the females in and a method of filtering males out. I applied their premise to the Allred Group and found that over a fifteen-

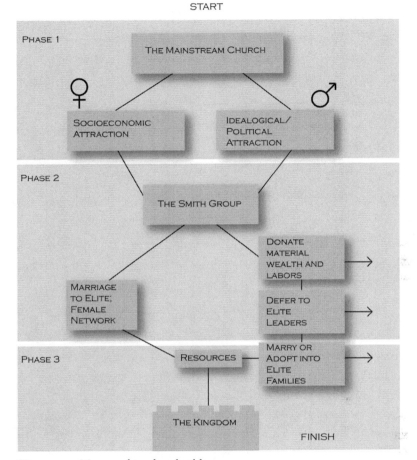

Figure 4. Mormon kingdom building.

year period, approximately 66 percent of the converts who stayed in the group were female; and approximately 60–65 percent of those who left or were expelled from the group were male (Bennion 1998). In other words, as many males were emigrating as females were immigrating. As many as 30 percent of young men were leaving Pinesdale, due to alienating competition over wives and stewardships or the promise of finding work in Utah. The flow of women at Pinesdale was directly tied to the conversion and to marriage practices. The flow of men out of the group fits the Misisi's template of elite polygyny beautifully (Misisi 1991).

Interestingly, the Isaiah scriptural mandate and Mosiah Hancock vision both predict skewed ratios in favor of women to provide optimal conditions

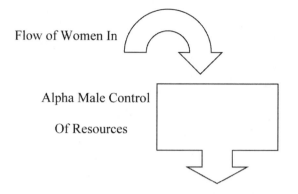

Flow of Women In

Alpha Male Control

Of Resources

Flow of Rogue Males Out

Figure 5. "Sink faucet" flow of men and women in polygamy.

for polygamy. Joseph Musser paraphrased Brigham Young's statement that women are more plentifully righteous than men, advising men *against* polygamy. "Only the best [men] are allowed to take more than one wife. Every man must first prove before the priesthood that he has the capacity, love and worthiness to assume the great responsibilities of this heavenly law (quoted in Hales 2006, 247). I use the image of a sink faucet (Figure 5) to illustrate how a skewed sex ratio and male alienation allows polygamy to thrive. Polygamy was never intended to be a widespread phenomenon; it cannot function with too many males in the system. In addition, there are never enough available women to make it work. Conditions are too limiting for the Principle to ever be the prevalent marriage structure.

The best example of the efficacy of this process is within the FLDS group. The natural birth rate provides enough females for the alpha males to marry but too many males. So when Warren Jeffs ousted 400 rogue males from the group, he provided the essential balance White and Burton (1988) wrote about: the number of born-in women who stay in the group is approximately the same number of rogue males who exit the group. If the FLDS proselytize for converts, as the AUB does, they could afford to keep more males in the system.

The final phase of kingdom building is designed to connect the individual's ideals with the socioeconomic realities conducive to managing a large and thriving family corporation. To advance in this last stage, each individual must access certain key religious and temporal resources, thus meeting certain essential standards of excellence on the path of God-making. These resources are a church calling (leadership role), a fruitful economic steward-ship, numerous wives, reproductive advantage (enough young wives to maxi-mize fertility), and adequate income-earning potential (enough wives in their twenties, thirties, and forties who are educated and employable). Note that not all men need to be the alpha leaders in this kingdom-building scenario. Many rogue males are welcome in the group as long as they are grafted onto the kingdoms of more powerful alpha leaders. They contribute as followers, workers, and supporters of the system dominated by the elite polygamists.

Disputes and Conflict Management

One sign of the strength of an individual's position in fundamentalist groups is his or her ability to rally support in a crisis. In 1994, I conducted a study of how the AUB resolved disputes and which tactics men used to gather political power. These processes are similar to the ones that are used in the FLDS and Kingston groups. Relationships that define the disputing process are primarily based on priesthood rank, kinship, and economic stewardship. Although the process of determining who has prestige and thus the power to settle conflicts is more overt for men than it is for women, even among the wives there are rules for managing disputes. A series of patron/client relation-ships determines the contours of power in relationships. These include elder brother/younger brother, senior wife/junior wife, husband/wife, born-in or "pureblood"/convert, councilman/member, senior councilman/junior council-man, prophet/councilman, Elohim/Adam.[5] In each set of relations, the pa-tron, or senior person, has access to valued resources and extracts deference from the client, or junior person. These patterned relations set up the condi-tions for cooperation, support, and advancement or, conversely, competition, avoidance, and isolation. The high-ranking priesthood bearers have the right to grant or deny converts new wives, priesthood keys, and jobs, all essential ingredients of exaltation and God-making.

Converts learn quickly that the successes they enjoy on earth will pave the way for their successful progression in the next life. The best strategy for both women and rogue males is to immediately solicit support from a patron who clearly has a position of importance in the group. They must also connect themselves to many other "seniors" through ties of blood, marriage, and economic exchange. Purebloods have a better chance of mobilizing sup-port from kin and elite councilmen than new converts do. Converts who can manipulate pureblood councilmen and their kin to their advantage win out over those who do not interact as skillfully. An individual can also increase his or her prestige and social advantage through working hard, bearing many children, expressing devotion, and cooperating with others, but the need to create ties with high-ranking individuals through kinship, marriage, priesthood, and economic advantage is paramount.

Barnes first introduced the idea of social networks to describe social relationships among parishioners in Norway (1954). The more linkages an individual in a network has with other network members, the greater the socioeconomic and political power that individual enjoys in the system. It is vital to note that linkages represent categories of power and a series of rights and privileges. Many of these linkages are expressed through direct exchanges or transactions, such as a conversation, a gesture, a ritual, or gift. Gluckman (1955) calls such relationships "multiplex," by which he means that they are based on status. Such relationships are likely to result in a senior person's ability to mobilize support. For example, one powerful woman in the Allred Group, Dauna Baird, has primary kinship, economic, and marital links with at least three members of the priesthood council; she also has five secondary links with four additional councilmen and female leaders.

Another way to mobilize support during disputes is to learn how to offset and manipulate negative relationships using a triad mechanism. Figure 6 represents triadic forms of social relations generated through the transfer of material and symbolic wealth. In this figure, the positive and negative nature of relations are expressed in (A) a man and his two wives and (B) a councilman and his two subordinate followers. In (C), all three triads are illustrated: a husband and two wives, a father and two sons, and a councilmen and his two appointees. In such triads a negative relation between a senior wife and a junior wife (A) can generate a positive relation between husband and either wife. Likewise, a negative relationship between an established group member and a convert (B) generates a positive one between a councilman and either appointee. Sometimes there is an unbalanced relationship triad between a husband and his two wives or a father and his two sons or a council patriarch and his two appointees (C), which creates conflict and further manipulation by all three members of the triad. All of these triads potentially parallel the symbolic relation of the Father (Elohim) and his two sons, Adam and Christ. The theory of negative balance relationships suggests that humans will try to balance and unbalance awkward situations (i.e., even numbers of negative

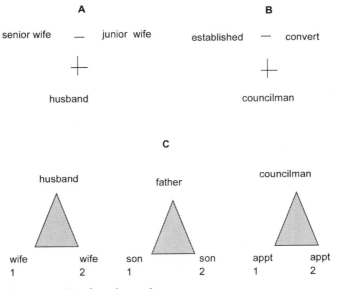

Figure 6.   Triadic relationships.

relations). Thus, in the case of the husband and wives, one wife will try to pit her husband against the other wife, causing a negative relation to exist between them. Likewise, a son will alienate his brother from his father in order to gain the father's resources, and a member of the sect will strive to convince his protector councilman of the unrighteous behavior of another member in order to win his favor.

Disputes develop because of the discrepancies between what members are promised and what they experience. For example, some men enter the group with grandiose schemes of royalty and kingship, only to find that they are alienated from those who have power over the priesthood keys. These novice kings sometimes take on the priesthood keys themselves, making covenants without the sanction of the council and even taking on new wives without permission. Such members quickly find themselves ousted from the group. Many men are reluctant to become subordinate children in another man's kingdom; they feel that this somehow diminishes their own exaltation. Those who have left the LDS Church because they felt powerless are reluctant to become servants on Mt. Zion in another's kingdom. However, the Abraham covenant links individuals to their hierarchical senior as well as to God, and the individual must please both their senior and God. The demands that the senior in the covenant makes on the junior, who must obey, is a major source of conflict in fundamentalist Mormon groups. Further, although fundamentalist ideology suggests that all are equal in the "fulness," some members are given more wives and greater economic stewardships than others, and this inequity can breed discontent.

Other disputes arise when a man cannot preside over his own family. His wives have to obey him only to the degree that he is consistent in the gospel or as long as they feel that he treats them equally. If he deviates from the codes and commandments in any way, he can lose his wives both in this life and the next to another, better man. Therefore, women have the power to identify a husband's flaws by way of witchcraft accusations (accusing their husbands of abuse) in order to rise to a better status for themselves and their children.[6] In some sects a woman can gain a release for any reason. In others it is a political issue that must be resolved by the council. One couple, for example, who had conceived out of wedlock, were later sealed by the priesthood after the baby was born. When the husband sought to take a plural wife, the first wife wanted to leave him and was told she must accept the new wife without complaint. She desperately wanted a release but was denied it, as the young man was a member of a pureblood family. Had she married a convert, she might have gained that release.

Conflict resolution also reaffirms cultural norms by weeding out disruptive elements, like cutting off a dead branch to make the tree stronger. For example, FLDS member Dan Barlow disputed the right of Warren Jeffs to become prophet after Rulon Jeffs died. Barlow essentially challenged Jeffs' priesthood authority. Even though Dan was the son of a prestigious family, Warren Jeffs had him quickly removed from the community, along with twenty others who either agreed with Barlow or whom Jeff saw as competitors in his attempts to gain control of the community's resources (including wives). Jeffs was able to achieve this victory over dissenters by virtue of his role as Holder of the Keys, which gave him undisputed rights of privilege and rule. In another example, the AUB expelled Councilman John Ray, who practiced a gruesome form of blood atonement. When his reputation for cruelty to children became known to local child protective services and law enforcement, the community saw him as a threat to the stability of the group in spite of his high rank, and they excommunicated him. This reaffirmed the rule in Pinesdale (which was new at the time) of revealing child abusers to law enforcement. By cutting John Ray off, the council fostered a stronger relationship with the Ravalli County sheriff's department.

The history of disputes in the AUB is a useful tool for pinpointing stress in the organization. Disagreements over valuable material and symbolic resources are the main source of conflicts between individuals and families and friction between co-wives. In my conflict resolution study, I weighed the various links between individuals in disputes according to whether they are advantageous or deleterious, using the graph theory criteria of density, betweenness centrality, and content multiplexity. Density qualifies the types of links a disputant has with others. If a member has blood and marriage links to another member, he has fairly strong density. But if he adds economic exchange to those links, his potential for mobilizing support becomes that much stronger because his ties with others are more dense. Betweenness centrality measures the location of a disputant in the path between others. An example of this is when a new convert presents an attractive investment opportunity to one councilman in order to win that councilman's niece or daughter in marriage. He then invites a second councilman, who is connected to the first investor by kin ties, to bring his family into the new business. This way, he is ideally located between two high-ranking councilmen, one of whom may become his father-in-law. Content multiplexity is used to distinguish between the meanings or types of links individuals use in the kingdom-building process, such as ties of friendship, affinity, consanguinity, and economic obligation. How is a member connected to another member? Is it by blood, marriage, or priesthood? If the ties are based on any of these three factors, he may be in good standing with that other member. However, if the tie is only economic, he may find himself being used or isolated if he is not also honoring his priesthoods. For example when Ron Bierer converted to the AUB, he gave the bishop $10,000 in cash to be used to buy wheat for the town. A few weeks later he found that the Jessop leadership had used the money for something else, which they labeled "priesthood business." Because Bierer was having trouble with the IRS, the priesthood told him to turn his hardware store over to Unified Industries, an AUB corporation. Later, when Beirer's tax troubles were behind him, he asked for his store back, but the Brethren refused to give it to him. In another example of how a member can be exploited when ties are solely economic, the AUB asked a convert to sign a quitclaim deed that gave his property in Panguich to the group. When he visited the property, he was threatened with arrest for trespassing (Llewellyn 2004; Bennion 2008).

Although mobilizing the support of as many elite members as possible is the key to an individual's success, this is sometimes difficult to do because the councilmen are often at odds with each other. Multiple council members may be vying for control of the council; each competitor would like to be next in line for the office of prophet. If an ambitious new convert aligns himself to the wrong councilman, he may be in a weakened position when he becomes involved in a dispute. For example, when Rod Williams converted to the polygamous community, he sought to rise to a satisfactory calling in the group and aligned himself with Councilman George Maycock. However, Councilman Lamoine Jensen accused Maycock of sex abuse, and Maycock was excommunicated. Rod also married the daughter of Councilman Joseph Thompson, who has also been excommunicated. These choices created two counts against Williams in his links to the priesthood council. Another issue was Rod's support of a "gentile" woman's cause at the direct expense of several top councilmen. When Rod brought an accusation of foul play against the council, he was immediately ostracized and disfellowshipped.

Whenever a convert goes against the prophet, his ties with the elite and others at all levels are threatened, even when he has a history of business success. John Putvin of the AUB experienced this when he conspired to rob Virginia Hill of $1.5 million dollars with the help of Dennis Matthews, another AUB man. He had told the prophet, Owen Allred, that a woman had generously donated a great deal of money. Putvin and Matthews used this money to pay off AUB debt and line some of their own pockets. During the official investigation of this swindle, John and his wife Karen Thompson—who was Councilman Joseph Thompson's daughter—battled for custody over their daughter. When Owen Allred supported Karen Thompson, Putvin tried to deliver him to the police for the money swindle. The AUB subsequently disowned Putvin (Llewellyn 2004; Bennion 2008).

Individuals who have a combination of locational advantage between others and multiplex ties of priesthood power, kinship, and favorable economic stewardship will be able to mobilize support. Under these conditions internal social stratification in favor of elite kingdom builders is sustained and the traditional norms and values of the community are reinforced.

SUMMARY OF CONFLICT CASES

In my study of dispute resolution, I found that most cases involved either convert men engaged in disputes with councilmen over access to priesthood and economic callings or councilmen, or purebloods, fighting among themselves over a variety of issues. Of lesser frequency were disputes between children and parents over economic stewardships and disputes between husbands and wives over obedience issues, access to financial goods and services, and lack of equality in the treatment of wives and children. Also less frequent, but still potent, were disputes among wives over domestic matters, particularly child care and sexual relations with the husband. I will briefly highlight one case from each category to illustrate the nature of the power structure in the groups and the way disputes are resolved. One convert, whom I call "Judd Clark," moved in with his wife, Amy, and their eight children, seeking a powerful stewardship through Amy's grandfather, Rulon C. Allred. Though Judd and Amy were promised a project in Bluffdale, Utah, they were actually moved to Pinesdale, Montana, against their will and put under the thumb of the Jessop leadership. Judd and Amy gave all their property and cash to the Jessop branch, including their Salt Lake City home. Judd worked in auto parts sales, and the Jessop brethren built them a home. But Judd was refused a plural wife. He and Amy declined to pay their tithe and were ostracized. When their house caught fire, they lost all their possessions. They handed over the insurance money from the fire to the brethren, who used it to help build the home of another councilman's daughter. Judd complained to Amy's uncle, Marvin Allred, who then discussed it with the Jessops, who said that Morris Jessop's son needed priesthood help more than the Clarks did, as they had a good job and would recover their loss. The council recommended that the Clarks leave the group. But if they did so, they would relinquish all their possessions to the brethren. Amy was invited to stay; she and her children could be connected to a man with higher priesthood authority, if she wished.

The pivotal factor in this case was Judd's failure to mobilize support from high-ranking priesthood officials. He had unorthodox doctrinal views and no network ties with pureblood families. He spent time with rogue convert males. His only council contact was the man who converted him, who lived far away in Bluffdale. He also accused one of the Jessops, a powerful family in Pinesdale, of abusing his daughter and laundering money. Although Amy had great potential through her bloodline to claim legitimate access to prestige, she was linked to an "apostate" and was unable to move any further while she was still married to him. The Judd Clark family eventually left the group and went back to the LDS Church.

Although most cases are resolved in favor of pureblood or established members, one possible exception is the case of Councilman Joe Thompson, one of the original councilmen under Rulon Allred in the 1950s. Despite his high status, he was ousted from the group by Rulon's brother Owen in 1994 after allegations of abuse. Because of this, his entire family's status was altered. If my theories about pureblood networking are valid, then his kinship status alone would have protected him from disfellowship. Yet new values can be introduced and enforced through the expulsion of a councilman, such as reinforcing the notion of social evolution and spiritual adaptation. Because Thompson had financial control over the Mexican branch and veto power in the distribution of funds for the Pinesdale branch, his position was coveted by others. In addition, Thompson often made statements from the pulpit in defense of incest, to the embarrassment of the council, which had taken a new progressive stance against underage brides and incestuous marriages. One Sunday, Owen Allred announced that the council had found Thompson guilty of sexually abusing his daughters and was thereby summarily excommunicated. Why was this expulsion made in 1994 instead of twenty years earlier, when the alleged abuse occurred? Many Thompson family members felt it was a political maneuver to allow other councilmen access to the Mexican stewardship and to allow Lamoine Jenson to get one step closer to becoming prophet. Joe had many ties to the old guard, yet he was still alienated. He failed to create new connections over the years, instead relying heavily on the compassion of an aging prophet to protect him. Thompson was not tied to the younger, ambitious members of the council and often offended them with doctrinal disputes and outdated notions. The timing of his excommunication provided new opportunities for the younger members of the council. This dispute demonstrates how the underlying set of recognized rights and responsibilities can change as new philosophies and needs emerge. But no matter how tolerant the system is, it will not tolerate certain breaches of conduct, such as sex abuse scandals, dark-skinned priesthood bearers, and doctrinal impurities.[7]

The second case involves a fight between two high-ranking councilmen. "Glen" Allred, the eldest son of the prophet's second wife, vied for control over a lucrative cattle operation known as the Granite Ranch (also known as the Red Cedar Corporation) with "Carl" Bronson, the eldest son of another councilman's first wife. Glen had two wives and twelve children, whereas Carl had one wife, Sally, and seven children. With the permission of the priesthood, Carl and Sally bought the 1,200-acre Granite Ranch in Juab, Utah, using priesthood funds for the down payment. Sally's mother, the daughter of a councilman, lived at the ranch and helped care for Sally's children while she taught school. Sally's father, a son of Rulon Allred, helped Carl with the cattle. After four years, Carl's younger brothers and wives joined the operation. Glen Allred, Owen Allred's son, also joined the ranch. In the fifth year, Glen and Carl began disputing over profits. The council decided, without Carl's father's vote, to hand the management of the ranch over to Glen, since he was the son of the prophet and had three wives. Carl and his wife were furious and went to Sally's grandfather, another councilman, to get Carl's jurisdiction back. This councilman then spoke to the prophet about the issue. The prophet said he wanted his boys to have a place out west, as his other sons and nephews were in charge of another ranch forty miles north of Salt Lake. Since Glen had more wives and children than Carl, his "need" was greater than Carl's. Further, since Allred's nephew (Sally's father) was at the ranch, it made sense to have an Allred in charge.

Carl accused Owen Allred of racism, stating that because Carl had "Lamanite" (Hispanic) blood, he was keeping him and his family away from the good stewardships. Carl said that because Lamanites have a closer relationship to Abraham as true Israelites, Carl should have the ranch stewardship.[8] Two other councilmen were angered over the change of guard at the ranch. One of the councilmen's granddaughter had married Carl in the sixth year of the operation, increasing his status slightly. Also, Carl's third brother had brought his wives out to the ranch to increase the family's size and justify their case for control of the holdings. This angered Glen, who hadn't authorized it, and he fought with Carl to remove his brother.

Carl took a leave of absence to live in Bluffdale on a part-time assignment for the council. While there, he met and married the prophet's brother's granddaughter, "Betty," and befriended Morris Jessop's son, "George," who happened to be Betty's father. In other words, Betty had blood ties to both the Allreds and the Jessops. In marrying her, Carl doubly increased his prestige; he now had three wives, fifteen children, and key allies in the Allred family. In the seventh year of the ranch, the council gave the control to both Glen and Carl equally, with Glen handling the marketing and irrigation and Carl managing the herd. This compromise preserved ongoing relations among several key pureblood families. Although they still have tensions, they have agreed to work together to keep their family's relative power in the sect stable and secure, including their own fathers' positions. The dispute was resolved primarily through strategic intermarriage and by the actions Carl took to create a balance with Glen by creating new and multiplex ties with important councilmen.

The third case of dispute concerned a disgruntled first wife from Pinesdale named "Alice," who married Earl and had five children. She was living in a two-bedroom trailer, crowded in with another family of two wives and children. The new family soon built their own home but shared this space with several other families during the "growing period" of the Pinesdale sect. Because they were converted by Councilman Morris Jessop, they were grafted onto a powerful kingdom. Earl even worked with Morris as a drywall installer for a while. Years later, Alice, who by then was in her late thirties, had thirteen children. She provided most of the labor to build their newest home, a shell of 2x4s with a plywood floor and no running water. She installed the plastic sheeting, doors, and fixtures herself. She learned about wiring and plumbing and installed a barrel stove for heat. She refused to hand over her earnings from part-time data entry work to her husband and as a result Earl disowned her, as the council advised him to do. Her ideas about her role as a potential Goddess further alienated Earl and some of the brethren. Alice's best friend, the second wife of Marvin Jessop, spread the word among the women in Pinesdale that Earl was mistreating Alice and convinced council members of his abuses. During the dispute, which lasted a few years, Alice had to sell Amway products and collaborate with other women to survive. Meanwhile, her husband married two additional wives, with whom Alice had to share space. His latest wife was younger than Alice's eldest daughter and could never be "put upon" to clean up after herself.

To resolve the dispute, the priesthood council convinced Earl to treat Alice with greater respect, give her the spirit child (that she had dreamt of from the Pre-existence) she sought, and give her some of his money for the home she was building. The network connections both Earl and Alice had secured were crucial in their ability to mobilize support in favor of their position. The support both sides received made compromise the best option. You could call this situation a "stalemate" rather than a blissful reunion of man and wife, but it was still considered by all in the community as a resolution. The prominent factors in the mobilization of support were priesthood, doctrine, kinship, and marriage.

The fourth, and final, case involves a conflict between two women. "Dolly," a high-ranking charismatic Relief Society president, and "Rita," the favored daughter of a councilman, were both married to the prophet Owen Allred.

Rita was first wife to Owen whereas Dolly was his third wife. Before Dolly married Owen, she and Rita had been great friends who met several times a week to gossip about the frailties of men. Rita was her father's "right hand"; she organized everything for him and traveled to various branches with him. Although she had been married before, when her husband died, she married Owen as a "time wife," which linked the prophet to the dead councilman in the hereafter. Rita has twelve children, twenty-three grandchildren, and many allies in the sect. She felt that Dolly, a convert from the LDS Church, was trying to transform the sect into a replica of the Mormon Church. Rita, a traditionalist, felt that Dolly was too liberal. Dolly also lived in a much nicer home than Rita. In a Relief Society meeting one Sunday the two women began a shouting match about Relief Society procedures and their sexual behavior with their shared husband. Rita went to her father, the councilman, and then to the prophet with a list of grievances against her co-wife. She called Dolly a lesbian and said she was destroying the sect. Rita announced in church that Dolly had no right to be the president of the Relief Society because she was not the first wife of the prophet. In response, Dolly went to the prophet and to other key councilmen with whom she had economic ties. She had helped arrange the marriage of one councilman's daughter to Owen Allred's son and was connected to a second councilman through the marriage of her son to his granddaughter. This relationship was further enhanced by the common interest that she shared with Owen in the programs of the Mexican saints. Rita gained support through her father and her uncle, who was the brother of another councilman. As second wife of Owen, she had seniority over Dolly who was a more recent wife. She was also best friends with the first wife of a councilman, and through this friendship she was good friends with the councilman.

The two women met with their husband, the prophet, explaining their two sides. Since Rita's father was away on business in Mexico during the meeting and her own husband was siding with her co-wife, Rita lost the dispute. Owen said that he had gone to the Lord on the matter and felt that the case was closed. The key factors in mobilizing support in this dispute among co-wives were charisma, access to priesthood keys, affinal ties, and economic advantage. Dolly's relative youth and charismatic personality, her business ties, and her organizational skills won her the place of "favorite wife." The council saw her as a better investment than Rita.

This case illustrates the pattern of disputes that occur between a husband

and his wife or wives and among the wives. Ideally, a man should live in love and harmony with each wife and they, in turn, should love each other. A husband should treat his wives equally. Oftentimes, especially when a new wife from a different background is brought into the family, jealousy, tension, and quarrels arise that stem from differing personalities and expectations. One grievance that often arises between wives happens when a female convert expects to become a queen who is free to voice her opinions and exert control over her life but finds instead that she must show deference to the senior wife or wives. Wives also often experience conflict about clothing, parenting styles, cooking methods, and decorating. They may argue about the time their husband is spending with one wife at the expense of another, or they may quarrel about which wife gets to go on a business trip with the husband. It is a sad reality that women and their children are often treated differentially by their husbands, even in the best of families. Wives usually shrug this off as part of a spiritual polishing process that builds character as they learn patience and understanding. But if it a pattern of favoritism or neglect becomes entrenched, it often leads to conflict.

A further source of conflict is that second and subsequent wives have no legal right to health insurance, the husband's pension, and or his estate upon his death. They also cannot take their husband's last name, even though it is the patronym they will be associated with in the celestial kingdom. Only first wives can claim these privileges. The economic status of converts without formal connections to pureblood families is also questionable. If they are suddenly disowned by the Priesthood Council, they must forfeit any rights to their home, their stewardship, or any property they gave to the sect when they converted. This happens more often to men than to women. For example, when Warren Jeffs expelled Dan Barlow, his properties and his wives were given to other men in the group. Yet disowning men and shuffling women from one man to the next is discriminatory toward the wives of that disowned man. This example presents a very clear picture of how women can be treated like chattel or property and how converts can be viewed as secondary citizens.

In spite of certain inequities, equilibrium and relative peace can be established through the elite's political control and the entire community's emphasis on core values and beliefs. Since the council controls the land and stewardships, holds the priesthood keys, has the ability to excommunicate deviants, and controls the distribution of plural wives, they have the power to maintain their status quo and disenfranchise any deviant element. Like the orthodox Mormon Church, fundamentalist sects are learning to deal with significant pressures such as the need to maintain solidarity as diversity increases, the need to respond to an increase in radicalism and pluralism among members, the need to include non-normative families more fully (such as mixed-race couples and single fathers), and the need to find a way to manage the contradiction between the core ideal of egalitarianism and the reality that women and "rogue" males are treated as subordinates.

Individuals who have strong, multistranded ties to the elite and who have roles that exhibit economic, religious, and kin-related centrality can successfully mobilize the support necessary for a favorable resolution of disputes they are involved in. People tend to align themselves with other members according to economic need, doctrinal interpretation, obligations and privileges associated with their kin group, and their role in the priesthood or family order—in other words, the most powerful ties one can have in kingdom building are those related to priesthood authority, family ties, and marriage.

CRITIQUE OF THE POLYGAMOUS POLITICAL SYSTEM

The seeds of discontent within polygamous Mormon groups lie in the failure of the United Order to distribute wealth and valued callings equally and its failure to encourage widespread cooperation. The hierarchy itself often pits councilman against councilman, discouraging true unity. Ironically, and to the advantage of women, the fierce competition among males and the time and energy this takes away from the household actually fosters opportunities for female empowerment in a patriarchal system. The structure relies heavily on matricentric residences, where women work with other women to meet their needs and spend their energies focusing on the welfare of their children and homes. Perhaps more than any other feature of polygamous life, this is what encourages female solidarity and interdependence, as exhibited in two-thirds of the AUB cases I observed.

The resolution process breaks down when conflicts occur within the same family kingdom or when conflicts arise between spouses and their affines. One challenge for the community is how to deal with recurring conflicts of interests between converts and established members. The fundamentalist political system can actually interfere with the prized ideology of the "eternal round" of Mormon perfection achieved through successful negotiation of daily challenges. Converts and established members have differential access to valued economic and priesthood resources, and the rigid patron-client relations (husband/wife, senior wife/junior wife, favored son/ignored son, established member/convert, and so on) often present obstacles to compromise. These challenges to the utopian ideal mean that it is essential that individuals learn to mobilize ties with others based on priesthood rank and prerogative, kinship, marital ties, and economic stewardship. Converts and born-ins alike must use shrewd strategies when they express their views about doctrine, investing their donations and tithes, and marrying into the right kind of families. The necessity for such Machiavellian strategies seems to run counter to the concepts preached in early Mormonism about equal access to the Kingdom of God.

PART TWO

How Do We Deal with Polygamy?

This section analyzes the impact of public opinion, the media, and the law on Mormon fundamentalist polygamy. How has the pre-dominantly negative view of polygamy since the 1800s affected the movement? How is the polygamy narrative evolving with the birth of television shows like TLC's *Sister Wives* that celebrate plural marriage? What is the legal history of polygamy, and should Canada and the United States repeal their bans on plural marriage?

5

Media and the Polygamy Narrative

> I just fell in love. Then I fell in love again, and I fell in
> love again.
>
> — KODY BROWN, TLC's *Sister Wives*

Americans are fascinated by polygamy, and the media has helped mold our images of those who practice it. Although the public often shows disdain toward plural marriage on television talk shows, in book groups, and in response to sensationalized newspaper headlines, people are drawn to its exoticism. Just as the *Brady Bunch* introduced the concept of divorce and the blended family in the 1970s and *Queer Eye for a Straight Guy* of 2000 created more acceptance of gay professionals at the turn of the twenty-first century, the new polygamy shows, HBO's television drama *Big Love* and TLC's reality program *Sister Wives,* paved the way for a new narrative about fundamentalist Mormonism.

This new narrative has enormous entertainment value. It evokes a dreamlike frontier utopia where men are tough and fatherly and women are feminine, courageous, and motherly. Plenty of children sing around the piano to give the family a *Waltons* flavor. Yet the television narrative also evokes an image of danger, sexual intrigue, abuse, and lawlessness. This dichotomous portrayal is what led 2.74 million viewers to watch the Season 1 finale of TLC's *Sister Wives* in 2010. The sensationalized narrative of polygamous life feeds into headlines about the horrors of the sexually outrageous behaviors of Warren Jeffs or Ron Lafferty, but it overlooks the rather nondescript, boring lives of most members of the AUB and most independent polygamists. In the twenty years I have studied the Allreds, the most benign of the groups, I can recall only a handful of stories in the media about little Pinedale, Montana, where I conducted my first research project, or the larger congregation in the Salt Lake Valley. There were no sex scandals (other than when a sex offender intruded into the Pinesdale community from Alaska), nor was there any swapping of underage brides, as took place in Bountiful, British Columbia, or Colorado City, Arizona. The Pinesdale community has a positive relation-ship with neighboring townships and works with the police on common goals. Pinesdale community members send their children to the same high school that the children of nonfundamentalists attend, and they shop at the same stores and work in the same industries as nonfundamentalists do. Because journalists were bored by Pinesdale, they ignored it, and most Americans have never heard of this particular banal, ordinary polygamous community.

According to sociologist Sarah Whedon (2010), the media purposefully makes a spectacle of polygamy-style sexuality and the potential within it for abuse. Journalists avoid focusing on polygamists' faith or the full complexity of life in the Principle. They use elaborate images of "outsiderness" to sell newspapers and attract readers on the Internet. We respond to these arche-typal threats to our innocence and our monogamous Victorian values; we "gawk in horror at their sexual practices and at the way they treat women and children" (ibid., 2). Ironically, once you live inside polygamy, as I have done, you find that most polygamists are essentially *Puritan* in their marital and sexual modesty. For example, I attended a priesthood meeting with married couples to discuss the proper decorum and behaviors in matters related to sex. I never saw such blushing and nervousness in my life; the discussion was painfully conservative and naïve and, above all, proper.

The American public is especially vulnerable to the "save the children" mentality, and the media often uses this idea to create mass hysteria about plural marriage. For many viewers and readers, the subject of pedophilia can be both disgusting and compelling. According to James Kinkaid, Americans are obsessed with the topic and are quick to shout "sexual abuse!" even where they cannot find it (case in point, the 2008 raid on the community in Eldo-rado, Texas). We are quick to label polygamist behavior as illness or deviance, especially if we don't quite understand it or if we allow a particularly nasty case of abuse within a polygamous family to represent all plural families in our minds. Jon Krakauer's book *Under The Banner of Heaven* focused on sensationalized cases of polygamous life that "fueled the fire of mass hysteria about polygamy" (Whedon 2010, 1). The book recounts one horror after an-other without providing a single glimpse of how *most* polygamists live their day-to-day lives. This type of one-sided profiling engages a large audience of Americans who are drawn to the topics of violence and mayhem, abuse, and the bizarre. It makes the public believe that all polygamy is inherently ugly and abusive and can lead to actions taken against polygamists such as the

1953 raid on Short Creek, the witchhunt for Utah polygamists prior to the 2002 Olympics, and the kidnapping of children from their families in Eldorado in 2008. According to sociologist Ryan Cragun and psychologist Michael Nielsen (2011), the media helped justify the raid in Texas with stories about Warren Jeffs' idiosyncratic abuses, such as him placing a bed in the FLDS temple that was supposedly used for the consummation of marriages to underage girls, according to the testimony of former FLDS witness Rebecca Musser at Jeffs' 2011 trial (Bentley 2011). Yet the media also created an alternative narrative about the injustices of the Texas government, which served the interests of the FLDS in pursuit of their civil rights. This media unreliability serves, on the one hand, to promote anti-polygamy sentiments that inform public policy against polygamy, and, on the other, promotes anti-government, pro-libertarianism policies. Neither serves the interests of most polygamists.

Yet in the last few years a different portrait of polygamy has begun to emerge, due in part to the growth of pro-polygamy weblogs and new television programs such as HBO's *Big Love*. This new image is positive and dynamic and has the potential to alter the way people think about the poly mindset. University of Utah law professor Ed Firmage states that series such as *Big Love* and *Sister Wives* can familiarize an exotic form of marriage and set the stage for the recognition of new legal rights (2006). For example, the pro-polygamy website Principle Voices, which was founded in 2003 by three women who favor polygamy, is quite positive about the poly lifestyle. Founders Anne Wilde and Mary Batchelor represent themselves as deeply committed to their faith and the culture of polygamy, but they are careful to align that position with a commitment to liberal American values of freedom, equality, education, and care for children. Along with the new television shows, these websites promote the normalcy of the day-to-day lives of polygamists. Blogs and television programs on national networks have the potential to spread positive information about polygamy in the United States and around the world so that people can discuss the pros and cons of this lifestyle just as they discuss any other controversial topic.

In their analysis of the social and psychological impact of the media coverage of the 2008 raid on the YFZ ranch in Eldorado, Cragun and Nielson (2011) noted how subtle biases tended to shape the public's view of polygamy. But media coverage has begun to change as journalists have become aware that more evidence of vile conduct is not likely to emerge. Polygamists use the media to present their own framing of events and promote pro-polygamy sentiments. They also use the media as a way to develop new and ever-changing views of themselves. Frantz Fanon ([1952] 1980) wrote about Algerian black men who developed identities from 1950s comics that depicted only white men. Likewise, polygamists who read the news begin to see their world as composed of dark, perverse villains. They see the predominantly evil depiction of themselves on talk shows and subtly adopt the mainstream view of themselves, further promoting isolation and alienation.

Recently, the media has produced a more progressive, sexy depiction of polygamy: charismatic Bill Henrickson of *Big Love,* Joe Darger of *Love Times Three,* and handsome Kody Brown of *Sister Wives* and their vocal, educated plural wives. But anti-polygamists such as anthropologist Stanley Kurtz (2006) believe that sympathetic treatments of polygamy on television will undermine cultural taboos and foster support for pluralist definitions of marriage and family. He points out that the authors of *Big Love* are gay men. This, he says, should indicate to us that the show is trying to destroy traditional family. "At the heart of the show," Kurtz worries, is the claim that "so long as people love each other, family structure doesn't matter" (ibid., 2). Survivors of polygamy abuse such as Vicky Prunty and Carmen Thompson, founders of the anti-polygamy group Tapestry Against Polygamy, agree with Kurtz that the shows do not fully represent the dangers of plural marriage and the threats to children growing up in that environment, which they see as tyrannical.

Which of the multiple viewpoints presented to us in the media about plural marriage should we believe? Is polygamy morally repugnant, or is it a "cool" alternative lifestyle that is admirable for the commitment of those who practice it to their religious ideals? Perhaps Whedon (2010) is right that these dual visions of polygamy represent our own internal battles and obsessions with love, sex, and marriage. As marriage in the United States continues to evolve and diversify in the new millennium, perhaps people are drawn to polygamy's creative nonconformity or, conversely, its return to traditional gender roles. Further, it is possible the responses to the new television shows about polygamy tap into larger anxieties about alternative family life and frustrations/fascinations with youth, sexuality in the twenty-first century, and nonnormative lifestyles. Our fascination with the Polygamous Other as represented in a variety of media venues reflects our own cultural interests in nonconformist individualism and a search for viable alternatives.

We also must recognize that the media generates our interest in polygamy because the practice is on the rise in North America. Mormon fundamentalists have extremely high natural birth rates, and some appeal to potential converts. In addition, the growth within Muslim populations in both the United States and Canada increases the possibility of more plural marriages among both immigrants and converts (Dixon-Spear 2009).

TV Dramas

Two venues that provide positive images of the relative normalcy of life in polygamy are HBO's *Big Love* and TLC's *Sister Wives*. In this section, I analyze whether these two programs truly represent life in Mormon fundamentalism or are just a Hollywood fabrication.

BIG LOVE

HBO's *Big Love* ran from March 2006 to March 2011, was produced by actor Tom Hanks, and was written by Mark Olson and Will Scheffer. The series presents fictional scenarios of members of the AUB, the FLDS, and independent groups. The writers crafted the series to promote the right of polygamists to live their beliefs without persecution. They present the many problems that arise within polygamy, including incest, sexual abuse, and patriarchal exploitation, while at the same time portraying a relatively normal, loving family that is struggling with the daily challenges of work and home life. The program draws connections between discrimination against same-sex marriage and plural marriage, pointing out that the children of polygamous families experience the same stigma and ostracism many children of lesbian or gay parents feel. Both groups of children attempt to conceal the nontraditional lifestyles of their families.

The writers have created an atmosphere that is reminiscent of the loving family life on *The Waltons* or *The Cosby Show*. The message of *Big Love* is that difference in form doesn't mean difference in content; the fictional Henrikson family provides affirmation, stability, and affection for its children. This message resonates with many alternative families today, whether it is a family of one man and three wives or two women and a child or two men and their children. *Big Love* is thus a vehicle for exploring all alternative forms of marriage and a political platform for decriminalizing plural marriage.

Although the series tends to celebrate more sex and mayhem than are appropriate, historians, like Anne Wilde, and ethnographers, like myself and

Phil Kilbride, have responded positively to the series because it introduces polygamy to the mainstream as a viable form of marriage (Lee 2006). Modern polygamy is less about sexual deviance and more about how to manage a rather colorful suburban family in a struggling economy and in the context of active discrimination. As the Henricksons try to balance work, home, family, and religion, they seem like any other family trying to achieve the American Dream. In the series, family members present themselves as orthodox Mormons to avoid arrest and scrutiny. Their cozy little neighborhood of Sandy, Utah, reminds me of Draper or the new developments in Eagle Mountain in Cedar Valley, where so many independents like the Joe Darger family and AUB-style polygamists are now living. And yet, the writers have given Sandy a distinctive orthodox Mormon feel to it, with the wives scurrying to make Jell-o and potato salads, the kids playing the piano and participating in sports, and the bills piling up to be paid at the end of the month. One FLDS woman reported that the series was so true to life that she didn't want to watch it: "It annoyed me and turned me off. I deal with the idiosyncrasies of our lifestyle all day long, every day. Believe you me, I don't want to watch it on the screen when I finally have a moment once in a blue moon to sit and relax with a good movie" (quoted in Sloan 2011, 3).

The Henrickson family includes Bill Henrickson; his wives Barb, Nicki, and Margene; and seven children. They live in the Salt Lake City suburb of Sandy, Utah, not far from the real-life Allred sprawl in Draper and Bluffdale. Sandy is like any western suburb with far too many stores and one of the highest fertility rates in the nation. The air is dry but there are plenty of malls with air conditioning. Parking lots are filled with SUVs and mini-vans (often called "Mormon assault vehicles"). The Henricksons live in three interconnecting houses with unfenced, adjoining backyards, an "open door" policy that allows both children and co-wives to move freely among the homes to share in paying bills, borrow cups of sugar, and collaborate in child care.

Bill Henrickson is an overworked forty-five-year-old polygamist who was raised in rigid patriarchal Juniper Creek,[1] a FLDS-like community ruled by Roman Grant, a patriarch with twenty-seven wives who bears a striking resemblance to Rulon Jeffs, the father of Warren, with a whisper of the megalomania of Ervil LeBaron of Mexico. Bill's history is that of a nonconformist rebel who challenged the prophet's hegemony over young brides and resources and left home as a teenager. Bill hates the backward poverty, child marriage, and secrecy of his youth and seeks to live as an independent, much like real-life Alex Joseph or Brady Williams, who left the larger group to live among mainstream Mormons. Like so many converts to fundamentalism, he enters into polygamy with his wife after twelve years of marriage in order to obtain the "meat of the gospel" because he felt dissatisfied in the mainstream LDS Church's "milk." This sounds like Rulon Allred, who originally sought to discipline polygamists and then returned to fundamentalism, reforming the doctrine and traditions so his group would blend with the Mormon mainstream.

Bill owns a Home Depot–like big box store (Henrickson Home Plus). He is constantly trying to develop branch stores and expand his business ventures into video gaming and casinos. He is on an endless treadmill to try to provide for his ever-growing family and his wives' appetites for material goods. Although the series is sympathetic toward polygamy, it doesn't glamorize Bill's role; he is struggling and frustrated most of the time. He is the one we feel sorry for after watching an episode. His life is like that of many men among the Allred group. The husbands lead lives that are not always to be envied: they are vagabonds, roaming from one home to the next without a space of their own, always being criticized by their wives for not doing enough, never bringing in enough money, never pleasing the wives sexually or emotionally.

Bill's first wife, forty-year-old Barb, was his college sweetheart. She was a member of the LDS Church, in which they raised three kids. For most of the series they pretend to be Mormons while they acquire two more wives, Nicki and Margene. When Barb was stricken with uterine cancer and was unable to have more children, Bill said God wanted them to increase their family by marrying women who were already present in the family circle; Nicki, in her twenties, was Barb's caretaker, and Margene, in her late teens, was the children's babysitter. The four spouses seem to live in a rather *singular* marriage, not in three separate marriages but in a marital community of sorts. Yet each wife has her own unique, dyadic connection to Bill and her own unique personality. Nicki, the second wife, is the patriarch Roman Grant's daughter. She was raised in the Juniper Creek compound and dresses in long skirts or pioneer-type dresses and wears her hair with a bent wave in her bangs and a long braid. She could easily fit in with the Allred and Jessop families; her long blond hair and blue eyes are quite common in those bloodlines. Margene is a convert to the LDS Church, and her mother is either a Catholic or a lapsed Mormon who drinks and gambles.

Barb struggles to fulfill her role as senior wife ("Boss Lady"), with all of its responsibilities for management and mediation, and hold a job as an

elementary teacher and raise two teenagers and an eight-year-old. Her monogamist orthodox LDS family disapproves of her polygamist lifestyle. She is
nominated for Utah's Mother of the Year but is banned from the competition
when it is discovered that she is a polygamist. She is eventually fired when
the school learns of her polygamist lifestyle, much like AUB polygamist Meri
Brown, who lost her job when her family "came out of the closet." Barb is the
one to keep the other wives in line; when Margene flirts with Barb's son, plays
rock music too loudly, or makes too much noise when having an orgasm, Barb
chastises her. Barb also reprimands Nicki for upsetting Bill and spending too
much money. She also has to deal with Bill's emotional needs, as he is most
comfortable dumping his problems in her lap. She resents it when he gives
her orders, especially when he steps on her toes as senior wife. He desperately
wants her to obey him, but she is a modern career woman who stands up for
herself and doesn't obey just for obedience' sake; she questions and challenges
Bill. She hates the corruption of Juniper Creek and how the old men prey on
helpless young girls. When she decides to get her master's degree, she finds
she is juggling far too much.

Like many first wives I met in the course of my research, Barb is the most
powerful wife. She displays both tyranny and compassion yet attempts to
live up to the ideal of the "eternal round," in which each wife is like a spoke
in a wheel, perfectly equal, surrounding the hub, their husband. Polygamist
women who are critical of the show say that Barb may be too powerful; that
it would be more realistic for the husband, who is the priesthood holder, to
set the rules; and that the senior wife's duty is to obey (Lee 2006). However,
during my research, I saw many examples of first wives who ruled the household, especially during prolonged absences of husbands and patriarchs. Nicki
resents Barb's status as the head wife who is always in the public light as the
legal spouse. Nicki can't use Bill's name, she can't accompany him to celebra-
tions, and she can't use his credit cards, since she is the hidden wife. Even
her own car is registered in Barb's name. She has a particularly hard time
picking up the slack when Barb works full time and has a chip on her shoul-
der because she is not Roman's favorite daughter or Bill's favorite wife. Nicki
desperately wants time with her father, but she is just one of fifty children.
She complains to her mother, Roman's first wife, who maintains order and
teaches other women to accept their life as handmaids to their husband's rule.
She is trying to balance her rigid upbringing and her love for her father with
her life in the materialistic suburbs. She succumbs to credit card spending

and gambling, upsetting the stability of the household in the process. Nicki is continually trying to get more "love" time with Bill, but she chastises Margene for enjoying sex too much. She is eventually disowned by her Juniper Creek family for siding with her husband over her father.

Margene, the third wife, always feels trapped in the wrong shoes; I have seen many younger plural wives in this same condition when first entering a family. Margene is accustomed to having fun and getting attention, but now she is dealing with postpartum weight and is trying to learn domestic skills and how to care for children. Although she is young and sexy, she is still the "lesser" wife; she doesn't have her own car or spending privileges. She tries to contribute but can't seem to get anything right. She always feels like she is the last one to know anything; Barb and Nicki are always sharing secrets that exclude her. Furthermore, her own mother flirts with her husband, and her family assumes that every enterprise she engages in is doomed to fail. At one point, she childishly tempts Bill to run away with her and spend more time with her than the other wives. She is unaccustomed to discretion, modesty, and communal living. She also seeks friendships with LDS neighbors, who see her life as a contradiction. Missing her old partying lifestyle, Margene sneaks an occasional cigarette. She also tells her Mormon neighbors that she is a surrogate mother when she conceives a child with Bill. In my opinion, Margene's "Gentile" persona is not at all indicative of fundamentalist converts. Her background is not orthodox Mormon, and she is not a pureblood fundamentalist. She also actively flirts and is immodest. She would never have been selected by a man who was interested in keeping his other wives happy. She is too sexy, too flighty, and has few domestic talents. They would not have tolerated her.

Bill is always contemplating taking a fourth wife (such as Ana, the Russian immigrant), much to the chagrin of Barb, his first wife. Like "Ann," Rod Williams's first wife, Barb was accustomed to having Bill to herself and her children but now must organize her household to accommodate more wives and their children. She uses the management skills and domestic talents she learned in the Relief Society presidency to deal with the challenge. At each step of the way, Barb challenges Bill's authority. The love she feels for her co-wives always brings Barb back into polygamy. If one member leaves the marriage, the bond will be broken for all of them. It is ironic that while most people believe polygamy to be a rigid misogynist, patriarchal system, the center of this polygamous family is a series of ties between the husband and his wives and among the wives. Barb reminds me of Sharon Jessop of Pinesdale, who no longer believes in polygamy but loves her husband, her co-wives, and all their children. She continues to live in the AUB branch in Montana to be with those she loves. Yet, she is also parallel of Jane Blackmore of British Columbia who became a surrogate mother to many of the young wives that formed a parade into her husband's life and bed.

Love for co-wives is balanced and tempered with jealousy among co-wives in almost every episode. Jealousy is often portrayed in very painful, somewhat unrealistic ways. For example, we see scenes where Bill leaves one sexual encounter with Margene to experience another encounter that same day with Nicki. Although the writers erred in this depiction of the schedule—men never sleep with two wives in one night—we are reminded repeatedly that each wife is constantly comparing herself and her relationship with Bill with the other co-wives and their relationship with their husband. Each wife is perpetually criticizing how the others cook and clean and care for children. The wives quarrel about everything. This type of competition among wives reminds me of Michael Comb's wives Debbie, Carlene, and Brenda in Colorado, who are continually comparing their huge mansions and fighting over the Honeycomb legacy. It is also seen in monogamous stepfamilies when an ex-wife criticizes her ex-husband's new wife, who is the stepmother to her children. Yet *Big Love*'s emphasis on competitiveness over homes, swimming pools, cars, household goods, and the right to be in the husband's bed is a bit unrealistic. Most polygamist wives are not that sexually obsessed with their husband. They are taught to realize that their husband is not to be owned. And the material competitiveness and emotional backstabbing by the wives is not as common as it is portrayed in *Big Love*. Women have to work together to survive, and they realize very early in the marriage that if they intentionally wound their co-wife, family life will be disrupted because there will come a time when a woman's survival rests in her co-wife's hands. However, the *Big Love* wives always make up in the end.

Bill's three wives provide an interesting window into the stages of marriage. The young Margene still has a youthful passion for her husband, which annoys her sister-wives, and she has trouble balancing motherhood and household management. Nicki represents the "seven-year-itch" phase of marriage, when the passion is gone and the drudgery of raising young children and balancing checkbooks prevails. She is the cunning and manipulative wife who is perpetually dissatisfied with her husband, her place in the family, and the lack of financial resources. She acts out through compulsive shopping and gambling. Barb plays the role of the mature older sister/teacher. She is the backbone, keeping the household system intact in the face of numerous threats.

Bill always seems harried, and he consumes large quantities of Viagra to keep up with his wives' voracious sexual appetites. His is a cautionary tale that men should think twice before entering into polygamy, since that way of life is stressful and requires an extraordinary amount of juggling to keep up with the responsibilities of work, fatherhood, and being a husband. Bill somehow meets the emotional, spiritual, social, and financial needs of his three wives and seven children, yet he often appears worried and overwhelmed and seeks refuge from the house in his plush office. Bill's situation of a polygamous man with two or three wives is much more common than the man with fifteen to thirty wives (Winston Blackmore) or even thirty to forty wives (Warren Jeffs). Such mega-families typically produce a setting where women have less power than the women in the smaller families like Bill Henrickson's. The children in the huge clans are organized by age and rank according to their mother's position in the family, and they rarely spend quality time with their fathers. It is common for men in these mega-families to forget names and birthdays, thereby alienating children who do not happen to be favorites.

We see Bill making love to his wives over and over. This emphasis on sex is typical of HBO, but it does help us see the complexities of trying to maintain three sexual dyads and a full-time job. HBO's indulgence in soft porn may parallel Jim Harmston's view of sex as a duty that goes beyond sex for procreation, but it disturbs some polygamists who say that the show should present more spiritual content (Lee 2006). Bill is always "bumping and grinding" with his wives without discretion or reserve, said one polygamist I interviewed about the show. "Our husbands are not that sex-crazed." In fact, women from Pinesdale said that sex was a minor part of their lives that was reserved for the purpose of bringing spirit children into the world. "Not my favorite part of polygamy," confessed one wife. She said that she was attracted to her elderly husband's priesthood powers, not his sex appeal. The nonstop groping and sexuality in *Big Love* is unrealistic in another sense; in real-life polygamy, the children are virtually everywhere and they are plentiful, so there is very little privacy. Further, many women told me that instead of fighting for the right to have sex with their husband, they fight for a "free" night apart from their husband so they can go to a movie, eat casually, or attend an evening class.

Bill is so stressed and overwhelmed that he experiences erectile dysfunction and is having stress over finances and political confrontations with Juniper Creek. When Bill leaves Nicki one morning, for example, does she wonder if he is as satisfied with her as he is with his new young bride, giggly and vivacious Margene? And yet, when he is with Margene, Bill can't achieve an erection. When Nicki begs him for money to pay off her debt, he calls her selfish. She is manipulative and whiney. She is torn between her loyalties to her husband and his nemesis, her father Roman. She is also offended by "nasty sex" that Bill thinks she'll like because Margene likes it. Many years ago, when Viagra first came out, one AUB member told me that it allowed him to finally satisfy his younger wives and feel potent again. When I mentioned this in a *New York Times* interview, the prophet Owen Allred wrote me a stern letter stating that absolutely none of his members ever used the drug. "We don't need it," he said.

Although the wives on *Big Love* have different styles and upbringings, they seem to somehow pull together in a crisis, and they truly love each other. This became apparent when Barb lost the Mother of the Year contest. This love and support among wives is realistic; it is typical of the many families I've seen and lived with. For example, the love Ann and Emily Williams shared was strengthened during the crisis of a custody battle over their co-wife's children. When Sharon Jessop had her hysterectomy, her two Pinedale co-wives came to her rescue without complaint. This kind of cooperation is depicted on *Big Love*. For example, Barb bails Nicki out of a problem at the superstore when she uses Barb's credit card. She also sides with her when Bill explodes about Nicki's heavy debts and comforts her when she is afraid that Bill will throw her out. The wives are always willing to "trade nights" when there is a crisis. On countless occasions, Barb has been a mother or older sister figure to the other wives, and when she faces a challenge, they come to her rescue. For example, Barb walked away one time when Bill angered her. Margene pleaded with her to return, saying "I don't know if I can be married to Nicki and Bill if I'm not married to you." Another time when Bill was being annoying, Barb and Margene kicked him out of their hotel room. The wives pray and eat together and have a weekly planning session to determine changes to Bill's sleep schedule, discuss budgeting issues, and engage in general troubleshooting. As Barb said, "We are not trapped, we're all here by choice; we've chosen to be a family." This depiction reminds me of the Hammons of Centennial Park, who say that all the wives care deeply about each other. "We have to take each other's feelings and needs and wants into consideration," said one wife (quoted in Phillips and Diaz 2007, 2). The Hammons wives take turns being with their husband, arranging a schedule that works for all. The problem with the show is that it focuses on the struggles of sister-wives, not on their joys and triumphs. The writers don't depict the many advantages of being a polygamist wife, such as sharing and friendship and saving money rather than spending it.

Bill Henrickson provides us with a clear example of the fallibility of the head of the household yet he is still lovable because he is trying so hard to please and succeed in polygamy. He often makes mistakes, however, such as when he made love to Nicki in Margene's bedroom on Margene's day. Co-wives hate that; their routine is set and should not be broken without their permission. He also favors Barb as the senior wife by having an "affair" with her when he is supposed to treat all wives equally. He gives more money to Nicki because she complains so skillfully. Further, his ambitions about franchising the store and entering the gaming industry take up most of his time.[2] His frustration over his failure to live up to his own economic ambitions translates into irritations at home and materialistic competitiveness among the wives and kids. He feels he has to keep juggling to the point of frenzy. He forces the gaming investment onto his wives, saying that "marriage is not a democracy," and he punishes his wives like children by taking away their "nights."

The Henricksons live in constant fear that people will discover their true lifestyle and Bill will lose his job. Neighbors continually try to "fellowship" them and missionaries try to convert them or determine how active in the church they are. They try to have some sense of normalcy by inviting their other polygamous friends, Don and his family, to their house. This reminds me of Bonnie, Brady Williams' wife, who said she had a hard time keeping a job when people found out she was a "polyg." The biggest moment for the television family is when they come out to the world about their plural marriage. This affects neighbors, co-workers, politicians, church-goers, and other fundamentalists. Again the parallel with the Henricksons and any lesbian or gay family that comes out to their heterosexual neighbors. Such families face the same set of concerns: worry about job loss, concern that their children will be ridiculed at school, and concern about the security of their homes.

The continual battle between Bill and the Juniper Creek leadership reminds me of the struggles between Warren Jeff and Dan Barlow over jurisdiction of stewardships and wives in the FLDS group. Eventually, like Bill, Dan

Barlow was ousted from the sect and his property was given to another man. Since the priesthood owns the land; builds many of the homes and structures; and requires that all members consecrate their lives, holdings, and talents to the United Effort, it has a legitimate lien on the future economic assets of its members. I found it interesting that Bill, a fundamentalist, is running a big business but no one knows he's a polygamist. Many real-life fundamentalists are businessmen in Utah, Idaho, Montana, and Oregon. Unbeknown to many people, they own construction companies, fireworks companies, and vending-machine companies. The FLDS leaders came to Eldorado as businessmen seeking to build a "hunting resort." Polygamists work in government, schools, and sales. They operate gambling resorts, build the Mormon chapels, and supply the government with airplane parts. People have no idea that these workers are fundamentalists, and the polygamists would like to keep it that way. Fundamentalists must lead secretive lives or they will lose their livelihoods, as Bill fears he will in *Big Love*.

The depiction of both Roman and of Juniper Creek, which is modeled on Colorado City, is quite accurate. In Juniper Creek, polygamists exist in an isolated desert compound with very little technology in order to polish the souls and remove them from temptation associated with the modern world. Members of the FLDS and AUB groups often don't trust doctors, who may draw attention to the group. Members of these groups are also known to carry guns to protect themselves and may use the threat of violence or the threat of loss of property to coerce others to conform to the leader's wishes. This kind of coercion is depicted on *Big Love*. For example, to get priesthood votes from Bill's brother Joey, Roman tells him he'll forgive his wife's attempts to kill her father-in-law. If that doesn't persuade him, he'll reassign his wife to another husband, which is in his power to do as prophet. This reminds me of how the AUB council removed Joseph Thompson from power and Warren Jeffs gave the wives of Dan Barlow and his followers to other men. Like the FLDS leadership, the leaders Juniper Creek contract marriages with underage girls. During the first season, Roman married Rhonda, a demanding fifteen-year-old girl who had her eye on a younger man from the compound. Rhonda eventually tries to escape the marriage by running away to Bill's house in the city. This scenario has real-life parallels in the stories of LuAnn and Mary Ann Kingston and Warren Jeff's niece, all of whom left restrictive environments for the mainstream. Rhonda's story is taken from two FLDS teens named Fawn who left because they didn't want to be married to older men. These twins appeared on a television talk show, as Rhonda did on *Big Love*. But these stories obscure the reality that more young men leave fundamentalism than females. For example, hundreds of boys and rogue males were forced to leave the FLDS over several decades. And in the AUB and LeBaron groups from 1985 to 1995, 27–30 percent of the males of the group exited the system by the time they were thirty-five (Bennion 1998). Young men are forced to leave to find work, and some leave because they don't want to enter polygamy. They see how difficult the life has been for their parents, and they don't want to continue it.

Although Mormon fundamentalists try to follow the ideals of the United Order, many groups actually create economic dependence through the demands that members consecrate their property to the group and give tithes regularly. The writers for *Big Love* may have gone overboard, however, in their portrayal of Juniper Creek's poverty. The FLDS group actually has quite a bit of money and its members do not live in abject poverty. It is true that many homes are in the process of construction, so you will see black roofing paper or exposed insulation, just as you do in Pinesdale, Montana. But FLDS members don't have any debt. Some of the homes are much nicer than the ones shown on the television show, and some are larger and include communal rooms for dozens of people. Since there is no debt and because the priesthood brethren pay for the construction of homes, some fundamentalists can afford to drive expensive SUVs or minivans and have luxurious home furnishings.

Big Love viewers learn of the United Effort Brotherhood, or UEB, a fictional version of the United Effort Plan (UEP) of the FLDS. This organization is run by the prophet and his priesthood council, which decides who lives where and who "owns" which wives. The UEB owns a plane, which council members use for business trips to Phoenix. The television version of this financial organization is fairly accurate, although the UEP, a trust worth about $110 million, is currently under government control, not in the hands of the FLDS. The Kingstons have a business trust worth about $150 million and run a gaming business. The Kingstons' ownership of diverse investments and multiple businesses is certainly used as a model for Henrickson's ambitions. Bill and some of the Juniper Creek members are attracted to the big bucks they can make in Wendover. Many of these assets are portrayed on the television show accurately.

Another accuracy is seen in the control the core groups have over men who have left the fold. In *Big Love*, Roman commands Bill to pay some kind of stipend or "tithe," since Bill was raised in the group where his parents and brother Joey still reside. Roman wants 15 percent of anything Bill makes in his business. Bill continues to get sucked into responsibilities at Juniper Creek because of his mother Lois, who is the third wife of his father. His parents are always reminding Bill of his roots: "Remember where you come from and who you are." Lois feels inferior because she is a third wife. When the first wife dies, she vies for top spot, flirting with her husband shamelessly when just a few months before the funeral she had badgered and annoyed him. Being tied to his family means that Bill and his wives must take care of his brother Joey and Joey's wife and their derelict and annoying father, Frank, who pees in the sink, along with other disgusting and erratic behaviors. This scenario of obligation and bondage to the father group is familiar to many independents who have married councilmen's daughters because of their strong ties to their family kingdoms.

When Roman pressures Bill to "pay up," Bill retaliates by setting up a surveillance system. Roman's attempt to control all the assets of his flock is similar to the behavior of Warren Jeffs, Winston Blackmore, Paul Kingston, and Lamoine Jensen, all of whom tend to run a one-man show in their respective groups. Such avarice and greed are also reminiscent of Ervil LeBaron, who claimed he was the mouthpiece of God and collected tithes and offerings for his own purposes. The Juniper Creek priesthood council tries to keep all their activities secret. For example, they cover up an attempted murder by Bill's sister-in-law and try to hide shady business deals. Roman has the power to eradicate whole families, and he excommunicates the entire Green clan.[3] Tension escalates between Roman and Bill to the point where Roman calls on his sons and nephews to put pressure on Bill. Roman also tries to sue Bill for the money he says Bill owes him. Bill is fiercely independent and fights back. This scenario reminds me of Winston Blackmore's refusal to do Warren Jeff's bidding; he eventually split off from the FLDS. It also reminds me of the AUB's surveillance of Rod Williams when he was investigating the Virginia Hill case. On more than one occasion, his life was threatened.

The show also depicts tensions between purebloods. Roman's son Alby would like to kill his father so he can take over the group. In one episode, Alby looks into a hat to see a vision about his future, a practice that is somewhat reminiscent of the "seer stone" Joseph Smith used to translate the Book of Mormon. Believing that he is meant to be the "one mighty and strong," Alby shoots Roman and has his wife Laura sedate him to finish him off.

Laura claims to have had a vision of Alby's ascension to the presidency. This is similar to how Warren Jeffs' wife said that she and Warren had received a "burning of the bosom"—a spiritual witness—about Warren taking over the leadership from his father, Rulon. (Interestingly, real-life polygamist Dan Barlow has said that he feels that Warren had something to do with his father's death.) On *Big Love*, when Roman recovers, Alby engineers his arrest for transporting women across state lines for sex. This storyline is accurate; for fifty years, the FDLS has transported underage girls from Colorado City to Bountiful, British Columbia. Further, emphasis on pureblood rule is depicted when one FLDS patriarch attempts to do genetic modification surgery, reminiscent of Elden Kingston's purification process, mentioned in Chapter 1.

This situation of wanting to be progressive and independent but also dealing with patriarchal ties to strict groups is a common paradox among independents. Bill exemplifies this conflict in the television series. On the one hand, he has been trained to dominate the household. On the other hand, he sees himself as a progressive, sensitive man who has escaped the cycle of tyranny between fathers and sons and between the prophet and group members. Barb knows this and won't tolerate his attempts to dominate her. Like many polygamous men, Bill sometimes forgets that the wives are not only married to their husband but also to each other. Bill attempts to pit one wife against another generally fail. He also sometimes forgets wedding anniversaries and scheduled nights with a particular wife, and he flirts with other women. In the independent sect in Centennial Park, Arizona, this behavior would not be tolerated. In addition, advocates of polygamy such as Anne Wilde and Mary Batchelor say that Bill's character is often weak. He mismanages his home life and his work and has not provided consistent leadership for his wives and children (Lee 2006).

The children's issues on *Big Love* are interesting and fairly representative. Sarah, Bill and Barb's daughter, is forced to lie to her friends and say that her father is married to only one wife. This rings true; I have seen children from independent families pretend they are not from a polygamist family because of the fear that their classmates will stigmatize them. On the television program, the fictional Sarah also has to deal with the "inactive" status of her family. This idea of "inactivity" is found throughout Mormondom. If you aren't active, you often are judged harshly. There is a desperate need by others to label your degree of membership, as depicted by a license plate I once saw that read "IM1RU2," meaning "I'm a member, are you one too?"

Sarah deals with the conflict between fundamentalism and orthodoxy by befriending an exuberant young Mormon girl whose father is a state trooper. She makes the mistake of bringing her home when all three wives are visiting. She hates the "hiding" part of their lifestyle. She rebels by falling in love with an older ex-Mormon boy who is now unaffiliated with fundamentalism. She gives up her virginity to him in defiance of her family's ways. This is where *Big Love* strays from the truth about young women. According to Quinn (1993), fundamentalist girls are prepared for the polygamist lifestyle and embrace it; they do not imagine any other kind of lifestyle. Media commentators consider this to be "brainwashing" but isn't any socialization behavioral conditioning? Why is this brainwashing and the way a monogamist family raises their child simply "child rearing"?

My research depicts the ease with which young women enter the Principle. For boys, the path is often more difficult. Yet *Big Love* suggests that young men will have an easier time adopting the Principle. Ben, the eldest son, who is dealing with his burgeoning sexuality, experiments sexually with a girlfriend who he realizes will never adopt polygamy. There is also sexual tension and horseplay between Ben and his father's young wife, Margene. He feels alienated and intimidated by the fact that he may never live up to his father's expectations that he will become a priesthood holder, a patriarch, and a polygamist. These anxieties accurately portray the coming-of-age experience of some fundamentalist males. Several young men left the AUB group because they could not meet the group's expectations that they would follow in their fathers' footsteps by marrying and supporting three or four wives. Both Sarah and Ben face the limits polygamy puts on them. Ben cannot enter the Naval Academy, and both are called "polyggy" by friends at school. Eventually, Ben considers adopting his father's lifestyle and begins dating twin girls from Juniper Creek. Since Ben is the eldest son, it makes sense for him to take on the "mantle" of priesthood authority.

An incongruous feature of the program's portrayal of the family's teenagers, however, is their overt sexuality. Both children are sexually active at seventeen or eighteen, which in polygamy is unheard of unless you are a teen bride. For example, in Centennial Park teen dating is not allowed and chastity is strictly enforced. Teenagers speak out against losing virginity before marriage because to have pre-marital sex is a sin next to murder. Very few youths kiss, much less make love to, a member of the opposite sex. Yet on *Big Love*, both Ben and Sarah explore their sexuality and try to imagine what kind of marriages they will build for themselves. Both clearly feel ambivalent about the family life their parents have chosen for them, and both feel ill at ease about the loss of the comfort and stability of the LDS community that used to be the foundation of their religious lives. As the show's second season ends, Sarah rejects polygamy, defies her parents openly, and sleeps with her boyfriend. Ben, however, chooses the path his father has taken, embracing the Principle and dating two sisters from Juniper Creek. The choices of both children put their parents in a quandary; they want to keep Sarah in the fold of the family and they want to keep Ben from practicing polygamy.

Seasons 4 and 5 of *Big Love* show how the family is eventually revealed to the world as polygamists and how this realization translates into fear and misunderstandings. Bill assures his wives that they don't need to fear immediate arrest, as they are not abusive to their children or on welfare. They have no underage brides, and the co-wives were not married in a civil ceremony. Yet people treat them with suspicion. The billboard on Bill's store is defaced, their neighbors ridicule them, and a state trooper asks the children if they've experienced abuse. Through all of this, the family continues to present a façade of normality to the outside world. The LDS gets involved, sending out statements to every ward to be wary of polygamists, requiring the family to hire a bodyguard, which further isolates them from their neighbors and further destroys their chances of earning a livelihood. Bill tries to convince other polygamists to join them in "coming out," but eventually Bill, who is a state senator, faces impeachment in the state senate and an LDS Church-sponsored witch-hunt targets Bill personally. Barb begins drinking wine (a taboo!) and Margene announces that she lied about her age when she married Bill, opening him to charges of statutory rape. Bill's interest in public office and "coming out" are similar to how Alex Joseph operated; he became the mayor of Big Water, Utah, and declared that all residents of the town had the freedom to openly pursue any family lifestyle they chose.

In the final season, Barb tells Bill she wants the priesthood, Bill is faced with the possibility of arrest for polygamy, and the family loses the hardware business because of persecution by the LDS Church. In the final episode, Bill dies suddenly when a disgruntled neighbor shoots him in the chest, and Barb is promoted to priesthood leadership of Bill's new church. This ending suggests that polygamy will keep growing and will need to be accommodated in the mainstream and that Mormon women will continue to demand their rights as priesthood bearers.

I applaud *Big Love* and its creative directors. I see the series as mostly accurate in its portrayal and in capturing the flavor of polygamous life in the Intermountain West. I would have liked to have seen a segment how crippling it can be for women to lose a co-wife when their husband divorces a wife. It would also have been nice for the show to depict how lesbianism sometimes arises in the context of poly love, especially during the long-term absences of husbands. But overall, *Big Love* depicted the close-knit world of shared emotions and finances sympathetically and accurately.

SISTER WIVES

Sister Wives is an unscripted American reality television series that began broadcasting on TLC in September 2010. It documents the life of a progressive polygamist family living in Lehi, Utah, comprised of AUB member Kody Brown (42); his wives Meri (thirty-nine), Janelle (forty), Christine (thirty-seven), and Robin Sullivan (thirty-one); and their sixteen children. Kody and his wives agreed to participate with TLC to make the public more aware of polygamy and to fight against discrimination. As Kody, an advertising salesman, said, "There are a lot of families much more like ours than what's being perpetuated in the media. . . . To be transparent makes us more safe to [the American public]. We're hoping that other fundamentalist Mormon polygamists will follow our example" (Episode 1).

Kody and his wives hope that their children will find the openness liberating. Surprisingly, his family even supports gay marriage, as long as it is between consenting adults. Unfortunately, this step toward openness has been publically criticized by Kody's prophet, current AUB leader LaMoine Jenson, who chastised Kody for participating in the show without his blessing.[4] Jenson says that he has twice asked the family to stop filming. Toward the end of Season 1, the Browns had problems with the local police as well, causing them to pack up their twenty-one-member household and move to Nevada. Kody tried to protect himself while in Utah using the same logic Mormon George Reynolds used in 1879 in *Reynolds v. United States*: he is legally married to only one woman and the other marriages are spiritual unions. That logic failed in the context of contemporary Utah Valley politics, where, as one local Lehi resident told me, any blight on the LDS Church could hamper proselytizing efforts and Mitt Romney's run for president in the 2012 election. Local Utahns have criticized the show because it works on the incorrect assumption that polygamy is accepted by the mainstream church, putting the "real"

Mormons in a bad light. In fact, the sentiment against nontraditional plural or gay marriages runs strong in the mainstream Mormon Church, which raised $25 million in support of Proposition 8 in California, which repealed the gay marriage law. The show also disparages the "The Family: A Proclamation to the World," an LDS document that validated monogamous, heterosexual marriage as the norm. The Utah attorney general's office has not ruled out seeking criminal charges against the Browns, but stated they it does not have the resources to go after polygamists who are not suspected of serious crimes such as child abuse or child trafficking. In Utah, bigamy is a third-degree felony with a possible penalty of twenty years' imprisonment. If the Browns were prosecuted and convicted, Kody might serve that sentence, and each of his wives might serve five years.

According to polygamy advocate Anne Wilde, "If it really goes to a court situation, then our people are going to go right back into isolation" (quoted in Telegraph 2011, 1). Over the past ten years, Utah's historically insular polyga-mist community has worked with state agencies to increase understanding of the unique aspects of polygamous culture, Wilde said. As a result, plu-ral families are now less hesitant to seek help and services when they need them. The Brown family's decision to do the reality TV show was in part an extension of that education work. If Utah officials arrest the Browns, all that work will be in vain. In spite of the current investigation against them, the Browns decided to continue filming the program. They hired constitutional law scholar Jonathan Turley a vocal critic of anti-polygamy laws, to prepare a legal defense in the event that charges are filed.

The Brown family has an interesting history. When the show began in 2010, Kody has been married to Meri for twenty years, Janelle for seventeen years, Christine for sixteen years, and Robin for a few months. Kody and Meri have a fourteen-year-old daughter; he and Janelle have six children; he and Christine have six children; and Robin has three from a previous marriage. Meri, Christine, and Robin were raised in polygamist families, but Janelle was raised in the Mormon mainstream. In Utah, the Brown family lived in a ranch-style home with three interconnecting apartments. Kody and Janelle are the breadwinners of the family and Christine is the homemaker. Meri is getting her degree in psychology and had a part-time job in social work, before she was fired.

Prior to the airing of the show, Kody and his family had kept their lifestyle semi-secret; some friends knew but most people were unaware. Then in 2010, their interpersonal struggles and polygamist beliefs were brought to prime time. Viewers were able to see that many of these struggles were common to any monogamous marriage. In Season 1, for example, Meri was distressed about her infertility problems and her daughter's rebellious embracing of goth culture. However, Meri's jealousy and feelings of self-doubt when Kody announced his intentions to marry a fourth wife, the young and beautiful Robin, was an issue that would only occur in a polygamous family. This new relationship created jealousy among the other three wives, but they ultimately accepted her and welcomed her into the family. Another feature of co-wife friendship is how the three co-wives helped Robin prepare for her wedding to *their* husband and their attempts to befriend her.

Kody is very proud of being a polygamist and is proud of his faith. He admits, "I'm a polygamist, but we're not the polygamists you think you know. I have three awesome wives — Meri, Janelle and Christine. I like marriage. And I'm a repeat offender. I have adopted a faith that embraces that lifestyle" (Grossman and Friedman 2010, 1). In spite of this bravado, Kody is often seen as naïve on the show because he needlessly upsets his wives. After sixteen years, like many husbands, he still doesn't understand the emotional limits of his wives. He points out during one episode, for example, that he secretly chose Robin's wedding dress himself, upsetting the other wives, especially Christine. It is a small betrayal, but represents other deeper issues: will Kody treat the wives differently now that he is marrying a young woman? Does he still love the older wives? In an effort to console herself about giving another piece of Kody to a younger, more attractive woman, Christine says, "I'm glad he's getting a trophy wife. He's a great guy. He deserves a cute girl." The first season culminates in the grand wedding of Kody and Robin at the Hidden Meadows gardens (where my own niece recently had her reception). During the ceremony, Meri and Christine present Robin with a Claddagh ring to welcome her into the family. This symbolizes their willingness to bond with Robin and work with her as a true sister wife.

Sister Wives is, of course, much more realistic and representative than *Big Love* in several ways. First, it is distinctly modest and therefore a bit boring to watch. You don't see sex in every scene or even the discussion of it. Second, there is little threat from rival fundamentalist groups, and the neighbors seem to be less threatened by the Brown family than the neighbors were in *Big Love*. Yet both shows illustrate the institutional opposition to the plural lifestyle. In *Big Love,* the LDS Church convinces the legislature to begin targeting polygamous families; likewise, the Utah Valley police are encouraged by the Town of Lehi to pursue the arrest of the Brown family in *Sister Wives*. Both shows depict the jealousy that arises among co-wives who share their husband sexually, economically, and emotionally. The wives seem to go through a series of fissions and fusions in each episode, although they eventually resolve their conflicts by talking them out.

The Brown family have what appears to be a natural honesty and they seem loving and good natured, although they bicker and experience normal upsets. They also seem to love and care for their children in a very Mormon way (families are forever) and try to reconcile any differences each day before they rest their heads on the pillow. Viewers see the small details of the family's everyday life, such as how the women divide the labor and child care and how they settle disputes. We see that at the heart of most polygamist families is a matrifocal structure that relies on the collaboration of all wives to provide a cohesive unit and that the husband is on the periphery of this structure. It also becomes obvious after a few episodes that the bonds between the wives are much stronger than the bonds of the wives with their husband, for whom the wives show an almost casual, second-hand affection. Kody often makes blunders that are difficult for them to forgive, always imposes his own ideas ahead of those of his wives, and always seeks to position himself in front of the camera. When he is not present, the wives seem more natural and relax. The minute Kody brings his ego into a situation, the wives begin to bicker with each other.

Kody, who is familiar with Allred-style polygamy, was anxious to begin building his earthly kingdom. He married two wives in the space of one year and married his third wife three years later. He first met Meri in 1989 and they became fast friends, watching movies and shopping together. They entered the typical Mormon dating scene—ice cream and pizza parlors—and became engaged on Christmas Eve of 1989. They were married the next April when she was nineteen and he was twenty-two. They have a committed, loving relationship, but they have only one child. In Mormon culture that is an anomaly, especially in fundamentalism. Thus, it was a foregone conclusion that a second wife would be brought into the family to increase the progeny. Kody met Janelle the same year he met his first wife. Since she was not raised in fundamentalism, she didn't think she had a chance with Kody, as he was already tied to Meri. She attended Meri and Kody's wedding reception and was friends with both of them. It was natural for her to be at their house from time to time. One year, she set up a tipi on Kody's parent's ranch (she is a fan of Native American culture). When Meri and Kody visited his parents, they ran into Janelle and struck up a valuable conversation about the future; Janelle and Kody were married the next year.

That same year, Christine and Kody met through her sister in the summer after Christine graduated from high school. Since they were both in the Allred Group, it was destined that they would see each other occasionally. Kody and Meri were actually Christine's chaperones at AUB youth camp. Christine was impressed with Kody's personality but thought him too short to marry. Yet during the winter of 1994, Meri and Janelle invited Christine to visit them in Wyoming and out of the blue, *she* proposed to Kody. They courted with the full approval of the other two wives and were married in March of that year. The family then moved from Wyoming to Lehi, Utah.

These courtship stories are typical of the Allred Group. Although the man is often the one to initiate courtship with a new wife, it is not uncommon for wives to initiate friendships and convince their husbands to marry a woman. It is also natural for a younger woman to show interest in an older man and arrange the courtship. This is a far cry from the arranged marriages of underage brides associated with the FLDS and Kingston groups. Kody's fully consensual courtship of and marriage to Robin, a divorcee, is well documented in the series.

The series focuses on how Kody and his wives manage a marriage that is both dyadic and communal; each wife has her own separate apartment in the same home. The wives often talk about the benefits of having sister wives. The arrangement allows Janelle to work long hours outside the home without having to worry about cooking and cleaning; it gives Meri the peace of mind that if anything should happen to her, the two other moms will be there to raise her daughter; and it allows Christine to stay home when she was pregnant and keep house without worrying about the need to generate more family income. "I never wanted to just be married to one man," says Christine, who recently had a baby. She's glad to be Kody's third wife because she never wanted to be alone with a husband and the third wife balances out the tension between the first two. "I always wanted sisterwives," she says. "There's too many things I wanted to do, to be free for" (quoted in Hall 2010, 1).

Sister Wives illustrates how the family deals with normal suburban problems: burning toast, pulling loose teeth, trying to get teenagers to rake the leaves, and so on. It shows how each of the wives has an individual sexual relationship with their husband with a rotation schedule. But the wives warn that he must come to them alone; they aren't into kinky threesomes. The wives elaborate on the arrangement during a confessional on their sectional couch, Kody wedged in the middle, nodding his head and chuckling awkwardly as they discuss sharing his sex life. "We know that that's required in each relationship," Christine says. On the topic of Kody having sex with his other wives, she remarked, "Gosh darn it, they better!" Meri prefers an out-of-sight, out-of-mind approach. "When he's off with somebody else, I just don't think about that part of it," she says. "Why would I want to do that to myself?" (Episode 2, Season 1).

In October 2010, as a result of the legal scrutiny that followed the program's debut, Meri, Kody's first wife, lost her job in the mental health industry even though her employer knew about the polygamist marriage before the show aired. The show had a negative impact on his company as some clients opted to take their business elsewhere because of publicity related to the show. Meri said she understood that her boss was trying to protect the company, but it broke her heart. The family moved to Nevada to pursue new opportunities shortly after Meri was fired. In the spring of 2011, the Kody Brown family appeared on the *Today* show in New York, initiating the next season of their prime time reality show.

Short Films about Polygamy

In the summer of 2010 a ten-minute documentary called *Sisterwife* appeared at the Utah Sundance Film Festival. Written by Booklocker and directed by Orschel, the film features DoriAnn, an FLDS plural wife and mother of twelve, who married her current husband at her younger sister's request. "This film is about honoring my culture, honoring other people's culture, about learning we don't have to be a threat to one another so we can live in a you-and-me world," said DoriAnn in a recent interview (quoted in Sloan 2011, 2).

DoriAnn had been married to a monogamist and divorced before entering polygamy. The film illustrates the ups and downs of a love triangle—two sisters and their husband—and raises many questions about sororal polygamy such as "whether there is more or less jealousy when the co-wives are sisters and whether kin selection plays a role in how one raises someone else's children. DoriAnn was born and raised in Colorado City by alcoholic parents. In the 1980s, she witnessed the deaths of two men. In spite of these hardships, she stuck with the Principle, believing that being a co-wife could teach her the way to reach the highest level of heaven and an opportunity to be an eternal mother (Sloan 2011, 1–2). She married her first husband when she was sixteen, and for many years it was just the two of them and their children. She wanted to enter polygamy, but the woman she wanted her husband to marry decided to join another family. DoriAnn began to get bored in the structure of monogamy; she wanted a co-wife. She was also poor, and she was living in Mexico, away from her family. At thirty-two, after eleven years of marriage and eight children, she divorced her husband and married her sister's husband. She and her sister are struggling with jealousy and insecurity, which is odd since it was her sister who encouraged DoriAnn to marry her husband. In spite of these problems, DoriAnn loves her sister and their husband deeply. She had connected with him as a child, when they lived in the same neighborhood; they are soul mates, she said. The three spouses all lived together for many years, then for the last four years they moved to separate communities. DoriAnn had four more children, and between the three of them they have twenty children. She is saddened by the fact that her children are leaving the Principle; some of them use alcohol and are sexually active. She has joined a few other women in forming a healing arts center to facilitate a place to explore self-expression through painting, dramatic arts, dance, music, learning life skills and more.

Another film production about polygamy is an Egyptian serial entitled *Ailat Al-Hagg Metwalli* that depicts a fifty-year-old man and his three wives. This show illustrates the ongoing struggles among the wives to prevent their husband from courting a fourth wife, who is quite young. Other films include the American drama series *Lone Star,* about a con man on the verge of entering into multiple marriage, which premiered on Fox but was quickly cancelled after two episodes; and *Escape,* with actress Katherine Heigl as Carolyn Jessop, a woman who fled from a polygamist sect. The documentary *Banking on Heaven* by Jon Krakauer (2006) stars the real Carolyn Jessop. The film includes vivid details of the lives of FLDS escapees and examines how welfare funds ($300 million a year) are turned over to Warren Jeffs while wives and children are neglected.

Escapee Narratives

Another medium that portrays the impact of polygamy on woman and children is nonfiction escapee literature. Interestingly, most books of this sort have been written about the abuses associated with the FLDS group, including books by Bistline (2004), Jessop (2007), Wall and Pulitzer (2008), Moore-Emmett (2004), Singular (2008), Western (2007), Hancock (1987), and Krakauer (2006). These books about the FLDS are written predominantly by women who have left the group. By contrast, only three volumes have been published about abusive conditions within the AUB. Two were written by men (Llewellyn 2006; Hales 2006) and one by the daughter of Rulon C. Allred, who left the group and went back to the mainstream LDS Church (Soloman 2004). Two books focused on the LeBaron group: Irene Spencer's account of her life as the second wife of the prophet Verlan LeBaron (2008) and Susan Ray Schmidt's book about her tumultuous marriage to Ervil LeBaron (Schmidt 2006). Two volumes reveal the abuses of independent fundamentalists; one tells about Jim Harmston and his alleged rape of Rachel Strong, who was his stepdaughter (Llewellyn 2006), and the other about the Lafferty brothers, who were convicted of murdering their sister-in-law and her daughter (Krakauer 2004).

The narrative voices in escapee books share one theme: coercion by priesthood leaders of young, vulnerable, teenage girls. For example, in *The Secret Lives of Saints* (2008), Daphne Bramham describes how Warren Blackmore, the former leader of the FLDS branch in British Columbia, "married" and impregnated nearly a dozen teens, some as young as 15. In *God's Brothel* (2004), Moore-Emmett describes Laura Chapman's story. Laura was married against her will and saw girls as young as twelve forced to wed their stepfathers. In *Stolen Innocence* (Wall and Pulitzer 2008), Elissa Wall recounts her struggle against Warren Jeffs, who forced her to marry her first cousin at age fourteen.

Other antipolygamy nonfiction is a book describing Warren Jeffs' "cult of fear," *When Men Become Gods* by Stephen Singular (2008) and Carole Western's *Inside the World of Warren Jeffs* (2007), which focuses on the theme of abuse and financial neglect. According to Bistline, a Colorado City historian and the author of *Colorado City Polygamists* (2004), Warren Jeffs is a dictator who surrounds himself with highly skilled businessmen and vulnerable women who are treated as chattel. Flora Jessop, a former member of the FLDS, agrees with this assessment in *Church of Lies* (2009), which recounts how her father began molesting her after she was baptized at age eight. Flora blamed her reluctance to report the abuse on the "Keep Sweet" mantra of the community. "'Keep Sweet' is the sacred song of the church, preached with relentless passion. . . . It covers a multitude of sins. It means be modest and pure; obey your parents; obey your husband. But to me and thousands of other abused kids, keep sweet meant keep silent as your father is molesting you. Say nothing as your mom or dad beats you with their fists, a belt, a steel pipe" (Jessop 2009, 17).

Melinda Fischer Jeffs is an FLDS woman who doesn't recognize the women depicted in the news and in these popular books. "Most all of what appears in the media, it makes us sound like we're somehow being kept against our will" (quoted in Anderson 2010, 7). Joe Darger, co-author of *Love Times Three* (2011), also challenges negative stereotypes of polygamy. But if this is the case, why have so many women tried to escape from this lifestyle? Is it another brand of hysteria that is sweeping up semi-disgruntled women desperately seeking some excitement in their lives, or are the abuses legitimate and widespread?

Scores of fictional accounts document Mormon life. These include David Ebershoff's (2008) imaginings of the story of Ann Eliza Young, the nineteenth wife of Brigham Young, which is richly woven into a modern-day tale of murder in a southern Utah border town that is very representative of the FLDS group. The book, *19th Wife,* is brave and entertaining but is full of stereotypes and errors about the Mormon culture. For example, Ebershoff's protagonist wore temple garments at the age of fourteen. Temple garments are not worn until one is ordained as an elder and enters the temple for the endowment at nineteen years. I yearn for the day when an ethnographic fiction about polygamy can be written to provide a more meaningful, accurate picture of Mormon language, culture, and history.

Websites

Many Internet sites now provide forums for discussions about polygamy. Topics range from how to stop FBI and state-funded raids on polygamy communities to advice on how to overcome sister wife jealousy. Most social media forums have a similar purpose of welcoming polygamists to join in civil dialog, exchange of ideas, and friendship. Bloggers strive for solidarity with others of the poly lifestyle and desire to increase support for and the advancement of many forms of polygamy/polygyny. Some of the sites are restricted to discussions of Mormon-based polygamy, such as Principle Voices, a site operated by a pro-polygamy group headed by Anne Wilde, Linda Kelsch, Marianne Watson, and Mary Batchelor, who are all from the Salt Lake City area. The site's purpose is to educate people about plural marriage and the fundamental teachings of Joseph Smith. It claims to represent thousands of polygamous families in the West, including those affiliated with the Kingstons, the Allreds (in Utah), the FLDS, and various independents (two of the founders are independents).

Many other Internet sites advocate for greater acceptance of polygamy through political activism and education, such as Mark Henkel's TruthBearer .org site, which provides a cross-national, cross-denominational venue for the modern social movement called Christian Polygamy. The movement, which began in 1994, claims to distance itself from Mormon, Islam, or even liberalized forms of polygamy. Henkel uses a distinctly Christian and biblical conservative argument for his pro-polygamy stance. He argues that polygamy protects women from "unkind, immature, or downright abusive husbands" (Henkel 2011, 1). Henkel also sponsors material on LoveNotForce.com and NationalPolygamyAdvocate.com. He claims to have paved the way for fellow believers to learn about polygamy and help dispel the myth that polygamy is synonymous with Mormonism, abuse, or underage marriage. He, like many other advocates of non-Mormon polygamy, often make the mistake of assuming that all Mormon polygamy is abusive.

Another website of interest is polygamyday.org, sponsored by a nonprofit group that promotes public education and political action with the goal of decriminalizing "freely consenting, adult, non-abusive marriage-committed polygamy" (2011, 1). Similarly, Pro-Polygamy.com is a polygamy-focused resource for the media and other information-gatherers. Timely, relevant reports from the pro-polygamy perspective are archived as news reports with links to other relevant websites. Their most recent agenda is the fight to legalize all forms of plural marriage. Other websites that discuss modern-day polygamy issues are Anti-polygamy.org, BiblicalPolygamy.com, ChristianPolygamy.info, and the site that provides resources so women can escape Mormon fundamentalism, Tapestry Against Polygamy, directed by Vicky Prunty.

One typical site that provides conversation about interpersonal issues in plural marriage is sisterwives.yuku.com, where there is a story of a man and his two wives who have adopted the true "poly mindset." Written by two sister wives, this site explains how the poly life is severely marginalized in America and gives advice on how to overcome co-wife jealousy. Here is a sample of one plural wife's struggle:

> Neither Antony, Jadez, nor I were prepared for what laid ahead of us when we fell in love and became poly. No one wrote about these things. We never had any warning. We were young and maybe even na-ive because we believed that others would be happy for us because we loved one another and this made us happy. Quite the contrary though, people wanted us to live our lives according to their beliefs and their ideals. We did not fit their mold, so they made us their enemies. They were out to get us and to make our lives miserable through rejection, isolation, humiliation, punishment, threats, familial control, gossip, slander, and evil deeds which influenced the lives of our children and our family. ("Steady" 2010)

Contributors to this website focus on the complexity and richness of sister wife relationships. They write that the poly mindset "remains vital in order to maintain these relationships and to help them to grow. Every individual person in a poly relationship needs to always care about all the other relationships within their family unit. Otherwise, one failing relationship can poison the whole" (ibid.).

The site also provides a list of cures for jealousy: It advises co-wives to stop, understand their feelings of fear and anger, learn to control their envy, and looking at what does not belong to them. It suggests that co-wives communicate their feelings by writing in a journal and then talking to the people they are afraid of losing or are angry with. It advises them to open up a dialogue using "I feel" statements rather than blaming statements. It also suggests the co-wives analyze their feelings of jealousy closely. Are they afraid that their husband has better communication with a sister wife? If so, then it is the co-wife's desire to have good communication with him also. If a co-wife is jealous that her sister wife has more money or nicer things than she does, she may need financial security or independence. Knowing this can help the co-wife take positive action to maintain relationships without negative emotion influencing her actions. The site also encourages co-wives to change any false beliefs that causes them to be jealous, such as, "Every female is out to get my husband" or "If he/she leaves me, I won't be able to survive" (ibid.).

Another contributor to the site MyDaily.com—whose co-wife was her sister—said that there was fierce jealousy in her marriage (Sloan 2011). She wrote that often the pain would set in when she saw her husband with her co-wife. "You get pulled . . . kind of like little kids in the sandbox, where someone has the toy that everyone wants" (p. 3). Sharing a man sexually is one of the greatest obstacles. "I have yet to meet one human who is thrilled to share a sexual partner (and I imagine there are a rare few), in this imperfect world with our imperfect bodies."

Another poly-friendly website is polygamylovescompany.com, which covers conversations about polygamy events in the news and provides data on day-to-day life within Mormon fundamentalism. Similarly, polygamy.now, written by Martin and his two wives, Karen and Lisa (last names are not provided), describes the day-to-day events in one poly family. Martin and Karen, his first wife, met at a dance convention in Palm Springs in 1995. They were both interested in dancing, biology, and building houses. They became dance partners and started competing together, winning championships in California and Washington in various dance styles. Karen joined Martin in Seattle, Washington, in 1998, where they built their dream home together. They met Lisa in 2002, when she moved into the neighborhood with her two sons. Lisa became a frequent visitor to Martin and Karen's home, where she played duets with Martin and learned to dance from Karen. The three started going out together. A year later, Martin and Karen added a wing to their home for Lisa and her sons and Lisa became Karen's sister-wife. Karen announced the relationship to the community at a general meeting in 2003; the state of Washington does not discriminate against polygamists. Lisa recalls her first marriage, to a man who cheated on her while she was sick and could have used the help of a second wife. If her first marriage had been an open polygamous marriage, it might have worked. Instead, the infidelity led to divorce. Now she's in an open plural marriage that works for all concerned. Theirs is a symbiotic relationship with honesty and open communication. As Lisa describes: "I like that I can support Karen in the things she loves to do. She likes to work outside in the yard for several hours at a time, and Martin likes to have someone nearby and not feel left by himself. So I can fulfill this need for the both of them, by being with Martin when Karen likes to work outside. Also Karen likes to take trips to see her daughter out of state frequently. I can stay at home with Martin so he doesn't feel left behind" (Lisa, Martin, and Karen 2010, 1).

Polygamy.com, another advocacy website, provides a wide range of articles and discourse on issues related to worldwide polygamy and polyamory. Although there is a section on Mormon fundamentalism, most of the resources are about Muslim, Jewish, and non-Mormon Christian polygamy in a variety of international contexts and all over the United States. The site is open to discussions about bisexuality in polygamy, which supports my theory that plural marriage fosters clandestine lesbianism. In fact, one contributor is encouraging bisexuality within her polygamous marriage. She writes that she wasn't happy in her one-male, two-female triad until she became intimate with her co-wife. This made the marriage more equal, she said.

There is also a "personals" website for women seeking to become a part of a polygamous family. This site, 2Wives.com, is a secular forum for "good people" who want to share a husband with another woman. Sisterwives.yuku.com also offers advice for the modern poly person about polyamory, polygamy, polygyny, polyandry, and other poly combinations.

The media has the power to generate support for the poly cause, as many websites, television series, and talk shows do, or encourage hatred and anger toward polygamists with hostile news articles, nonfiction accounts of abuse and exploitation, and anti-polygamy websites. A new narrative of plural living is emerging that emphasizes the right of poly families to live freely and openly. This narrative has the potential to generate support for legislation that will decriminalize polygamy and other nonnormative forms of marriage in the United States and Canada.

6

Polygamy and the Law

> Let it be published to the four corners of the earth that
> in this land of liberty, the most blessed and glorious upon
> which the sun shines, the law is swiftly invoked to pun-
> ish religion, but justice goes limping and blindfolded in
> pursuit of crime.
>
> —GEORGE Q. CANNON (1879)

This chapter examines polygamy legislation in North America over 150 years. It covers major legal action about plural marriage in the United States and Canada from 1856, when the U.S. Republican Party initiated legal sanctions against polygamy, to the current trial in British Columbia to determine whether Canada will lift its ban on polygamy. The chapter addresses the question of how fundamentalists who practice plural marriage deserve to be treated by the law and highlights a handful of recent "true crime" stories involving poly lifestyles, including the 1988 Singer/Swappe shootout in Marion, Utah, and the 2008 lawsuit against the Allred Group for money laundering. The chapter discusses petitions by polygamists for greater liberties, such as the right to marry, the right to adopt, and the right to purchase real estate; and cases where polygamists have been prosecuted for child abuse, violence, illegal possession of arms, and kidnapping. The final section analyzes the pros and cons of three legal options for dealing with polygamy in North America.

Relevance of the Law

A growing number of social scientists and lawyers have begun to explore the issue of polygamy and the law (Song 2010; Driggs 2011; Smith 2011; Stacey and Meadow 2009; Bailey 2007; Strassberg 2010; Turley 2004; Duncan 2008; and Davis 2010). My interest stems from a desire to remove the stigma of polygamy and provide greater rights for poly families. Yet unlike my great-great uncle, George Q. Cannon, who fought to live his faith in its "fullness" and "to exclude from the land prostitution, bastardy and infanticide" (Cannon 1879, 2), I do not believe in faith-based polygamy, nor am I overly fond of patriarchy.[1] I fight for the right of polygamists to practice religion free from government intrusion for the same reason I fight to remove legal obstacles for lesbigay relationships and other marginalized forms of marriage. Like other nonnormative women, I want to live in a land where everyone can freely choose who they marry without harassment by the media, public discrimination, or scrutiny from law enforcement. Though I would not choose this form for myself or my daughters, I will fight for the right of individuals to choose plural marriage without fear of arrest or persecution.

In North America, judicial and legislative systems are archaic. According to University of Michigan sociologist Arland Thornton (2011), the perception of polygamy as backward and uncivilized plays a role in promoting traditional family forms and the use of legal tactics to discriminate against poly communities. U.S. family law still favors heterosexual monogamous marriage, as seen in the flurry of recent actions to protect traditional marriage: the Defense of Marriage Act, the Healthy Marriages Initiative, and a proposed Federal Marriage Amendment to the Constitution. This legislation does not serve the needs of a growing, dynamic populace. The United States seeks to impose monolithic, normative values on all families, regardless of the cultural, economic, or psychological context. U.S. law resists supporting family forms beyond the ideal model of marriage from the 1950s and withholds legal protection from the majority of American families. Americans are simply too diverse in how they express their sexuality and form marriages to be limited to one type marriage that is now archaic. Alternative forms of marriage are becoming more prevalent, partially because of the pressures of an evolving socioeconomic environment and a growing cultural tolerance for difference (U.S. Census 2006, 2010).[2] In addition to lesbian or gay marriage,[3] single parenthood, or the blended family or stepfamily, polygamy should be viewed in its appropriate, fully modern cultural landscape. Scholars must begin to see polygamy with its various conundrums and attributes as the new intellectual challenge of our day.

As proof of how marriage is evolving in the United States, the Supreme Court struck down a Texas law that criminalized sodomy in 2003 (*Lawrence v. Texas,* 539 U.S. 558),[4] ending the possibility that male homosexuals in that state could be arrested for their sexual behavior.[5] This ruling and the Massachusetts decision legalizing gay marriage that preceded it (*Goodridge v. Department of Public Health,* 798 N.E.2d 941, 2003) supported the general movement toward more openness to alternative marital arrangements, including polygamy. Always a step ahead of the United States, Canada decriminalized homosexuality in 1969, legalized lesbian and gay marriage in 2005, and commissioned a study in 2006 to investigate whether to decriminalize polygamy (Campbell et al. 2005).

Yet legal policy on polygamy in the United States is often fractious, cumbersome, and contradictory. From the outset, at least for white male Europeans, America has recognized the rights of individuals as long as they did not interfere with the legal system. Since polygamists are in violation of the law of the land, law enforcement agencies and the courts are torn between the need to intervene, protect, and prosecute and the need to preserve the rights of citizens to act freely on their beliefs. This legal dance between the rights of polygamists and the rights of the larger society is confusing. Some years polygamy is the enemy and must be eradicated; other years, it is honored as a religious right and is ignored. What has guided polygamy legislation over the past 150 years? Further, what are the financial, legal, and ethical consequences of recognizing the marriage of one man to several women for individuals and for the broader society?

History of Polygamy and the Law in North America

NINETEENTH-CENTURY LEGISLATION

In 1852, Brigham Young revealed the practice of plural marriage as a Mormon doctrine. He established an impressive nation-state along Utah's Wasatch Range within the first decade of his arrival in Emigration Canyon. Young was free to marry his twenty-three wives without any retribution from the federal government because there was no federal law that banned polygamy in the territories. Polygamous suffragists in Utah claimed that "polygamy was the only reliable antidote for prostitution" (Davis 2010, 1974). Many Mormon women felt that monogamy was associated with many societal ills and that polygamy would prevent an increase in fallen women, mistresses, and prostitutes and the need for sexual outlets for men outside marriage (Gordon 2001).

This freedom ended in 1856, when the Republican Party condemned the "twin relics of barbarism" (polygamy and slavery) and began taking action to ban the practice nationally. Yet since the territory of Utah didn't register plural marriages, the Republicans couldn't enforce the law and new plural marriages continued to be performed. According to Gordon (2001), Mormons tried to use local sovereignty as their argument for polygamy, while opponents of Mormonism justified efforts to use the authority of the federal government to outlaw polygamy on the basis of "common morality." To Mormons, polygamy was their moral and legal right.

In 1862, the federal government outlawed polygamy in the territories with the passage of the Morrill Anti-Bigamy Act. Yet, Mormons, who were the majority residents of the territory, ignored the Act and enjoyed their freedom to practice polygamy based on their religious beliefs. Mormons held all the political power in the territory and had increased the number of voters by granting women the vote. For example, when my ancestor Angus Cannon cast his vote in federal elections, his six wives voted as he did.[6] Multiply this scenario by the thousands of polygamists in the territories and you have a significant, even formidable voting force. The federal government sought to diminish this voting power by seeking to outlaw polygamy, using the promise of statehood as bait. In 1874, Congress passed the Poland Act, which transferred the battle about polygamy from the territory of Utah to the federal arena and in 1879, in *Reynolds v. United States,* the Supreme Court upheld the bigamy conviction of George Reynolds.

Reynolds was the first polygamy case to reach the U.S. Supreme Court. George Reynolds, Brigham Young's private secretary, was convicted of polygamy under the Morrill Anti-Bigamy Act and was sentenced to two years' hard labor. In his appeal, Reynolds claimed that if he ignored his religious duty to marry his second wife he would be eternally damned. The courts denied his appeal, stating that the First Amendment pertaining to religious freedom did not override anti-bigamy laws. Chief Justice Morrison Remick Waite, a founder of the Republican Party, said of the case: "To permit this would make the professed doctrines of religious belief superior to the law of the land, and in effect to permit every citizen to become a law unto himself. . . . government could exist only in name under such circumstances" (quoted in House 1998, 2).

Yet the practice of polygamy continued despite prosecutions and incarcerations. No law official could accurately discern who was married to whom. Because plural marriages were not registered, they did not legally exist. However, in 1887, the Edmunds-Tucker Act made polygamy a felony offense, and scores of polygamists, including my ancestor, Angus Cannon, were put in jail (we have a picture of him in his black-and-white striped outfit in the Sugarhouse Jail). This law criminalized unlawful cohabitation and denied polygamists the right to vote and to hold office, essentially killing two birds with one stone: most polygamists were the "alpha males" who held positions in the church and in public office as legislators, mayors, and magistrates.

The final blow came that same year, when Congress dissolved the corporation of the Mormon Church and confiscated most of its property. Within two years, the government also denied the church's right to be a protected religious body. This policy created a large group of single and impoverished mothers, as polygamous women who were no longer tied to their husbands religiously or economically. As a result of these actions in 1887, the LDS Church renounced the practice of polygamy in 1890 with church president Wilford Woodruff's manifesto. Utah was admitted into the Union in 1896. As a condition of statehood, Utah was required to write into its constitution that polygamy is forever outlawed. It is unclear whether Utah could remove this provision from the state constitution (Smith 2011).

When the U.S. government began its assault on polygamy in 1887, a small community of members in the Mormon Church fled to Canada. They sought permission from Parliament in 1888 to bring their plural wives with them. (These members later became affiliated with the FLDS after polygamy was banned in the United States.) The Canadian government officially denied polygamists this right and in 1890 passed its first legislation against plural marriage. The law sought to convict Mormons "on the basis of cohabitation, attacking the Mormons' private ceremonies" (Macintosh, Herbst, and Dickson 2009, 7). Incidentally, only two polygamy convictions have taken place in the Canada since 1890; one was a case in 1899 involving a native man in the Northwest Territories named Bear's Shin Bone. Shin Bone's case was not excluded from the Criminal Code and he was jailed, in part due to broad tribal marriage norms and in part due to missionary efforts to civilize and convert aboriginals to Christianity.[7] And in 1906 John Harris was convicted of polygamy after he cohabited with a married woman whom he believed to be divorced.

The nineteenth-century bans on polygamy by the governments of Canada and the United States were intended to check the power of the Mormon Church (Song 2010). Canadian law was passed under pressure from the U.S. Congress, which argued that polygamy violated Christian and American public morals and subordinated women. Yet the Victorian norm of monogamous marriage also has been shown to subordinate women. Suffragist Elizabeth Cady Stanton listed three types of sexual behavior that she considered to be equally problematic: Mormon polygamy, bigamy based on fraud, and polygamy involving one wife and many mistresses, which she said was "everywhere practiced in the United States" (ibid., 154). The complaint of Congress that polygamy was too patriarchal and therefore undemocratic was fueled by the contempt members had for the Mormon Church rather than a concern for vulnerable females. According to Berkeley scholar Sarah Song (2010), the outrage about dangers to the moral character of the United States and concerns about prostitution, divorce, lax morality, and sexual perversion were really an outcry against the fact that women in Utah had been given the vote. Women's voting rights, which Mormon polygamous women strongly supported, created two problems for most congressmen: 1) it threatened the principle in common law that a woman's identity was subsumed by that of her husband upon marriage; and 2) it created more voting power for the Mormon Church, which was seen as a political and military threat to the Union.

In supporting heterosexual, monogamous marriage, Congress presented a softer image of patriarchy; it portrayed polygamy as a deviance from marriages formed with mutual love and consent. Polygamist wives such as Martha Hughes Cannon, Zina Young Williams, and Emmeline Wells were portrayed as the innocent victims of lustful, undisciplined male supremacists, when in reality most polygamist women were very outspoken and had active careers in medicine, law, and government. The criticism that linked polygamy with divorce and women's suffrage clearly revealed the anxieties of mainstream men; both of which are related to an *increase* in women's status. Anti-polygamists went so far as to try to racialize polygamy, referring to the practice in Africa and Asia (including Turkish harems) as "on par with human sacrifice, barbaric, and uncivilized" (Song 2007, 148). In short, the dominant culture's rejection of polygamy was about controlling and restricting the political power of the church while reaffirming the "true" American family form: monogamy. Congress thus protected their own brand of patriarchy by shielding America from polygamy.

Song has suggested that Mormon polygamists are an oppressed minority and that their arguments in favor of plural marriage are a demand for accommodation. Yet as in the nineteenth century, advocates of traditional marriage are asking for federal intervention to dismantle this deeply patriarchal practice. It is a test of how a liberal democracy deals with a right-wing, essentially nondemocratic, enclave. Perhaps nineteenth-century women's rights activist Elizabeth Cady Stanton's viewpoint can offer us a feminist perspective on our twenty-first-century attempts to decriminalize polygamy once and for all: "We offer a simple, loving, sisterly clasp of hands in order to help abolish the whole system of women's subjection to man in both polygamy and monogamy" (quoted in Song 2007, 154).

TWENTIETH-CENTURY LEGISLATION

At the beginning of the twentieth century, the legal status of polygamy in Utah was still not clear. In 1904, the U.S. Senate held a series of hearings after LDS apostle Reed Smoot was elected as a senator from Utah. The controversy centered on whether or not the LDS church secretly supported plural marriage. In 1905, the LDS issued a second manifesto that confirmed the church's renunciation of the practice, which helped Smoot keep his senate seat. Yet, the hearings continued until 1907, the Senate majority still interested in punishing Smoot for his association with the Mormon Church. By 1910, Mormon leadership began excommunicating those who formed new polygamous alliances, targeting underground plural movements. From 1929 to 1933, Mormon fundamentalist leadership refused to stop practicing polygamy and were subject to arrest and disenfranchisement. In 1935, the Utah legislature elevated the crime of unlawful cohabitation from a misdemeanor to a felony. That same year, Utah and Arizona law enforcement raided Short Creek after allegations of polygamy and sex trafficking. U.S. Supreme Court Justice William O. Douglas saw polygamy as debauchery, but Justice Frank Murphy saw it as one of the basic forms of marriage, not sexual enslavement.

Although U.S. legal judgments are not binding on courts in Canada, the influence of U.S. law has led to changes in marital policy in Canada.[8] The last prosecution in Canada for polygamy occurred in 1937 (*R v. Tolhurst; R v. Wright*). This case involved a couple who were married to other parties while cohabiting with each other; the two were acquitted later that year. In 1944, fifteen Utah fundamentalist men and nine of their wives were arrested on charges of bigamy and jailed in Sugarhouse, Salt Lake City. Then in 1953, officials raided Short Creek and took 263 children away from their parents in Arizona and Utah.[9] Two years later the Utah Supreme Court held in *Utah v. Black* that the Black polygamous family was an immoral environment for rearing children because of the parents' practice and advocacy of plural marriage, and it upheld the decision of the Juvenile Court to remove their children. After this ruling, the mother promised to give up polygamy and got her children back, but she went back into polygamy after that.

After the 1953 raid on Short Creek, most polygamists went underground or fled to Mexico or Canada. However, many stayed in the United States and sought to practice their religious beliefs in the open. For the most part, the police did not enforce the anti-polygamy law.[10] Although state courts occasionally convict individuals of polygamy, in the last fifty years, government officials have more often focused on individual crimes by polygamists, such as child abuse, statutory rape, welfare fraud, and incest. The official position of the Utah Attorney General's office was not to pursue cases of bigamy between consenting adults. A spokesperson for the office said, "We want to use our resources wisely" (quoted in Dobner 2010). Utah also sought to reduce the bigamy charge from a felony to misdemeanor, as in Montana, to encourage people to provide information on abuse in secretive families. This relative tolerance is exemplified by the 1991 Fischer adoption case (*In the Matter of the Adoption of W. A. T., et al.*), where the Utah Supreme Court ruled that a polygamous Hildale family could adopt children, essentially reversing *Utah v. Black.*

When Republican Mike Leavitt, who was a member of a "pioneer" Mormon family, was elected governor in 1992, he initially stated that Utah might overturn the *Reynolds* decision. Yet he and other faithful members of the orthodox Mormon Church felt torn about polygamy. On the one hand, they knew that polygamy was once a cornerstone of LDS faith and was responsible for huge numbers of offspring for the Church. On the other hand, as conservative Republicans, they believed in the sacredness of the traditional monogamous bond and condemned polygamy as heresy.[11] In the early 1990s, Leavitt amended his earlier position of tolerance and stated that polygamy was actually a crime or a sin. LDS apostle Gordon B. Hinckley recommended the wholesale purging of undesirables from Mormon membership, especially polygamists and their sympathizers (or researchers, as was my case). He appeared on *Larry King Live* and said that polygamy was not a part of Mormonism. The "purges of the 1990s" sent a message that the LDS Church would have zero tolerance for nonnormative behaviors throughout the political and religious constituency. The LDS First Presidency passed out documents to all the stakes and wards of Zion entitled "Is Your Church Membership in Danger?" and "Profile of Splinter Group Members or Others with Troublesome Ideologies." These documents listed behaviors of deviants for Mormons to watch for: home schooling of children, a preoccupation with the end of the world, membership in the John Birch society,[12] being unemployed, and meeting in clandestine groups to study the "mysteries." The list also warned against listening to tapes by government conspiracy theorist, Bo Gritz, being preoccupied with food storage, adopting government conspiracy theories, reading books by Avraham Gileadi,[13] receiving state welfare, and, of course, practicing plural marriage (First Presidency 1990a, 1990b).

TWENTY-FIRST-CENTURY LEGISLATION

As a new millennium approached there was a sudden increase in fundamentalism and apocalyptic teachings. I remember several of my AUB informants insisting that the entire Salt Lake Valley would be flooded on January 1, 2000, and that I should make preparations by stocking up on food and other survival supplies. The paranoid murmur of Armageddon was heard in various cottage meetings and town halls throughout the Intermountain West (Bennion 2008). It became essential for fundamentalists and law enforcement to reach a new cultural understanding. A coalition was formed between polygamous leaders in Arizona and Utah and the attorney general's offices in both states that produced an agreement: law enforcement promised not to raid or arrest polygamists unless laws beyond polygamy were violated, particularly laws about child abuse. Utah law enforcement realized that when it comes to investigating and intervening, it is best when both sides speak a common language. Yet this soft truce was broken during preparations for the 2002 Olympics when state officials tried to sweep the "embarrassment" of polygamy under the carpet (interestingly, they also scooped up the homeless, marijauna-smoking members of drumming circles, and Hells Angels from Pioneer Park and sent them, in air-conditioned buses, to Portland, Oregon). As a result of this cleansing process, the Utah Supreme Court issued three opinions about Utah's bigamy statute that criminalized the religiously motivated practice of plural marriage. In all three cases, the court upheld the bigamy law. In 2004, in *State v. Green,* the state Supreme Court upheld the conviction of a rather benign yet outspoken independent polygamist, Tom Green, and declared the bigamy statute constitutional. In 2006, in *In re Steed* (131 P.3d 231), the court upheld the recommendation of Utah's Justice Conduct Commission that a polygamist Justice Court judge from Hildale, Walter K. Steed, should be removed from the bench. That same year, in *Utah v. Holm,* the court again upheld Utah's bigamy statute in a case that involved polygamist Rodney Holm, who had been convicted for violating the law for his participation in a 1998 "spiritual marriage" to Ruth Stubbs.

While American courts were upholding bigamy statutes, Canadian policies were embracing increased tolerance for alternative sexuality and marriage. The Canadian Parliament legalized same-sex marriage in 2005. Law professors Angela Campbell, Martha Bailey, Beverly Baines, and six other scholars at the Alberta Civil Liberties Research Centre were commissioned to investigate polygamy and report their findings to Status of Women Canada (Campbell et al. 2005). The group recommended that Canada decriminalize polygamy and change legislation to better regulate the conditions of plural living for the benefit of women and children (Campbell 2005, 25). They argued that a challenge to the ban on polygamy on the basis of human rights violations might be successful and that the ban itself would be found unconstitutional because it infringed directly on religious freedom. The report noted that immigrants could more easily achieve their rights if criminal sanctions against polygamy were removed (Bailey et al. 2005). A challenge on the basis of human rights would likely succeed, they argued, because the antipolygamy statute would be found to violate the guarantee of human rights in the Constitution.

For the United States, however, progress toward changing attitudes and policies about plural marriage was thwarted by the April, 2008, removal of over 400 children from their parents at the FLDS compound in Eldorado, Texas, after an allegation of sexual misconduct. The Texas Supreme Court later declared the raid unjustified because of the absence of evidence that the children faced immediate danger to their physical safety.[14] The next month, the California Supreme Court issued a historic decision in favor of same-sex marriage, but voters overturned it the following year after a campaign by the political right (including the Mormon Church) that was supported with millions of dollars. This ban on gay marriage reaffirmed that only one form of marriage, between two heterosexual people, would be valid in the state of California. This set a precedent that had implications for the legal struggle to overturn laws against polygamy.

Finally, in the fall of 2010, the Chief Justice of the British Columbia Supreme Court began weighing the efficacy of Canada's 121-year ban on polygamy. The Canadian legal system has never had the same appetite for criminalizing sexuality as the U.S. system has, and Canada is considering striking down its polygamy law. This would call into question the continued validity of *Reynolds v. United States* under modern religious freedom laws. It would also bring into question the fairness of liberalizing the legal treatment of nonmarital sex, extramarital sex, divorce, and same-sex relationships while retaining harsh penalties for polygamous marriage.

We have reached a point in the twenty-first century of legally guaranteed sexual autonomy that would have been unthinkable to the anti-polygamists of the nineteenth century (Gordon 2001). Indeed, even the polygamists of that era probably would have been shocked at the extent of liberty people have today. Yet polygamy remains illegal even as people are fighting to legalize gay marriage. The arguments in both cases sound familiar: opponents of alternative marriage insist that heterosexual monogamy is the cornerstone of civilization. Those in favor of expanding the definition of marriage argue that traditional marriage does not accommodate every person's needs or fit appropriately within a progressive view of marriage. In July 2011, Vermont senator Patrick Leahy proposed that the Defense of Marriage Act be replaced with the Respect for Marriage Act, which would creative a more accepting environment for alternative marital structures. This move was in response to President Obama's withdrawal of support for the Defense of Marriage Act in February.

Ethnographic Cases of "True Crime"

This section examines how various polygamous communities discussed in this book have been affected by the legal system with an emphasis on the following questions: How do polygamists feel about the way the law intersects with their lives and how they use it? How does the threat of prosecution shape their behavior? Are women able to manipulate and improve their position by threatening to go the police or the courts or are they, in effect, alienated from the legal process because of their status as polygamists' wives? Do polygamist men have the same rights in the workplace as monogamist men? Can polygamist families buy homes and adopt children even though they are guilty of a third-degree felony? Can polygamists hold public office and participate fully as citizens of the United States?

At least six of these cases intersect with my life as a researcher or as a member of the LDS Church. One involved an immigrant who wanted to bring his plural wife to Canada, one involved illegal possession of arms, another involving money laundering, and others involved child sexual abuse in the Kingston and AUB groups. The most significant case that affected my early fieldwork was the 1990s raid on the Branch Davidians of Waco in February 1993. I was living in a Montana Allred commune with my daughters when I heard the news: four Bureau of Alcohol, Tobacco, and Firearms (BATF) agents and six Davidians had died in a shootout. Twenty-one children and fifty-three adults suffered fiery deaths when FBI agents assaulted their home in a botched raid fifty-two days later. The members were followers of David Koresh, who claimed to be the reincarnated Christ. Koresh had exclusive sexual rights to all the women in the community. The FBI justified the raid with claims of child abuse and illegal firearms possession. This action played into the community's radical belief, inspired by the Book of Revelations in the Bible, that the saints would have to defend themselves against an invading enemy (Shepherd and Shepherd 2011), and the event further alienated other fundamentalists from mainstream society. My informants, the Allredites, were afraid that they would be the next target of the FBI. The Waco affair became the catalyst for a string of criminal investigations, seizures, and home invasions, including the FBI's attack on the Montana Freemen Christian Patriot movement of Jordan, Montana. This series of events culminated in the raid on the Eldorado YFZ ranch in 2008.

These confrontations were all handled poorly. Authorities often assumed that they were dealing with deviant and/or brainwashed members of a cult with criminal tendencies. They paid more attention to the grievances of former members than to statements made by members in good standing or the research of social scientists. Officials rarely sought cultural or historical data before acting, and often suspended normal legal procedures to justify their raids and arrests (Bennion 2011b; Shepherd and Shepherd 2011). Hopefully, analysis of the following cases will contribute to increasing the understanding of government officials and the public of the cultural context of crime and how to better investigate claims against nontraditional religious movements in isolated areas so that violence and further alienation of fundamentalist groups can be avoided in the future.

Criminal Prosecution

PROSECUTIONS FOR POLYGAMY AND BIGAMY

Typically, polygamists avoid arrest in western states by legally marrying just one wife while living with their spiritual wives in consensual relationships. This is the method the Allred Group used in Pinesdale, Montana, where polygamists do not want to bring attention to themselves by recording plural marriages or any unrecorded births or deaths with civil authorities. Pinesdale men do not marry underage brides and there are few cases of sexual misconduct, so the town rarely has any confrontations with the law. Once polygamists attempt to marry legally or civilly, they face legal action and all the media attention and public scrutiny that are associated with being arrested and incarcerated. Avoiding the law by marrying spouses in secret ceremonies without a paper trail has been the preferred method of existence for most polygamists.

This was not the modus operandi for polygamist Tom Green of Salt Lake City, Utah, who spoke openly about his lifestyle to the press and to neighbors. Green's bravado would have easily been ignored were it not for three factors: 1) the 2002 Olympics were coming to Salt Lake; 2) he made the mistake of marrying an underage girl; and 3) he promoted his poly lifestyle on national television. In Utah, if a bride is under sixteen, it is not legally possible for her to consent, even if she seeks the marriage, as was the case in this instance. Therefore, cohabitation does not trump or override bigamy laws. The case was used to ignite a campaign against polygamy. Opponents of plural marriage focused on the vulnerability of the wife, who was too young to know what she was doing, and emphasized the exploitation of women and children and issues of sexual impropriety within polygamous communities. Green's wife was only fourteen when they married and had been already pregnant. In addition, he had once married her mother, too. Although this underage bride, now in her adult years, is adamantly in favor of her marriage to Tom, he was convicted of statutory rape. In 2001, Green was also convicted of four counts of bigamy and sentenced to five years in prison. The Supreme Court upheld the conviction in 2004 and Green served his sentence; he was released in 2007.

To other fundamentalists, Tom Green is both celebrated and viewed with disdain. On the one hand, he was brave enough to live polygamy openly and flamboyantly, making a statement to the world that he should be given equal rights as a full citizen (Bennion 2011b). On the other hand, because he was guilty of a crime beyond that of polygamy, many feel that he should have kept his mouth shut and remained hidden instead of parading his brazen relationship to a girl and her own mother in public. He was a poor choice for the poster boy for plural marriage.

In 2003, Rodney Holm, thirty-two, a Hildale police officer, was arrested and convicted under the bigamy statute for his spiritual marriage to his third wife, Ruth Stubbs. Holm was also charged with unlawful sex with Ruth, who is Holm's first wife's sister; she was sixteen when she slept with Holm to conceive their first child. Holm, who fathered twenty-one children with the three wives, challenged the constitutionality of the bigamy statute, arguing that his private union with multiple spiritual wives is an expression of his religious beliefs as a member of the FLDS. The Utah Supreme Court felt that that because Holm was guilty of sexual conduct with a minor, his case that polygamy was a fundamental liberty was not valid (*State v. Holm,* 137 P.3d 726). Holm invoked *Lawrence v. Texas* (539 U.S. 558)to argue that the state could not interfere with his choice to be intimate with Ruth Stubbs. He argued that criminalizing this intimacy violated the due process clause of the Fourteenth Amendment and that consenting adults have the freedom to define their private intimate relationships within "the confines of their homes and their own private lives," as the *Lawrence* decision stated. Four Utah judges rejected Holm's argument, stating that his behavior was criminal according to *Reynolds v. United States* and that the *Lawrence* decision was based on homosexual acts, not on marriage, which in Utah is defined as a union of one man and one woman. Chief Justice Christine Durham dissented in the Holm decision, stating that the bigamy statute "oversteps lines protecting the free exercise of religion and the privacy of intimate, personal relationships between consenting adults" (*State v. Holm,* 137 P.3d 726). Although Holm sued for custody of his children, the court decided that they should live with their mother.

Early in 2011 the Kody Brown family from TLC's *Sister Wives* was threatened with arrest by the Lehi, Utah, police for polygamy, after growing concern in the neighborhood about the family's airing of Mormonism's "dirty laundry" to the world. Lehi law enforcement stated that Utah defined cases of bigamy on the basis of cohabitation, not just legal marriage contracts. The Browns moved to Nevada and have now have brought suit in federal court to have the Utah bigamy law declared unconstitutional. Their case is based on the "due process clause" argument in *Lawrence v. Texas.* In that case, the court said that a "crime against nature" statute was unconstitutional when the sexual activity in question was between consenting adults in private (539 U.S. 558, 564, 123 S. Ct. 2472, 2003). Yet the *Reynolds* court ruled that private consensual sex in cases of bigamy is not legal. Honoring *Reynolds,* the Utah Code states that a "person is guilty of bigamy when, knowing he has a husband or wife or knowing the other person has a husband or wife, the person purports to marry another person or cohabits with another person" (Utah Code 2003). The law applies not just to individuals with multiple marriage licenses but also to those who are legally married to only one person but are participating in other marriage-like relationships that are not recognized by the state. This code is unnecessarily broad in three ways: first, it criminalizes the behavior of both purported spouses, not just the one who is already married; second, it says that religious ceremonies undertaken without a civil license fall under the heading of "purporting to marry"; and third, it criminalizes cohabitation (as well as actual marriage) with a second person while an individual is married to someone else.

This broadness is designed to forestall actions by polygamists to get around the law, such as men who try to divorce each wife before marrying the next while continuing to live with all of them as "husband and wife." Other maneuvering is also prevented, such as a man who marries one legal wife and religiously marries additional wives (most polygamists use this strategy). Although Kody is legally married to Meri but only religiously bound to Janelle and Christine, he (and they) are still in violation of the Utah's code. Interestingly, if all three were merely religious marriages, not legal ones, then Kody and his wives might be safe from prosecution. Yet even in that case, the Utah statute would define the relationships as common-law marriages; according to the code, when one man and one woman cohabit and consider themselves to be husband and wife, they are in a common-law marriage (Utah Code 30-1-4.5). Thus, cohabitation with multiple spouses is not protected. Kody could divorce his first wife, Meri, and then impregnate many women that he has no commitment to with no risk of arrest. Yet Kody's public avowal that he will live in legal marriage with all four wives is seen as illegal. Further, if he divorces Meri, they cannot share health care and tax benefits. (Utah common-law couples do have beneficial rights if it is just one man and one woman.) Despite the investigation of Kody Brown for bigamy, it is unlikely that any charges will be brought against him. Paul Ryan of the Utah Attorney General's office said that they are not focused on crimes involving consenting adults. Nonetheless, the Brown family decided to relocate to Nevada, in part because Nevada laws are more lenient and in part because Meri lost her job when her lifestyle became public knowledge.

PROSECUTION FOR UNDERAGE MARRIAGE

Perhaps the most publicized feature of polygamist communities in North America is underage marriage. Although the Utah State Legislature has raised the legal age of marriage from fourteen to sixteen and raised the age of statutory rape to sixteen, underage marriages continue to occur. Warren Jeffs, who often coerced teen girls into marrying much older men, was convicted for this crime in 2005. John Daniel Kingston was also convicted for forcing his teenage daughter to marry her thirty-two-year-old uncle by beating her unconscious until she complied. Kingston and his brother pled no contest to charges of child abuse, incest, and unlawful sexual conduct, but no polygamy or bigamy charges were ever filed against the uncle (Duncan 2008). The Jeffs and Kingston convictions highlight the new direction in enforcement: prosecutions for child abuse and underage marriage with little attention paid to violations of polygamy laws. The fact that most Kingston women are married by sixteen and that FLDS women are often married to much older men is not reason enough for investigations in Utah. A 1987 study of the FLDS group showed that 60 percent of 224 wives were married before age eighteen. A 1996 study showed a decrease in this trend; 55 percent of women married in their teens, typically to men over thirty (Duncan 2008).

This particular criminal offense is the most challenging obstacle to obtaining rights for most polygamists who wish to live "quietly alongside their monogamist neighbors" and who are law-abiding fundamentalists (4The Family.us 2008). Underage marriage generates bad press for all poly families as it is claimed to be a violation of young girls' sexual autonomy and causes high-risk pregnancies, maternal mortality, and severe birth defects, including mental retardation, as a result of incest (Duncan 2008). The misguided raid on the FLDS compound in Eldorado, Texas, was motivated by the goal of saving children from harm. Officials sought to prosecute men guilty of statutory rape by identifying teenage mothers who had been coerced or brainwashed into sleeping with these men. "There is a culture of young girls being [made] pregnant by old men," said a Child Protection Services official (Blumenthal 2008, 2). Yet Texas officials did not focus their efforts on teenage girls who might have been at immediate risk of sexual abuse; they removed all children, regardless of age. Further, there was no evidence of an "emergency," an often-required prerequisite for pursuing Child Protective Services inquiries of such magnitude (Smith 2011). The FLDS mothers petitioned the state Court of Appeals for a writ to return their children to them. The Court of Appeals ruled in their favor, but the state's Child Protective Services asked the state Supreme Court to overturn that ruling. The Supreme Court declined to do so, ruling that the state had not presented evidence that the children were in immediate physical danger. The state returned the FLDS children to their parents, but Child Protective Services retained the right to visit polygamist homes unannounced to examine the medical, psychological, and economic well-being of the children. The FLDS families also had to agree to never again allow women under eighteen to marry.

Although Texas officials claimed to be protecting teen girls from sexual abuse, their larger agenda was to rescue children from an authoritarian religion (Smith 2011). This created paranoia among polygamists about their parental and constitutional rights. Although authoritative parenting is considered to be a superior parenting style over authoritarian child-rearing (Benokraitus 2009), it hardly justifies removing children from parents.[15] According to law professor Linda Smith (2011), the state should have left the young children with families that had not consented to underage sexual unions of their daughters. Further, she stated, it is unwise to pursue criminal prosecutions without the support of the victims. This just serves to unite the community against the state instead of providing support for families who make appropriate choices for their teenage daughters. If a group must be investigated, the less disruptive method is to intervene on a case-by-case basis and to arrest only men who have a history of marrying underage girls or of sexually assaulting minors.

When a child is abused or neglected, including a teen minor who is subjected to underage marriage, the state decides whether to litigate a protective case, a criminal case, or both; it is up to their discretion. In the Texas case, DNA samples were taken to match parents with children. The DNA data and family records were used to identify women who gave birth before they were seventeen and the men who sired children with underage wives. This evidence was used to indict Warren Jeffs and four other men for sexual assault of a minor. The Texas ranch's doctor, Lloyd Barlow, was also charged for failing to report abuse in his role as obstetrician to underage women. In March 2009, the number of men indicted for sexual assault increased to twelve. In retrospect, although the Texas government sought to end child sexual abuse, it went too far when it removed children from their parents (Smith 2011). They should have had the support of the victims and ample DNA evidence of abuse first. The aggressive community-wide approaches that were used in Texas are unsuccessful because the polygamists see this as an attack on their way of life. They see the action as a threat to their families and their beliefs, and this further unites them against the state. Any rational plan to end abuse must also provide social and legal support for families who make appropriate choices for their teenage children.

One of the first fundamentalists to be arrested in the post-Eldorado era was Raymond Merril Jessop, who was found guilty and sentenced to ten years in 2009 for the rape of a sixteen-year-old girl (Roberts 2009). In 2010, there were five more FLDS convictions: Michael Emack was sentenced to seven years, Merril L. Jessop to seventy-five years, Lehi Barlow Jeffs to two eight-year terms, and Abram H. Jeffs to seventeen years. The Pinesdale, Montana, community prefers to deal with the criminal activity of its members by appointing a liaison between the Ravalli County sheriff's department and Pinesdale's leadership. From time to time, the AUB has requested my services as a cultural liaison in cases relating to accusations of sex abuse and illegal firearms possession. The Montana AUB has a relatively low rate of criminal activity due, in part, to the knowledge that their leaders cooperate with civil authorities. They are not at risk for seizures or raids and maintain open channels of communication with local and state officials.

In 2004, an investigation of underage marriage was initiated by the British Columbia Human Rights Commission after decades of allegations of abuse in the FLDS town of Bountiful, located near Creston, British Columbia, in the East Kootenay Mountains. Over the past fifty years, patriarchs of the town have been accused of "sexual exploitation of girls, polygamy, physical abuse, cross-border trafficking of women, and racism" (Beatty 2004, 2). Winston Blackmore, the bishop, has twenty-six wives and eighty children and actively promotes the right of men to rule over their wives and children, a philosophy typically promoted by the FLDS under the leadership of Rulon Jeffs (Beatty 2004). Blackmore's wife, Jane, told reporters that young women of fourteen and fifteen are often married off and are having babies in Bountiful. Another report by Tim Dickson, a court-appointed lawyer (Bart 2010, 1), used in a court hearing in December 2010, found that 10 percent of the teenage women are pregnant or have already had children. Former FLDS member Debbie

Palmer accused Bountiful leaders of impregnating minors; she claims to have been physically and sexually abused and forced to have sex with three different men, whom she bore seven children.

Carol Anderson, a border patrol officer, has turned away many of the young women sent from the FLDS church in the United States. She says, "There is no class under Canada's immigration law by which they can be sponsored in as a plural spouse. The law prohibits it" (CBC News 2003). FLDS girls who do enter Canada are awarded a full range of welfare benefits, including health care and child credit. Canada's laws allowed consensual sex between children aged twelve to fourteen as long as the partner is less than two years older. The law is designed to prevent the exploitative sex often associated with much older men and underage teen girls. Yet the law allows a sixteen-year-old to marry an older man if she obtains her parent's permission and a signature from a judge.

In 2005, Winston Blackmore changed his earlier pattern by offering his congregation more freedoms and organizing a national polygamy summit in Creston, British Columbia. At the summit, his wives urged the government to increase the age of consent from fourteen to sixteen. Later that year, one of Winston's wives, Edith Barlow, who came to Canada from the Colorado City group, faced deportation. Although she had five children with him, her visitor's visa was rejected. If she had been his first wife, she could have received permanent residency. Eventually, another of Blackmore's wives, Jane, left the community and divorced him. She had worked as a midwife for many years but felt that the marriages of underage girls were wrong. She wants her daughter to have a better life and more education than she had (CBC News 2006). Robert Blackmore, Winston's nephew, is another apostate from Bountiful. He told me that he is bitter about the fact that Winston controls his father's land and has ten homes, whereas he is a single father struggling in Creston to make ends meet (Bennion 2008). Another Creston resident stated that no one wants to prosecute Blackmore because nonpolygamists in the area believe that it would lead to the arrest of other alternative groups, such as Sikhs, homosexuals, and Native Americans who use peyote in their religion. Most important, arrests would also hurt business, as the Bountiful community has helped support Creston's economy (CBC News 2003).

In 2009 Blackmore and James Oler, who has three wives, were charged under the Criminal Code of Canada for practicing polygamy. Each leads a separate faction within the FLDS in Bountiful. A British Columbia Supreme Court judge dismissed the charges against the Bountiful leaders, stating that former attorney general Wally Oppal had overstepped his authority in shopping around for a prosecutor who would take the cases to court. Two previous special prosecutors whom Oppal had personally selected considered the charges and told him that while Section 293 of the criminal code is constitutionally valid, the most efficient test of the law would be to refer it to British Columbia's provincial Supreme Court rather than testing it at the national level. Oppal, who had been the subject of repeated investigations by the RCMP at Bountiful, chose instead to appoint a third special prosecutor, who eventually agreed to take the charges to court. Both that prosecutor and the charges were dismissed by Judge Sunni Stromberg-Stein in the B.C. Supreme Court in 2010. Rather than attempt to retry Blackmore and Oler, Oppal petitioned the British Columbia Supreme Court to provide a reference case for the courts to determine the constitutionality of Section 293 of the Criminal Code which began in November 2010.

Two previous studies have examined the issue of whether Section 293 of the Criminal Code of Canada is consistent with the Canadian Charter of Rights and Freedoms. The first study, which was crafted by Status of Women Canada, recommended the decriminalization of polygamy (Campbell et al. 2005). The other was written by Rebecca Cook and Lisa M. Kelly (2006). Cook, a professor at the University of Toronto, urged British Columbia to prosecute polygamists in Bountiful. Both studies explore the essential conundrum related to polygamy in North America: How do we respect human rights and individual freedoms that permit citizens to set up cults, live undisturbed to practice their religion, and even, if they so wish, deviate from mainstream ethical codes and at the same time protect vulnerable citizens and the state itself from harms perpetrated by these cults and individuals within them? And in what ways do these groups threaten the larger society, its laws, and stability of the North American way of life?

PROSECUTION FOR INCEST

In 1991, a staff member of the Utah Attorney General's office met me in my Salt Lake City home to discuss problems associated with the Kingston group. He showed me pictures of incestuous sexual activity and asked me if I knew anything about the patterns of couplings. I told him I had no firm data about dangers associated with the Kingstons, only hearsay. Years later, I did find patterns of incestuous marriage among the Kingstons (Bennion 2008, 2011a), though I neither saw nor heard of the type of pornography the Attorney General's office claimed was happening. John Daniel Kingston forced his sixteen-year-old daughter to secretly marry her thirty-two-year-old uncle, David Ortell Kingston, which launched an investigation into the clan's activities. John Daniel and the mother of his sixteen-year-old daughter, Susan Nelson, were half-siblings who were fathered by the same man. They have ten children.

Of 150 sex crimes investigated each month in Utah, about 60 percent involve close relatives, according to statistics from the state's Division of Child and Family Services (DCFS).[16] Katy Larsen, regional director of the northern division of DCFS, says that most of the cases involve a perpetrator of incest who is a caretaker, a sibling, or a member of the victim's extended family. She stated that the reason her department is involved is because of the need to protect teen girls. "Incest is a prevalent problem, one that doesn't get the exposure because investigators and the media, out of kindness, want to protect the parties involved" (Burton 1998, 1). The motive for not exposing crimes of incest may be kindness, but this strategy conceals the problem within the Kingston group. John Ortell Kingston, who died in 1987, had a history of incest. He fathered more than 65 children, one of whom was a child born with severe birth defects that Kingston likely conceived with a close relative. Because matings with siblings, cousins, and uncles are frequent in the Kingston group, the genetic pool lacks the necessary variability for healthy offspring. Brother/sister marriage produces a greater pool of recessive genes, and this means a higher-than-average rate of birth defects and a variety of other problems, such as low intelligence, weak immunity, problems with fertility, and mental retardation. According to genetics professor Lynn Jorde, approximately 35 percent of the Kingston children have problems attributable to genetics (Burton 1998).

Discussions about incest among polygamists are strained, as many have some history of inbreeding in their family tree. For example, the Jessops, the Allreds, and the Barlows intermarried to a great extent, often creating bonds between first and second cousins that were nearly impossible to avoid. This was also true of nineteenth-century Mormons. In the history of my own poly family, the Cannons and Bennions often intermarried, creating thousands of offspring who continued the cycle of intermarriage. It was no surprise to me when I learned that my college sweetheart, Bruce Cannon, was my relative; he and I were both second and third cousins. Our common great-great-grandfather, Angus M. Cannon, married two sisters, Amanda and Sarah; Bruce came from Amanda's line, and I came from Sarah's.

PROSECUTION FOR VIOLENCE AND SEXUAL ASSAULT

Other publicized criminal cases linked to polygamists have involved violent behavior in the home or community in the form of corporal punishment, sexual abuse, domestic violence, and emotional abuse. A Kingston woman reported living in fear of being beaten. Others described being emotionally distraught and suffering from eating disorders and depression. Still others said because of the required childbirths, they suffered from obesity and stress (Bennion 2008). According to Vicky Prunty, a co-director of Tapestry Against Polygamy, women are emotionally hurt by being "forced into allowing their husbands to take on other wives in the name of religion, getting married too young to men much older, being hit or worse" (Scharnberg and Brachear 2006, 2). One woman said that co-wives are sometimes abusive to each other and to each other's children. Yet another woman described how in her group "children were beaten and locked in rooms. On one occasion a younger child was smothered by one of the mothers until they choked or gasped for air" (Dougherty 2003, 2). In the FLDS group, after the "lost boys" incident (Bistline 2004), some members were afraid that their children would be given to another family.

Other extreme accounts emerged from the Allred Group. Councilmen were said to have set up a torture enterprise in Oregon in the 1960s where they would join in molesting and beating pre-pubescent children. Though I heard this story from two different sources, I could not verify any such "enterprise" with Oregon law enforcement. One of the AUB councilors accused of abuse preached that God told him to take his daughters and other children to his bed. (For a more full account of child sexual abuse in Mormon fundamentalist groups, see Chapter 7.)

In a 2006 study, I traced the causes of the sexual abuse of females, particularly father-perpetrated rape, in rigid patriarchal communities in Montana, Mexico, and Utah. Certain cues make incidents of abuse more likely, such as when low socioeconomic status of the perpetrator; social and geographic barriers to female autonomy within a community; and the cultural beliefs that allow and, in some cases, encourage the rape of women and children without punishment (Bennion 2007). I predicted that female sexual abuse would be more prevalent in environments characterized by male supremacy, isolation of females, and economic deprivation. I looked at sex offender profiles in 1999 provided by twenty-two licensed sex abuse counselors in the State of Utah, focusing on father-daughter incest. Of 320 perpetrators, 120 were fundamentalists. The typical perpetrator was a male aged thirty to fifty who had himself been victimized as a child. These men often exerted formal control over a large, overcrowded household and often traveled away from the home on business or to visit other families (in the case of polygamists). Many of the perpetrators were religious and had high expectations of righteousness for themselves and their families. Yet despite their religious beliefs, the perpetrators often had a history of using pornography and were described as having sexual addictions. Furthermore, perpetrators typically lived with their families in relative poverty in a rural, isolated region. In sum, these Utah cases revealed that the offender had a high level of eroticism and tended to take out his economic frustration on a submissive wife and vulnerable children in a confining, troubled household. The man of the house reinforced his dominion over his wife and children through physical and sexual abuse, in addition to restricting their access to the larger world outside the home.

Interestingly, while I was investigating cases of mental and physical abuse in the poly world, Utah therapists and social workers told me that many of the same characteristics are to be found among perpetrators in the monogamous LDS congregation. In other words, the sexual molestation and battery of children is not an exclusive problem among fundamentalist Mormons. Studies also found that monogamous Mormon women from Utah have the highest consumption rates of Prozac in the nation (Ponder 2003), primarily because of the stress of repeated childbirth, their expectation of perfection, and the fact that they have relatively little adult conversation during their very busy days. It is well known that mainstream Mormons also suffer from physical and sexual mistreatment while in the care of their leaders, scout masters, bishops, or spiritual mentors (Melloy 2008).

PROSECUTION FOR KIDNAPPING AND RAPE

In June of 2002, fourteen-year-old Elizabeth Smart was kidnapped from her home in Salt Lake City by an independent fundamentalist street preacher named Brian David Mitchell, a self-proclaimed prophet who worked as her family's gardener. The case was of great interest to me as the Smarts are distant relatives.

Mitchell, fifty-six, was convicted in December of 2002 of kidnapping and unlawful transportation of a minor across state lines for sex. He was then sentenced to life in federal prison without parole. Mitchell believed in many of the tenets of Mormon fundamentalist doctrine but stole his wives from the Mormon subculture instead of recruiting them from polygamy enclaves. Rather than claim authority through Woolley and Musser, Mitchell believed that he was directly chosen by God to be prophet. He was a bizarre prophet who altered his temple garments into Islamic-styled *djellaba* cotton robes and sought out girls he could train in obedience. He trained these girls to wear the *hijab* (face covering) and the *abayas* (the head-to-toe garment some Muslim women wear).

Mitchell called himself a visionary and created his own scripture, the Book of Immanuel David Isaiah, that is filled with biblical warnings and references to Joseph Smith. He called himself the "one mighty and strong" who would set the church "of the Firstborn" in order. He used his "wife" Wanda to help kidnap Elizabeth Smart. Wanda washed Elizabeth's feet and prepared her for marriage to Brian Mitchell. Mitchell then raped Elizabeth.

After a huge search effort, Elizabeth was eventually found about eighteen miles from her home in Sandy, Utah, traveling with Mitchell and Wanda. Mitchell was indicted but was initially found not competent to stand trial because of insanity. He claimed to hear revelations from God and was committed to a psychiatric hospital. But after many months of psychiatric testing, Mitchell was convicted and sentenced to life in prison (Associated Press 2011).

Warren Jeffs was sentenced to life plus twenty years in prison for his sexual assault of a twenty-three-year-old and a pre-adolescent girl. Evidence for the conviction was provided by audio and video tapes of Jeffs engaging in sex acts with a twelve-year-old girl, teaching her how to satisfy him. Witnesses claimed that Jeffs typically raped girls and boys in his home, threatening them with physical punishment and eternal damnation if they did not comply.

Women have often been abducted to feed the needs of polygamy. White and Burton (1988) argue that wife capture is one way to ensure that the poly condition survives in many cultures around the world. In my 1998 book I suggested that this need is often filled by wife conversion, or the proselytizing of women. Perhaps on some level, this was Mitchell's intent, to forcibly convert Elizabeth into his kingdom for the purpose of procreating heavenly subjects. Many polygamists rely on the natural flow of women into fundamentalism that occurs as mainstream women lose their socioeconomic foothold in the orthodox church. That is how most polygamists find their plural wives (see Chapter 4).

PROSECUTION FOR WELFARE FRAUD

The reports on welfare abuse within polygamous communities are contradictory and confusing at best. On the one hand is the familiar story of widespread fraud in which men use their wives to obtain public assistance by having them pose as single mothers. On the other hand are statements by authorities that there is no fraud but simply great need (Adams 2009). In the scenario of widespread fraud, polygamists tell themselves that abusing welfare is justified as it helps God defeat the government. Three reports of welfare fraud typify this pattern. The FLDS Hildale/Colorado City order ranks in the top ten cities in the Intermountain West for the amount of federal aid they receive, primarily for poor women and children. They pay very little tax ($651 for each adult who files a tax return), have the highest average household count in the Intermountain West (8.5 people), and yet they get the most benefits ($8 per each tax dollar). According to the Utah Department of Workforce Services, in 2002, 66 percent of Hildale FLDS residents received federal assistance, and according to the Arizona Department of Economic Security, 78 percent of Colorado City residents received food stamps. Although Arizona hasn't charged any fundamentalist with welfare fraud, in Utah, the Washington County Attorney's Office charged Jared L. Barlow and his wife Linda with fraud in 2006. The couple was forced to repay $37,319 to the Utah Department of Workforce Services and perform community service.

Tom Green, who was also found guilty of using the government to support his lifestyle, owes Utah nearly $80,000 in welfare payments fraudulently collected to support his five wives and twenty-six children. The Kingston family also relies on food stamps and subsidies, in spite of a net worth of more than $150 million (Duncan 2008). In 1983, their prophet John Ortell Kingston was found guilty of perpetrating the largest welfare fraud in the nation. By that year, four of his wives and twenty-nine of his children had received hundreds of thousands of dollars in public assistance over a ten-year period. Utah recovered $250,000 from John Ortell and $100,000 in judgments against various other members for welfare benefits they had received. The investigation also showed that the John Ortell Kingston family had received $1 million in food stamps, Medicaid, and Supplemental Security Income for nearly ten years, from 1972 to 1983. They collected Social Security disability benefits. A few years before, Kingston had been found guilty of tax evasion; he reported $30 million in land sales but only paid $800 in income tax.

Yet some assumptions about fraud among members of fundamentalist groups are unfounded. A recent U.S. Senate Judiciary Committee hearing found that the facts do not fit claims of widespread polygamist welfare fraud, at least not for the FLDS group (Adams 2009). Although the group received food and medical assistance, they did not receive cash assistance. Further, the assistance given was legal Temporary Assistance for Needy Families aid. The value of food assistance for recipients in Colorado City tends to be higher because "families in that area tend to be larger," said a spokesperson for Arizona's Department of Economic Security (ibid.). The large size of fundamentalist families allows more community households to meet the poverty guidelines of Medicaid and food stamp programs. This means that polygamists living in poverty will use more public funds than the average monogamous family living in poverty.

According to Jerry D. Jaeger, deputy attorney with the Washington County Attorney's Office, the perception that welfare fraud is rampant in fundamentalism is a myth. A former FLDS man, Ezra Draper, suggests that the myth was generated by the language "bleeding the beast," which is mostly used by anti-FLDS people in the mainstream. Contradictorily, I spoke with members of the FLDS group who did, indeed, use this term, so Draper is incorrect in suggested that it came from outside the group. Paul Murphy, spokesman for Utah Attorney General Mark Shurtleff, said that there is enormous resentment in the public about the fact that taxpayers fund polygamy. He stated, "If you are going to have three wives and 15 children, you need to figure out a way to support three wives and 15 children" (Adams 2009).

How do we sort out the confusion about welfare fraud? First, the media and hearsay have created a powerful vehicle for misinformation about fraudulent misuse of welfare funds. The media have relied heavily on statements by Carolyn Jessop and Stephen Singular. Jessop used the term "bleeding the beast" when she testified before the Senate Judiciary Committee in 2009, and Singular claimed that Colorado City residents received "eight times the welfare assistance of comparably sized towns in the area" in his 2008 book about the FLDS (Adams 2009). Second, during my observations of the fundamentalist lifestyle, I saw how easy it is to deceive government officials when providing documentation for applications for welfare, as plural wives use their maiden names and do not claim to be married at the time of the application. State officials can't always show that a father is able to support his family because paternity is difficult to establish. Plural marriages are not recorded, nor are birth records always available (polygamists typically deliver babies at home and file no paperwork to document the birth). Without proof of paternity, the state continues to provide assistance. Social services departments typically do not investigate the situations of plural wives because they are not legal wives.

I have documented welfare abuse in my research among both the Allred group and the FLDS. The typical explanation I heard from both wives and patriarchs was that using the government is justified as it is the enemy and that the greater goal in this life is to raise as many righteous seed as possible in the fulness of the gospel. This may require, at certain times, using public assistance to reach the final goal in kingdom building. Welfare, or creative financing, is essential for vulnerable plural wives who do not have any other means of support, either from the group or from their husbands. In posing as single mothers to obtain resources, these polygamist women are doing the same thing that many single mothers in mainstream American do--using the system as a way to cope in the absence of husbands/partners and fathers.

PROSECUTION FOR ILLEGAL POSSESSION OF ARMS

The 1993 raid on the Branch Davidians in Waco and the raid on the Freemans (a family that promoted separatism and anti-government sovereignty through violence) ignited a series of investigations of fundamentalist arsenals in Montana. The AUB was a target of one such investigation. In 1991, I was subpoenaed to appear before the Third Circuit court as a reluctant expert witness against the AUB after members of the Pinesdale order had been charged with illegal arms possession. I refused to testify in order to protect my informants' anonymity. Although there were allegations of a mysterious bunker where government-issue weapons were stored, the prosecution failed to provide any evidence of such firearms at the Pinesdale ranch. As this incident took place twenty years ago, I can now speak freely about the rumors of a hidden store of guns to be used in defense of the enemy during the first stage of Armageddon. Though I found no physical evidence of such a bunker, I believe that many of the group's members sought to protect themselves with such weapons.

This case illustrates the political and ideological views of many fundamentalists regarding firearms. As Alex Joseph of Big Water did, many polygamists believe in their right to live as sovereign communities, to separate themselves from the larger wicked world, and to use their weapons in the appropriate defense of their homes and families. They believe in their constitutional right to bear arms and fight what they believe to be a corrupt government that may be intruding into the private lives of people who are simply trying to live their religious convictions. Fundamentalists see possessing illegal arms in the same light as they see homeschooling or building a home without the consent of city engineers. Each of these acts is an expression of libertarianism, sovereignty, and constitutionally based patriotism. It was also the Freeman premise that every man has a right to take up arms in defense of his religious belief. Government raids on fundamentalist compounds only reinforce the fundamentalist beliefs that Big Brother is out to get all nonnormative communities and that the only recourse to begin storing up weapons, along with adequate foodstuffs and toilet paper, to prepare for the impending clash between government-based tyranny and the free citizenry.

PROSECUTION FOR MONEY LAUNDERING

In 1994, I was working closely with Rod Williams, my key informant with the Allred Group (AUB). Rod introduced me to his friend John R. Llewellyn, a retired Salt Lake County Sheriff's Department lieutenant and a former member of the AUB. In 1995, Mr. Llewellyn became an investigator for Virginia Hill in a civil action (*Hill v. Allred*) to recover $1.54 million in cash members of the AUB had stolen from her. Williams helped him in this investigation and explained the whole story to me on several occasions; it was his favorite story.

Virginia Hill was once the wife of Harry Hilf, a big Detroit gambler. When the Allred polygamists were retained to purchase the Desert Inn Ranch, the Las Vegas mob's recreational ranch in southern Utah, Virginia loaned them the money they needed, expecting full repayment at a later date.. One Allred polygamist, Jeffery J. Norman, was imprisoned for money laundering in connection with the Hill case, but at the time of my 2008 interview with Williams, the case had yet to be resolved.

It took three years for Llewellyn Williams to build a case against Owen A. Allred, leader of Apostolic United Brethren, and his two followers, Dennis E. Matthews and John C. Putvin. Some of the Hill money was eventually traced to the purchase of a used car lot, Diamond Automotive Specialties Inc. Putvin negotiated the sale, and the business was managed by James E. Sandmire (Llewellyn 2010). The business was shut down in 2009 by the Utah

Motor Vehicle Enforcement Division for selling stolen cars smuggled into Utah from Canada.

This case illustrates how some polygamists attempt to expedite the kingdom building process. Growing movements like the Allreds and the FLDS have both used creative methods for obtaining cash to purchase new buildings, provide housing for new members, and pay for travel expenses for priesthood leaders and missionaries. This was true of the orthodox LDS Church as well, whose leaders occasionally used illicit means to acquire funding for projects deemed vital to the cause of building up Zion. One such venture was initiated by LDS apostle Erastus Snow, who presold worthless land to migrating pioneers, such as my ancestor Titus Mousley.

CRITIQUE

These criminal cases reveal that larger agendas are at play when state governments pursue polygamy convictions, such as the desire to clean up Utah for the Olympics or the political need to reinforce normative, monogamist, family values. Some perpetrators believe they are living the higher law of God, even when their actions break the law of the land. In some instances this means marrying child brides to gain more progeny for one's kingdom. In other cases it means using fraud or laundering money to cope with a growing population of converts and offspring. It may also mean that violence and emotional tyranny is used to keep children and wives from straying from the path of heaven and to use illegal weapons to protect temporal and spiritual investments. With an "eye single to God," polygamists often rationalize their use of criminal action to attain a higher Celestial purpose.

These criminal actions are not representative of the larger fundamentalist population. They are perpetrated by individuals with a particular fanatical ethos. These individuals do not follow the common moral code outlined by Taylor, Woolley, and Musser; instead, they pursue a more radical version of kingdom building with themselves as the masters of the enterprise. Many feel rejected by the outside world and their fellow fundamentalists and seek to resist any form of tyranny that disempowers them. Such self-proclaimed prophets—such as Brian Mitchell, who kidnapped and raped Elizabeth Smart; accused sex offender Joe Thompson, who believed in mating with his daughters; or John Ortell Kingston, who was guilty of promoting welfare fraud, incest, and child marriage—claim to be above the law, accountable to no one but God.

Most criminal prosecutions reflect deep-seated cultural beliefs in very specific geographic, structural, and situational contexts, often produced in an environment of resistance and revolution (Fanon [1952] 1980).[17] Proper responses to polygamy require a keen awareness of cultural relativism (Campbell 2005, 36) and an examination of cultural cues tied to the perpetrator's own set of personal beliefs and religious ethos (Bennion 2007). Sociologists Christopher Ellison and John Bartkowski suggest that "when assessing competing claims, it is important to link competing claims . . . to the ideological, psychological, and material interests and agendas of the adversarial parties" (1995, 140). Concepts such as "child abuse" and "welfare fraud" should be defined very carefully to "avoid loose and ideologically laden uses of [a] stigmatizing label."

> Children who are physically punished, or raised in an unusual set of circumstances (e.g. communally) are not necessarily being abused by their caregivers. Authorities who must adjudicate the various claims and counterclaims about marginal religious groups should solicit and take seriously the input of social scientists who are familiar with the theology, history, and collective dynamics of such groups. . . . At each step in the investigative process, it must be the responsibility of authorities to weigh carefully the tradeoffs between the preservation of religious liberty for minority groups and the welfare of the children. (Ellison and Bartkowski 1995, 140−141)

Yet how do we reconcile the competing claims of law and culture? The cultural defense argument should not be invoked to exonerate criminals from verified instances of abuse or to dismiss concerns about women's rights to equality. Nor should cultural difference exempt these groups or individuals from the law, especially when irreparable harm has been done. However, in the absence of any real harm or threat, cultural minorities should have the right to follow their rules and traditions, free from governmental interference. Why should polygamists be punished for obeying the rules of their culture?

Even when "irreparable harm" is done, there are legal and ethical complications. Harm itself is a culturally relative term; no two people can define exactly what they mean by it. Contrary to Barbara Costello's (2009) premise, the definition of harm is not objective and universal. For example, no two cultures can agree on what constitutes female subordination and how best to deal with it. The veiling of Muslim women and girls may not be a symbol of women's oppression but may be a vehicle for female empowerment, depending on the context. Likewise, the marriage of a young fifteen-year-old to an already married man may not be an act of sexual abuse but a culturally approved venue for increasing offspring for the lineage and fulfilling a valued role for young women as "Handmaids of the Lord," just as it was a hundred years ago and is still today among traditional Indian, Muslim, and African families. It is not the path my daughters or granddaughters would ever take, but does that make it wrong for those raised in such a context to believe that the practice can fulfill them?

Further, fundamentalists themselves cannot agree on what constitutes irreparable harm. Even from prison Warren Jeffs continues to mandate female subordination, whereas Owen Allred preached female autonomy; the two prophets interpreted the rules of gender quite differently. So in the FLDS context, polygamy is associated with low status for women and potential abuses of them, while in the Allred context, polygamy is equated with benign patriarchal rule with a sprinkling of feminism. And even within the FLDS there is diversity in how the "victims" of male supremacist ideologies respond to it. Carolyn Jessop felt exploited as young girl when she was groomed against her will to fit her expectations and desires to the will of her father, her husband, and the prophet. Yet Carolyn's daughter Betty, who was raised in the same environment, wanted to remain in the male-dominated world of the FLDS. She feels that it is truly her path to God, a protected haven from the dangers of Babylon. How do we protect the rights of one without violating the rights of the other?

Without an understanding of cultural differences in the expression of polygamy, we are guilty of labeling all polygamy as equally harmful. We are misguided in believing that there is a single definition of abuses against women and that all abuse is of the same magnitude. Angela Campbell has stated that we must reject narrow interpretations of the law and polygamy:

Women's experiences in polygamy are extremely varied. Whether a woman, and often her children, thrives or suffers within a plural marriage often depend[s] on the socio-cultural context in which her marriage is situated, as well as the relationships that exist within her family unit. This being the case, it would be contrived and inappropriate to imagine that a single policy response to polygamy would be effective in all plural marriage societies and families. Solving the dilemmas that women may experience in this family structure requires respect for diversity. (Campbell 2005, 34)

I suggest that laws should be redrafted to acknowledge cultural integrity, context, and diversity. The new law should reflect the "human right to culture" as a fundamental principle that "inheres in such constitutional guarantees as equal protection, freedom of association and religion, the right to counsel, and the right to a fair trial" (Renteln 2004, 49). This does not mean fundamentalists should be exempt from the law, but that their culture should affect how their cases are handled; it should be seen as a mitigating circumstance that is weighed against the seriousness of the offense and their behavior should be viewed in the context of the strength of the person's ties to his or her cultural norms. Special accommodations for cultural minorities such as polygamists should be made in the law, even at the expense of our western notion of gender equality. Law professor Sarah Song recommends resolving gendered cultural dilemmas through intercultural democratic dialogue that is "sensitive to the particularities of context" and includes all the voices of those affected by the traditions in question (Song 2007, 172).

Cases Brought by Polygamists

LEGAL RIGHT TO POLYGAMY

In 2007, a Utah AUB couple, the Cooks, requested that the Salt Lake County clerk issue a marriage license for a third person, Miss Bronson (interview with AUB member, 2008). The clerk refused, so they sued the county, claiming that polygamy is a religious belief and that they should be able to practice their beliefs. All three were consensual adults and they felt it was their right to bring in another woman into their lives without hiding it. The Cooks did not get the marriage license they wanted in part because of the legal precedent of *Reynolds v. United States* (1879), where the Supreme Court was asked to interpret the free exercise clause as it related to religious belief and the federal law prohibiting polygamy in the territories. The court ruled that an individual's religious beliefs were not adequate reason to overturn the federal bigamy law. The case began a dispute in legal policy that is still not resolved today: how does the decision distinguish between beliefs, which are not restricted, and practice, which can be regulated by law? The Cooks will have to be content to live in polygamy as consenting adults but still in violation of

Utah law, which puts them at risk for arrest. This case is one of many similar petitions to have plural marriage civilly recognized.

In July 2011, Kody Brown and his four wives filed a suit in U.S. District Court in Salt Lake City to petition for their right to live in polygamy. Jonathan Turley, their lawyer, argues that the bigamy statute as applied to the Browns is unconstitutional, and he challenges the state's right to prosecute people for what they do in private. He told a reporter:

> The Browns are asking for nothing more than for rights that are extended to other families in living their private lives according to their own values and faith. . . . There are no allegations of child crimes or child abuse; what remains is simply a lifestyle that many citizens find obnoxious. The Supreme Court, in Lawrence vs. Texas, emphasized that a homosexual couple was neither accused of crimes nor seeking recognition of their union. The same can be said of the Browns. One of the things we argue in the lawsuit is that the state [of Utah] has been fully aware that the Browns were a plural family long before the show . . . they only put the Browns under criminal investigation after they became openly polygamous through their show. (Starr 2011)

In *Lawrence,* the Supreme Court ruled that the state cannot criminalize private intimate relations without a good reason. It sets a high threshold for legislation that penalizes immoral conduct, so this case could be a basis for challenging laws that make polygamy a crime. The *Lawrence* decision would not require the state of Utah to recognize Kody's plural marriages in any way. So far, no formal bigamy charges have been filed against the Browns, but the Lehi police threatened to do so in late 2010.

THE RIGHT TO EMPLOYMENT

This case, like the Cook petition, involves a law-abiding citizen who wants to live his polygamous lifestyle without legal retribution. Royston Potter was a police officer in the Murray Police Department in Salt Lake County. He had a reputation for being an outstanding police officer and had been awarded numerous commendations at work. Like Tom Green and Kody Brown, Roy spoke openly of his poly relationships, even to fellow Murray police officers. After three years on the force, in November 1982, he was terminated by the City of Murray because he had two wives. . Roy sued to get his job back and took his case all the way to the U.S. Supreme Court when he lost in the lower courts. But the Supreme Court refused to hear the case, upholding the decision of the lower courts that polygamy is still illegal according to Utah state law (Kraut 1989). The court said: "The prohibition of polygamy as provided by [Utah's] Constitution and laws, continues to be its settled public policy as does its commitment to monogamy as the cornerstone of its regulation of marriage" (quoted in ibid., 23). Roy was never formally charged or sentenced for violating Utah's law, but since he was fired he has not been rehired as a police officer or hired in any other public office because he broke the bigamy law.

In 2006, Hildale judge Walter Steed was also removed from his job because of polygamy. When the town council appointed him in 1980, he had two wives, but when he got a third wife, the Utah Supreme Court removed him from the bench. Steed married all three women when they were adults. Though Steed had a private, consensual cohabiting relationship with his wives, the court refused his constitutional challenge to the bigamy law, stating that a sitting judge must abide by the law, regardless of his beliefs (*In re Steed*, 131 P.3d 231).

Meri Brown, the first wife of AUB polygamist Kody Brown, was in a similar situation when she and her family came out to the world on national television. She was fired from her job in the mental health field because of her poly lifestyle, and she and her family moved out of the Lehi area.

However, not all stories about polygamists and employment are the same. In 1992, the Arizona Law Enforcement Officer Advisory Council recommended that Hildale town marshal Sam Barlow not be decertified for having three wives unless his polygamy jeopardized public trust. Barlow hoped that the case would go to the Supreme Court to allow him to fight for the rights of polygamists but was content with the recommendation. So although polygamists have lost jobs in Utah, in Arizona, at least in law enforcement, it is possible to be openly polygamous and still keep a job. Perhaps the stringent rules that are applied when unionized public officers are fired through legally mandated procedures are part of the explanation for the Barlow recommendation. As a part-time social worker, Meri Brown didn't have such protection.

THE RIGHT TO HOME-SCHOOL CHILDREN

Few subjects are as sensitive for Mormon polygamists as the education of their children. One of the biggest threats to the well-being of their offspring is government interference in the form of mandatory secular instruction and a group of social workers dictating how polygamists should be raising their children. Yet from a government perspective, young children are disadvantaged by fundamentalist doctrine, which breeds mistrust and contempt for mainstream America and federal authority. Advocates of public education fear that the absence of a solid, secular education will lead to hardships for children in later life; they are concerned that the children will not be able to develop into healthy adults who can live and work in the mainstream world. The women in these insular communities are seen as having limited access to educational and employment opportunities: they have no jobs, no licenses to drive, and no birth control. Since their duty is to serve their husbands and have as many children as possible for their family's kingdom, some wives have few options. A proper secular education would provide women and children with valuable opportunities to identify their interests and learn about the world.

On the other side of the issue, many fundamentalist believe that home schooling provides a much better education than the public school system offers (Bennion 1998). They also seek a more "pure" environment for their children, one that is free of drugs, video games, pornography, and commercialization, all of which they believe corrupt the mind and soul. Some, like the LeBarons of Chihuahua, believed in religious instruction from kindergarten to twelfth grade with an emphasis on vocation agricultural and construction for the boys and homemaking and training in child care for the girls. The AUB uses Montessori training for children from the ages of three to five, and a blend of religious and secular instruction in elementary school. They send older children to a secular public high school in a nearby town. In Utah in the 1980s, it was illegal to home school children, which meant that polygamists/fundamentalists had to send their children to a secular school with mixed races. Both the secularism of the school and the mixing of the races offended them.

With a purist vision of education in mind, in 2000, Warren Jeffs required all FLDS families to remove their children from the Colorado City public school, yet he kept the government funding that typically went to the district to use for priesthood traveling expenses. Some FLDS members have reported that the FLDS preaches against sex education and teaches historical errors such as that the Holocaust never happened and that the moon landing was a government conspiracy.

One conflict about home schooling ended in a violent confrontation with the Utah State police and the FBI. In 1979, fundamentalist John Singer was killed in a standoff with state government authorities, who were trying to arrest him for refusing to send his children to public school. Singer had married Vickie Lemon in 1965 and had had seven children with her. The family lived on a farm in Marion, Utah. In 1970, he was excommunicated for his support of polygamy, and in 1978 he married a plural wife, Shirley Black, who was still married to another man, with whom she had four children. Singer objected to public school as both black and white children attended, but authorities did not approve his request to home school his children. In 1979, after Singer refused to give up his children to state authorities, Utah law enforcement officers returned to arrest him and surrounded his home. After refusing to surrender, he reportedly pointed his pistol at the officers, who then shot him multiple times, killing him (Weinriter 1994).

In 1988, Adam Swapp, Singer's son-in-law and "spiritual heir," bombed an LDS Stake Center (large regional parish) at Marion with dynamite and ammonium nitrate. He then retreated to the Singer-Swapp compound, and a thirteen-day stand-off with state authorities, the FBI, and the Bureau of Alcohol, Tobacco, and Firearms began. Swapp believed his actions would lead to the resurrection of John Singer and the downfall of the government. During the standoff, Singer's son, John Timothy Singer, shot and killed a police officer. Both John Timothy Singer and Addam Swapp were convicted of manslaughter and the bombing of the church, and both went to prison. Vickie Singer was also sentenced to five years in prison.

THE RIGHT TO ADOPT A CHILD
OR GAIN CUSTODY OF A CHILD

One of the first cases I studied during my fieldwork among polygamists was the petition of Hildale FLDS polygamists Vaughn and Sharane Fischer to adopt the six children of Vaughn's third wife, Brenda Johanson Thornton, who had died two months after their wedding. At first, Judge Dean Conder denied the petition, saying that polygamy is a crime, that it constituted immoral conduct, and that it would not be in the best interests of the children to be raised in "such an atmosphere" (Spangler 1988, 1). The Fischers and the Utah Department of Social Services argued that the issue should not be about plural marriage but about whether the parents had the skills and willingness to care for the children. A social worker from the Division of Family Services visited the Fischer home and reported that the family was highly qualified to adopt the six children, who at the time were aged five to nineteen. Although

Brenda Thornton had signed over custody of the children to the Fischers before her death and had requested they legally adopt the children, her two monogamous sisters, Pat and Janet Johanson, opposed the adoption. They did not want the children to be raised in polygamy because it is illegal. The Fischers' attorney, Steven Snow, argued that there was no law that banned a polygamous couple from adopting. Based on this argument, 5th Circuit Judge Conder granted the Fischers the right to adopt the children on March 26, 1991. Utah justice Christine Durham stated that although Utah's Constitution requires the state to prohibit polygamy, this "does not necessarily mean that the state must deny any or all civil rights and privileges to polygamists" (House 1998). Utah's highest court overturned Judge Conder's decision and decided the Fischers could not be prohibited from adopting purely because of the polygamist lifestyle; that the trial court must make a determination as to the child's best interests considering all the factors, polygamy among others. Yet Supreme Court justice Richard Howe disagreed with the ruling, stating that a child should not be raised by parents who are engaging in criminal activity. He felt that it would "breed in the children a disrespect for other laws" (ibid.).

Prior to the Fischer case, in 1987, a Cedar City case was heard, *Sanderson v. Tryon* (739 P.2d 623, Utah 1987). A judge had followed *Black* and ruled that a mother could not have custody because she was still in a polygamous relationship, even though the father was not (two wives had left him). This case also went to the state Supreme Court, which ruled, in a badly reasoned decision, that *Black* did not preclude the court from granting custody to whichever parent was in the child's best interests, reasoning that juvenile court is different than a case of parent vs. parent.

The *Sanderson* case paved the way for a favorable custody ruling for a polygamist man in Washington state. In 2005, I received a call from my friend and key informant, Rod Williams, formerly of the Allred Group, now living with his three wives and four children in the Olympic Peninsula. He said his third wife had discovered that she was really in love with another woman and wanted a divorce. She wanted custody of their three children. Eventually, this situation exploded in disharmony between the third wife and her two co-wives and husband, to the deep disappointment of the two wives, who loved her and her children. When all the evidence was presented before the Washington judge, primary custody was awarded to Rod and his two wives and not to the birth mother. The Clallam County judge based his decision on the quality of care the children would receive in the Williams home, not on the fact that the mother was a lesbian. This suggests that, at least in the state of Washington, a polygamist can be granted custody in a fair trial without discrimination against his/her beliefs in plural marriage.

Another custody battle occurred in a polygamist compound in Concho, Arizona (Crawford 2008). Sarine Jessop, the mother of eight, left her husband when he sought to bring teenage girls into the marriage. She took her husband to court to sue him for custody of their children, which pitted her against the high-ranking Jessop family in the FLDS group. According to a Jessop informant, Sarine was not a good mother; she was said to have locked her children outside so she could nap and to have used them as indentured servants. In the end, though, she was awarded custody of her children because of the FLDS reputation for marrying underage girls.

THE RIGHT TO CHILD SUPPORT

In 2005, Michael Combs of Colorado was forced to pay child support to his plural wife after she left him (Frazier 2005). In 1978, when she was just seventeen, Brenda Tibbitts, who at the time was living in Estes Park, Colorado, met Michael and his wife, Debbie. Brenda and her sister Carlene, who was nineteen at the time, agreed to both marry Michael in a "celestial" ceremony performed by Alex Joseph. The sisters' father had just died, and they were promised that if they married Michael, it would draw them closer to their father. Their mother sought to have Michael arrested for polygamy, but as long as there were no complaints by his wives and they were of age to marry, the law couldn't do anything. Shortly after the wedding to Michael, Brenda became pregnant, at which point Michael took her car away from her and sold it, preventing her from leaving the marriage. Many years later, Brenda claimed he threatened to take her children away from her if she left him and restricted her from having friends outside the clan.

Brenda eventually left the marriage, taking her children with her, but she was destitute. She had lived with Michael in a luxurious 9,000-square foot home in Sanborn Park, Colorado but she soon had nothing. Her co-wife and sister, Carlene, also lived with Michael in a separate 9,000-square foot log cabin, and Debbie, who was content to stay in the marriage, had her own home in Montrose, Colorado. Although Michael eventually sent $4,000 each month in child support payments to Brenda, in 2004 he stopped making payments. Brenda took Michael to court, basing her case on the fact that polygamy is illegal in Colorado and on his duty to her children as their biological father. His case was based on a dissolved relationship and the fact that she knew that he had a wife when she married him. Though Michael was initially charged with bigamy, Judge Kirk Samuelson eventually ruled that Michael and Brenda had been married in the context of their religious faith and ordered Michael to pay $48,000 in back child support, plus attorney's fees. Brenda also sought a decision about her demand for $2.5 million for her share in HoneyCombs Industries, the family's vitamin business, which had been promised her in the marriage agreement (Frazier 2005). The judge awarded her this money. The judge in Colorado set a precedent by honoring religiously sanctioned polygamous unions and taught a vital lesson to polygamist men: even though their plural wives are not legal in the eyes of the state, they can petition for financial support if they leave the marriage. The judge's ruling also shows that child support payments are not dependent on marital status. Generally, married couples and common-law couples that have separated are treated equally by the courts in cases of child support.

THE RIGHT TO BUY A HOME

Do polygamists have the right to buy any home they wish? Do they have the right to sue someone who refuses to sell them a home because of their religious beliefs and family style? In 1996, Henry, Mark, and Hyrum Barlow of the Allred Group sought to buy $468,070 worth of land in a Lehi subdivision to build homes for their families. But the sellers of the land broke the contract of sale when they became suspicious that the buyers were polygamists. So the Barlow family sued the sellers, claiming that they had violated the federal Fair Housing Act by refusing to sell to polygamists, using the argument that it was religious discrimination. Judge Dee Benson found against the Barlows, stating that polygamy is unlawful and cannot be protected, citing the 1878 *Reynolds* decision. Benson also stated that polygamy is "one of those rare religious practices that is contrary to the interest of society and undeserving of constitutional protection" (House 1998, 2).

Many polygamists avoid such conflicts by buying land as a group and living in homes built by the community in isolated areas. But those who seek integration and want to live near work in larger towns and cities must hide their status as polygamists in order to get a better price on their homes, live in a neighborhood of orthodox Mormons, and keep their jobs. There is no protection for polygamists in this integration process, yet it is the very charge given to them by law enforcement and state officials: avoid living in remote areas and act as true citizens by integrating with the mainstream.

THE RIGHT TO IMMIGRATE AS POLYGAMISTS

In the fall of 2010, I became a witness in *Maikudi v. Canada,* a case that offers evidence of both the inward and outward faces of the polygamous lifestyle. Maikudi, an immigrant from West Africa, sought to bring his second wife into Canada through the Canadian Charter of Rights and Freedoms, which guarantees freedom of conscience and religion under Section 2(a). Maikudi's lawyers charged that Canada's Immigration and Refugee Protection Act and Section 293 of the Criminal Code both violate this guarantee of freedom of religion. The case is still unresolved. It raises questions about the rights of immigrants to protect their families, practice their faith, and maintain cultural integrity.

Queen's University law professor Martha Bailey has argued that we should continue to expand the longstanding practice of recognizing valid foreign polygamous relationships. In 2005, she and her Status of Women Canada colleagues stated that the Canadian legal principle of "universality of status" should be recognized.[18] This means that both foreign and domestic polygamous unions should be allowed and that although there is an association between some polygamy and gender inequity, the concern should be to defend an individual's right to marry as they wish. Bailey told reporters that criminalizing polygamy serves no good purpose. She asked: "Why criminalize the behavior? We don't criminalize adultery. In light of the fact that we have a fairly permissive society, why are we singling out that particular form of behavior for criminalization? . . . No one is actually being prosecuted but the provision is still being used in the context of immigration and refugee stuff. People are not being admitted to the country" (Leong 2006).

THE RIGHT TO RUN FOR PUBLIC OFFICE

On the television program *Big Love,* fictional Bill Henrickson served as a state senator. Is this achievement possible in the real world? If polygamy is a felony, is it illegal for any polygamist to hold a public office? Both Roy Potter and Judge Steed were fired from public office. But some polygamists have held elected positions of public service. Alex Joseph was elected as mayor of Big Water, a southern Utah town, while he was married to seven women. Joseph, who was known for his libertarian politics and fundamentalist ideals, simultaneously promoted women's liberation and gun rights. Dan Jessop, the man who was ousted from the FLDS by Warren Jeffs in 2004 and whose wives were assigned to other men in the group, was the mayor of Colorado City, Arizona, for 19 years. While he was in office, Barlow often acted as the spokesmen for the group to the press and authorities. Finally, a small number of Allred men have served as deputy sheriffs in Ravalli County, Montana.

The advantages of polygamists holding public office are many. They can assert their political opinions more effectively if they hold positions of power in the towns, counties, and states where they live. They can influence policies and strategies to better care for vulnerable people in their communities and submit new bills in the legislature to overthrow *Reynolds* and various other prohibitions against the poly lifestyle. One of the disadvantages, of course, is that polygamy is officially illegal and it sets a poor standard if elected officials are felons. Polygamists are in direct violation of the criminal code and should not be in a position of political, or legal, leadership because their ability to uphold the law will be sorely compromised. Another negative is that fundamentalist polygamists represent such a small, insular population that any elected official above the level of township would be so out of touch with mainstream needs that their positions would be incongruous with their constituents. They would advocate for policies that are too extreme for the American public such as home schooling of children, school prayer, relaxed firearms laws, lower taxes, the removal of restrictions on land use, and the eradication of sex education from public schools. These are policies that, even in a conservative state like Utah, might alienate the mainstream voting public.

Weighing Legal Options in North America

The history of polygamy legislation is replete with hidden agendas and cultural misunderstandings. In the 1800s the agenda was to fight the threat of a Mormon nation-state. In the 1900s the government sought to combat the threat of a non-normative religious sect to the traditional American family. Yet in the twenty-first century, law enforcement has been at times tolerant and progressive and at other times overaggressive and intolerant. Since polygamists have an undeniable place in American society, we cannot afford to ignore their needs. These are a people who want the freedom to mesh their lifestyle with their beliefs without having to continually battle the state for the right to practice those beliefs. And there is no indication that they will yield (Altman and Ginat 1996). So what are our options in evaluating the 150-year-old legal ban on polygamy? Should we maintain the anti-polygamy law? Should we decriminalize polygamy, as other western democracies have done? Or should we legalize polygamy in order to better monitor and regulate the practice?

In determining our course in this debate, we need to clarify the definitions of decriminalization, legalization, and legal recognition. According to Martha Bailey, decriminalization means eliminating the criminal prohibition against polygamy, but it does not mean that polygamous marriages will be permitted or regulated by the state or that parties to polygamous marriages will be entitled to the legal benefits or burdens of marriage. Legalizing polygamy means changing civil marriage laws to include polygamous marriages (e-mail correspondence, July 2011). Brandeis professor Lisa Fishbayn Joffe adds that both decriminalization and legalization would mean that people would not be punished for polygamous relationships but they not mean that polygamous relationships would be legally recognized or that any marriage-like rights would be attached to them. However, legal recognition of polygamy as a valid form of marriage would attach marriage rights to the relationship and would allow these relationships to be regulated through laws of marriage and divorce, as in South Africa (e-mail correspondence, August 2011).

MAINTAINING THE CRIMINAL BAN AGAINST POLYGAMY

Many logical arguments have been expressed about the dangers of polygamy by scholars, politicians, and former members of polygamist groups, but by far the most compelling arguments come from law professors Maura Strassberg (2010) and Rebecca Cook and Lisa M. Kelly (2006). These arguments can be summed up as follows: polygamy fosters crimes against women and children, polygamy is a danger to a democratic society, and legalization would open up Pandora's box.

Point No. 1: Polygamy fosters crimes against women and children. This argument suggests that polygamy is inherently evil and creates an environment that fosters male supremacist ideologies and misogyny, giving rise to some of the worst characteristics of human barbarism: incest, underage marriage, sexual abuse, rape, physical abuse, nonconsensual marriage, birth defects, welfare fraud, poverty, and educational deprivation. Those who take this position argue that these traits directly threaten the health and well-being of women and children, and since they produce harm, they should be universally banned.

In 2006, Cook and Kelly recommended that the anti-polygamy law be maintained based on a series of assumptions about harmful abuse perpetrated against polygamous women. They found that polygamy uniformly: "violate[s] women's right to freedom by requiring obedience, modesty, and chastity codes that preclude women from operating as full citizens and enjoying their civil and political rights. Further, women can often be socialized into subservient roles that inhibit their full participation in family and public life. The physical, mental, sexual and reproductive, economic, and citizenship harms associated with the practice violate many of the fundamental human rights recognized in international law" (Cook and Kelly 2006, 6).

Cook emphasized that polygamy is a violation of women's right to equality within marriage and the family. She seeks to legally prohibit polygamy based on the following factors:

- Male supremacy/patriarchy
- Female subordination or treatment of women as property
- Complex sexual relations
- Competition between co-wives
- Family-related stress and mental illness among women
- Dangers to women's mental, physical, and sexual, and reproductive health
- Women's economic instability and vulnerability
- Isolation and alienation of women and children
- Low levels of socioeconomic status, academic achievement, and self-esteem for children

Cook recommended that polygamy continue to be illegal in perpetuity and that the government ban it in both its patriarchal and egalitarian forms.

In August 2007, based upon Cook and Kelly's report, the National Council of Women of Canada issued an official statement opposing polygamy. They stated that polygamy is a crime and that it is abusive. The council condemns polygamy, and "the immigration and emigration of women and female children for sexual and breeding purposes, and the abuse of women and children in polygamous communities" (as quoted in Cook and Kelly 2006, 6). They asked the government to immediately attempt to enforce the criminal code, rejecting the argument that criminalization of polygamy conflicts with the guarantees of freedom of religion in the Canadian Charter. They noted that the Charter of Rights and Freedoms is often cited as a reason not to intervene on behalf of girls at risk for abuse. They feel that there are reasonable limits of the freedom law that are justification for protecting the rights of female minors. Further, they wrote that polygamy has already been condemned as a contravention of women's equality rights by the UN's Office of the High Commissioner for Human Rights.

Tapestry Against Polygamy, a refuge organization for escapees from polygamy, claims that most polygamist women are trapped in a lifestyle that is abusive and disempowering. Its position is that polygamist communities violate the rights of women, children, and men, especially those who dissent or oppose those in power. The leaders of such groups coerce underage girls into marriage and they conduct wholesale deportation and alienation of young males. In some cases, polygamist groups sanction corporal punishment and violence as a tool to facilitate obedience and restrict the access of women and children to valuable educational and economic opportunities (Kenworthy 1998). This lack of education, in turn, limits women's ability to join the work force, forcing them to become financially and emotionally dependent on their husbands and forcing them into roles as dutiful wives and mothers. Further, because few men can support such large families and because favorable economic stewardships are given to select men who have connections to the leaders of the group, there is considerable economic inequality, leaving many families impoverished. Polygamy also means inbreeding, dependence on welfare, and extreme fertility, compounding the problems of poverty and inequality (Duncan 2008).

Lawyer Maura Strassberg (2010) has stated that the victimization of young women associated with polygamy must be criminalized. There is considerable pressure for girls and women to enter a polygamous marriage. Should a girl refuse, she is told that she could jeopardize her salvation and let the whole community down as well as lose financial and social security. She is encouraged to have as many children as possible and to get pregnant very soon after marriage. Strassberg's position is that this kind of tyrannical control over young women is intolerable. She also points out that if the state decriminalizes polygamy, the male perpetrators of statutory rape will not be prosecuted.

Law professor Linda Smith (2011) argues that forcing a fifteen-year-old into a "spiritual union" with an older male is abusive because it denies that girl the time and freedom to develop an autonomous identity. It is inappropriate to force or control an adolescent's sexuality, whether that be denying the right of lesbigay youth to express their sexual selves or forcing FLDS adolescent girls into early sexual unions. Psychologically, it is the same sort of inappropriate and unhealthy control of the emerging self. In some groups, a plural wife is apt to lack a high school diploma because of her early motherhood. She is also likely to have little or no financial support from a husband who has other families as well and to be surviving economically only through the formal assistance of the church and informal support networks of sister wives and other plural wives who are in similar situations. She may well lose these critical sources of support if she seriously reconsiders plural marriage and has no connections outside the isolated community that makes plural marriage "its defining ideology and practice" (Strassberg 2010, 4). Having many children of her own may make her feel that she cannot escape the group, especially without independent socioeconomic resources to help her obtain a divorce, custody of her children, and child support payments from the biological father. In many extreme cases, if a woman does have the courage to try to leave an abusive situation, she knows that she may have to leave her children behind under fundamentalist religious doctrine.

Finally, Strassberg says, criminalization would deter both men and women from entering into an outlaw lifestyle that required them to hide. It would also discourage naive experimentation, saving many women from the dangers of marital entanglements. Polygamist groups use a "masochistic ideology of plural marriage, not amenable to external influence at all" (Strassberg 2010, 3). For many women, especially those who have tapped into media outlets and community resources, escaping from abuse has trumped their beliefs in a religion that sanctions unhealthy conditions; they are willing to leave this way of life behind forever. Other women wish to "martyr" themselves for religious reasons, embracing their suffering as part of their journey toward polishing the soul.

Point No. 2: Polygamy is a danger to a democratic society. Strassberg (2010) wrote that Mormon fundamentalism is a cultural enclave that is a political lifestyle that has the potential to contribute to the demise of our democratic system. She feels that because polygamy operates in a tyrannical, patriarchal fashion, it is inappropriate in a nation that fosters equality and justice. Plural marriage injures our liberal democratic state and the people who practice it. She argued: "Polygyny not only fails to produce critical building blocks of liberal democracy, such as autonomous individuality, robust public and private spheres, and affirmative reconciliation of individuality and social existence, but promotes a despotic state populated by subjects rather than citizens. [Polygamists] have retreated from civil society, cloaking their members in insular, theocratic-fundamentalist polygamous enclaves that segregate themselves from society and perpetuate both abuse against their members and fraud against the state" (ibid., 3).

Strassberg felt that unless there is a war or a mass migration that shifts our current sex ratios, polygamy is a "zero sum game" where some men have many wives at the expense of others. Polygamy is unregulated and, therefore, incompatible with our democracy and human rights agenda. Because she believes that polygamy poses a significant political threat, Strassberg feels that criminalization is not only justified, it is constitutional, just as it was in the nineteenth century. Polygamy is also a danger because it is often associated with crimes, including welfare fraud and child abuse, that draw upon the a state's child protection, law enforcement, and judicial resources.

Point No. 3: Legalizing polygamy opens Pandora's box. James Dobson (1991), who sees a template for monogamy in the Bible, is a well-known warrior for traditional family and gender roles. He promotes the "natural" division of male and female worlds, basing his argument on biology, and advocates policies that would punish those who deviate from heteronormative monogamy. Dobson, who has mobilized public outrage about both same-sex marriage and polygamy, encouraged Congress to pass the Defense of Marriage Act and state-level "baby DOMAs," including Proposition 8 in California, which repealed that state's gay marriage law. He and other DOMA advocates are worried that if gay marriage is adopted, other deviant forms such as polygamy will follow suit (Pro-Polygamy.com 2005). He has said, "It's only a matter of time before the homosexual agenda in South Africa reaches an even more radical level, as it already has in the U.S.A., where certain groups are seeking to legalize pedophilia, polygamy, and polyandry" (Dobson 2004, 1).[19] Columnist Stanley Kurtz (2006) agrees: "If we are going to argue people ought to be able to marry who they want and have plural marriage, how different is that from saying you ought to allow homosexual marriages?" (ibid., 3). Utah's House Speaker, Marty Stephens, has warned that tampering with anti-polygamy laws is dangerous. Once the United States legalizes lesbian and gay marriage, all deviant forms of marriage will come out of the woodwork, he fears (Stacey and Meadow 2009). Dobson, Kurtz, and Stephens all voice the growing fear—common among those who advocate that the ban on polygamy be maintained—that legalizing polygamy or any other marginal form of marriage will make it possible for other nonnormative forms of marriage to gain a stronger foothold, further destroying the traditional American family.

Critique The history of polygamy and the law shows an intolerance of plural marriage based on a variety of arguments, ranging from the belief that polygamy poses a threat to public morality and liberal democracy to the belief that polygamy violates human rights of women and children and that the system carries the potential for the abuse of vulnerable persons. In the end, however, a bigger threat to a true democracy is intolerance itself. As long as individuals and groups meet certain minimal conditions, including the absence of child marriage, the absence of sexual abuse, and clear exit policies for wives, poly forms of marriage could easily coexist with serial monogamy, grandparent parenting, sister motherhood, cohabitation, and lesbian and gay marriage. These minimal conditions could be achieved by decriminalization or legalization.

North American anti-polygamy laws reflect the ethnocentric myth that all polygamy is abusive and harmful. These laws fail to take into account the rich and varied experiences of polygamous women, who are often marginalized by the monogamous, mainstream. The assumption that all polygamy is abusive lacks substantive evidence of abuse. Such assertions fail to acknowledge data that finds that many plural families around the world appear to operate successfully. The cases of polygamy Rebecca Cook (2006) cited to support her argument that polygamy is inherently abusive are primarily sensationalized instances of abuse reported by former members of polygamous groups. These stories are associated with a few very isolated fundamentalist groups; they do not represent the norm of family life within fundamentalist polygamist society. Indeed, the only longitudinal ethnographic study of women's lives in polygamy is my own work, which Cook felt offered helpful insights into the relative benefits of polygamy: "Indeed the networking Janet Bennion outlined in her scholarship on contemporary Fundamentalist Mormon polygamy signals that this type of social framework is already being used by women." Cook also felt that more scholarship on the topic can help "women within the Fundamentalist Mormon communities to re-define religious doctrine that subordinates them while still being able to embrace faith components that are normatively valuable" (ibid., 7).

I question Cook's assumption that polygamy unequivocally "violates women's right to equality within marriage and the family" (Cook 2006, 6). Rather, my research reveals that some polygamous families achieve long-term satisfaction and longevity in the context of the North American plural experiment. This evidence also shows that polygamists are not all alike, a significant portion of polygamists—such as Joe Darger—marry adult women with their full consent and live within their means without government aid. Part of the problem in the discourse about polygamy is the dichotomous view of it as either evil, patriarchal, and Mormon or good, egalitarian, liberating, and non-Mormon. Many are more familiar with the non-Mormon version of polygamy that is based on an egalitarian family structure in which there is little exploitation and in which progressive, secular men and women of their own free will form poly families in an environment that is conducive to collaboration and individual freedom. In spite of my work to provide evidence of the variability in Mormon polygamy, most observers see only the oppressive, exploitive version. I argue that both forms exist within Mormon fundamentalism, as well as every shade of gray in between.

Polygamy itself poses no risk to modern democracy; instead, it is the criminalization of polygamy that is undemocratic. If any family form that "inconsistent with the values of the mainstream" is disallowed, that would mean that families where two women or two men raise a child and grandparent-headed families should also be disallowed. You would also have to make informal polygamy illegal, where a man marries a woman, bears children, abandons his wife and children, and repeats the cycle. You would also have to safeguard against the father absence associated with serial monogamy. Should adultery and neglect also be criminalized? Both pose challenges to female empowerment and equality.

Prohibiting plural marriage opens other forms of marriage to question, such as those based in cultural customs. Such prohibitions would endanger the custom of arranged marriages that is common in African, Indian, and Middle Eastern cultures. Such customs have been proven to create marriages that are longer lasting and are more satisfying overall to the marriage partners than the serial monogamy that is prevalent in the United States (Hayyat 2011).[20] It is ethnocentric to assume that people should reject this form of marriage in order to adopt a more "romantic" version promoted by Hollywood.

These nonnormative forms should not pose a threat to our moral and social schema for the very reason that we do not agree on any single social schema when it comes to marriage. We are in a state of dynamic fluctuation regarding sexuality and marriage today, and the tendency toward tolerance and experimentation is growing. In this context, we must see the polygamy experiment as one of many forms of marriage that may succeed or fail within the larger context of the modern world.

A final critique is that the criminalization of polygamy makes all polygamists criminals. Such laws feed into stereotypes that there is a causal relationship between polygamy and abuse. If polygamy as a marriage form is a crime, then it doesn't really matter what a polygamist does. He or she could live a law-abiding lifestyle but would still be a criminal. If polygamy is legalized, individual abusers would be prosecuted for their crimes and entire communities would not become targets of government raids. Polygamous men who are older than their teenage plural wives would automatically be vulnerable to prosecution under statutory rape laws. At the same time, polygamous husbands and their plural wives who marry as consenting adults would no longer be at risk of prosecution for violating the law.

DECRIMINALIZING POLYGAMY

Arguments about decriminalization typically follow several lines of logic: 1) polygamy will be practiced whether we like it or not; 2) banning polygamy is unconstitutional; 3) criminalization further isolates and alienates fundamentalist movements; 4) many democracies decriminalize polygamy; 5) monogamy is no better than polygamy; and 6) laws against polygamy are hypocritical.

Point No. 1: Polygamy will be practiced whether we like it or not. Although most western nations, like the United States and Canada, do not permit either bigamy or polygamy, such laws are rarely enforced. Polygamy is practiced by 30,000 to 100,000 people in North America (Altman 1996; Bennion 1998). Further, the number of polygamists in the United States is growing. In Utah alone, the poly community has grown tenfold over the last fifty years and now makes up 2 percent of Utah's population. In Colorado City, Arizona, the polygamist population has doubled every decade since the 1930s. Polygamists maintain their high numbers because of their extraordinarily high natural birth rates and because people continue to convert to Mormon fundamentalism (Duncan 2008). According to Attorney General Mark L. Shurtleff of Utah, the poly population has every intention of continuing their lifestyle. He has stated, "You can't incarcerate them all. You can't drive them out of the state. So they are here. What do we do about it?" (quoted in Pomfret 2006, A1).

One reason for the increase in polygamy is the growing appeal of the lifestyle for single mothers looking for a home for their children. These women are economically vulnerable because of an extremely high rate of absentee fathers and because of discrimination against working mothers (the "mommy tax"). Another reason is that polygamy appeals to Mormon women who are searching for their "savior on Mt. Zion." Men who refuse to defer to an oppressive government or a bureaucratic church structure are drawn to polygamy by the Mormon fundamentalism's promise of political and ideological power. Polygamy gains in popularity after government raids and mass prosecutions. These events "deepen [polygamists'] sense of persecution and community solidarity" (Driggs 2011, 94). The fact that polygamy is illegal is irrelevant to many insular groups, as they believe that civil law is corrupt and Satanic. In short, people will continue to live in polygamy whether it is banned or not, just as people continued to drink during Prohibition.

Point No. 2: Banning polygamy is unconstitutional. Is the polygamy ban in direct violation of constitutional government? Does it violate the rights of citizens, including those that wish to immigrate from lands where polygamy is fully legal? The Status of Women Canada report by Angela Campbell and other legal scholars stated clearly that criminal sanctions against polygamy are a violation of the Charter of Rights and Freedoms, including the principles of freedom of religion and freedom from discrimination based on marital status (Campbell et al. 2005).

Campbell and her colleagues challenged the limitation clause of the Criminal Code, which states that a law prohibiting polygamy may be constitutional even if it violates Charter rights such as freedom of religion if the violation is otherwise justified in a free and democratic society. In the report, Queens University professor Nicholas Bala and his colleagues (2005) argued that the strongest argument for fundamentalist Mormons is that their faith requires polygamy as directed by their prophet, whereas Islam merely allows it (ibid., 30). The scholars who contributed to the Status of Women Canada report suggested that various Canadian laws should be changed to protect polygamous women by providing them with spousal support and inheritance rights (Campbell et al. 2005, iv). One of the authors, Martha Bailey, explained to a reporter how the current law violates polygamists' rights: "They are denied access to our divorce law. . . . You have a great deal of difficulty claiming your rights with access to children, custody of children and financial support for the children. . . . We are starting to make accommodations for some small things in some of the provinces [such as] extending support law to women and children in any kind of marriage" (quoted in Leong 2006).

Another possible constitutional argument comes from a dissenting opinion in *Lawrence v. Texas* (2003), which held that the Texas statute criminalizing sodomy was unconstitutional because it violated the due process clause. In his dissenting opinion to the majority ruling in that case, Judge Antonin Scalia wrote that "state laws against bigamy, same-sex marriage, adult incest, prostitution, masturbation, adultery, fornication, bestiality, and obscenity are likewise sustainable only in light of *Bowers'* validation of laws based on moral choices."[21] Yet moral offenses are very difficult to define in this day and age; any laws referring to morality seem antiquated and inappropriate in the modern era where sexual appetites are tolerated. Martha Bailey had stated that Canada, for the most part, does not intrude into the bedrooms of the nation by imposing criminal sanctions for private, noncommercial sexual activity among consenting adults. Adultery, group sex, and sexual relations between adoptive fathers and their adult children may be considered immoral or repugnant to many or even to most Canadians, but these activities are not crimes. Since these activities are not outlawed, why should plural marriage be criminalized? Further, Canada has a law-free space within which parties may engage in sexual activity without criminal sanction though they are not legally permitted to marry (Bailey 2010). Thus, it is hard to justify intervening in polygamous relations involving consenting adults.

U.S. Chief Justice Christine Durham also used the *Lawrence* case in her argument against the polygamy ban, which she stated should cover more than one type of sex act. According to Durham, that the cohabitation portion of the anti-bigamy law is in clear violation of *Lawrence*. If cohabitation is allowed, why wouldn't polygamy also be allowed? Which would be more offensive to the American conscience, she asked, a man who sleeps with many women without his wife's consent or a man like Tom Green who has several wives who gave their full consent to the plural marriage? Durham argues that *Lawrence* held that the constitutional right to privacy includes the right of adults to enter into consensual, intimate relationships without interference from the state.[22]

George Macintosh, the court-appointed amicus curiae in the Bountiful case about the constitutionality of the polygamy provision in the Criminal Code of Canada, argues that the Code itself is an act of discrimination perpetrated by the government because it makes any sexual relationship involving more than two people a crime, regardless of whether that relationship is harmful. The Code acts against women and children, whom the government claims are victims, as well as vulnerable religious minorities, such as the self-described fundamentalist Mormons of Bountiful. He stated, "The criminalization of polygamy is perpetuating prejudice and perpetuating stereotyping . . . used to target groups that are already disadvantaged. The clearest examples are fundamentalist Mormons and aboriginal persons" (Macintosh, Herbst, and Dickson 2009, 106).

This prejudice against a marginal religious movement is promoted by labeling polygamy a cult. The term "cult" is laden with negativity and is often by the media when describing paranoid, suicidal, or murderous groups. Yet a cult is also a group of gentle, creative, and peaceful people who simply have a cause that is outside the norms of mainstream society. The depiction we see of polygamists is often rooted in the dissatisfaction of former members and in political agendas rather than in representations of real life.

Finally, Martha Bailey argues that decriminalization would not threaten Canada's cultural commitment to monogamous marriage, which is sufficiently protected by the civil laws of marriage and the criminal prohibition of bigamy (Bailey 2010, 3). Decriminalizing polygamy would simply mean that Canada would follow the example of other monogamous, democratic countries and that polygamy no longer be a criminal offense.

Point No. 3: Criminalization further isolates and alienates fundamentalist movements. Rendering polygamy illegal may actually exacerbate some problems associated with closed religious communities (Bailey 2010; Duncan 2008; Bennion 2011b). Criminalization promotes fear and isolation, leading to greater secrecy. It is in these conditions that the abuse associated with "outlaw" fundamentalism can emerge. Thus, greater isolation makes women more vulnerable and more susceptible to male domination. A woman is more fully under the thumb of her tyrannical husband when other women, relatives, or social support networks are not around to help her, as is often the case in insular polygamous family life. Fear of prosecution or arrest causes groups to go deeper into rural isolated areas and discourages women and children from getting help and education. Isolation also enables sexual abuse, neglect, underage marriage, and welfare fraud to flourish because such practices are unregulated and unmonitored when families hide. The illegal status of polygamy feeds a fear and loathing of the government, dooming any attempt at intervention. Members of such families tend to see the government as an evil entity that violates constitutional rights by separating children from their mothers. This fear further isolates the fundamentalist community and unifies members in their hatred of authority.

According to George Macintosh, rendering polygamy illegal has the following negative effects:

- Offending the dignity of women who choose polygamous lifestyles
- Impeding the open expression of religious identities and values, or lifestyle choices
- Harmful and unnecessary stress from the impediment of open expression and the fear of prosecution
- Stigmatizing members of polygamous relationships and communities
- Justifying abuse toward polygamous communities and their members
- Causing or heightening insularity for polygamous communities, making their members less likely to access (or know about) outside social and police services, and potentially making them more vulnerable to abuse
- Jeopardizing the incomes and support structures of polygamous families whose members could be fined or incarcerated
- Diverting energy and funds from improving polygamous communities and the lives of their members to legal proceedings (Macintosh, Herbst, and Dickson 2009, 9)

Point No. 4: Many democracies have decriminalized polygamy. Nearly fifty countries recognize polygamy as a lawful form of marriage. Most of these are Muslim and African nations, although Israel, Turkey, Tunisia, and recently Egypt also have such laws (El Alami and Hinchcliffe 1996). Many western democracies such as Britain, Jamaica, Australia, France, and New Zealand recognize polygamous marriages entered into in countries that permit them. These countries also do not criminalize bigamy defined as open cohabitation with more than one person. Although France has adopted stricter immigration laws regarding polygamists, Britain grants welfare benefits to foreign polygamists (Wynne-Jones 2008). Britain also handles its Muslim immigrant population with relative grace; even though the country's moral standard is monogamy, it has not made polygamy a criminal offense. Thus, Britain is in full compliance with United Nations human rights principles.

South Africa has granted legal recognition to both polygamy and lesbian and gay marriage (Stacey and Meadow 2009). In 1998, the South African Parliament passed the Recognition of Customary Marriages Act, which respects customary law and protect women's rights. This act recognizes all past customary unions as marriages but also reforms the marriage so that women and men are formally equal in the marriage. The state thus regulates open and officially legal polygamous marriage. In order to take a second or subsequent wife, a man must make a written contract with existing wife fairly dividing the property accrued at that point and persuade a family court that the contract is fair for all involved. Legal recognition of polygamy subjects its practice to a standard of gender equality and prevents the abuses against women so often associated with the Mormon fundamentalist condition (ibid.).

The United States and Canada, by contrast, do not recognize or sanction polygamous marriages, although Canada recognizes some types of foreign polygamy as valid in certain circumstances, defined as those that do not undermine the monogamous character of the nation (Bailey 2007). If Canada and the United States were to adopt South Africa's policy, the conditions of entry into and exit from a plural union would be monitored and regulated by the state. Obtaining consent from the previous wife would be an essential legal step in this process. The next step would be to require a document or contract that ensured equal distribution of property and that the husband was economically prepared to support all of his wives; all parties to the marriage would sign this contract. Perhaps a third step would be to obtain approval of a family court judge to secure the rights of current and future wives as well as evaluate the state of the well-being of the children. Finally, some form of regulation should be in place to secure the exit rights of any of the wives, should they wish to quit the marriage. As in South Africa, some form of qualified recognition of polygamy can better protect the basic rights of women and children in polygamous households than the current illegal status. Young women, especially, would enjoy increased benefits in this qualified recogni tion, such as freedom from abuse and coercion and access to health care and nutrition, education, and social support networks. Above all, prenuptial legal contracts would require new brides to demonstrate that they were of legal age and that were entering the union with their full consent.

Point No. 5: Monogamy is no better than polygamy. Many scholars (Dixon-Spear 2009; Bennion 2008; Kilbride 1994) question whether monogamy and other forms of sexuality are free from human rights violations. There is ample evidence to show that serial monogamy, the prevalent form of marriage in the North American context, is associated with many severe problems, including male absence, feminization of poverty, physical abuses against women and children, and so on. Most Americans are involved, at one point or another, in secondary or tertiary alliances, especially in the context of consecutive marriages. Most Americans are, in fact, incapable of true monogamy, defined as sexual loyalty to only one individual for an entire life. As libertarian John Tierney has stated: "Polygamy isn't necessarily worse than the current American alternative: serial monogamy" (Tierney 2006, 1).

Feminist Elizabeth Joseph of Big Water, Utah, who is also a lawyer and polygamist wife, argues that polygamy is a potential weapon in the ongoing battle of the sexes caused by dyadic monogamy. Joseph has called plural marriage "the ultimate feminist lifestyle" (Joseph 1997, 26) because it permits men's basic (or is it base?) instincts to express themselves while using the marital structure to domesticate and discipline them. Following this logic, within polygamy men can serve their biological impulses for multiple partners but may not be deceitful or disrespectful. They can have multiple sexual partners, but they may not turn women into prostitutes. Joseph thus defends plural marriage as preferable to the alternative of men's inevitable adultery and infidelity. Yet she points out that it is also a venue for the empowerment, freedom, and liberation of women.

Anthropologist Phil Kilbride of Bryn Mawr has suggested that we reevaluate our phobia of polygamy so that we can pass legislation that is appropriate for our changing socioeconomic needs. He states that frequent divorce and remarriage, separation of children from parents, multiplication of step-relations, and total breakdown of parental investment all suggest that serial monogamy is in trouble and may not be any better than polygamy. Pro-polygamy activists such as Mary Batchelor and Anne Wilde agree that monogamy is not a shining example of successful family life. They both believe that the healthy, child-loving, healing atmosphere of polygamous lifestyles is the perfect place to raise a family (interview with Batchelor and Wilde, 1993).

Some family scholars find the problems inherent in monogamy to be greater than those associated with polygamy (Benokraitus 2009). In my own research, I saw examples of women who found refuge in polygamy because they were deprived of socioeconomic resources within monogamy (Bennion 1998). Decades after Betty Friedan's *The Feminine Mystique,* even after substantial changes in gender roles, many women continue to complain that conventional monogamy leaves them craving deeper emotional intimacy and more equitable divisions of household labor. Thus far, frustrated wives have had three options: surrendering and consigning themselves to gender inequity and personal exhaustion, remaining locked in battle with their husbands, or divorce. Polygamy presents another option. For some women, increasing the ratio of women to men in a household might be more effective than pressuring husbands to "change" and conform to women's expectations. Done properly — that is, among women committed to feminist principles — polygamy can provide a "sisterhood" within marriage, provide more adults committed to balancing work/family obligations, and allow more leisure time for each wife.

Point No. 6: Laws against polygamy are hypocritical. This point suggests that if society is accepting of adultery, cohabitation, and homosexuality, it cannot in good conscience reject polygamy. That is, North American anti-polygamy laws are hypocritical when other forms of marriage are protected. Macintosh argued that if a nation decriminalizes homosexuality, it must also decriminalize polygamy. He believes that removing polygamy from Canada's Criminal Code would have the same positive effect as the decriminalization of homosexuality in 1969. He wrote, "In this sense, [the anti-polygamy law] is precisely the same as the law against homosexual sex, which was struck down in Canada 42 years ago" (Bramham 2011:2). Court cases linked to gay rights have opened the door to changing that what constitutes a lawful union a bit further.

University of Michigan law professor David L. Chambers drew attention to the connection between modern polygamous and lesbian households in the *Hofstra Law Review* stating, "Little Heather has two mommies, and more and more Americans believe that if Heather is doing well, then having two [or more] mommies is just fine" (quoted in House 1998, 1). Shortly after the *Lawrence* decision, in 2004, Brian Barnard, a civil rights attorney, filed suit to overturn Utah's ban on polygamy on behalf of a married couple wishing to enter into a plural marriage with another woman.

Interestingly, the creators of the HBO program *Big Love,* Mark Olsen and Will Scheffer, who are romantic as well as business partners, are advocates of alternative forms of marriage. They explained that they were intrigued by polygamists' enthusiastic response to the *Lawrence* decision: "We thought that just made such interesting, strange, and perverse bedfellows that it was just too delicious to not use" (quoted in Davis 2010, 1980). In other words, in a social and political climate where homosexuality is accepted, the *Big Love* writers ask, why should it matter how many women a man has sex with outside of marriage? And further, why should it be a crime to claim these women as "wives?" Yet, as lawyer Jonathan Turley states, "It is unlikely that any network is going to air *The Polygamist Eye for the Monogamist Guy* or add a polygamist twist to *Everyone Loves Raymond.*" However, Turley concludes, "No matter. The rights of polygamists should not be based on popularity, but principle" (Turley 2004, 1).

Columnist Charles Krauthammer argued that "it is utterly logical for polygamy rights to follow gay rights" (Krauthammer 2006:1). Although the two forms are somewhat antagonistic, they have come to share some surprising political affinities in the United States (Stacey and Meadow 2009). Both challenge the normative definition of monogamous heterosexual marriage that historians have shown to be central to the American identity. And both expose the inconsistencies between mainstream sexual and familial ideology and widespread intimate practices in the United States.

LEGAL RECOGNITION OF POLYGAMY

This option involves not only removing the criminal sanctions against polygamy (decriminalization) and changing the civil law to include plural marriage; it goes further to legally recognize marriage-like rights for polygamy and would allow poly relationships to be regulated. The stakeholders in the pro-legalization debate are Mormon fundamentalists, non-Mormon Christians, non-Christian polyamorists, Muslim immigrants, non-Muslim African immigrants, and African American converts to Islam, all of whom have a voice and agenda in the larger legal debate. Others are lawyers such as Jonathan Turley and Emily Duncan, who believe that laws against polygamy are unconstitutional and that legalization provides positive benefits, including protection for women. Scholars such as Debra Majeed and Patricia Dixon-Spear who are advocates of African American women who are adopting polygamy by consent, are also stakeholders in the debate (Majeed 2010; Dixon-Spear 2009). Additional stakeholders include theologians and leaders of religions that mandate or permit plural marriage, such as evangelical and fundamentalist Christians, African Hebrew Israelites of Jerusalem, and Muslims affiliated both with the Nation of Islam and Sunni sects.

Many of the arguments for legal recognition are the same as those for decriminalization; that is, most of the world's cultures practice it, people will continue to practice plural marriage whether it is illegal or not, and so on. Yet some arguments specifically apply to legal recognition: 1) polygamy represents a viable option for some women; 2) anti-polygamy laws are difficult to enforce; and 3) legal recognition will allow greater regulation of the practice.

Point No. 1: Polygamy represents a viable option for some women. Pro-polygamy feminists such as Anne Wilde, Elizabeth Joseph, and Christine Brown uniformly agree that if poly families do not practice abuse, fraud, or marriage to underage girls, their lifestyles should be legally recognized. Debra Majeed (2010), representing African American Muslim women, argues that polygamy should be legal to accommodate the needs of Islamic women. As the West increasingly welcomes Muslim immigrants from the Middle East and Asia, democratic governments must make plans to provide for poly families. More and more black Muslim women are adopting polygamy as a tool to preserve the integrity of the male-headed household, an anomaly in many inner-city black enclaves. Polygamy replaces the weak, matrifocal households that are often associated with black communities that suffer from imbalanced gender ratios, a lack of economic options, and the absence of fathers. In this view, polygamy is seen as a "pragmatic" or "charitable" solution to a socioeconomic crisis. Polygamy provides black women with (black) husbands and black children with fathers who are present and committed. Within such a context polygamy is seen as viable, practical, and of benefit to the larger community in dealing with a particular social problem. If the basis for reforming marriage laws becomes social pragmatism, viability, and individual happiness, then "arguments against incestuous, adolescent and polygamous marriages must also fall aside" (Witte 2004, 1).

Attorney Jon Turley also speaks for the legalization of polygamy as a viable choice, stating that though he personally finds plural marriage repugnant, it should not be illegal (as quoted in Pomfret 2006). Law professor Judith Stacey states that Americans yearn for a "creative panoply of intimacy and kinship arrangements" (2009, 185), pointing out that many would prefer families "we choose" rather than families that are "thrust on us" because of tradition or law (Weston 1997). The Progressive Family Values Conference (2007) recently posted a statement on its site that since most families are now alternative, policy makers should be concerned with how any family provides a context conducive to satisfaction, good health, and feelings of contentedness or well-being, regardless of form.

If polygamy was legally recognized, women could benefit from greater educational and occupational opportunities in the world outside their polygamist enclaves. They will learn to drive and hold legal drivers' licenses. They can get high school diplomas and attend college and vocational schools and apply for work that best matches their skills without risk of being fired.

Point No. 2: Anti-polygamy laws are difficult to enforce. Not a single polygamist was criminally prosecuted in the United States for polygamy from the 1950s to 2001, and in Canada there have been no convictions against polygamy since 1906. Even in 1992, in the context of allegations of abuse and sex trafficking, Canada authorities chose not to charge leaders of a fifty-member polygamous commune in Creston, British Columbia, concluding that laws banning plural marriage unconstitutionally restricted religious freedom. Some polygamists and social scientists believe that this decision is another "signpost on the road to legalizing polygamy in the United States" (House 1998, 2).

There are so few convictions because laws against polygamy are difficult to enforce. Current efforts at enforcement are ineffective for many reasons. First, any attempt to help people living in polygamy deal with problems is difficult because of their illegal status. If polygamy is legally recognized, these issue would be resolved. Second, enforcement requires evidence of criminal activity, which is incredibly hard to obtain. Utah Chief Deputy Attorney General Kirk Torgensen has argued that substantial evidence that would be believable in a court of law is very difficult to obtain because witnesses do not come forward (Winslow 2008). Duke lawyer Emily Duncan summarizes the many obstacles to prosecuting for polygamy: 1) you can't ask family members to testify against each other; 2) children are taught to fear and distrust the law; 3) there is no paper trail for births or unlawful marriages; 4) it is nearly impossible to obtain accurate evidence about abuse or about which jurisdiction perpetrators should even be prosecuted in; 5) local police and doctors in the fundamentalist communities often aid and abet residents engaged in criminal activity; 6) law enforcement and political officials are concerned about acting too aggressively against a practice some see as a protected religious activity; 7) busy prosecutors place greater focus on more serious offenses, ignoring polygamy; 8) many Mormon law enforcement officials are simply unwilling to charge consenting adults for religious beliefs their Mormon ancestors shared (Duncan 2008, 325).

Effective enforcement also requires public resources. Even if a state had unlimited funds to pursue inquiries and was able to gather irrefutable evidence for conviction, what would it do with all the guilty polygamists? They would have to build new prisons for tens of thousands of people, which would cost millions in taxpayers' money and leave a hundred thousand children on welfare, not to mention the thousands of polygamists' wives that would be left without their breadwinners. And what of all those guilty polygamists who are not guilty of any other crime? Victimless crimes draw manpower and funds away from crimes that do hurt innocent parties. Torgensen has stated that fighting polygamy is no longer feasible or manageable. The attorney general's office has stopped seeking the arrest of "truly consensual adults," which means that polygamy in Utah is in effect already decriminalized (Winslow 2008). This policy is in keeping with changing public opinion about plural marriage. In 1998, the Salt Lake Tribune published a survey that found that only 54 percent of 1,000 residents polled voiced concern about polygamy; around 46 percent felt there was no need for criminal prosecution.

Point No. 3: Legal recognition allows greater regulation of the practice. Legal recognition would encourage polygamists to come out of hiding and would make it possible to regulate polygamy. This would promote freedom for polygamists to have greater access to jobs and educational resources.

Recognizing polygamy would also allow law enforcement to pursue the criminal actions of individuals, such as child marriage and incest, not the culture itself. The "rights versus actions" argument of *Reynolds* v. United States will be refuted (Duncan 2008). Rather, polygamy would be legitimated as a "right" and abusive actions often associated with polygamy will be illegal regardless of their religious foundation, including family actions against minors. For example, Federal Senate Bill 146 should be passed and enforced, making it a felony for parents or religious leaders to solemnize or condone unlawful marriages to minors. Since most polygamists are not guilty of crimes against the state (other than polygamy), most would benefit from legal recognition. Those that do commit crimes would be prosecuted more fully and easily with the support of law-abiding polygamists who seek to remove the tarnish from their lifestyle. According to one FBI official, "At least 99 percent of all polygamists are peaceful, law-abiding people, no threat to anybody. It's unfortunate that they're stigmatized by a band of renegades" (Stumbo 1988, 1).

Mormon law enforcement in Utah and Arizona would be more likely to prosecute crimes against their peers if they believed it was polygamists' actions, not religious beliefs, that were being targeted for prosecution. New policies would also encourage cooperation between polygamists and law enforcement and more reliance on the Safety Net Program (a collaboration between government and polygamous groups) and other resources for individuals who wish to leave polygamy of their own volition. This cooperation would be enhanced by the fact that more polygamists could come forward without fear of incarceration. Collaboration with state and federal authorities would help officials defeat problems associated with underage marriage, incest, abuse, and nonconsensual marriage. Social scientists could engage in more open analysis of poly communities so they could identify the factors that contribute to abuse and other crimes and help law enforcement identify patterns of behavior and intervene to prevent problems, just as is attempted in monogamous society.

Legal recognition would prevent abuse before it occurs. The federal guidelines for sex abuse reporting don't work unless members of communities are willing to cooperate. One policy that has worked in the AUB of Montana is to have each branch track its own sex offenders in cooperation with the county sheriff's office. Following the example of U.S. tribal sovereignties, this policy requires communities to comply with the Adam Walsh Child Protection and Safety Act by publicizing the whereabouts of registered perpetrators. In Pinesdale, they have achieved an admirable compliance with this act. They have one registered sex offender who is under continual monitoring by their own Ravalli County detective, Jesse Jessop, who is assigned specifically to investigate sex crimes.

Also, legalizing polygamy would create a paper record of celestial marriages by requiring proper certification and licensing through a town clerk or a judge. This documentation would help prevent underage marriage and welfare fraud. Young women under 16 in the state of Utah would not be given licenses to marry, and plural wives would not be able to claim themselves as single mothers who have been abandoned by boyfriends in order to get welfare payments. The economic and social benefits of registering their marriages would replace the tendency toward welfare fraud; it would make it unnecessary. Births would also be publically recorded and children would be required to be immunized by law. Tax codes would be rewritten and social welfare benefits would be tailored to fit multiple spousal relationships and communal family needs.

If polygamy was legally recognized, more responsibility would be placed on the husband to take care of his economic responsibilities before taking subsequent wives, as is required in South Africa. It would make a fundamentalist man acknowledge his multiple wives and force him "to provide independently for his family or to marry fewer women" (Rower 2004, 728). This measure would require well-constructed plans for dealing with a poly family of multiple spouses with multiple needs and opinions. This would include laws requiring the formal consent of all wives and age of marriage laws, planned parenthood facilities, and access to educational resources for plural wives. Adrienne Davis (2010) has suggested bringing polygamy into the full light of scrutiny. She argues that family law already accommodates intimate multiplicity, or what might be thought of as "de facto" and "serial" polygamy. She recommends establishing baseline behaviors that would define multiple relationships, acknowledge ongoing entrances and exits, and identify life-defining economic and personal stakes. She also suggests turning to commercial partnership law to propose tentative default rules that would accommodate marital multiplicity and at the same time address some of the costs and power disparities that polygamy entails.

If polygamy was regulated, women would have the legal option of divorce to dissolve an unhappy or abusive alliance. In contented marriages between fully consenting adults, legalization would provide a symbolic and legally binding contract between all spouses concerned that would be recognized by society and the law. This would reinforce commitment and responsibility in marriage and parenthood. As it is now, woman who are guilty of a felony offense related to polygamy are unlikely to go outside the group for help when they need it; they have no legal recourse but to stay in an unwanted marriage (Song 2010).

I argue that polygamy must be legalized in order to ensure protection for men, women, and children who believe it is their religious right. Legal recognition will level the playing field for individuals and institutions in fundamentalist communities by enhancing their "life chances."[23] This might include finding ways to help teenage girls finish high school, with or without family support, and providing the economic and legal resources to allow individuals to assert their rights against powerful individuals and institutions. It would also hold fundamentalists accountable for following state and federal law related to employment, the environment, and taxes. Additional policies should be adopted to provide exit strategies for women and children and to require youth who are most at risk in isolated groups to attend public schools and access counseling.

Legalizing the polygamist family would allow it to be regulated with the same force of law as monogamy is regulated, including registration and documentation of marriages, societal tolerance and acceptance, and appropriate legal models that provide for multiple-spouse families. These measures will make women and children feel less marginalized and alienated by abusive conditions within polygamy and by prejudicial conditions outside polygamy. Regulation can "create and adapt a legal framework around polygyny to better regulate truly deviant practitioners" (Duncan 2008, 337) and would give law-abiding polygamists the freedom to practice their religion and marital practices without fear of prosecution.

Critique Some may argue that if polygamy was legalized, it might create an overwhelming burden on the American taxpayer if plural wives should become impoverished. If a man is married to three to four women and they have eight children on average each, that would be twenty-eight to thirty-six people in one family that would need financial support. In addition, the state would bear the cost of monitoring and regulating multiple relationships with many children. If polygamy is legalized, will wealthy groups like the FLDS and Kingstons continue to use taxpayers' money to fuel their religious beliefs (Perkins 2003)?

Further, some polygamists do not seek legal recognition as it will draw too much attention to their way of life. They resent outspoken polygamists such as Tom Green and Kody Brown as it opens polygamy up to scrutiny and criticism. Many leaders, such as Lemoine Jensen, Brent LeBaron, and Marvin Jessop, detest the limelight and see their isolation from the mainstream as crucial to living the Gospel. These are men and women who seek the mountains and deserts, away from Babylon, to renew their connection to God, and embrace the simplicity of hard work and clean air. Isolationism when it is a choice is not necessarily evil, nor is it always synonymous with criminal behavior. Some people are simply attracted to peace and quiet and autonomy.

Another potential issue with legalization of polygamy is that it might bring more attention to the legal issues related to extramarital sexual liaisons, such as the right of an unmarried partner in the affair and any offspring she may have. In other words, if a married man has an affair with his secretary, he might be legally responsible to pay for the expenses associated with that relationship, including the cost of health care, child care, and so on. Some might argue that this would make people think twice before entering into "adultery" because of the potential expense and legal headache.

This chapter reviewed the many legal battles related to polygamy in the North American context and demonstrated the impact of polygamy on the state and the effect of criminalization on the lives of polygamists. Twentieth-century polygamists have begun to experience a legal metamorphosis that is complicated by shifting social, political, and religious alliances but that has the potential to open up newfound freedoms for their families and communities. Yet if polygamy is decriminalized it would bring the responsibility to marry and raise children within the guidelines of the law along with new freedoms. Some fundamentalists might be unwilling to adapt their lifestyle to the rules of the government, while others will never approve of integration and collaboration.

In short, the First Amendment and the due process clause of the Fourteenth Amendment should allow us to define the contours of our sexuality and express our religious beliefs freely, as long as we do not harm the state or other people. I agree with the premise of the national ACLU (2006) that the anti-polygamy law violates these constitutional guarantees. The twenty-first-century pattern of increasing tolerance and acceptance of poly families calls for a change in the law that reflects the direction most democratic nations are taking: legal recognition, or at the very least, removal of legal sanctions against polygamy. Law and policy approaches to plural marriage must be guided by the "goal of facilitating meaningful choices for women" (Campbell 2005, 37). Because it criminalizes consensual, fully adult sexuality motivated by religious beliefs, the United States fails to fulfill the constitutional promise that consenting adults will be free to define love and marriage without fear of government intervention.

7

The Anna Karenina Principle

Bringing Abuse into the Light

Perhaps sunlight is the best disinfectant against fraud.

—ADRIENNE DAVIS (2010, 1964)

Although polygamy in North America can lead to satisfactory conditions for many men, women, and children, there are many cases of abuse, dissatisfaction, and alienation within the poly mindset. This variability in polygamy requires us to examine which factors contribute to abusive conditions. This chapter provides a heuristic, known as the Anna Karenina Principle, to provide clarity about favorable and unfavorable practices often associated with polygamy. By identifying the risks associated with dysfunctional polygamy, we can better inform law enforcement agencies and child protection services where to seek out and regulate cases of harmful polygamy. These agencies can then identify such cases for the purposes of intervention and prevention instead of using the highly unsuccessful and unconstitutional methods of raiding communities and seizing children.

Alean Al-Krenawi (2006) of Memorial University, who interviewed ten polygamous families in a Bedouin village south of Israel, found that some families are prone to function well and others are prone to failure. He determined that the relatively successful families had the following characteristics: 1) religious sanction of polygamy (God's wish or destiny); 2) equal allocation of resources among families; 3) separate households for each wife; 4) avoidance of minor conflicts and disagreements, including maintaining an attitude of respect toward the other wives; and 5) open communication among all wives and siblings and among children and other mothers. Al-Krenawi highly recommends a program of intervention called "multi-bonding," by which an intra-familial discourse is created to avoid discord and resolve conflict. His criteria for "well-functioning" families mirrored some of the precursors for success that I observed while living in the Pinesdale branch of the AUB from 1989 to 1993, which included a religious sanction for polygamy related to celestial glories and strong economic and emotional female networking. In 1998, I described this branch in glowing utopian terms. I saw their isolation and separation as a virtue that protected them from the evils of the mainstream. After visiting the LeBaron community in the Chihuahua Desert and the FLDS on the border of Utah and Arizona, I realized that such isolation can be more of a hindrance than a help. When I wrote about the AUB, I also assumed that most wives would enjoy living together in one communal home; I romanticized the notion of female sharing within the context of a large integrated whole. This also proved to be naïve, as I later learned that most women seek their own compartment, which they share only occasionally with their husband. After the Chihuahua fieldwork, I observed the factors that contribute to hardships for women and children in polygamy. These include 1) male supremacy; 2) absence of female networking; 3) the absence of secular education; 4) an emphasis on endogamous marriages; and 5) circumscription (Bennion 2004, 4–11). In 2006, after I had collected more stories of women's lives in Arizona, the Salt Lake area, Washington, and Montana, I understood that those factors included overcrowding and economic hardship; it is important for each wife to live in her own separate space. I also began to see how important Al-Krenawi's factor of open communication was for the happiness of women who share a husband. If a family has no periodic gab-sessions between wives, women begin to feel isolated and start bickering and trying to pit one against the other. Open communication is also vital between wives and their husband; it is important that all parties concerned become immediately aware of any grievances or any other issue in marital relations that need to be sorted out before the end of the day. I also added factors that relate to the outside world's perception of polygamy. Are polygamists viewed as outlaws or as citizens with rights? Further, if we opened up the practice to legal, public scrutiny, could we overcome some of the risks associated with abuse? In short, are groups uniformly alike in the way they abuse the rights of women and children, or do they abuse in a variety of different ways?

Taking my revised list of criteria into account, in 2008, I made the assumption that polygamy does not create dysfunction unless it is coupled with the following conditions: rural or structural isolation and female circumscription, prolonged absences of the father or husband, the absence of a vibrant female financial and emotional network, overcrowded housing where wives and their children are living "on top of each other," economic deprivation of both the wives and their husband, and the presence of rigid patriarchy or a mandate that males have supreme power.

The Anna Karenina Principle

To generate discourse on the factors that contribute to healthy functioning or failure in plural marriage, I use the concept of the Anna Karenina principle, which is based on Tolstoy's premise that "happy families are all alike; every unhappy family is unhappy in its own way."[1] This principle was popularized by Jared Diamond (1999) to describe an endeavor in which a deficiency in any one of a number of factors dooms it to failure. The principle allows us to classify a list of factors that promote healthy functioning. The absence of any of these factors could create a poorly functioning family or make family life intolerable.[2] Successful polygamous families are not successful because they have a particular positive trait; they are successful but because of the absence of any number of negative traits, such as the lack of a loving home environment with emotionally and economically stable parents and the presence of neglect, physical or sexual abuse, poverty, substance abuse, overcrowding, and inequality. Based on my analysis of the literature and my own observations, here is a working list of seven key reasons that polygamy fails:

1. Illegality: Because polygamy is illegal, many polygamists hide their lifestyle.
2. Isolation and circumscription: Many polygamist groups live in social, geographic, and religious isolation.
3. The equality quagmire: Men and women in polygamy can rarely achieve true equality, especially in the context of male dominance ideologies and co-wife jealousy.
4. Male domination: Often males are in control of all valued resources, including women and children, and females have a subordinated role in society.
5. Economic deprivation: Many individuals in polygamous households suffer from poverty issues that may also relate to father absence, overcrowded households, and substance abuse.
6. The absence of a female network: Women who are isolated from other women are less able to stand up to abusive husbands or tap

into economic opportunities, and they experience more depression and alienation.

7. Abuse: Some forms of polygamy are more conducive to the abuse of women and children.

Many items on this list overlap or intersect with others. Illegality, for example, influences where families live and how men treat their wives in the absence of legal protections. It contributes to economic deprivation by limiting legal opportunities for employment and reducing women's ability to use the female network to their advantage. Illegality also means that internal abuses go unnoticed and are not monitored and that external discrimination and violence are tolerated and endorsed by mainstream society. Isolation, also defined as seclusion, circumscription, and alienation, has been correlated with abuse (An-Na'im 2010). Geographic isolation connects to poverty; poorly maintained roads and remote mountain regions and vast desert landscapes can create obstacles to transacting business. In short, for the Karenina principle to be effective, we must see how these factors represent pitfalls that discourage healthy functioning in Mormon fundamentalist polygamous groups in many overlapping ways.

Illegality, or Criminalization Previous arguments for legalization have focused on the political issues of viability, enforcement, regulation, and human rights. But the illegal status of polygamy directly impacts the family structure. Wives and children in families that are living in hiding are at risk of abuse, economic hardship, and circumscription. The illegality of polygamy pushes the practice further and further underground, exactly where potential abuses are likely to occur. If the fear of incarceration were to be dispelled, polygamists would be more free to live in the mainstream, where women and children would have access to counseling, education, and opportunities for economic and emotional autonomy. If polygamy were to be legally recognized, or at least no longer carried the risk of arrest, several key questions relating to family security and individual rights could be addressed: Are spouses and children stigmatized by their neighbors and larger culture? Are the spouses of legal age and did the wife give full consent to the marriage? Is there a commitment to provide for each wife equally, including health care and insurance benefits? Do vulnerable parties have access to social and legal recourse should they need it? And is an exit strategy in place for dissatisfied parties?

The illegality of polygamy creates severe prejudice against poly families within the media, in local neighborhoods, at school, and in the larger mainstream. Legal recognition would legitimize polygamy as a faith-based lifestyle to neighbors, employers, and the state, which would meet Al-Krenawi's second factor for wellness—that polygamy be religiously sanctioned. Legal protection for religious rights would serve not only Mormon fundamentalists but also the growing number of Muslims who believe they are allowed four wives according to the Quran. For the LDS Church, which has enormous influence on how people react to polygamy in Utah, Arizona, and Idaho, the issue is not just that plural marriage is grounds for excommunication, but that it is also against the law of the land, or the civil law. If plural marriages were to become legal contracts between consenting adults, the stigma would be diminished, even in orthodox Mormon communities. Polygamists could "come out" to their neighbors and co-workers without fear of arrest, being fired, or being ostracized. They would be able to show affection to their wives in public and enjoy meeting with them in parks, at school, or at the mall without having to continually watch for the police or a man in a dark suit with sunglasses. The Kody Brown family, for example, could return to their home in Lehi, Utah, where many of their friends and family live. This process would certainly take time; people would need to become accustomed to the new law. Much like gay/lesbian marriage, polygamy would eventually be viewed as yet another potentially viable alternative family type that should not be treated as immoral. Legality would also reduce teasing and ostracism for children who are living in an illegal situation. Over time, classmates would stop ridiculing children in polygamous households about how many mothers they have or whether they live on welfare. Further, openness would reveal how to better protect "rogue" males from abuse and provide them with opportunities outside tyrannical movements so they could more easily live as "independents."

Because of illegality, polygamy is unmonitored and is prone to failure because it restricts the access of vulnerable individuals to social and economic support. If polygamy were to be legalized, "spiritual" wives would be transformed into legal wives and thus would gain access to their husband's work-related health benefits and pensions, hospital visiting rights, and life insurance. Wives could also, potentially, inherit and benefit from each other as well. Since wives are married through the Law of Sarah, they should have some claim on each other's job benefits, as with any typical husband/wife dyad. That way, wives who remain at home to care for the children and the house would be protected through their co-wife's employment. At present, Kody Brown's job provides only his first wife, Meri, with employee benefits; his other wives must either buy their own policies or go without. Another benefit would be hospital visiting rights for all spouses and the ability to access the pension funds of any adult married partner.

If legally recognized, law enforcement officials, academics, and legislators could examine more carefully the pros and cons of any poly situation. Polygamous families would be treated no differently from monogamous families; both would be subjected to scrutiny about domestic violence, welfare fraud, or "deadbeat dads." Further, the process of being a polygamist wife would be altered. If polygamy was legal, women could achieve self-actualization and confidence in their marital choices.[3] A woman considering entering a poly environment could ask rational questions, knowing the law would protect her in these queries. These questions might include: Are the women in the marriage relatively content and friendly? Do they make their own decisions and experience autonomy? Are they overworked without any supportive economic and emotional network? Are they or their children abandoned, abused, or mistreated in any way by the patriarch of the family? Are there clear exit strategies in place should the marriage fail?

The illegality of polygamy prevents women and children from accessing the socioeconomic resources that mainstream American families now enjoy: societal recognition, life insurance and health insurance, public education, full employment, protection from criminal abuse, and access to legal recourse for dealing with divorce and child support.

Isolation and Circumscription In a Utah Valley study, 95 percent of the abuse cases gathered from county abuse-relief centers occurred in a rural environment (Bennion 2007). Isolation can be used as a way to conceal sexual and physical abuses against women and children (Chamberlain 2002). Many abusers deliberately choose remote places in order to maintain control over their victims. When a woman is isolated, she also experiences circumscription, in which the physical or social environment blocks dissidents from leaving the group (Carneiro 1980). In the cases of polygamous groups, the desert creates barriers of heat, drought, natural predators, poor soil, and imposing sierras against escape. The isolating mountains where one often finds fundamentalist groups also contain geographical and climactic barriers, particularly for women and children, who are isolated in the winter months, from October to June. People who leave their abusive environment risk hunger, economic hardship, and possibly even death on the outside. This geographic hindrance combines with a harsh social boundary to ensure that people stay put. Fears of ostracism, of losing one's soul, of spiritual death, and of betraying the family keep people within the group. Women, especially, experience this type of circumscription because they have been raised to value relationships, loved ones, and solidarity. They also risk losing their children if they attempt to leave (the offspring of a man belong to his patrilineage in the next life). Thus, if a mother is aware that her daughter is being abused, she is not likely to tell anyone about it for two reasons: her husband and the brethren would condemn her for telling; and she would have to travel a great distance to locate an appropriate venue for such a grievance. Warren Jeffs' speech to his young ladies (Adams 2007) cautioned them against betraying family members in times of abuse. "What do many people do? They run to their friends or someone they think can give them counsel. You run anywhere else besides your Priesthood head, you could run into trouble. . . . Don't ever go beyond your bounds and try to rule over him." Jeffs' speech sanctions the abuse of vulnerable individuals by powerful ones—a cue that the leadership will not punish abusers.[4]

Equality Issues Al-Krenawi stated that equality is necessary for healthy functioning in a polygamous family structure. Although he specifically mentions equal allocation of resources to all wives, this issue of equity should be expanded to all stakeholders or parties concerned: the equality between men and their wives, the equality among wives, and the equality among men, especially in the general treatment of "rogue" men and boys.

How the husband treats his wives is often a question of righteousness. Mormon polygamists follow an ideological code of conduct to guide them in dealing with their wives (as mentioned in Chapter 3).[5] Both the Mormon Doctrine and Covenants and Muslim scripture contain verses that discuss the nature of polygamy and when it is allowed. In both cases, the ideology warns men that they may not be fit for polygamy because it is so hard to ensure that each wife will be treated with equity. At a recent Brandeis conference, law professor Dr. Abdullahi An-Na'im asserted that polygamy and the seclusion of women have done more harm to woman than the benefit conferred on her by bestowal of property rights. The fact is that a great misunderstanding exists based on the premise in the Qur'an that monogamy is the rule and polygamy is the exception, subject to certain conditions. It says, "If you fear that you will not do justice between them, then marry only one or what your right hands possess: this is more proper that you may not deviate from the right course" (Surah An-Nisa 4:3).

Men are allowed up to four wives under Islamic law, a practice that was intended to provide for widows and orphans during war and disaster. Yet the Qur'an clearly states that if a man cannot treat his wives with equality and if he is not acquiring multiple wives for the purpose of helping widows and orphans, he should steer clear of polygamy. Obviously, in both the Muslim and Mormon cases, men like to marry beautiful young women who have never married before. As long as the men can prove that they will treat them with equity, they are allowed these indulgences. In South Africa, the law requires that a man show proof of his ability to care equitably with all wives before the marriage can be sanctioned. It also requires men to gain written permission from the first wife. This law is an insurance policy for a woman against economic hardship in the future, especially in cases where their husband begins to prefer one wife over the other. In such a situation, each wife has the legal right to demand equity.

Part of treating any woman with equality, whether she be monogamist or polygamist, is to provide her with options. If a woman is career oriented, is she is able to work to provide additional income for the family outside the home, or must she stay within the confines of home and compound? Does she have access to a vehicle and an active driver's license? Are computers and telephones available? Isolating a woman in the home without an outlet for employment or outside resources can be oppressive. Feminist polygamists such as Elizabeth Joseph state that the poly mindset allows women "to have it all," the ability to work hard and have a great arrangement with co-wives who will look after children while they work or attend college. Monogamy is not so flexible, since there is only one wife who has to "do it all." Certainly there are other ways to achieve this flexibility, such as hiring a nanny or having a grandmother help with child care, but polygamy seems to provide this automatically.

If a man treats his wives equally, it is obviously much easier for wives to get along with each other. Equality among women means that each wife has equal resources and equal time with their husband and collaborate with each other for the benefit of the whole. In each advice blog on polygamy that I've read, there is a section on how important it is for wives to treat each other with equality and respect. When a new wife enters a polygamous relationship, existing wives can expect an initial period fear about sharing their husband or not getting anything for themselves. The husband gets another wife, gets to feel love for two women, and experiences twice as much intimacy. At this point, many wives suffer from an acute sense of injustice and jealousy—that is, until they overcome their jealousy and build strong friendships, thus creating the valuable economic and emotional network that is available in many of the polygamist groups. These networks are essential to women's happiness, especially because they give women who aren't with their husbands every day an outlet for their energy and affection.

Rivalries between co-wives are often based on the desire of one wife to obtain resources for her children instead of allowing resources to be given to another wife's children. In many cases, co-wives can use economic transactions among themselves to their advantage in the form of reciprocal exchanges. One wife provides garden produce, another provides child care, yet another provides profits from crafts for tourists. The pressure to get along comes not so much from ideology or social rules as from economic necessity. The problem is that one wife can have control over favored resources, to the disadvantage of one or more other wives, as in the case of the wives described in both Saitoti's *Maasai Warrior* (1988) or Achebe's *Things Fall Apart* (1959). When this divisiveness occurs, the children suffer mistreatment and become ranked in a hierarchy based on the ranking of wives. If, on the other hand, the husband creates an atmosphere of equality and the co-wives to do not dispute over resources among themselves but share freely and exhibit reciprocity and respect, the family will have greater chances of success and longevity. Children will look at their mothers and see that they are getting along beautifully; they will see a cooperative parenting coalition. By example they will exhibit the same sharing paradigm with their step-siblings and half-siblings, as true brothers and sisters.

Sororal or cousin polygamy may be more conducive to an environment of widespread sharing. Such a system benefits women, who can get household help from a kin member with whom she can easily form a coalition and at the same time retain significant power in her own household. Just as important to inclusive fitness is a woman's ability to share with another woman, insuring her sister's children will thrive, too. In West African polygamous contexts, such as the Ijaw tribe of Nigeria that Nancy Leis (1974) studied, disenfranchised women form an opposing unity against their husband should he ever treat any one of them poorly. It empowers them and fosters solidarity. Similarly, Robert Netting (1969), who studied polygamy among Kofyar women of Nigeria, found that when women share a residence, their status increases because of their ability to collectively oppose patriarchy. My own studies show that female bonding in Mormon fundamentalist communities is the most vital foundation for the existence of successful family and community economies (Bennion 1998). Without the collaboration of women, communities of self-oriented, isolated, and competitive patriarchs would fail.

The plural wives in the Altman and Ginat study (1996) experienced co-wife jealousy. Senior wives experienced a sense of "loneliness, sometimes to the point of feeling abandoned," and "feelings of inadequacy and low self-esteem," while new wives also experienced jealousy and feelings of inadequacy. Altman and Ginat identified several strategies women used for coping with jealousy. Wives said they turned to prayer "for solace, guidance, and the strength to help them adjust to the new family situation and abide by their religious beliefs" (Altman and Ginat 1996, 170). Husbands became more sensitive to their wives' feelings of loss and inadequacy and made greater efforts to give them love, commitment, and support. Wives "aired their adjustment stresses with husbands, sometimes only after suffering frustration and emotional turmoil alone" (ibid.). And wives reached out to one another, learning that they all experienced similar negative feelings and providing mutual support. The women interviewed seemed to find it possible, with much personal and interpersonal work, to establish and maintain romantic dyadic relationships with their husbands and at the same time share them with other wives, thus accomplishing the fantasy of monogamy within a polygamous setting. Negative experiences were primarily the result of either a lack of coping strategies or strategies that did not work because of individual personalities and the ethos and experience of the family and its members. Consequently, negative experiences were the result of particularly dysfunctional plural families rather than inherent and inevitable experiences of plural marriage in general (Altman and Ginat 1996).

The author of the polygamy.com website uses the word "compersion" to describe the "feeling of joy associated with seeing a loved one love another; contrasted with jealousy" (polygamy.com 2009b). Compersion is not possible in a monogamous relationship. When it happens, each member of a plural marriage functions without competition, feelings of inadequacies, insecurities or jealousies. If women can get over their jealousies, they can become very close to their co-wives, who, after all, share everything with them. As DoriAnn from *Sister Wives* put it, "It's a beautiful thing—that's what I longed for, because that's what I saw as a child growing up. That's the most beautiful part of the whole thing. That is the gift—that circle. Yes, the camaraderie of the women and the children is bar none" (Sloan 2011).

Equality issues are also important for relations among polygamist males. Kingdom building requires competitiveness among kings and rulers, which means that alpha males are more successful than rogue males, who are often marginalized and alienated. There is also the issue of alienation for an overworked, overwrought husband with multiple wives to please. Some polygamous men feel their wives are always fighting over them, which requires exactitude from them in terms of resources and time. One man told me, "It's impossible to be fair to both of them. Who do you go to if two wives get sick?" He further explained, "If anyone tells me they are seeking polygamy, I always tell them, you better think twice about it. My first wife never used to complain, but now she gets worried and frustrated all the time" (e-mail correspondence 2011).

Al-Krenawi's fourth and fifth preconditions for a healthy polygamous family are best fulfilled in an environment of equality and respect. These points require "the avoidance of minor conflicts and disagreements, maintaining an attitude of respect toward the other wife" (and all other parties); and allowing open communication among "all wives, siblings, and among children and other mothers" (and husbands) (Al-Krenawi 2006, 3).

Male Dominance Patriarchy, or male supremacy, is often associated with abusive conditions for women and children (Bennion 2004; Sanday 1981; Cook and Kelly 2006). When the husband is open to female decision-making and autonomy and has a more progressive, democratic approach to family structure and policies, women often can find satisfaction and become self-actualized. In some homes however, I discovered cases of alienation, verbal abuse, subordination and ridicule, as well as adherence to restrictions for females against travel, education, and hospitalization.[6] In a few cases in my 2006 study (Bennion 2006), patriarchs used their priesthood powers to rationalize the sexual abuse of their daughters.

A patriarchal ideology requires men to be ultimately responsible for the leadership of the family and control of the household. Those in my study who engage in sexual offenses felt that they could not live up to that masculine

ideal (Bennion 2006). These men were also in charge of the spiritual salvation of their kingdoms through the patrilineal pathway to heaven that runs
through them to God. They used their priesthood powers and the biblical
blueprint of the Abrahamic covenant, with its promise of infinite progeny,
as their exemplary tool for the practice of selecting child brides and abusing
their own daughters. Abraham was promised that his seed would be more
plentiful than the "sands of the seas" if he obeyed God's commands. Male supremacists dominate others by coercion; they invoke God's authority to sanction sexual abuse and threaten anyone who challenges them with damnation,
the removal of economic resources, and physical abuse. The victims become
strongly convinced that their father is justified in raping them, "refusing to
equate it with incest" (Myers and Brasington 2002, 4). The offenders may also
require that their children be home schooled so that they will not be exposed
to the evil of the secular schools of the mainstream world.

Females often have less access to schooling than males. For example,
the LeBaron colony offers a high school education for boys, who will need
rudimentary math and science skills to work in the agricultural and drywall industries. But LeBaron girls are not encouraged to finish high school
and stop their education after sixth or seventh grade. After that point, they
are rigorously taught homemaking skills and reverence for male authority
in their homes through the examples of their mothers and their mothers'
co-wives. They begin to use these skills early because they marry at age
seventeen or eighteen. Since few women have a driver's license, they rarely
travel outside their own family compound. For example, Irene Spencer had
only a ninth grade education. She was impoverished but didn't want to go on
welfare because she was afraid that the government would take her thirteen
children away from her. She had no job training, so she stayed in the group
(Garza 2007).

Analyzing male dominance is complicated, especially for western feminist
anthropologists. On the one hand, we see how a male tyrannical perspective
can lead to abuses against women and children. On the other hand, what we
call "negative" may actually be quite functional from an emic perspective.
For example, elite polygyny or male supremacy may be viewed by some as an
essential construct so that alpha males can rid themselves of rogue males in
order for plural marriage to thrive. In this social system, it is also essential to
solicit or capture wives, perhaps often against their will, in order to maintain a
healthy ratio of women to men (White and Burton 1988). Further, as one male

described it, men are naturally polygamous and dominant; whereas women are biologically submissive. His blog entry expressed admiration for men like Tiger Woods who live up to the hypermasculine standard: "Here you have an alpha male, sexy, rich, and talented, who has twelve young, beautiful females running after him. . . . Shouldn't Bill Clinton have been allowed to marry Monica and enjoy his polygamy? And what about all the other 'alpha' males out there like Pavarotti, Berlusconi, Shane Warne, Nick Faldo, Boris Becker, and all the other 'testosterone-rich males that have fallen by the wayside'?" (polygamy.com 2009a). Elite polygyny is also designed to cement friendships between elite males; one elite male gives the other his daughter.

However, there are tangible, negative consequences of such unchecked dominance. Although Al-Krenawi does not include male dominance as an element that contributes to poor-functioning polygamy, I have seen how it can lead to the physical and emotional abuse of women and children when it exists in conjunction with unequal distribution of resources and isolation.

Economic Deprivation The issues of father absence, abuse, and economic deprivation are all intertwined. Thornhill and Palmer (2000) wrote that most male abusers are raised in poverty and then use sexual force to gain access to women with good genes. They predicted that ameliorating the poverty of males would also decrease the incidence of sexual abuse and rape. In my Utah Valley study (Bennion 2007), abuse occurred in the context of lower-income households, where the offender was unemployed or underemployed. In polygamous orders, most people live well below the official U.S. poverty level of $17,000 a year for a family of four. John Ray of the AUB who was accused of abuse was a self-proclaimed scholar with little to no income. Chevral Palacios, also of the AUB, convicted of sexual assault,was in and out of construction work. Ervil LeBaron was a penniless farmer and religious leader.[7]

Poverty creates many disadvantages for plural wives, who are often dependent on their husband's priesthood stewardship or the charity of the community for food and clothing for their children. Such women are not likely to leave an abusive situation unless they have an outside relative who can support them economically. However, if they have a job of their own, they are more able to leave the sect. For example, Irene Spencer grew up in a poor polygamous family where her mother had to rummage through garbage cans to feed her children (Garza 2007). In her own marriage to Verlan LeBaron, she lived a lonely and exhausting life below the poverty level in Mexico. She bore her husband thirteen children in a home with no electricity. Once they had the funds to do so, she and her mother eventually left polygamy.

Impoverished parents often vent their frustration on their children by beating them, verbally abusing them, and sexually abusing them. In an overcrowded poor household, sibling abuse may also be a problem and a father's violence against his wife and other children is often ignored. Poverty can also lead to father absence. Poor men often go long distances to find work and are away from home for long periods. Male/father absence during a child's formative years can also lead to sexual abuse in later years; because the father doesn't play the father role to his children as they grow up, he may see them as potential sexual partners when they enter puberty (Parker 1976).

Economic difficulties also limit individual personal living space, causing discord and malaise. As Al-Krenawi writes, women must have "separate households for each wife" (2006, 311). Ideally, the various households should provide ample bedrooms and space for children so that they can develop autonomy and a personal identity. Each woman and each child should feel that they are important and not just a number, or, as one wife puts it, "one of his many wives" (interview with an anonymous wife, 2008).

Absence of a Female Network Women suffer in isolated households because of the absence of other women to talk to and work with. Where a female solidarity network is present, such as in Pinesdale, it may be harder for abuses to go unnoticed as everyone knows everyone else's business and the women are "always watching." The Pinesdale women are proud that their community is "abuse-free."[8] The network can provide child care for women who need to work outside the community and economic assistance for women who are not able to work or who have young children at home. It can help reduce the number of hours per day that women must work to provide for their families, thus creating more leisure time and therefore greater contentment (Kimmel 2008, 145). Women who do not have a protective emotional and financial safety net are more dependent on their husband for these resources. Women are more likely to choose divorce because of overwork than are men.

The network can also provide the means for open communication about any number of issues: the family budget, the sexual rotation schedule, the division of labor in the households, and interpersonal grievances. Women need to talk things out in order to work through feelings of low self-worth and jealousy. As Al-Krenawi writes, successful polygamous families "create intra-familial discourse to avoid discord and resolve conflict" (2006, 311). The female network can help alleviate anxieties, provide support in times of illness or hardship, and mediate disputes. Of great importance is its role in providing an opposing unity structure for women in cases where men are abusing their wives' rights. If one, or even two, women complain against an abusing husband it may not carry that much weight in a rigid patriarchal system, but if ten to fifteen women stand up for the victim, their voices will most definitely be heard.

Abuse Many of the factors associated with male supremacy and poverty overlap into physical, sexual, and emotional abuse of women and children. Most of the data about abuse in the media comes from a small group of investigators or from a handful of polygamists and plural wives who left fundamentalism. My data are drawn primarily from qualitative sources: 1) informant testimonials; 2) gossip sessions recorded through participant observation; 3) records provided by Child Protection Services and Attorney General's offices in Montana, Utah, and Arizona; 4) newspaper accounts; and 5) personal narratives written by apostate members. The last category, in the form of published books, contains rich and vivid descriptions of dissatisfaction, abuse, and neglect.

Although the FLDS is the group that is most often labeled abusive, virtually every other polygamous sect practicing in Utah today has been somehow, at some time, linked to financial, sexual, or spiritual improprieties (Scharnberg and Brachear 2006). Yet accurate statistics about abuse within polygamy are hard to come by. How do we know that reports of abuse are valid? The call that was the catalyst for the raid on the FLDS in Eldorado, Texas, was a hoax. Further, because many women and children may be prevented from contacting outside help in situations of abuse, we can never know the true extent to which abuse takes place in secretive settings.

From data in newspaper reports and government agency reports, I estimated that more than 158 different cases of abuse have been brought up in the last decade in reference to the FLDS group alone. According to Arizona Child Protective Services, from January 2000 to April of 2008, sixty-one reports of abuse involving children were recorded. Of the twenty-one reports from 2006 to 2008, only three were sexual in nature; the rest involved physical abuse or neglect (Deibert 2008). In July 2008, Texas Rangers investigated twenty cases of abuse and fifty cases of bigamy tied to Warren Jeffs and five other FLDS men: Raymond Merril Jessop, Allan Eugene Keate, Michael George Emack, Merril Leroy Jessop, and Dr. Lloyd Hammon Barlow (Texas Attorney General 2008). Jeffs and four of the men were charged with the sexual assault of a child, one follower was charged with bigamy, and the sect's doctor was charged for failing to report child abuse. Thus, 131 cases have been brought against the Texas/Colorado City orders during an eight-year period, in addition to the fifteen reports of abuse of the "lost boys" and the twelve cases reported against Winston Blackmore in British Columbia.

The rate of abuse in the Kingston group and the AUB seems to be lower. For the period 1996–2008, I counted twenty-seven reported offenses linked to the Kingstons (predominantly related to the Mary Ann Kingston case) and only fifteen reports of abuse perpetrated by members of the AUB (including in-house accusations of abuse). In the LeBaron clan, there were four cases in the last ten years and seventeen reports of abuse reported in the earlier period of 1969 to 1977, primarily in relation to Ervil LeBaron's "reign of terror."[9]

In one case involving an independent fundamentalist, a father indoctrinated and "groomed" his twelve-year-old biological daughter and thirteen-year-old stepdaughter to marry him. After having sexual intercourse with both of them, the first girl's mother turned the father in to the police, but the twelve-year-old refused to testify against her father (Myers and Brasington 2002, 2). Where polygamy is linked to sexual molestation (Bennion 2007), the families tend to be large and overcrowded and are rigidly controlled by a patriarchal figure. These groups are also generally isolated and provide little or no secular education for the children. With approximately 50,000 fundamentalists practicing polygamy, it is difficult to gauge how many families are incestuous. What is possible, however, is a thorough scrutiny of profiles of men who have been arrested or publicly identified as sexual offenders. In 2003, I began gathering surveys of sex offender profiles in the State of Utah. I found that 30 percent of perpetrators were associated in some way with one of the fundamentalist organizations. The other 70 percent were associated with monogamist living conditions.

In some cases, abuse consists of forced marriage, statutory rape, and co-wife cruelty. In other situations blood atonement was used. Several groups use this punishment as a way to deal with certain sins that they believe aren't covered by the atonement of Jesus for the sins of the world. To attain salvation, a person must spill their blood, that the "smoke thereof might ascend to heaven as an offering for their sins" (Young 1856, 53). Brigham Young first taught this practice around 1850 in the Utah Territory. Some believe this teaching led to such practices as execution by firing squad and the Mountain Meadows massacre, where Mormons killed a group of non-Mormon pioneers heading to Oregon. Although the AUB had trouble with blood atonement under the direction John Ray in the 1970s, since his excommunication, the practice has stopped. Under the leadership of Warren Jeffs, however, members are required to atone for grievous sins with physical punishment or even the sinner's death. Ervil LeBaron also practiced blood atonement in Colonia LeBaron during his reign of terror in the mid-1970s.

Although the AUB has fewer problems with abuse (Llewellyn 2004; Bennion 1998), I am more familiar with the stories from this group, which I heard in interviews, from the pulpit, and in cottage meetings. AUB councilor John Ray is featured in many of these stories. He was married to twelve women and was said by his son, a lawyer in the Salt Lake area, to have molested three young women outside his family and at least eight of his own children. To John this abuse was a natural, sacred enterprise. He would travel a great deal away from the order on priesthood business and then come home to find that a daughter had blossomed "as a rose." He would then ask her to join him in the shed out back, where he would rape her and "school" her on two vital topics: 1) she was now connected to him through blood and sex, which meant he would be her Savior on Mt. Zion; and 2) if she told anyone, he would torture her through the blood atonement, which allows fathers to physically punish their children. These abuses took place in the 1970s; John Ray is now dead.

In 1994, Joseph Thompson was charged by fellow councilman Lamoine Jensen on several counts of child sexual abuse and was excommunicated from the AUB (Hales 2008a). George Maycock was likewise accused of sex abuse in 1998, but no proof was provided to substantiate this charge. In both cases, evidence was presented to the AUB priesthood council, but the two councilmen were never prosecuted by the state because the victims would not testify and Owen Allred would not allow any evidence to be turned over to the officials. The state of Utah closed the case, claiming the AUB had started false rumors. The charges brought to the AUB council were based on the testimony of several of Joseph Thompson's daughters while under hypnosis and the discovery of soft porn and "girly" magazines in his home. One daughter said he lifted her dress when she was twelve years old. His eldest daughter said her abuse was confirmed by Abraham, Isaac, and Jacob in a dream. A former member of the AUB suggests that this removal was the result of a witch hunt designed to allow Lamoine to take over the priesthood. Joe also was said to have set up a torture enterprise in Oregon with a fellow councilman in the 1960s; this accusation led to his temporary arrest. He allegedly took young brides and beat preadolescent children (Bennion 2008).[10]

It is still unclear whether Joe actually abused children; he died in 1998, shamed and excommunicated from the Salt Lake Order. Yet Joe often preached his beliefs, rationalizing incest from the pulpit during Sunday meetings, which I personally witnessed. He believed that God asked him to mate with his own daughters. He referred to the Law of Lot, stating that God asked Lot to have sex with his children in order to build up a more righteous seed after his wife had been turned to salt outside Sodom. In addition, when Lot and his daughters sought refuge in a cave near Zoar, his daughters got him drunk with wine and lay with him in order to preserve their family line (Genesis 19:31–32). The Kingston clan has often used this same scripture to justify incestuous relationships. Thompson said that as a direct descendant of Joseph Smith and Jesus Christ, he had to keep the blood lines pure via inbreeding. He knew his daughters were pure; therefore, if they could produce a child who was also pure, he would ensure the continuation of the Thompson family kingdom. I also heard Joe use the story of Sarah and Abraham to sanction incest. Abraham said, "Because I thought, surely the fear of God is not in this place; and they will slay me for my wife's sake. And yet indeed she is my sister; she is the daughter of my father, but not the daughter of my mother; and she became my wife" (Genesis 20:11–12).

I met Chevral Palacios, then age seventy and a councilman in the Allred Group, years after he had left the Mexico order. A few years later, I read in the Salt Lake Tribune that he was charged with four counts of child rape that included three counts of sodomy on a child and one count for having sex with his young stepdaughters (Cantera 2001). I learned from an informant that he had also given two other daughters away to other councilmen as payment for favors they had done for him and encouraged his young son of thirteen to have sex with his youngest wife, who was twenty-four. He was excommunicated from the Salt Lake Order in 2002.

It should be noted that after John Ray's expulsion from Pinesdale in the early 1980s, the town has been paranoid about abuse, and rightly so. Strangers are not welcome there; the town experienced one of the most grievous cases of sexual molestation in Ravalli County, perpetrated by a stranger from outside the area. Fifteen years ago, Amber Jessop, then 6, biked to the store to buy candy. She was accosted by a man unknown to her, who kidnapped and raped her. The perpetrator was forty-two-year-old Kenneth Whitlow, a convicted sex offender from Alaska (Backus 2008). In 2007, Pinesdale housed one registered sex offender, thirty-nine-year-old Michael Nuttall, which brought the ratio of number of residents to sex offenders to 830 to 1, lower than in monogamous culture.[11] Chris Hoffman, the Ravalli County sheriff, told me that Pinesdale is a peaceful, law-abiding place; he has a good relationship with the people there. Further, the county attorney John Robinson stated that he has heard no complaints about the town. The case of the registered sex offender presents evidence that some polygamous towns are doing everything in their power to prevent abuse from happening in their midst. Thus, in spite of two authenticated cases of abuse in the AUB and one accusation relatively few complaints have been lodged against perpetrators. In fact, only one current issue of abuse is unresolved in Pinesdale.

Ervil LeBaron of Galeana, Mexico was convicted of murdering his own brother, Verlan LeBaron, and many other members of the Firstborn order. He used the doctrine of blood atonement to justify his killing spree. In addition, he was said to have taken teenage women to bed, whom he later married in the "covenant." Ervil's daughter, who described her father's actions in the film *The Godmakers* (Hunt and Decker 1980), said that her father's thirteen wives created a house full of jealousy and perversion, "as he would take several women to bed with him at one time." She claimed that preadolescents were often reserved for older men who would have a harder time securing wives because of their age. Ervil considered himself to be the Lamb of God and used blood atonement to keep his wives, children, and other members of the group in line. Ervil believed that he was the right hand of God with the authority to pass judgment on all sinners of the order. In his mind, that right also gave him the authority to mate with adolescent girls as compensation for his good deeds and to build up his mighty family kingdom. Like King Solomon with his 800 concubines, Ervil LeBaron believed his eleven wives represented his power and authority to spread his seed in righteousness. Another polygamist of Mexico, Orson W. Black, is following in Ervil LeBaron's footsteps; he has several wives including two teenage brides, the youngest of them just thirteen (Kocherga 2005). Black was not convicted of marrying underaged brides. Both Ervil LeBaron and Orson Black claimed to be following Joseph Smith, who sanctioned the law of polygamy in his own household in 1835, the same year that Fanny Alger, a seventeen-year-old orphan living in his home, became pregnant (Cairncross 1974).

There are scores of stories about abuse in the FLDS group, but I will recall only the more famous cases of the abuses against Elissa Wall and Carolyn Jessop. In 2007, Elissa Wall recalled how she had been forced by Warren Jeffs at age fourteen to marry her cousin. She was described as a strong-willed girl who was living with twelve siblings and her parents in their home in Salt Lake City. At fourteen she was married to her eighteen-year-old cousin to help her learn to submit to the group and to her husband in "mind, body, and soul" (Wall and Pulitzer 2008, cover). Prior to the marriage, Warren Jeffs had excommunicated her father and reassigned her mother and children to Fred Jessop of Colorado City. After a few years life in the larger family of twenty-two children, Elissa was informed by her stepfather Fred that she would wed Allen Steed, her cousin. When she rebelled against this request, the priesthood told her to try to be a good wife. During the next three years she endured Allen's physical abuse and what she describes as marital rape. She had several miscarriages and began to sleep in her car rather than share a bed with Allen. She eventually tried to leave the community but had no money and was naïve about the world beyond Colorado City. She took refuge in a lover, Lamont Barlow. Pregnant with Barlow's child, she left the group and filed a suit against Allen, Warren Jeffs, and the FLDS.

Like Elissa, Carolyn Jessop grew up in the FLDS group. Seventeen years after she became a plural wife, she left the group with her eight children. She was born into what she calls a "normal" polygamous family with only two wives, yet she was raised to believe that young women will eventually be married to older men who may also have as many as fifty, sixty, or even one hundred wives. These young women are assigned to husbands at the whim of the prophet. At eighteen, she was assigned to become the fourth wife of Merril Jessop, a prominent FLD leader who at fifty-five was three times her age. Merril eventually married six other women. During fifteen years of marriage, she bore eight children, all the while suffering perpetual physical and sexual abuses at the hands of her husband and her co-wives. When she tried to leave the group, she was threatened by FLDS members and the priesthood hierarchy.

Carolyn records a somewhat unique sexual paradox in fundamentalism: though the wife may not like her husband, she often seeks to have sex with him to acquire power. A wife who gains sexual favor with her husband can manipulate him to get resources and favors and, in the process, gain an advantage over the other wives. This can create anger and jealousy among the wives, of course, but it allows the wife, for one shining moment, to be empowered; therefore, it can be addictive. Associated with libidinousness is another vehicle for power: the bearing of many children. Because Carolyn became pregnant nearly every year, she increased her opportunity to manipulate, but ironically, she simultaneously struggled against patriarchal oppression from her husband, his other wives, and the priesthood brethren. Carolyn eventually left the group and won full custody of her eight children.

One of the most disturbing cases of abuse occurred in the Kingston group. At sixteen, Mary Ann Kingston of Salt Lake City left the Kingston group and filed a lawsuit against her family, seeking millions in damages for abuse. She named 242 family members in and around the Salt Lake Valley to validate her claim. Mary Ann was born and raised in the Kingston group, which she described as a "secretive religious society and economic organization" (Hummel 2003, 3) that promoted the sexual abuse of young girls "through illegal and under-age marriages, incest and polygamy" (ibid.). At thirteen she was pulled out of school and told to prepare for marriage. In 1998, at sixteen, she was told by her father, John Daniel Kingston, that she would become the fifteenth wife of his brother, David Kingston, thirty-three, her biological uncle. After the wedding to David she tried to run away, stating she did not want to have sex with him. She was subsequently taken to a remote ranch in northern Utah and beaten with a leather belt by her father. After twenty-eight lashes, she lost consciousness. When she revived, she ran away from the "ranch" and called the police. She filed a lawsuit against the group for sexual abuse of a child, seduction, assault, battery, false imprisonment, emotional distress, negligence, sham marriage, and conspiracy (ibid.). She won the case, and her father was sentenced to twenty-eight weeks in jail for arranging the underage marriage and the beating. Her husband-uncle was imprisoned for four years for incest and unlawful sexual conduct with a minor.

These narratives suggest that Mormon fundamentalist polygamy as a marriage form may be at some risk for abuse, a suggestion that support the observations John Llewellyn made while he was a polygamist. He spent twenty years investigating sex crimes and found a greater frequency of child molestation—including sibling sexual abuse—in polygamous communities (Llewellyn 2004). On the other hand, according to FLDS lawyer Rod Parker, women "enter those relationships voluntarily with the consent of their parents and extended family," and "although their model of marriage by revelation runs counter to traditional notions of romantic love and marriage, the model works for them because they have confidence in it" (quoted in Hummel 2003, 4.). Who do we believe, then, Llewellyn or Parker? Are the abuses described in the narratives isolated occurrences or they are typical? Do any of the women actually love their husbands and find contentment or they all miserable, brainwashed victims of male tyranny?

While I acknowledge that the abuse in these cases is disturbing and appears to have been systematic and while I realize that not all marriage arrangements are "consensual," I insist that the abuse described above does not happen in all polygamist families. In fact, my research shows that many families do not experience this type of abuse unless certain conditions that tend to lead to abuse are present. This question of prevalence of abuse requires careful analysis of sex offender cases in both monogamous households and polygamist communities. Ideally, such a study would sample and compare small Mormon communities and Mormon fundamentalist enclaves in the Intermountain West. Not all polygamous families exhibit the behaviors that contribute to abuse and neglect; likewise, many monogamist families do exhibit these behaviors that put women and children at risk. Further, many of the abuses against men often go unnoticed, with the exception of the expulsion of the "lost boys" from the FLDS (Bistline 2004).[12] To avoid reductionism and bias, I suggest that we begin to ask whether these abuses are unique to fundamentalism or whether we can identify similar problems in a wide array of other family configurations, such as single mother households, traditional monogamous homes, or blended family units.

Conclusion

I suggest that the Anna Karenina principle is a useful heuristic for identifying conditions that lead to abuse within polygamy. The following factors when combined with polygamy produce a greater risk for failed family environments: 1) the illegality of polygamy; 2) the isolation of polygamous households; 3) inequality within polygamous families; 4) male domination; 5) economic deprivation; 6) the absence of female networking; and 7) abuse. The results of this examination and other future studies of the contemporary polygamous lifestyle may help identify the conditions that may lead to cases of abuse. Such research can help inform policies to protect victims and prevent future abuses. It may also clarify when abuse is not present, and this can provide data about the viability of this alternative form of family life, inform policy on legalization rights and procedures, and provide evidence to support the passage of anti-discrimination laws that would protect all nontraditional marriages. If women and children are at risk of abuse or are being abused, the attorney generals of Montana, Texas, Arizona, and Utah must be alerted. Polygamy, as is often the case in monogamy, may also intensify the risk of sexually transmitted diseases, sibling battery, and psychosexual problems inherited by victims of sexual incest. Cases of abuse must be followed up with investigations of individual families instead of targeting a whole religious community or cultural enclaves.

Although I believe that the FLDS and Kingston groups may be at higher risk than the other groups for abuse and family dysfunction, this does not mean that entire communities should be held at gunpoint, nor does it mean that all underage marriage is abusive. Further, if Texas is able to target a whole culture because that culture encourages teenage girls to marry and bear children, should not other cultural enclaves that encourage child brides be seized, such as in my old high school community of Tooele, Utah, made up of immigrant white Mormons and Latino Catholics, where 20 percent of the senior class was pregnant or had already borne children? Or should we raid predominantly black communities, where, according to the Guttmacher Institute, 134 pregnancies occurred per 1,000 girls aged fifteen to nineteen (2006)? Perhaps we need to redefine abuse or at least consider cultural differences in the definition of abuse and be aware that the average age of menarche in the United States is now 12.5 years, which shapes the possibility that girls may be willing and prepared to take on motherhood earlier, as in sub-Saharan Africa, where 143 of every 1,000 teen girls is a mother (UNICEF 2001). In addition, the philosophy of teaching young girls that they must submit their will fully to a man isn't unique to Mormon fundamentalism. The solution is to make sure that there are constitutional and legal ways for women to exercise their free will and to leave a group easily if they wish to do so. This will empower young women like eighteen-year-old Carolyn Jessop, who had dreams of a career, or fifteen-year-old Mary Kingston, who was forced to marry her uncle, to have strength and support to say "no."

Future discourse on how well or how poorly polygamous families function should include an examination of best practices that are effective in terms of preventing, intervening in, and combating the conditions that lead to coercion, rape, brainwashing, and tyranny in isolated communities. Data should also be provided about early menarche, socialization patterns, psychological predispositions, and gender dynamics within fundamentalist communes. Analysis of the prevalence of lesbianism in fundamentalism might also be of interest. Furthermore, investigations of abuse in monogamous cultures should be undertaken with the same vigor and intensity that is now being visited upon polygamous groups.

Poly Families in the Twenty-First Century

Expanded Interest in Polygamy

Hopefully, this book has opened the door to further inquiries about North American polygamy for a diverse audience of readers. Plural marriage has great appeal for students of media and law as well as for social scientists, historians, theologians, and the general public. The public regards polygamy with both overt disdain and amused sympathy, as expressed by my ex-husband's wife, who finds Bill Henrickson' juggling act on *Big Love* "fascinating," and by my nineteen-year-old Lyndon State College students, who find the exotic notion of "sexual sharing" intriguing. As public interest in polygamy increases, new research possibilities emerge. Scholars are generating dialogue on a number of "poly" topics: the discrepancy between state law and group rights, the role of poly sexuality in population dynamics, and the ethics of government raids of religious groups. A recent collection of papers published by Oxford University Press attempts to provide a balanced history and cultural comparison of the various Mormon groups in response to the 2008 raid on the YFZ ranch in Eldorado. This anthology, called *Modern Polygamy in the United States: Historical, Cultural, and Legal Issues* (Jacobson 2011), is an example of the new trend of interdisciplinary analysis of polygamy.

New publications are also expressing the interests and experiences of other communities that practice plural marriage, such as African American women and Islamic immigrant groups (Majeed 2010; Dixon-Spear 2009). New light is also being shed on how polygamy is declining in East Africa (Bennion 2006) yet is gaining ground in other areas of the world such as Malaysia, South Africa, Mali, and Indonesia, where women practice polygamy by consent (Stacey and Meadow 2009; Anderson 2000; Madhavan 2002). Anthropologists are especially drawn to cross-cultural analysis of polygamy that focuses on how the situational context gives rise to varying forms of plural marriage.

Some of these forms benefit women and children, and others create disadvantages for them. By observing cross-cultural trends, we find that polygamy is an economic buffer in times of war, when racial/economic stratification characterizes a society, and when significant numbers of men are migrant workers. When soldiers or migrant workers leave their wives behind for months, or even years, women earn money through garden work, in-house industry, and livestock production to provide for their families. But this trend is changing. Land that was once used for subsistence farming is being purchased and used for large agribusiness plantations, factories, or tourist parks. Women are no longer associated with "land wealth" and are often left destitute. Now when their men leave the area for war or work, many turn to prostitution.

To combat this economic marginalization, the government of Kelantan, Malaysia, is encouraging elite politicians and businessmen who are already married to marry single mothers (including reformed prostitutes with children). The men must have good, stable jobs to enter into polygamy. This policy arose in response to the increase in unmarried, single mothers. Malaysian women say that the legalization of polygamy would be a godsend: it would give them rights to a man's financial and physical support, legitimacy for their children, and rights to state benefits. Interestingly, to facilitate courtship between vulnerable women and would-be polygamists, a polygamy club in Rawang was launched in August of 2009 (Malaysian Insider 2009). The founder of the 300-person club is Madam Hatijah Aam, the second wife of a wealthy polygamist in the area. She wants to target the problems of prostitution and adultery and help "old maids" and former sex workers find mates, even if those mates are already married to other women.

Historians have noted correlations between early Indo-European plural marriage and current U.S. trends. In both time periods, two types of plural liaisons were typical: a man has a relationship with two or more women or a man has a wife and another women, a mistress or informal wife, who the first wife does not know about. The "other" wife, who was known as the hetaera in Greco-Roman society, provided intellectual, romantic, and sexual stimulation that the first wife did not provide (Dixon-Spear 2009). Maillu, author of *Our Kind of Polygamy* (1988) called the hetaera relationship a form of simultaneous polygyny where one woman has the legal rights and the other is the secret, disadvantaged wife with no legal, economic, or social claims to the husband. Today it is seen as appropriate and normal for a man to fulfill his sexual needs within the general framework of monogamy, yet such arrangements leave both the wife and mistress disenfranchised. The wife and must deal with the shame of her husband's infidelity and the potential loss of financial and emotional security while the mistress is "legally, financially, and socially vulnerable," subject to rejection at a moment's notice (Dixon-Spear 2009, 54). This same pattern of disenfranchisement existed in early America for both the white legal wife and the African American enslaved concubine/"Mammy."

Africanist Phil Kilbride (1996) believes that functional frameworks for plural marriage still exist in traditional African and Islamic nations, where wives and children are granted legitimacy and economic status with socially sanctioned plural marriages. The women are not sexual objects but are legally recognized wives, a status that guarantees their ties to their husband and to their lineage. This system has a long history in Africa and works particularly well in areas where there is a shortage of eligible males, such as during war or where there are high rates of homicide, disease, or migrant labor. The problem with polygamy initially occurred when Europeans began to dominate the continent; they raised monogamy on a pedestal as the only acceptable form under God. Polygamy was practiced in a "peculiar" way, marginalizing both the first wife and the enslaved or vulnerable "other" wife, disempowering all females involved and undermining their marriages and families (Dixon-Spear 2009).

Legal scholars are entering the discourse about legislation about polygamy and the consequences of removing the ban in a variety of venues, including the *Columbia Law Review,* the *Duke Journal of Gender Law,* and the *Journal of Law and Family Studies.* Some challenge the efficacy of legal bans against polygamy (Duncan 2008; Turley, as quoted in Pomfret 2006, and Campbell et al. 2005); and others argue against polygamy for moral and ethical reasons, stating that polygamy does not provide an appropriate environment for children (see the quote by First Amendment scholar, Marci Hamilton Kirt in Winslow 2008; and Strassberg 2010). Theologians are also divided on the issue. Some argue that the Old Testament provides an appropriate template for family structure, reaffirming a poly ethic. Others feel that Mosaic law has been fulfilled and that Christ embraced monogamy as the true standard.

Gender scholars are also divided about polygamy. Some feel that any form of patriarchy dissolves a woman's power and that polygamy is a patriarchal form of marriage. They note that the areas of the world where polygamy thrives—the Middle East, Africa, Indonesia, and Latin America—are also places where patriarchal culture dominates. In such regions, polygamy is accompanied by male supremacist ideologies. Yet gender humanists like myself recognize that even women in patriarchy have access to informal power.[1] Many such women, who are found in Mormonism, Islam, and traditional Africa, have created a unique world within the patriarchal matrix that provides them with ironic access to empowerment and autonomy and resources (Friedl 1989). Further, women are empowered when they are around other women like themselves, engaging in similar temporal and spiritual work. Gender scholars are recognizing this "womanist ethic of care" as a new developing framework for women to meet the challenges they face (Dixon-Spear 2009). And libertarian polygamist Elizabeth Joseph (1997) has said that the poly ethic is an example of the most sublime form of feminism.

Family and marriage scholars are also examining polygamy and its impact on women and children. In America, heterosexual monogamous women suffer from a variety of problems (Benokraitis 2009); they are more likely to choose divorce and to have emotional and physical health problems than are their male counterparts. Most working women begin a second shift of housework after they return from a full day at the office or in the factory. They, more than men, are in a position of "service" to their spouses' emotional and physical needs and are often more responsible than men for caring for children. There is also a serious problem with father absence and neglect; most husbands do not follow through with their obligations to their sexual partners or any children born to that union (ibid.). In these kinds of conditions, is it no wonder that some women choose to have a sister wife who can contribute to the workload, a structure that enables one woman to stay at home with the children and the other to earn a living outside the home. One polygamist woman chose to live in a polygamist union with her biological sister rather than face life as a single mother on food stamps. She also loved the way it revealed things about herself that she would never have known with just a husband around. "Much more has been required of me than I could have ever imagined was possible for a human being. If you could have told me then who I would be now, I couldn't have comprehended it. It requires development, fast and hard and quick: emotionally, mentally, physically, spiritually" (Sloan 2011, 3).

In addition to reducing divorce rates and providing single women with more options, polygamy may enhance family life by providing more parents to care for children. During the FLDS raid, many children who were asked to identify their mothers replied that they have many mothers (Roberts 2008). In a healthy polygamist environment, children will always be surrounded by loving caregivers. Another benefit to children is the socialization they receive through the intense friendships they forge within the large family network. According to anthropologists Bill Jankowiak and Monique Diderich (2000), when children are raised in polygamy they develop sibling solidarity; they develop bonds with full and half-siblings based on inclusive fitness. In his study of Centennial Park, Arizona, and found that siblings produced from several wives in one family typically created friendships and loyalties and bonds of love through a unique ethos that downplays genetic differences (half versus full blood) in order to create communal harmony, or a clustering of feeling and affection.[2] Polygamy is also a productive way to guarantee a labor force and an insurance plan against hardship. It also ensures that children will have a better chance to reach adulthood to care for their parents.

A growing, diverse group of scholars is examining polygamy from the fields of law, media, gender, theology, and culture. Of great concern in the twenty-first century are the socioeconomic pressures for North American women that force them to consider alternative forms of sexuality, marriage, and family. Polygamy is one of the options that appeal to certain types of women in certain contexts. I find it frustrating that most people tend to lump all polygamy together without considering the rich variability of lifestyles, beliefs, and behaviors within that family structure. No single perspective captures the experiences of all women in polygamy. Like any other alternative family form, polygamy does not easily fit into mainstream society, yet because it is adopted by some women in our society to meet their evolving needs, it must be legally protected and socially tolerated.

A New Face of Polygamy

One of the most profound moments in the *Big Love* series was in Season 5, when Bill and his family came out of the closet to live the Principle in full view of the public eye. Bill told his polygamous friends, neighbors, and congressional constituents that there was a "whole new face of polygamy" and that they had better prepare for it. It is my belief that this "new face," presented on weekly television shows, will help decrease the stigma associated with plural marriage. *Big Love* and *Sister Wives* will educate the mainstream about the idiosyncrasies and the challenges of the poly lifestyle. They will provide evidence of its viability and, it is to be hoped, provide support for the reform of laws regarding polygamy. Just as the U.S. Supreme Court's overturning of sodomy laws in 2003 followed the appearance of television programs about lesbian and gay life, so too, I predict, the decriminalization of polygamy will follow the recent poly media phenomenon.

Toward that effort, we should begin viewing the rights of poly families as every bit as important and intrinsic to human rights as the rights of lesbian or gay, blended, or single-parent families. The rights of those who practice poly sexuality should be just as protected as the rights of lesbians and gays, those who practice serial monogamy, or even prostitutes. In fact, prostitution has more legal protection in some parts of the United States than religiously sanctioned polygamy. In Nevada, where female prostitutes have unionized, the state legislature has passed laws that give prostitutes the resources to protect themselves and their children, including health benefits and child care programs. Their activities are regulated and monitored for their own protection, by their own volition. The name of the organization that spearheads such legal rights, which could very well be the new pledge of advocates of legalizing polygamy, is C.O.Y.O.T.E., Call Off Your Old Tired Ethics.

If we begin seeing poly families in this same progressive light, perhaps the public will begin to accept polygamy as an option, or at the very least treat it with the same benign insouciance that they treat the blended family. Within such an atmosphere of tolerance the Kody Brown family could return to Utah, the ex-wives of Merril Jessop could get child support payments, and pro-polygamist Anne Wilde could be run for state senator if she wanted to. Any privileges enjoyed by the monogamist mainstream would be offered fully to polygamists.

As a scholar who has studied the minutiae of poly relationships for two decades, I reject the claim that all polygamy contributes to abuse and female subordination. Rather, I embrace the anthropological view that human behavior, seen in its situational context, can be appropriate, functional, and even satisfactory. As both an insider and outsider, I have tried to give voice to the broadly diverse population of Mormon women: fundamentalists, orthodox Mormons, liberals, conservatives, divorced women, lesbians, single mothers, and polygamist wives. For many of these women, especially those who are disenfranchised by the mainstream, plural marriage seems a reasonable choice. As a democratic people, we need to create and adapt a sociocultural and legal framework around polygamy to better provide for this choice. Such a framework would regulate deviant polygamists and at the same time protect the rights of women who actually prefer polygamy to monogamy, who are in plural marriages that function well and enjoy the benefits of a women's network, assistance with child care and housework, and intimate relationships that meet their psychological, spiritual, and emotional needs.

Postscript

On November 23, 2011, when my book was already in production with Brandeis University Press, I learned that a British Columbia trial court had upheld Canada's anti-polygamy law (Sec. 293 of Criminal Code of Canada), in spite of the many challenges it poses to the Canadian Charter of Rights and Freedoms. In other words, the court found the Canadian polygamy ban to be *constitutional*. Chief Justice Robert Bauman stated that although the law violates the religious freedom of fundamentalist Mormons, Muslims, and African immigrants, polygamy's potential harm against women and children outweighs that concern.

The arguments made against polygamy were based predominantly on negative stereotypes, largely ignoring the widespread variability in the expression of poly love and poly family structure. Also ignored was the evidence that many polygamist unions involve consensual sexuality with no presence of abuse. The B.C. court assumed that all polygamy is equally and uniformly abusive. "Polygamy's harm to society includes the critical fact that a great many of its individual harms are not specific to any particular religious, cultural or regional context. They can be generalized and expected to occur wherever polygamy exists." The court dismissed evidence about successful polygamy, assuming a positive correlation between polygamy and the decline of civil liberties.

Thus, in agreement with America's legal opposition to polygamy, Canada is maintaining its original statute, that polygamy is inappropriate in a democratic nation and may be associated with abuse. My prediction that Canada would adopt a progressive stance on polygamy was proven wrong. Yet, there is still hope that this ruling may be appealed to the higher courts in Canada, and eventually in the United States. Toward that end, I would argue that South Africa continues to set a prime example for managing plural unions and protecting women and children against the harms associated with polygamy. I would also direct our gaze to the current struggle in the state of Utah, where lead counsel Jon Turley is challenging the constitutionality of Utah's statute criminalizing plural or polygamous marriage. After a December 2011 hearing, a federal judge ruled that there was sufficient evidence to allow

Sister Wives' Brown family to pursue a lawsuit challenging Utah's bigamy law. The task ahead for Turley and the Browns is to show that there is a real and viable threat to their constitutional rights, in order for the lawsuit to hold up in court.

Rather than criminalize polygamy, which will continue to exist whether we like it or not, we should acknowledge the rights of individuals to pursue their own unique pathways to love and marriage, so long as those choices do not harm other people and so long as they occur with free, informed, and full consent.

Appendix

THE 27 RULES OF CELESTIAL MARRIAGE

By Apostle Orson Pratt

From *The Seer* 1 [November 1853]: 173–176; 1 [December 1853]: 183–187.

Inasmuch as the saints in Utah consider it moral, virtuous, and scriptural, to practice the plurality system, they should seek by every means to eradicate, not only from their own minds, but from the minds of their children, every erroneous improper prejudice which they have formerly imbibed, by their associations with the nations of modern Christendom. Parents who have daughters should seek to instil into their minds, that it is just as honorable for them to be united in marriage to a good man who is already a husband, as to one that is single: they should be taught to reject the society and proposals for marriage of all wicked men, whether single or not. A father should be impartial to all his children, and cultivate the same love for them all; while each wife should instil into the minds of her own children the necessity of loving the children of each of the others, as brothers and sisters. Each wife should, not only care for the welfare of her husband and her own children, but should also seek the happiness of each of his other wives and children· And likewise, the children of each wife should not only represent, honor, and love their own mother, but also the mothers of all their brothers and sisters. By observing these precepts, peace and tranquility will reign throughout every department of the family, and the spirit of God will flow freely from heart to heart.

Nothing is so much to be desired in families as peace, love, and union: they are essential to happiness here and hereafter. And, in order to promote these desirable objects, we would recommend the observance of the following rules.

Rule 1st.—Let that man who intends to become a husband, seek first the kingdom of God and its righteousness, and learn to govern himself, according to the law of God: for he that cannot govern himself cannot govern others: let him dedicate his property, his talents, his time, and even his life to the service of God, holding all things at His disposal, to do with the same, according as He shall direct through the counsel that He has ordained.

Rule 2nd.—Let him next seek for wisdom to direct him in the choice of his wives. Let him seek for those whose qualifications will render him and themselves happy· Let him look not wholly at the beauty of the countenance, or the splendor of the apparel, or the great fortune, or the artful smiles, or the affected modesty of females; for all these, without the genuine virtues, are like the dew-drops which glitter for a moment in the sun, and dazzle the eye, but soon vanish away. But let him look for kind and amiable dispositions; for unaffected modesty; for industrious habits; for sterling virtue; for honesty, integrity, and truthfulness; for cleanliness in persons, in apparel, in cooking, and in every kind of domestic labor; for cheerfulness, patience, and stability of character; and above all, for genuine religion to control and govern their every thought and deed. When he has found those possessing these qualifications let him seek to obtain them lawfully through the counsel of him who holds the keys of the everlasting priesthood, that they may be married to him by the authority of Heaven, and thus be secured to him for time and for all eternity.

Rule 3rd. — When a man has obtained his wives, let him not suppose that they are already perfect in all things; for this cannot be expected in those who are young and inexperienced in the cares and vicissitudes of a married life. They, as weaker vessels, are given to him as the stronger, to nourish, cherish, and protect; to be their head, their patriarch, and their saviour; to teach, instruct, counsel, and perfect them in all things relating to family government, and the welfare and happiness of themselves and their children. Therefore, let him realize the weighty responsibility now placed upon him, as the head of a family; and also let him study diligently the disposition of his wives, that he may know how to instruct them in wisdom for their good.

Rule 4th. — Betray not the confidence of your wives. There are many ideas in an affectionate confiding wife which she would wish to communicate to her husband, and yet she would be very unwilling to have them communicated to others. Keep each of your wives' secrets from all the others, and from anyone else, unless in cases where good will result by doing otherwise.

Rule 5th. — Speak not of the faults of your wives to others; for in so doing, you speak against yourself. If you speak to one of your wives of the imperfections of the others who may be absent, you not only injure them in her estimation, but she will expect that you will speak against her under like circumstances: this is calculated to weaken their confidence in you, and sow division in the family. Tell each one of her faults in private in a spirit of kindness and love, and she will most probably respect you for it, and endeavor to do better for the future; and thus the others will not, because of your reproof, take occasion to speak reproachfully of her. There may be circumstances, when reproof, given in the presence of the others, will produce asalutary influence upon all. Wisdom is profitable to direct, and should be sought for earnestly by those who have the responsibility of families.

Rule 6th. — Avoid anger and a fretful peevish disposition in your family. A hasty spirit, accompanied with harsh words, will most generally beget its own likeness, or, at least, it will, eventually, sour the feelings of your wives and children, and greatly weaken their affections for you. You should remember that harsh expressions against one of your wives, used in the hearing of the others, will more deeply wound her feelings, than if she alone heard them. Reproofs that are timely and otherwise good, may lose their good effect by being administered in a wrong spirit, indeed, they will most probably increase the evils which they were intended to remedy. Do not find fault with every trifling error that you may see; for this will discourage your family, and they will begin to think that it is impossible to please you; and, after a while, become indifferent as to whether they please you or not. How unhappy and extremely wretched is that family where nothing pleases — where scolding has become almost as natural as breathing!

Rule 7th. — Use impartiality in your family as far as circumstances will allow; and let your kindness and love abound towards them all. Use your own judgment, as the head of the family, in regard to your duties in relation to them, and be not swayed from that which is right, by your own feelings, nor by the feelings of others.

Rule 8th. — Suffer not your judgment to be biased against any one of your wives, by the accusations of the others, unless you have good grounds to believe that those accusations are just. Decide not hastily upon partial evidence, but weigh well all things, that your mind may not become unjustly prejudiced. When one of your wives complains of the imperfections of the others, and endeavors to set your mind against them, teach her that all have imperfections, and of the necessity of bearing one with another in patience, and of praying one for another.

Rule 9th. — Call your wives and children together frequently, and instruct them in their duties towards God, towards yourself, and towards one another. Pray with them and for them often; and teach them to pray much, that the Holy Spirit may dwell in their midst, without which it is impossible to maintain that union, love, and oneness which are so necessary to happiness and salvation.

Rule 10th. — Remember, that notwithstanding written rules will be of service in teaching you your duties, as the head of a family, yet without the Holy Ghost to teach and instruct you, it is impossible for you to govern a family in righteousness; therefore, seek after the Holy Ghost and he shall teach you all things, and sanctify you and your family, and make you one, that you may be perfected in Him and He in you, and eventually be exalted on high to dwell with God, where your joy will be full forever.

Rule 11th. — Let no woman unite herself in marriage with any man, unless she has fully resolved to submit herself wholly to his counsel, and to let him govern as the head. It is far better for her not to be united with him in the sacred bonds of eternal union, than to rebel against the divine order of family government, instituted for a higher salvation; for if she altogether turn therefrom, she will receive a greater condemnation.

Rule 12th. — Never seek to prejudice the mind of your husband against any of his other wives, for the purpose of exalting yourself in his estimation, lest the evil which you unjustly try to bring upon them, fall with double weight upon your own head. Strive to rise in favor and influence with your husband by your own merits, and not by magnifying the faults of others.

Rule 13th. — Seek to be a peacemaker in the family with whom you are associated. If you see the least appearance of division arising, use your utmost efforts to restore union and soothe the feelings of all. Soft and gentle words, spoken in season, will allay contention and strife; while a hasty spirit and harsh language add fuel to the fire already kindled which will rage with increasing violence.

Rule 14th. — Speak not evil of your husband unto any of the rest of the family for the purpose of prejudicing their minds against him; for if he be informed thereof, it will injure you in his estimation. Neither speak evil of any members of the family; for this will destroy their confidence in you. Avoid all hypocracy; for if you pretend to love your husband and to honor and respect his wives, when present, but speak disrespectful of them when absent, you will be looked upon as a hypocrite, as a tattler, and as a mischief-making woman, and be shunned as being more dangerous than an open enemy. And what is still more detestable, is to tattle out of the family, and endeavor to create enemies against those with whom you are connected. Such persons should not only be considered hypocrites, but traitors, and their conduct should be despised by every lover of righteousness. Remember also, that there are more ways than one to tattle; it is not always the case that those persons who are the boldest in their accusations that are the most dangerous slanderers; but such as hypocritically pretend that they do not wish to injure their friends, and at the same time, very piously insinuate in dark indirect sayings, something that is calculated to leave a very unfavorable prejudice against them. Shun such a spirit as you would the very gates of hell.

Rule 15th. — If you see any of your husband's wives sick or in trouble, use every effort to relieve them, and to administer kindness and consolations, remembering that you, yourself, under the same circumstances, would be thankful for their assistance. Endeavor to share each other's burdens, according to the health, ability, and strength which God has given you. Do not be afraid that you will do more than your share of the domestic labor, or that you will be more kind to them than they are to you.

Rule 16th. — Let each mother correct her own children, and see that they do not dispute and quarrel with each other, nor with any others; let her not correct the children of the others without liberty so to do, lest it give offence. The husband should see that each mother maintains a wise and proper discipline over her children, especially in their younger years: and it is his duty to see that all of his children are obedient to himself and to their respective mothers. And it is also his duty to see that the children of one wife are not allowed to quarrel and abuse those of the others, neither to be disrespectful or impudent to any branch of his family.

Rule 17th.—It is the duty of parents to instruct their children, according to their capacities in every principle of the gospel, as revealed in the Book of Mormon and in the revelations which God has given, that they may grow up in righteousness, and in the fear of the Lord, and have faith in Him. Suffer no wickedness to have place among them, but teach them the right way, and see that they walk therein. And let the husband and his wives, and all of his children that have come to the years of understanding often bow before the Lord around the family altar, and pray vocally and unitedly for whatever blessings they stand in need of, remembering that where there are union and peace, there will also be faith, and hope, and the love of God, and every good work, and a multiplicity of blessings, imparting health and comfort to the body, and joy and life to the soul.

Rule 18th.—Let each mother commence with her children when young, not only to teach and instruct them, but to chasten and bring them into the most perfect subjection; for then is the time that they are the most easily conquered, and their tender minds are the most susceptible of influences and government. Many mothers from carelessness neglect their children, and only attempt to govern them at long intervals, when they most generally find their efforts of no lasting benefit; for the children having been accustomed to have their own way, do not easily yield; and if peradventure they do yield, it is only for the time being, until the mother relaxes again into carelessness, when they return again to their accustomed habits: and thus by habit they become more and more confirmed in disobedience, waxing worse and worse, until the mother becomes discouraged, and relinquishes all discipline, and complains that she cannot make her children mind. The fault is not so much in the children, as in the carelessness and neglect of the mother when the children were young; it is she that must answer, in a great degree, for the evil habits and disobedience of the children. She is more directly responsible than the father; for it cannot be expected that the father can always find time, apart from the laborious duties required of him, to correct and manage his little children who are at home with their mothers. It is frequently the case that the father is called to attend to duties in public life, and may be absent from home much of his time, when the whole duty of family government necessarily rests upon the respective mothers of his children; if they through carelessness, suffer their children to grow up in disobedience and ruin themselves, they must bear the shame and disgrace thereof. Some mothers, though not careless, and though they feel the greatest anxiety for the welfare of their children, yet, through a mistaken notion of love for them, forbear to punish them when they need punishment, or if they undertake to conquer them, their tenderness and pity are so great, that they prevail over the judgment, and the children are left unconquered, and become more determined to resist all future efforts of their mothers until, at length, they conclude that their children have a more stubborn disposition than others, and that it is impossible to subject them in obedience. In this case, as in that of neglect, the fault is the mother's. The stubbornness of the children, for the most part, is the effect of the mother's indulgence, arising from her mistaken idea of love. By that which she calls love, she ruins her children.

Children between one and two years of age are capable of being made to understand many things; then is the time to begin with them. How often we see children of that age manifest much anger. Frequently by crying through anger, they that are otherwise healthy, injure themselves: it is far better, in such instances, for a mother to correct her child in a gentle manner, though with decision and firmness, until she conquers it, and causes it to cease crying, than to suffer that habit to increase. When the child by gentle punishment has learned this one lesson from its mother, it is much more easily conquered and brought into subjection in other things, until finally, by a little perseverance on the part of the mother, it learns to be obedient to her voice in all things; and obedience becomes confirmed into a permanent habit. Such a child trained by a negligent or overindulgent mother, might have become confirmed in habits of stubbornness and disobedience. It is not so much in the original constitution of children as in their training, that causes such wide differences in their dispositions. It cannot be denied, that there is a difference in the constitution of children even from their birth; but this difference is mostly owing to the proper or improper conduct of parents, as before stated; therefore, even for this difference, parents are more or less responsible. If parents, through their own evil conduct entail hereditary dispositions upon their children which are calculated to ruin them, unless properly curtailed and overcome, they should realise, that for that evil they must render an account. If parents have been guilty in entailing upon their offspring unhappy dispositions, let them repent, by using all diligence to save them from the evil consequences which will naturally result by giving way to those dispositions. The greater the derangement, the greater must be the remedy, and the more skilful and thorough should be its application, until that which is sown in evil is overcome and completely subdued. In this way parents may save themselves and their children; but otherwise there is condemnation. Therefore, we repeat again, let mothers begin to discipline their children when young.

Rule 19th. — Do not correct children in anger; an angry parent is not as well prepared to judge of the amount of punishment which should be inflicted upon a child, as one that is more cool and exercised with reflection, reason, and judgment. Let your children, see that you punish them, not to gratify an angry disposition, but to reform them for their good, and it will have a salutary influence; they will not look upon you as a tyrant, swayed to and fro by turbulent and furious passions; but they will regard you as one that seeks their welfare, and that you only chasten them because you love them, and wish them to do well. Be deliberate and calm in your counsels and reproofs, but at the same time use earnestness and decision. Let your children know that your words must be respected and obeyed.

Rule 20th. — Never deceive your children by threatnings or promises. Be careful not to threaten them with a punishment which you have no intention of inflicting; for this will cause them to lose confidence in your word; besides, it will cause them to contract the habit of lying: when they perceive that their parents do not fulfil their threatenings or promises, they will consider that there is no harm in forfeiting their word. Think not that your precepts, concerning truthfulness, will have much weight upon the minds of your children, when they are contradicted by your examples. Be careful to fulfil your word in all things in righteousness, and your children will not only learn to be truthful from your example, but they will fear to disobey your word, knowing that you never fail to punish or reward according to your threatnings and promises. Let your laws, penalties, and rewards be founded upon the Principles of justice and mercy, and adapted to the capacities of your children; for this is the way that our heavenly Father governs His children, giving to some a Celestial; to others a Terrestrial; and to others still a Telestial law, with penalties and promises annexed, according to the conditions, circumstances, and capacities of the individuals to be governed. Seek for wisdom and pattern after the heavenly order of government.

Rule 21st. — Do not be so stern and rigid in your family government as to render yourself an object of fear and dread. There are parents who only render themselves conspicuous in the attribute of Justice, while mercy and love are scarcely known in their families. Justice should be tempered with mercy, and love should be the great moving principle, interweaving itself in all your family administrations. When justice alone sits upon the throne, your children approach you with dread, or peradventure hide themselves from your presence, and long for your absence that they may be relieved from their fear; at the sound of your approaching foot-steps they flee as from an enemy, and tremble at your voice, and shrink from the gaze of your countenance, as though they expected some terrible punishment to be inflicted upon them. Be familiar with your children that they may delight themselves in your society, and look upon you as a kind and tender parent whom they delight to obey. Obedience inspired by love, and obedience inspired by fear, are entirely different in their nature; the former will be permanent and enduring, while the latter only waits to have the objects of fear removed, and it vanishes like a dream. Govern children as parents, and not as tyrants; for they will be parents in their turn, and will be very likely to adopt that form of government in which they have been educated. If you have been tyrants, they may be influenced to pattern after your example. If you are fretful and continually scolding, they will be very apt to be scolds too. If you are loving, kind, and merciful, these benign influences will be very certain to infuse themselves into their order of family government; and thus good and evil influences frequently extend themselves down for many generations and ages. How great, then, are the responsibilities of parents to their children! And how fearful the consequences of bad examples! Let love, therefore, predominate and control you, and your children will be sure to discover it, and will love you in return.

Rule 22nd. — Let each mother teach her children to honor and love their father, and to respect his teachings and counsels. How frequently it is the case, when fathers undertake to correct their children, mothers will interfere in the presence of the children: this has a very evil tendency in many respects: first, it destroys the oneness of feeling which should exist between husband and wife; secondly, it weakens the confidence of the children in the father, and emboldens them to disobedience; thirdly, it creates strife and discord; and lastly, it is rebelling against the order of family government, established by divine wisdom. If the mother supposes the father too severe, let her not mention this in the presence of the children, but she can express her feelings to him while alone by themselves, and thus the children will not see any division between them. For husband and wives to be disagreed, and to contend, and quarrel, is a great evil; and to do these things in the presence of their children, is a still greater evil. Therefore, if a husband and his wives will quarrel and destroy their own happiness, let them have pity upon their children, and not destroy them by their pernicious examples.

Rule 23rd. — Suffer not children of different mothers to be haughty and abusive to each other; for they are own brothers and sisters the same as the children of the patriarch Jacob; and one has no claim above another, only as his conduct merits it. Should you discover contentions or differences arising, do not justify your own children and condemn the others in their presence; for this will encourage them in their quarrels: even if you consider that your children are not so much in the fault as the others, it is far better to teach them of the evils of strife, than to speak against the others. To speak against them, not only alienates their affections, but has a tendency to offend their mothers, and create unpleasant feelings between you and them. Always speak well of each of your husband's wives in the presence of your children; for children generally form their judgment concerning others, by the sayings of their parents: they are very apt to respect those whom their parents respect; and hate those whom they hate. If you consider that some of the mothers are too lenient with their children and too negligent in correcting them, do not be offended, but strive, by the wise and prudent management of your own, to set a worthy example before them, that they, by seeing your judicious and wise course, may be led to go and do likewise. Examples will sometimes reform, when precepts fail.

Rule 24th. — Be industrious in your habits: this is important as fulfilling the law of God: it is also important for those who are in low circumstances, that they may acquire food, and raiment, and the necessary comforts of life: it is also important for the rich as well as the poor, that they may be able more abundantly to supply the wants of the needy, and be in circumstances to help the unfortunate and administer to the sick and afflicted; for in this way, it is possible even for the rich to enter into the kingdom of heaven. A family whose time is occupied in the useful and lawful avocations of life, will find no time to go from house to house, tattling and injuring one another and their neighbors; neither will they be so apt to quarrel among themselves.

Rule 25th. — When your children are from three to five years of age, send them to school, and keep them there year after year until they receive a thorough education in all the rudiments of useful science, and in their manners, and morals. In this manner, they will avoid many evils, arising from indolence, and form habits that will render them beneficial to society in after life. Let mothers educate their daughters in all kinds of domestic labor: teach them to wash and iron, to bake and do all kinds of cooking, to knit and sew, to spin and weave, and to do all other things that will qualify them to be good and efficient housewives. Let fathers educate their sons in whatever branch or branches of business, they intend them respectively to follow. Despise that false delicacy which is exhibited by the sons and daughters of the rich, who consider it a dishonor to labor at the common avocations of live. Such notions of high-life, should be frowned out of the territory, as too contemptible to be harbored, for one moment, by a civilized community. Some of these bogus gentlemen and ladies have such grand ideas, concerning gentility, that they would let their poor old father and mother slave themselves to death, to support them in their idleness, or at some useless fanciful employment. The daughter will sit down in the parlour at her painting or music, arrayed in silks and fineries, and let her mother wash and cook until, through fatigue she is ready to fall into her grave: this they call gentility, and the distinctions between the low and the high. But such daughters are not worthy of husbands, and should not be admitted into any respectable society: they are contemptible drones, that would be a curse to any husband who should be so unfortunate as to be connected with such nuisances. Painting, music, and all the fine arts, should be cherished, and cultivated, as accomplishments which serve to adorn and embellish an enlightened civilized people, and render life agreeable and happy; but when these are cultivated, to the exclusion of the more necessary duties and qualifications, it is like adorning swine with costly jewels and pearls to make them appear more respectable: these embellishments, only render such characters a hundred fold more odious and disgustful than they would otherwise appear.

Rule 26th. — Use economy and avoid wastefulness. How discouraging it would be to a husband who has a large family, depending mostly upon his labor for a support, to see his wives and children carelessly, thoughtlessly, and un-necessarily, waste his hard earnings. Let not one wife, for fear that she shall not obtain her share of the income, destroy, give away, and otherwise foolishly dispose of what is given to her, thinking that her husband will furnish her with more. Those who economize and wisely use that which is given to them, should be counted worthy to receive more abundantly than those who pursue a contrary course. Each wife should feel interested in saving and preserving that with which the Lord has entrusted her, and should rejoice, not only in her prosperity, but in the prosperity of all the others: her eyes should not be full of greediness to grasp every thing herself, but she should feel equally interested in the welfare of the whole family. By pursuing this course she will be beloved: by taking a contrary , course, she will be considered selfish and little minded.

Rule 27th. — Let husbands, wives, sons, and daughters, continually realize that their relationships do not end with this short life, but will continue in eter-nity without end. Every qualification and disposition therefore, which will render them happy here, should be nourished, cherished, enlarged, and perfected, that their union may be indissoluble, and their happiness secured both for this world and for that which is to come.

Let these rules be observed, and all others that are good and righteous, and peace will be the result: husbands will be patriarchs and saviours; wives will be like fruitful vines, bringing forth precious fruits in their seasons: their sons will be like plants of renown, and their daughters like the polished stones of a palace. Then the saints shall flourish upon the hills and rejoice upon the mountains, and become a great people and strong, whose goings forth shall be with strength that is everlasting. Arise, O Zion! clothe thyself with light! shine forth with clearness and brilliancy! illuminate the nations and the dark corners of the earth, for their light is gone out—their sun is set—gross darkness covers them! let thy light be seen upon the high places of the earth; let it shine in glorious splendour; for then shall the wicked see, and be confounded, and lay their hands upon their mouths in shame; then shall kings arise and come forth to the light, and rejoice in the greatness of thy glory! Fear not, O Zion, nor let thine hands be slack, for great is the Holy One in the amidst of thee! a cloud shall be over thee by day for a defense, and at night thy dwellings shall be encircled with glory! God is thine everlasting light, and shall be a Tower of strength against thine enemies; at the sound of His voice they shall melt away, and terrors shall seize upon them. In that day thou shalt be beautiful and glorious, and the reproach of the Gentiles shall no more come into thine ears; in that day, shall the sons of them that afflicted thee come bending unto thee and bow themselves down at the soles of thy feet; and the daughters of them that reproached thee, shall come saying, We will eat our own bread and wear our own apparel, only let us be joined in the patriarchal order of marriage with the husbands and patriarchs in Zion to take away our reproach: then shall they highly esteem, far above riches, that which their wicked fathers ridiculed under the name of Polygamy. Amen

Notes

PREFACE

1. LDS leaders targeted polygamists, gays, intellectuals, and/or feminists in the purges of the early 1990s.

2. See Bourdieu's sociological reflexivity and self-conscious inquiry (1992) and Weber's use of subjectivity (1949), where he describes *verstehen,* a process of subjective interpretation by the social researcher, a degree of sympathetic understanding between researcher and subjects of study whereby the researcher shares the situated meanings and experiences of those under scrutiny.

3. The term "ethnography" refers to the anthropological research tool of immersing oneself within a culture and systematically and holistically recording the day-to-day life of humans within a particular cultural environment. The dominant methodologies used in ethnographic research are participant and naturalistic observations and informal interviews.

4. At one point in my unhappy marriage to my first husband, I pondered sharing him with my sister Sue (whom he was fond of anyway), romanticizing about how we could save money and raise our children together.

5. Cannon stated publicly that "short-lived, debased nations like Rome" are all monogamous and that the United States should rise above them and become polygamous (Cannon 1872).

6. The term was coined by O'Dea (1957, 225) and I find it applies to my professorial Bennion roots. I would like to think I take after my esteemed cousin, author and teacher Lowell Bennion, who admonished Mormons to continually reevaluate their beliefs, question authority, and update their spiritual connections to the gospel (see his *I Believe,* published by Deseret Books, 1983).

7. I coined the phrase "Jill" Mormons at a 2002 Mormon History Association conference in Salt Lake City. It refers to inactive Mormon women, like myself, who do not embody the Mormon ideal of traditional marriage and family required in the Proclamation of the Family.

8. The term "emic" refers to an anthropological "insider" approach perfected by Franz Boaz in the early 1900s. It requires the researcher to walk in the shoes of his/her subjects, seeing the world the way they do and attempting to understand their ethos and lifeways from the native perspective.

9. In Part One I draw upon several chapters from other works. In Chapters 1 and 2, where I discuss the history, culture, and ideology of the polygamists, I

draw upon the fourth and seventh chapters of the Oxford University compilation, edited by Cardell Jacobson (2011). A section of Chapter 3 comes from my "Mormon Women" article in Jacobson (2008a), and Chapter 4 contains work also featured in both my Chapter 9 of *Women of Principle,* and my Chapter 5 of *Evaluating Polygamy* (2008). All are used by permission.

INTRODUCTION

1. A setback to this ruling occurred in 2009 with the passage of California Proposition 8, which banned homosexual marriage. Later, however, in 2010, the "don't ask don't tell" law was repealed, allowing gays in the military to be open about their sexual preference. Then, in February 2011, President Obama publicly stated that he no longer supports the Defense of Marriage Act, which seeks to ban alternative forms of marriage across the United States (Nakamura 2011).

2. There were, of course, government-sponsored raids of Native American villages throughout the history of colonization, such as the 1904 Spanish raids of the Navajo, when women and children were killed (Bonvillain 2001) or the famous U.S. cavalry raid on Wounded Knee in 1890, when 300 men, women, and children were massacred.

3. National data on child abuse fatalities show that a child is nearly twice as likely to be abused in foster care as in the general population (National Coalition for Child Protection Reform 2008).

4. Interestingly, this was brought out very clearly in the last episode of Season 5 of *Big Love,* when the show depicted the Mormon Brethren making a statement that asked all four million members of the LDS Church to decry any polygamist organization that claims to be "Mormon." After the publication of my first book on polygamy in 1994, I was also asked by the Brethren to avoid using the word "Mormon" in affiliation with fundamentalism. Rather, I was asked to simply call them fundamentalist polygamists.

5. He also referred to high teen birth rates in Mississippi among monogamous African American women.

6. Interestingly, Carolyn Jessop's fourth daughter, Betty, decided to return to the FLDS group, saying that her mother had exaggerated the abuses of the group.

7. President Gordon B. Hinckley contested this definition of Mormon fundamentalism on *Larry King Live* on September 8, 1998, stating that polygamists are no longer Mormon. Many fundamentalists, however, see themselves as Mormon, and since they follow the nineteenth-century Mormon doctrines and have more cultural traits in common with Mormons than with members of any other religion, scholars also feel justified in calling them "Mormon fundamentalists."

8. These women reported their experiences to me during informal interviews that took place in their homes and workplaces. It is possible that what they say about their lives may be a product of heavy scrutiny by patriarchal leaders. However, I chose to interview them at times when their husbands and male leaders where away at construction sites or on priesthood business and only after several months of building a strong rapport with them. Therefore, I trust that what they say merits our attention and is what they truly believe to be fact.

9. Interestingly, in 2006, South Africa also legalized lesbian and gay unions.

10. Different countries have varying criteria for would-be polygamists. Kuala Lumpur requires written consent from existing wives. In Perak, a man's promise to treat wives fairly is sufficient.

11. The Journal of Discourses is a twenty-six-volume compilation of apostles sermons during LDS conferences compiled by George D. Watt, later published in the church-owned *Deseret News*. It was later printed by the LDS in Liverpool, England, containing 1,438 speeches delivered by prophets and apostles.

CHAPTER 1. HISTORY OF THE PRINCIPLE

1. According to a new census put out by Anne Wilde and the pro-polygamy group Principle Voices (Wilde et al. 2010), a growing number of polygamists (15,000) are "independents" who have no central leader. The FLDS Church reports 10,000 members; about 7,500 belong to the AUB; 2,000 are members of the Centennial Park community on the Utah- Arizona border; another 2,000 are members of the Davis County Cooperative Society (also known as the Kingston group); and 1,500 were listed on the census as "others."

2. The head God, Elohim, spawned millions of worlds and spirits, permitting the latter bodies for occupancy of these worlds. God himself had once been a man who advanced to divinity by the same means. This idea of eternal progression from "mortal coil" to Godhood appealed to both rich and poor.

3. The Adam-God doctrine refers to the evolution of humans to deific states. I explain this in more detail later.

4. In 1874, Leroy Johnson, leader of the FLDS group, told the story of Brigham Young's visit to the Arizona-Utah border with George Q. Cannon. Young said that the spot would one day house the Saints and feed them. Johnson regarded this statement as a prophecy about the gathering of fundamentalist saints (Driggs 2001).

5. Louis Kelsch, the last man ordained to the Priesthood Council under Lorin Woolley, had the distinction of spending more time in "crowbar college" (as he termed it) than any other Mormon man. He spent seven years in jail for having

five wives and thirty-one children. Louis later told a friend that he would rather "rot in prison" than sign a statement renouncing plural marriage (quoted in Kraut 1989, 22).

6. Interestingly, the LDS Church collaborated with law enforcement officials to raid Short Creek. Although mainstream Mormons practiced polygamy in their pioneer past, they became fierce opponents of the practice in the modern day. Part of this objection stemmed from the tenacious belief in modern revelation by a living prophet. If God has told the prophet to abandon something, it then becomes abhorrent and defiled.

7. The rules of the Priesthood Council (Council of Friends) stated that all members must vote before adding new members. Further, when Musser called Rulon to be his successor, he breached the protocol of seniority. Those opposed to Rulon were Charles Zitting, Rulon Jeffs, Alma Timpson, and Guy Musser. It should be noted that Musser never really intended Short Creek to be the center of polygamy; that was John Barlow's idea.

8. See *Child Bride of Short Creek* (1981), a film that depicts this tarnished reputation. In it, Diane Lane plays an underage woman married to an old patriarch.

9. In the 1980s, the AUB sent Priesthood Council members Joseph Thompson, William Baird, and David Watson and Watson's wife, Marianne, to the United Kingdom to gain British converts. They won over eighty people. This group was intending to migrate to Utah, but they were stalled by a failed prophecy of a catastrophic event in 1997 that would wreak havoc with the AUB and the 2002 Olympics. When the event failed to occur, many converts left the AUB.

10. The Jessops and the Allreds have intermarried for many decades and are members of the LeBaron, Allred, and FLDS groups. One example of the original affinal links occurred in Colonia Juarez, where Byron Harvey Allred, Rulon's father, forged a friendship with Dayer LeBaron. Two Juarez girls, Beth Allred and Winnie Porter, married Joseph Lyman Jessop, who became a leader in the AUB. Another interesting link is between the two Allred sisters, Irene and Carolyn, who married Verlan LeBaron before the 1952 split, creating in turn hundreds of grandchildren and great-grandchildren who are connected to the two prominent family kingdoms.

11. Ervil LeBaron went on a killing spree in the mid-1970s in order to eliminate competition for his title as the "one mighty and strong." He used his wives and followers to assassinate those who threatened his position, including Rulon C. Allred and his own brother, Verlan LeBaron. Rena Chynoweth, who assassinated Rulon, was following Ervil's orders.

12. Right after I published my first ethnography, in 1994, Joseph Thompson was released from the Priesthood Council on charges of sexual molestation. Two

others on the Council were later accused of the same offenses: George Maycock in 1998 and Chevrol Palacios in 2002.

13. In 1995, John Llewellyn and Rod Williams, both former members of the AUB, conducted an investigation on behalf of Virginia Hill to recover millions of dollars in cash taken by the AUB priesthood leaders (see Chapter 6).

14. Interestingly, his brother Rulon married girls younger than seventeen, including his wife Ethel, often keeping the marriage secret from the other wives and the young girls' mothers.

15. When Elden died in 1948, his brother Merlin Kingston was listed as the formal head of the organization. However, another brother, John "Ortell" Kingston, made most of the day-to-day leadership decisions and was soon revered as God's prophet and presiding priesthood leader on earth by Kingston followers.

16. Many Mexicans practice a form of polygamy whereby a man is sexually connected to several women. He marries his first wife in the Catholic tradition. Then, in full use of the cultural requirement of virility (machismo), he takes on lovers who become informal wives when they begin having children. This is especially common among migrant farm workers, some of whom have one wife in Chihuahua and another in Utah or California during the picking season.

CHAPTER 2. FURTHER LIGHT AND KNOWLEDGE

1. Mormons generally use the spelling of the King James Bible, with only one letter "l" in the word "fulness."

2. According to Murdock, only 22 percent are restricted exclusively to monogamy (1967).

3. Just as in a cattle herd, where too many bulls in the pasture can create serious stress, in polygamy too many viable males creates antagonism, jealousy, and fierce competition for scarce resources and wives. White and Burton (1988) wrote that polygamist societies that rid themselves of excess males are more stable.

4. "The Mormon Talmud" is a phrase coined by teacher and philosopher Vance Allred, who describes the changing cultural habits of fundamentalists — such as wearing the skinny 1950s-style tie or the sausage curl — as nondoctrinal norms that come and go with each new leader.

5. Through baptism there is a "transmission of the blood" when one enters the covenant to become a member of the Chosen, the literal descendants of Israel. Often members find through their patriarchal blessings that they are the sons and daughters of Ephraim, who is associated with the birthright of the covenant (Doctrine and Covenants 133:26–32). Those who are adopted into the fold can rise to prestige as servants to literal descendants.

6. The Law of Sarah is the process by which Sarah gave her handmaid, Hagar, to her husband, Abraham. It refers to the first wife's full awareness of her husband's plans to mate with a second woman. The law of Sarah requires that a woman, usually the first wife, give another woman of her choosing to her husband in marriage. Placement marriage is held in the highest regard and those who are able to practice this principle are revered as the most faithful among the people.

7. This event occurred just after my entrance into the Allred Group. I remember keenly the celebration among mainstream Mormon women of their newfound spiritual autonomy in the temple ceremony. I also remember how upset some fundamentalists were about the fact that one of their treasured ordinances had been altered.

8. A good source for understanding the Mormon fundamentalist perspective on changing ordinances and laws is found on http://mormonfundamentalism.org compiled by Brian C. Hales.

9. This quote is from a series of recordings that were secretly made during the period 2001 to 2003 by an FLDS member who hid an audio recorder in his boot and recorded dozens of sermons given by FLDS leaders (Smith 2005).

10. Some Mormons believe that the east bluffs above the Grand River in Davis County is where Adam and Eve lived after being kicked out of the Garden and that this location will be the gathering spot for the meeting of the true priesthood leadership just prior to the Second Coming.

11. See the recent work of historian Kathryn Daynes (2011), which elucidates additional differences between nineteenth-century and present-day fundamentalists.

12. This phrase comes from the portion of the LDS endowment ceremony in which Adam is waiting for the additional light and knowledge Elohim promised to send him in the Garden of Eden.

13. In other words, no man can enter the highest glory unless he is sealed to more than one righteous female.

14. The opposing argument comes from Mark 10:11 ("And he saith unto them, Whosoever shall put away his wife, and marry another, committeth adultery against her") and from 1 Timothy 3:2 ("A bishop then must be blameless, the husband of one wife").

15. Interestingly, women in the early Mormon Church once had their own magazine, *The Women's Exponent*; they raised their own money in bazaars and bake sales; and they ran community business through the Relief Society, which was once regarded as an autonomous power equivalent to the priesthood. Much of this autonomy had been taken away by the beginning of the twentieth century.

16. Although most would agree that sustainable living is a positive goal in this era of global warming and high oil costs, not everyone will see libertarian values as positive. I place these two concepts together because most polygamists adhere to these ideals in combination, often relating them to patriotism, anti-government sentiment, and an ethic of saving money.

17. After several years of researching the group, I purposefully cut my long hair as a test to see if I could produce an etic, or distancing, effect. I was immediately shunned for the loss of my virtue.

18. Since alcohol is prohibited (except on occasion in the FLDS group), fundamentalists must find alternative outlets to "set the mood" before coitus. At a priesthood meeting in Pinesdale, one young man protested the Word of Wisdom rule, stating that a few beers really helped grease the wheels of lovemaking. He was promptly told to eat ice cream or try soft, romantic music instead.

19. In these conversion studies, 13 percent of the respondents were "undecided," not truly happy but not truly miserable. These families described having some doubts about whether they fit with the group but remained in the group until something else came along or they found a stronger connection to the group's doctrine and principles.

CHAPTER 3. GENDER DYNAMICS AND SEXUALITY

1. The 2004 data suggest that there are approximately 12 million Mormons in the world. Armand Mauss predicts that there will be nearly 240 million in the year 2080, but this seems to be a fantastic figure given current information on fertility. We are actually seeing a decrease in the number of children born each year (Soukup 2008).

2. Though Utah, which is 70 percent Mormon, continues to have more traditional households that the nation as a whole, 37 percent of couples are not living in a heterosexual monogamous family unit (Utah–Census 2000). Further, according to Heaton (1992), only 20 percent of LDS families are actually members of a temple-sealed family structure.

3. Mormon templegoers in the period of 1990-1995 are far less likely to divorce; 6 percent were found to have dissolved their temple vows. This is an indication of the diversity within the Mormon population, which includes both conservative templegoers and inactive members. Further, Judd found that only 13 percent of LDS couples had divorced after five years of marriage, compared with 20 percent of religiously homogamist unions among Catholics and Protestants and 27 percent among Jews (Judd 2000).

4. Incidentally, he also neglected to acknowledge the enormous pressures

on twentieth-century males to conform to the extraordinary expectations of a righteous priesthood-oriented life.

5. This issue has never been satisfactorily resolved among Mormons: was God polygamous or monogamous? Many orthodox and all fundamentalist Mormons believe that God had at least two wives, Eve and Lilith. But according to the Proclamation document, God and Christ *have* to be monogamous, as they are the blueprint for others to follow.

6. O'Dea does not recognize notable Mormon feminists such as Emma Smith, Joseph's first wife, who wrote about the active role of women in the priesthood in the early days of Nauvoo, or Dr. Martha Hughes Cannon, the first female senator in the United States.

7. Michael Quinn (1992) states that Joseph Smith issued the right of the priesthood to women, giving them endowment rights to become priestesses and queens in the church. Other scholars have argued that women have always held the priesthood by virtue of the Relief Society, which they claim Joseph Smith intended as a "kingdom of priestesses" in which women would receive ordination and perform temple rites. In addition, nineteenth-century Mormon women were ordained as healers with the power to anoint and lay hands on the sick (Radke 2004).

8. Yet the FLDS regularly exiles young unmarried men from their community, as in the case of the 400 "lost boys" who were excommunicated by Warren Jeffs. Because of the practice of expelling men, more males than females leave this group. The difference lies in whether one is an "apostate," or one who desires to leave the fold, or an "exile," one who has been expelled from the fold. Because young women are considered a reproductive resource, they are rarely expelled.

9. The reference to "Stepford wives" comes from a film directed by Bryan Forbes in 1975 about a little town called Stepford, Connecticut where the female residents appear too perfect, happily pleasing their husband's every whim; it is soon discovered that the town's wives have been replaced by robots.

10. This is also true in the orthodox Mormon Church. Part of my title as "black sheep" in my own family is because I have only given birth to only two children and have no grandchildren.

11. Sociologist Robert Merton refers to this form of social deviance as "innovation," because its adherents choose unorthodox ways to achieve the American dream of wealth and family (as quoted in Ritzer 2007).

12. This woman's statement could be considered specious or ingenuous: serial monogamy is quite different from plurality of spouses. I doubt that she is speaking of "serial polygamy." This would involve one man marrying several women then rejecting them all and remarrying several new women, whom he would then live with at the same time.

13. Typically, the intervals between husband's and wives' ages in the FLDS are large, but there is a new trend toward smaller intervals in ages between husband and first wife, suggesting a "peer"-style marriage.

14. "Sisterhood" was a term used by one ex-Allredite who spoke of clandestine sexual liaisons with other women who were alienated by their husbands. These were, she explained, extremely rare dyads formed in conditions of duress and male dominance.

15. Elite polygyny is present in each of the three major Mormon fundamentalist movements--the FLDS (led by Warren Jeffs, the Latter-day Church of Christ (led by Paul E. Kingston), and the AUB (led by Lemoine Jensen). In all groups it defines the operational structure of the priesthood leadership. Each group uses some form of elite polygyny within the Priesthood Council to maintain control over economic and (to some extent) reproductive stewardships. Not all groups have the same type of control, however. The FLDS and Kingston groups have absolute jurisdiction, whereas the AUB and many independent polygamists often leave this leadership up to the patriarchs of each family kingdom.

16. Colorado City residents get eight times more government aid than they pay in taxes (Cart 2001).

17. In some African cultures, however, such as the Nuer, birth rank, not competition, determines the likelihood that a man will marry many wives (Evans-Pritchard 1940).

18. The difference between this form of hyper/elite polygyny and the typical form of polygyny is that in Mormon groups, each male is vying to build his own kingdom, whereas in typical polygamous societies only males entitled to political leadership and wealth by kinship/clanship status are polygamous. Other males do not actually compete in these types of kin-based systems. Therefore, Mormon fundamentalism is unique in the ethnographic record for its practice of kingdom-building polygyny within isolated families. Yet, like other African cases, younger males in Mormon fundamentalist societies do not have access to the wives unless they have a financial advantage, which is unusual. The system sometimes uses primogeniture to determine who among brothers will be given access to the beneficial stewardships and therefore the right to marry.

19. In the secular world, however, women have not achieved the ideal of full gender equity. However, the mainstream education system is evolving to provide more autonomy and opportunities for full access to valued resources.

20. In her study of "domestic networking" in a black inner-city neighborhood (1974), Carol Stack argues that women who are not fully separated from their husbands cannot be labeled as "matrifocal." She would use "matri-centric" to describe the polygamous households in my study. I disagree because of the large segments of time that women in Mormon fundamentalist societies are left on

their own. During these weeks, months, and sometimes years, the household is fully matrifocal.

21. Emma Smith, Joseph Smith's first wife, spoke adamantly against polygamy, denying that her husband engaged in plural marriage until 1853 (Newell and Avery 1994).

22. Compton wrote that one lingering myth about plural marriage was that lustful old men forced vulnerable young women into harems. He said, "While undoubtedly there were abusive husbands, and many older men did indeed unite with younger women (a tradition beginning with Joseph Smith's marriage to the fourteen-year-old Helen Mar Whitney in Nauvoo), most Mormons practiced the Principle for religious reasons and viewed sexuality almost from a Puritanical perspective, although child-bearing was, in fact, actively encouraged. As has been well documented, many plural wives were very intelligent and capable women" (Compton 1997, 2).

23. Recent data brought forth in the Canadian polygamy trial show that 10 percent of the FLDS teenage women in British Columbia are pregnant or have already had children (Keller 2011).

25. In Kenya, there is an informal wife market, especially for polygamous women who must stay behind with the cattle or in the markets while their husband travels to visit his other wives. The men shop for the perfect female companion who will help them care for children and keep their beds warm at night during this long absence.

25. In my AUB study (Bennion 1998), I found that women who had been abandoned by their husbands in emotionally and financially stressful homes would occasionally turn to another woman in the group for companionship, including sexual relations. Thus, it is not so difficult to believe that a woman could foster her lesbian tendencies in a polygamous environment, surrounded primarily by other women and very few men.

26. This custody battle also touches on sensitive ground by questioning whether a lesbian household is better or worse for a child than a polygamous household. The judge said the decision would rest on who could provide the child with constant, familiar care.

CHAPTER 4. OF COVENANTS AND KINGS

1. Each Mormon child is given a patriarchal blessing at age sixteen that gives them the name of the tribe of Israel they belong to. This reinforces their commitment to obey commandments and devote themselves to the lineage. For example, my blessing said that I came from the House of Reuben.

2. This is similar to what happens in the orthodox Mormon Church. When LDS prophet Ezra Taft Benson was aging and showed signs of senility, many of the brethren rallied to the side of Apostle Gordon B. Hinckley, preparing him for his role as new prophet.

3. "Spiritual wifery" is a term coined by Jacob Cochran, a non-denominational preacher who promoted free love in 1818. It often refers to free love, but it was later used in Mormonism by John C. Bennett to refer to plural marriage; any woman who entered polygamy was referred to as a "spiritual wife" (Compton 1997). The concept of spiritual wives was used as early as 1842, when Emma Smith, Joseph Smith's wife, spoke against the "spiritual wife system" (polygamy), referring both to Bennett's comments and her own husband's practices (Newell and Avery 1994).

4. To this day there is dispute in Mormon scholarship over whether Joseph Smith's "spiritual wives," with whom he actually slept while they were lawfully married to other men, belong to his patrilineage for eternity or to the patrilineage of their legal husbands. Mormon doctrine states that Smith was sealed to his wives, whether he slept with them or not.

5. Fundamentalists believe that each man has an office that he must fulfill. Adam is the first example of this responsibility. Adam left his station as the Angel Michael in the Pre-Existence to come to earth to fulfill his office as first man in the Garden. He then died and became exalted as the next Father, or Elohim.

6. Witchcraft accusations have also been used by men to maintain control over "upstart" women and by women to rise to positions of strength in a patriarchal world. They label these women as overly ambitious or poor mothers. For more insight into this form of dispute resolution, see Nadel (1952).

7. For example, one convert from the LDS community taught that God the Father is actually Christ (Jehovah), and not Adam (see John 8:58). This is a doctrinal deviation that will not be allowed in fundamentalism.

8. Mexicans are considered Lamanites, who, like other Native Americans, are said to be descended from the House of Lehi, who is a direct descendant of the House of Judah. According to the Book of Mormon, Lehi brought his family from Jerusalem to the New World around 500 b.c.

CHAPTER 5. MEDIA AND THE POLYGAMY NARRATIVE

1. Juniper Creek is named after a combination of Juniper Street and Short Creek.

2. Bill's interest in gaming is interesting. In Utah, there is no gambling, but in nearby Nevada, fundamentalists and orthodox Mormons have invested a huge

amount of money in the industry. Ironically, Mormons are taught that gambling is a sin, yet most of the shareholders in the industry are LDS (see *New York Times,* August 21, 2008). Nicki's gambling seemed incongruous to me. She would have had to drive all the way to Wendover to do so and had no car; further, few fundamentalists would dabble in gambling; it is considered a grave sin.

3. The Greens are taken from the story about Ervil LeBaron, who was the founder of the Lamb of God church, who sent two women to kill Rulon Allred.

4. According to one AUB member, Jensen has a reputation of embracing isolationism and male supremacy; more so than his predecessor, Owen Allred, who opened Allredite communities to reporters and researchers in the 1990s (Bennion 1998, 2008).

CHAPTER 6. POLYGAMY AND THE LAW

1. George Q. Cannon predicted (years before the LDS Church banned the practice in 1890) that polygamy would be outlawed by the state but would eventually restored in the latter days.

2. The U.S. Census (2006) shows an increase in alternative, or nontraditional, family forms, comprised of 52 percent of all forms of marriages in America. The 2010 census found that the traditional family form is in decline. Only 21 percent of homes in the United States consisted of a married couple with children under 18 living with them, down from 24 percent in 2000 (U.S. Census 2010).

3. Anthropologists use the term "Lesbigay" to include lesbians and bisexuals who often feel excluded by the term "gay." It is a contraction of "lesbian, bisexual, and gay," developed by the Association for Queer Anthropology.

4. A recent lawsuit filed by the *Sister Wives* cast in U.S. District Court in Utah seeks to have the bigamy law declared unconstitutional. They are basing their case on *Lawrence v. Texas.* Their lawyer is constitutional law scholar Jonathon Turley.

5. *Lawrence* dealt with the question of whether a law that criminalized sodomy was a violation of due process under the Fourteenth Amendment. It found that due process covered a right to engage in intimate relations that could not be denied simply because the state wanted to send a message that it disapproved of the behavior involved. Although the ruling does not say anything about marriage, it deals directly with sexuality. Justice Scalia commented that if laws against sodomy could not be upheld based on moral disapproval for behavior, then other sexual practices which are prohibited from moral reasons might also have to be allowed, including same-sex marriage and polygamy (Lawrence V. Texas (02-102) 539 U.S. 558 (2003) 41 S. W. 3d 349, available at http://www.law.cornell.edu/supct/html/02-102.ZD.html).

6. Unfortunately, Utah women lost their voting rights in the 1880s because of federal intervention in an effort to defeat Mormon polygamy. In January 1896, however, Utah entered the Union as a state and reintroduced full woman suffrage in its constitution.

7. The Canadian government demonstrated very little respect for aboriginal cultural values and no recognition of tribal sovereignty over most issues until the 1970s. Native customary marriage was formed by two people agreeing to live together, which made Natives more vulnerable to conviction under the polygamy law (Drummond 2009).

8. Canada's criminal law on polygamy, for example, did not come from Europe but was enacted in response to the 1890 criminalization of plural marriage in the United States (Bailey 2010).

9. In Arizona there was an appeal. In the trial courts, all the mothers promised to give up polygamy and got their children back.

10. There was only one arrest of a polygamist in Utah, Robert Foster, who in 1974, spent several weeks in jail (Kraut 1989). He had been an LDS seminary teacher for many years and married several of his former students.

11. Mormons, for the most part, have supported the Defense of Marriage Act, which defines marriage as a legal union between "one man and one woman," presumably because it also prevents the legal recognition of gay marriage, which violates the Proclamation of the Family.

12. My mother's uncle, the prophet Ezra T. Benson, was actually a member of the John Birch Society.

13. Avraham Gileadi is a Hebrew scholar and literary analyst who was excommunicated by the LDS Church for challenging the exclusive right of LDS leaders to define "doctrine."

14. The Texas opinion dealt only with the mothers who had younger children and had never consented to an underage marriage. After the opinion was issued, the state could have gone forward with the children of mothers who *had* so consented, but it is possible that the state had little evidence that these mothers would put their minor children at risk, and teenage girls would have been the only ones for whom evidence of immediate need could be shown (Smith 2011).

15. Authoritative parenting is democratic and child centered. In this style of child-rearing, parents try to understand their children's feelings. In contrast authoritarian parents are demanding and strict and offer no opportunities for dialogue (Benokraitus 2009).

16. I found no comparative study of incest in polygamous and monogamous families. In 2006, when I conducted a study of abuse cases in Utah by reviewing perpetrator profiles in each county, I found just as many cases of incest in monogamous households as in polygamous ones (Bennion 2007).

17. Fanon was an advocate of *negritude* resistance to the evils of colonialism; the fundamentalist mind is likewise contextualized around the notion of resistance, in this case, to the evils of the mainstream.

18. "Universality of status" means showing respect for the cultural practices of individuals from other nations by recognizing *valid* foreign polygamous marriages. It does not imply endorsement of polygamy or the gender inequality associated with the practice (Bailey et al. 2005).

19. Apparently Dobson was not informed that same-sex marriage has been legal in South Africa since 2006 and some rights were granted to those in polygamous unions in 1998.

20. I am not referring to forced marriages, which are a violation of human rights; I speak of traditional arranged marriage with the consent of the bride and groom.

21. *Lawrence v. Texas* (02-102) 539 U.S. 558 (2003) 41 S. W. 3d 349, Scalia, J., dissenting, 5, available athttp://www.law.cornell.edu/supct/html/02-102.ZD.html.

22. Justice Durham's views are recorded in *State of Utah v. Rodney Hans Holms,* 2006 UT 31, No. 20030847, available at http://www.utcourts.gov/opinions/supopin/Holm051606.pdf.

23. The term "life chances" refers to the opportunities and potential each individual has to improve his or her quality of life. Weber felt that life chances are positively correlated with one's socioeconomic and political situation (Weber 1958).

CHAPTER 7. THE ANNA KARENINA PRINCIPLE

1. Aristotle constructed this same principle in the *Nicomachean Ethics* (Book 2, translation by W. D. Ross): "It is possible to fail in many ways (for evil belongs to the class of the unlimited, as the Pythagoreans conjectured, and good to that of the limited), while to succeed is possible only in one way (for which reason also one is easy and the other difficult — to miss the mark easy, to hit it difficult); for men are good in but one way, but bad in many."

2. Jared Diamond used this same approach to explain why so many wild animals were rendered undomesticable.

3. Smith (1992) points out that women's concrete experiences have a significant impact on feminist thinking. Women's standpoint is an extralocal abstraction, but an actualized part of the experiential self

4. Of course there are examples of abuse among monogamists that also involve isolation and circumscription, such as in northern Maine (Zoll 2004), which has high rates of sex abuse, or in remote areas of small town Midwestern states.

5. In some cases, however, such as with Warren Jeffs, the code of ethics can be rewritten to suit a more patriarchal agenda. For example, Jeffs told a group of young women to obey his word above that of their husbands or fathers.

6. This was the case in 22 percent of the households of AUB converts; see Bennion 2007.

7. An exception to this rule is Warren Jeffs, a convicted sex offender who had access to large bank accounts.

8. Still, women can be singled out and mistreated by other women in the network, as some of the cases of disputes I discussed in Chapter 4 illustrate.

9. Utah Child Protection Services has stated that they are not allowed to release the names of perpetrators, but they were able to state which areas of the state are at high risk. By using this information and reviewing court hearings concerning abuse, I was able to make an estimate of the number of abuse cases.

10. This data was derived from the written testimony of one of the victims of abuse in Klamath Falls, Oregon, in reference to the AUB group.

11. According to the Family Watchdog website, New York and Arizona have 600 sex offenders per million population, a lower ratio than is found in Pinesdale (www.familywatchdog.us).

12. Of 1,024 individuals recorded as having joined the AUB from 1953 to 1993, 250 men left the group, obviously dissatisfied with their experiences there. By contrast, during that same period, only 110 women were recorded as having left the group (Bennion 1998, 132).

CHAPTER 8. POLY FAMILIES IN THE TWENTY-FIRST CENTURY

1. I coined the phrase "gender humanism" to depict postmodernist gender analysis that goes beyond the traditional feminist framework, examining gendered phenomena relating to both males, females, and transgendered individuals.

2. Jankowiak (2008) further explained that there is sibling solidarity across mothers but the quality of the interaction depends upon whether the siblings are full or half. Connectedness between siblings is vital, but the degree or intensity of the emotional bonding varies between members of the birth mother's own family and members of the family into which she married.

Glossary

Some entries adapted with permission from Utah Attorney General's Office and Arizona Attorney General's Office, *The Primer: A Guidebook for Law Enforcement and Human Services Agencies Who Offer Assistance to Fundamentalist Mormon Families* (Salt Lake City: Utah Attorney General's Office, 2009), available at http://attorneygeneral.utah.gov/cmsdocuments/The_Primer.pdf.

Adam/God doctrine: Some fundamentalists believe Adam is God the Father and came to the Garden of Eden with Eve, who was one of his many wives. There are disputes about this belief, but many practicing polygamists still adhere to this doctrine.

aunt: A biological aunt, a "sister wife," "another mother," or a title of respect and endearment for an elderly woman in the family or community.

bigamy: Bigamy is the practice of marrying or purporting to marry or cohabit with one person while being legally married to another. This includes those living in common-law marriages.

bishop: The ecclesiastical authority over a group of members who represents the church president in his leadership position. Bishops are appointed by the church president or the council.

bleeding the beast: An expression used by some fundamentalists as a rationale for accepting assistance (i.e., financial grants, WIC, TANF, food stamps, housing, medical assistance, etc.) from governmental agencies that they might not otherwise trust. Occasionally, the same term is used to justify the abuse or exploitation of such systems. Within certain groups it is taught that "bleeding the beast" will assist God in destroying the "evil" U.S. government and is considered a righteous endeavor.

blood atonement: A doctrine some groups teach that requires a person to have his/her blood "spilt upon the ground" or be executed to make up for what are considered to be unforgivable sins. Some victims of domestic violence are told that breaking a sacred covenant or leaving a relationship or family are unforgivable sins. Some victims may choose to stay in the abusive relationship out of fear for their lives.

Brethren: The vernacular name for the male priesthood leaders of either the LDS Church or any of the schismatic sects: FLDS, AUB, and so on.

Celestial Kingdom: Another name for the highest of the three levels of heaven. The Celestial Kingdom is reserved for the most righteous, and some groups believe that polygamy is an essential practice to dwell in this kingdom.

celestial marriage: The term adherents prefer for plural marriage, polygamy, or polygyny. Many polygamists consider celestial marriage to be a requirement for entering the highest level of the Celestial Kingdom.

circumscription: A term coined by Robert Carneiro (1970) referring to environmental obstacles that inhibit emigration from a place of tyranny or control. It is used in this volume to refer to the blocks imposed by patriarchy as well as geographic structures that inhibit females from leaving the sect.

constitutional law: Some fundamentalists believe that the Founding Fathers were divinely inspired when they wrote religious freedom into the Constitution and the Bill of Rights. They also believe the United States will fall by the hand of God because of sin. Some believe that the current federal and state governments and many of their laws are corrupt and that every action that takes freedom away from the individual and adds power to the government is unconstitutional and must be weighed against the "original intent" of the Constitution. Even though the U.S. Supreme Court has ruled that polygamy is not protected by the Constitution, they claim that plural marriage is protected under the freedom of religion clauses.

corrected or handled: The disciplining of an FLDS member by kicking him out of his home or reassigning his wives and children to another man.

covenant: A binding and solemn agreement made by two or more individuals with God.

Creekers: Members of the FLDS who live in Colorado City, Arizona, and Hildale, Utah, are often called "Creekers." The nickname "Creekers" began when this area was called Short Creek.

curse of Cain: Some fundamentalists believe that African Americans are an inferior race. They also believe that black people are descendants of Cain and have been cursed by God and are therefore ineligible to hold the priesthood.

Doctrine and Covenants: The title of religious scripture used by both the LDS Church and fundamentalist groups. This book contains revelations concerning polygamy (Section 132) and the Word of Wisdom (Section 89).

Doctrine of Consecration: Some fundamentalist groups ask or require members to consecrate, or give, money and legal ownership of property to church leaders.

Doctrine of Total Commitment: The Church of the First Born uses this term to refer to the belief that members must give everything to the church or church leader. This includes money, land, possessions, and even the right to have sexual intercourse with other men's wives. For a woman, it can mean she must give her body and choices to her husband.

double cousin: A person to whom one is related through both the mother's and father's families.

Elect of Israel: Righteous people who are chosen by God to be saved in the last days of the world. Some polygamous groups believe they are God's elect.

endowment: See temple endowment.

eternal family: Many fundamentalists believe that their legal and spiritual marriages are bound forever when a priesthood holder in their community seals them. Some fundamentalists make a marriage covenant between themselves without a priesthood holder, believing that at the correct time the proper authority will seal them. Having a righteous eternal family is often their ultimate goal.

exaltation: Most fundamentalists believe that those who have kept all of God's commandments (including plural marriage) will become exalted and reach the highest level of the Celestial Kingdom. Fundamentalist believe that those who are exalted will be granted eternal life, eternal increase, and greater glory and power and will ultimately become Gods or Goddesses. Many polygamist men believe they cannot reach this level of the Celestial Kingdom unless they have at least three wives. Women believe they cannot be exalted unless they are married.

excommunication: Some members are excommunicated from their group or ostracized for disobedience, incorrect beliefs, or sin. Those who are excommunicated lose blessings, privileges, and the rights of association. In some cases, families have been kicked out of their church-owned homes and wives and children have been reassigned and given to other men.

first rate or second rate: Some fundamentalists are considered "first rate" or elite because of their bloodline. Women and their children can also be considered first rate and receive special privileges within the family if they are favored by the husband. "Second rate" fundamentalists are those who lack economic, social, or consanguineal powers in the group.

fundamentalist Mormon, or Mormon fundamentalist: People who believe they are following the original principles and doctrines, including plural marriage, taught by early LDS Church leaders. The LDS Church opposes the use of this term and excommunicates members who practice plural marriage. Fundamentalists reject the authority claims of contemporary LDS leaders and consider the LDS Church to be in a state of apostasy.

Gentile: Anyone who does not have the priesthood or is not a member of the various fundamentalist groups. Some fundamentalists also refer to them as "outsiders."

God squad: This slang term refers to a group that is believed to be within the FLDS community to monitor and report the activities of its members to the church leadership.

half-sibling, half-brother, or half-sister: In Mormon usage, siblings with the same father but not the same biological mother; in general American usage, siblings who share one biological parent, whether father or mother.

head: A man who holds a position of respect, authority, or leadership, such as "head of the family, head of the Priesthood, or head of the group.

house mother: A sister wife who stays home to care for the children of other wives who may work outside the home.

joy book: Girls are said to be listed in this book while they wait for the FLDS prophet to have a revelation about whom they will marry.

"keep sweet": An admonition to be compliant and pleasant despite the circumstances.

keys: Fundamentalists believe that the original LDS Church was endowed with priesthood authority by receiving certain "keys" from God to administer certain rites and ordinances. These keys are rites and ordinances that supposedly set it apart as the "true" church. But most fundamentalists believe that before the LDS Church abandoned the practice of plural marriage, God passed specific "keys" of authority to others to hold and exercise on earth. (*See also* Mother Church; priesthood.)

Law of Abraham: Some fundamentalists refer to plural marriage using this term. This law gives men the right to take additional wives, as Abraham did. (*See* Law of Sarah.)

Law of Gathering: Calls for believers to live in close proximity to each other in order to collaborate, which sometimes includes acting as an economic unit. (*See* United Order.)

Law of One Above Another: A doctrine held by the Kingston group that establishes clear lines of authority and states that an individual is supposed to obey and please the person "above" him or her. Mothers are above children, fathers are above mothers, church leaders or church employers are above fathers, and the church president or head is above everyone. It is reported that the Kingstons believe that a person should obey any request of the "one above." Other groups believe in this line of authority but may not have a name for it.

Law of Placement, or placement marriage: A type of arranged marriage that evolved in Colorado City, Arizona, and Hildale, Utah, in the 1940s and 1950s. Under this system, young men (and sometimes women, depending on the group) decide when they are ready for marriage. They then discuss this with the religious leader, who assumes the responsibility for "placing" a young woman with a man based on the leader's "insight" or "revelation." In some instances, some allowance is given for individual preference, while in other cases decisions are made entirely by the leader. In some communities, parties interested in marriage are instructed to spend significant time in prayer and fasting so that they and their leader will both receive divine guidance or direction. The religious or priesthood leader, who is expected to be obeyed as God's representative, makes the ultimate decision. This type of placement is often used in the FLDS church. The Law of Placement is also used to reassign a man's wife/wives and children to another man when he is excommunicated or dies.

Law of Sarah: Fundamentalists relate this term to the biblical account of Sarah giving consent to her husband Abraham to marry other women. Some believe this law gives a woman the opportunity to accept the addition of another wife. However, even if the wife does not give consent, the husband may be allowed to take another wife under the Law of Abraham.

LDS Church: This is a shorthand term for the Church of Jesus Christ of Latter-day Saints. Historically, members have been referred to as Mormons because they consider the Book of Mormon to be scripture. Today, LDS Church leaders discourage the use of this nickname.

lifting up: On three separate occasions, the FLDS Church predicted that members would be lifted up into heaven while God destroyed the wicked and then would be returned to earth to peacefully live in polygamy. When no one was lifted up, the members were blamed for sinning and lacking faith.

Little Known Discourse: In the 1960s a pamphlet entitled "A Little Known Discourse" was distributed in Mormon circles. Its content was based on the first chapter of *The Peace Maker*, a book supposedly written by Joseph Smith, which was published by Paul Harrison of Manchester, England. While most fundamentalists have denounced "The Little Known Discourse" and the alleged source for the book, a small minority still adheres to its teachings. The discourse teaches that once a woman is married to a man, she cannot divorce him for any reason short of adultery. It is not considered adultery if a man has sexual relations with any woman who is supposedly "meant to be his," even if she is not married to him or is married to another man. A wife who rebels against her husband or "refuses to cheerfully submit to her husband in all things" commits a sin against him and can be told to leave. The children of such a union must stay with the man. It also states that the wife is the property of the husband and should obey his will: "The wife has no right to teach, admonish, reprove, rebuke, or to exercise any kind of dictation whatever. He is her head and she should be guided by the head. If the wife wants to know anything, let her ask her husband at home." According to the discourse, "the wife is pronounced the husband's property as much so as his manservant, his maidservant, his ox, his horse." Those who follow this doctrine may use it as an excuse to sexually abuse children and spouses or commit adultery, believing it is a God-given right.

Lost Boys: Young, unmarried men who are exiled from fundamentalist communities. They usually have little education and few skills to help them live on their own. Some are susceptible to drug abuse and other problems because they have been told they are going to hell. Some have been told they were asked to leave because they were a bad influence, but most believe it is because they provide competition for older men who are looking for wives.

The Manifesto: A document issued by LDS Church president Wilford Woodruff in 1890 that advised members to henceforth "refrain from contracting any marriage forbidden by the law of the land." While the Manifesto did not void existing plural marriages, the LDS Church eventually stopped recognizing and authorizing them. Many practicing polygamists consider the Manifesto to be a contradiction of earlier doctrine and often describe it as marking the beginning of their separation from the LDS Church.

Mother Church: Fundamentalists use this term for the current LDS Church. They believe that they are custodians of certain keys to rites and authority and that they will eventually reunite with or replace the LDS Church.

multiple mortal probation: Jim Harmston, leader of the True and Living Church, teaches that this doctrine is a form of reincarnation. Members are told of their previous lives during priesthood blessings.

"My Son John" revelation: Fundamentalists believe that the third LDS Church president, John Taylor, received a revelation from God in 1886 in which he was promised that the New and Everlasting Covenant (practice of plural marriage) would never be revoked. The LDS Church has not canonized this alleged writing of Taylor's and does not recognize it as legitimate or binding. However, fundamentalists consider it to be a primary authority and a vindication for the continuing practice of polygamy.

New and Everlasting Covenant of Marriage: Another term for plural marriage.

numbered men: The Kingston group uses this term to refer to male members who hope to be numbered among the Lord's people. They are believed to be part of the 144,000 people mentioned in the Bible's Book of Revelation. Kingston leaders select the most obedient men in good standing with the church to receive their actual "number" in public meetings.

one-man rule: Some fundamentalists interpret Doctrine and Covenants 132:7 to mean that only one person on earth can hold the keys of the priesthood. They believe that this leader has direct contact with God and can send a person to heaven or hell, since his authority extends into the next life. Therefore, an individual's very survival in eternity depends on his/her relationship with that leader and his/her absolute support of him. Others believe that the leader has direct contact with God but that only God can judge whether a person is going to heaven or hell.

outsider: A person not considered to be part of that individual's culture, including excommunicated members, nonmembers, customers, and especially government agencies, government officials, and the media. They are sometimes called apostates or Gentiles. Fundamentalists do not trust most outsiders.

patriarch: A title of priesthood authority given to men as the head of their families or to men who live in plural marriage (sometimes called the Patriarchal Law of Plural Marriage). This title is sometimes perceived as the ultimate right to rule in a family without regard to the feelings or well-being of the wives or children. However, many polygamous groups and families say that a patriarch is more magnanimous, more charitable, and more skilled as a husband and father than men who do not have plural wives.

patriarchal marriage or patriarchal law: Another term for plural marriage.

plural marriage: The marriage of one man to more than one woman, in some groups with the special permission of or by the command of group leaders. Interchangeable terms for plural marriage are celestial marriage, The New and Everlasting Covenant, The Principle, The Work of the Priesthood, and patriarchal marriage. The term *polygamy* may have a negative connotation within the culture and is used more frequently by the general public.

plyg (or polyg): A highly offensive and demeaning term for those who practice polygamy. Care providers should be aware that this term is never acceptable and would hinder efforts to provide help.

polygamy: The term (which means "many marriages") is widely used to describe the marriage of one man to many living women at the same time. It is often used in place of the more correct term "polygyny." Some groups believe the term has a negative connotation.

polygyny: The practice of one man being married to more than one wife at the same time.

poofers: A slang term for girls who suddenly disappear from their community in order to take part in an arranged marriage. The girls are either kept hidden or are moved to another state or country. This is most often done by the FLDS Church.

prayer circle: A special kind of prayer that is held in a circle formation by a family or group.

priestcraft: A derogatory term for the use of priesthood or religious authority to inflict abuse or exert power or unrighteous dominion over another person.

priesthood: Fundamentalists believe the priesthood is the power and authority of God delegated to man. They believe that only a man can hold the priesthood in order to enter the highest degree of heaven. Therefore, a woman must be married to someone with the priesthood or she will go to a lower level of heaven or to hell.

priesthood garment: Many fundamentalists, male and female, wear a white undergarment that covers the body from their neck to ankles and wrists. This garment has sacred and spiritual symbolism for the wearer. It also encourages modesty. Some FLDS Church members may be reluctant to get help from someone who is not wearing clothing that covers their ankles, wrists, and body up to the neckline.

priesthood law, priesthood teachings, or Law of the Priesthood: These phrases refer to priesthood ordinances or special teachings that are interpreted or implemented differently among fundamentalist groups. For example, some fundamentalists consider baptism to be a requirement before marriage. The term "priesthood law" is sometimes used specifically to refer to plural marriage.

priesthood sealing: Many polygamists believe priesthood holders must "seal" or bind their relationships for all eternity in order for a family to be together after death. It is also another term for a marriage ceremony performed by a member of the priesthood.

prophet: The prophet can speak with and/or receive direction from God for all members of a group. The FLDS call the leader of their church "the prophet," but it is not generally used in other groups or among independent fundamentalists who have no designated leaders.

reassignment of wives: Some fundamentalists interpret Doctrine and Covenants 132:44 to mean that a wife does not belong to the husband but to the priesthood. If the husband is out of favor with priesthood leaders or with his wife or wives, his family may be reassigned to another man.

rebaptism: The practice of being baptized again to renew covenants, restore health, or wash away sins.

red: Some FLDS members believe Jesus Christ will return to the earth wearing red robes and that He is the only one who should wear red. They also believe that Satan wears red to imitate Christ. They may thus be offended when people wear red or offer red clothing.

release: The Apostolic United Brethren use this term to refer to divorce. Only priesthood leaders can "release" a spouse from a marriage.

"repent from afar": Former members say that when an FLDS member is "corrected" or "handled," they must leave their homes and family to repent. Before the person can return, he must submit a list of sins that matches what the prophet claims was revealed to him by God.

revelation: God's communication with humans to offer guidance, answers to prayers, or insight concerning doctrinal issues. Generally, fundamentalists believe that individuals can receive revelations for themselves; heads of families can receive revelations for their families; and heads of organizations or churches can receive revelations for the congregations over which they preside. They believe that personal revelation can come in the form of a strong impression, a dream, a voice, a vision, or a "burning of the bosom." Some believe that when a woman's revelation contradicts a man's revelation, the man's revelation usually takes precedence. Others believe that women are not entitled to revelation at all.

righteous seed or righteous children: "Righteous children" refers to sons and daughters who stay in a fundamentalist group and live in plural marriage. Parents believe that bearing children and raising them to be honorable, industrious, and religious is the very purpose of plural marriage. If children do not conform to high standards the parents set, they often feel that they are failures. Parents may use extreme disciplinary measures to force obedience. In some of the stricter groups or families, a nonconforming child may be asked or forced to leave. Some children may be ostracized by their family and decide to leave on their own.

saints: Righteous followers of God. Individuals usually use this term to describe members of their group.

Second Ward or 2nd warder: A derogatory slang term for families who left Hildale, Utah, and Colorado City, Arizona, in the 1980s to start their own community in Centennial Park. However, members of the Centennial Park community do not like this term because it suggests an association between the two groups. Members of the FLDS church in Hildale/Colorado City are also called "first warders."

sister wives: Women married to the same man. Other terms that identify this position are "other girls in the family," "other mothers," or "other ladies."

sons of Helaman: A group of young men in the FLDS community who dress in uniforms, perform marches, and act as watchdogs in the community. At times, they have been instructed by FLDS leaders to enter houses without knocking and report if members own computers, television sets, novels, or other outside materials banned by church authority. The name is taken from a group of warriors in the Book of Mormon.

spirit child: Mormon fundamentalists believe that a woman may dream of a "spirit child" that wishes to leave the Pre-Existence and come to earth to be tested. This dream or vision encourages such a woman to become pregnant so that she can facilitate the transition of this spirit child into a human baby.

spiritual union: Another term for plural marriage.

spiritual wife: A plural wife who is not legally married to her husband. Polygamist men sometimes marry one wife lawfully and then cohabit with their other wives in what are sometimes called spiritual unions. They believe that spiritual wives or spiritual unions are as binding as legal marriages.

stewardship: A sacred responsibility within a fundamentalist community, such as owning land or a business, the care a husband provides for his wives, or even a woman's work in the home. Fundamentalists believe that a person's stewardship offers spiritual blessings or consequences.

temple endowment: In certain groups, endowments are considered special spiritual blessings that are given to "worthy" members. These practices include special words, symbols and teachings that are believed to be sacred and necessary for spiritual progression or exaltation. The True and Living Church (TLC) believes that these endowments are necessary during every prayer.

The Principle: Another term for plural marriage.

Third Ward: This refers to fundamentalists originally related to the Barlow family who live in the south part of Centennial Park, Arizona. They are no longer affiliated with the Centennial Park group or the FLDS Church. They do not claim to have the priesthood and only commit to live polygamy. They often meet together in group member's homes.

true order of prayer: The way some fundamentalists pray to God, especially members of the True and Living Church (TLC). When members of the TLC use certain symbols and words, they believe it allows them to pierce the veil to speak with God and/or with deceased individuals.

United Order: The concept of giving all individual possessions and assets to the church to be distributed according to need. The distribution is sometimes called a stewardship or inheritance. Participants say the goal is to eliminate poverty and establish income equality and self-sufficiency among group members. However, some groups receive only limited financial help, food, and necessities from the church and are taught that living in poverty is Christ-like. They are taught that their "inheritance" will be received in heaven.

Word of Wisdom: A general health code found in the Doctrine and Covenants, Section 89. It discourages consumption of alcohol, hot or strong drinks, and tobacco. Groups interpret this differently, but many believe it encourages the use of herbal medicine and discourages the use of conventional medicine. Some fundamentalists consider the Word of Wisdom to be a "lesser law" given to the weak and thus feel that obedience to it is not necessary for their salvation or exaltation.

Work of the Priesthood: Sometimes shortened to "The Work," this term refers to plural marriage and other religious principles believed to be practiced under priesthood authority. Many groups do not identify themselves with a specific organization, but instead identify with the mission to work toward living and teaching these principles of the priesthood. Thus, it is called the "work of the priesthood" or "the priesthood work." The Allred Group, the Centennial Park group, and the FLDS probably use the term "The Work" more than other polygamous communities.

References

Abu-Lughod, Lila. 1997. "The Interpretation of Culture(s) after Television." *Representations* 59 (Summer): 110–136.

Achebe, Chinua. 1959. *Things Fall Apart.* New York: Doubleday.

Acker, Joan. 2005. *Class Questions, Feminist Answers.* Walnut Creek, CA: Altamira Press.

ACLU. 2006. "Utah's Bigamy Statute and the Right to Privacy and Religious Freedom." Available at www.acluutah.org/bigamystatute.htm.

Adams, Brooke. 2001. "Rules for Plural Marriage." *Salt Lake Tribune,* February 25.

———. 2006 "Chicago Scoop: Eagle Mountain Is a Polygamous Enclave." *Salt Lake Tribune,* September 27.

———. 2007. "Jeffs Preaching Will Be Dissected Word by Word." *Salt Lake Tribune,* August 30.

———. 2009. "The Facts Don't Fit Claims of FLDS Welfare Fraud." *Salt Lake Tribune,* January 4.

Al-Krenawi, Alean, et al. 2001. "The Psychosocial Impact of Polygamous Marriage on Palestinian Women." *Women and Health* 34(1):1–16.

———. 2006. "Success and Failure among Polygamous Families." *Family Process* 45(3):311–330.

Allred, Rulon. 1981. *Treasures of Knowledge.* Hamilton, MT: Bitterroot Publishing.

Allred, Vance. 1993. "How to Raise Your Children." Unpublished document in author's possession.

Altman, Irwin, and Joseph Ginat. 1996. *Polygamous Families in Contemporary Society.* Cambridge: Cambridge University Press.

Anderson, Barbara. 2000. *Doing the Dirty Work? The Global Politics of Domestic Labor.* London: Zed.

Anderson, Lavina F. 2001. *Lucy's Book: A Critical Edition of Lucy Mack Smith's Family Memoir.* Salt Lake City: Signature Books.

Anderson, Scott. 2010. "The Polygamists." *National Geographic,* February, 34–61.

An-Na'im, Abdullahi. 2010. "Polygamy and Gender Justice in the 21st Century: Reflections on Basic Principles." Keynote address at the conference "Polygamy, Polygyny, and Polyamory," Brandeis University, Waltham, Massachusetts, November 7.

Anthony, Paul. 2008. "Court Ruling Puts Everyone on Hold." *Standard-Times* (San Angelo, Texas), May 26. Available at http://www.gosanangelo.com/news/2008/may/26/court-ruling-puts-everyone-on-hold/.

Aristotle. 350 B.C.E. *Nicomachean Ethics*, translated by W.D. Ross, Book II, Chapter 6. Available online: http://classics.mit.edu/Aristotle/nicomachean.2.ii .html.

Arrington, Leonard. 1961. "Religion and Economics in Mormon History." *BYU Studies* 3(3):31–32.

Associated Press. 2011. "Utah: Street Preacher Gets Life Sentence for Abduction." *New York Times,* May 25.

Austin, S. B., et al. 2008. "Disparities in Child Abuse Victimization in Lesbian, Bisexual, and Heterosexual Women in the Nurses' Health Study II." *Journal of Women's Health* 17(4):597.

Backus, Perry. 2008. "Long Road to Justice: After 15 years, Pinesdale Rape Case Is Closed," *Missoulian,* June 16. Available at http://missoulian.com/news/ local/article_574aa24e-8cd8-5e40-8ea3-80c48e387942.html.

Baer, Hans. 2008. "Foreword." In Janet Bennion, *Evaluating the Effects of Polygamy on Women and Children.* New York: Edwin Mellen Press, iii–v.

Bailey, Martha. 2007. "Dossier: Should Polygamy be Recognized in Canada? Ethical and Legal Considerations." *Printemps* 2(1):18–21. "Polygamy, Polygyny, and Polyamory," Brandeis University, Waltham, Massachusetts, November 7.

Bailey, Martha, Beverley Baines, Bita Amani, and Amy Kaufman. 2005. "Expanding Recognition of Foreign Polygamous Marriages: Policy Implications for Canada." Queen's University Legal Studies Research Paper No. 07-12. Prepared for Status of Women Canada. Available at http://papers.ssrn.com/ sol3/papers.cfm?abstract_id=1023896.

Barnes, J. A. 1954. "Class and Committees in a Norwegian Island Parish." *Human Relations* (7): 39–58.

Bala, Nicholas et al. 2005. "An International Review of Polygamy: Legal and Policy Implications for Canada." In *Polygamy in Canada: Legal and Social Implications for Women and Children: A Collection of Policy Research Reports.* Ottawa: Status of Women Canada. Available at http://www.vancouversun .com/pdf/polygamy_021209.pdf.

Bart, Brett. 2010. "Religion, Not Polygamy, May Explain Teen Pregnancies in Bountiful: Lawyer." *The Canadian Press,* February 9.

BBC News. 2001. "Divorce Study in Saudi Arabia." *BBC News,* April 30. Available at http://news.bbc.co.uk/2/hi/middle_east/1304886.stm.

Beaman, L. 2001. "Molly Mormons, Mormon Feminists and Moderates: Religious Diversity and the Latter Day Saints Church." *Sociology of Religion* 62(1):65–86.

Beatty, Jim. 2004. "Rights Tribunal Agrees to Hear Polygamy Case." *Vancouver Sun,* September 4.

Beck, Martha N. 1994. "Flight From the Iron Cage: LDS Women's Responses to the Paradox of Modernization." Ph.D. dissertation, Harvard University.

Bennion, Janet. 1991a. "The Dynamics of Polygyny: Kinship, Residence and Flow of Women in Mormon Fundamentalism." Unpublished paper. In author's possession.

———. 1991b. "Living Arrangements as a Form of Symbolic Communication among Contemporary Mormon Polygynists." Unpublished paper. In author's possession.

———. 1997. "Female Networking as a Factor of Female Status in Mormon Polygyny." In *Mixed Blessings: Gender and Religious Fundamentalism Cross Culturally,* edited by Judy Brink and Joan Mencher. New York: Routledge, 73–90.

———. 1998. *Women of Principle: Female Networking in Contemporary Mormon Polygamy.* Oxford: Oxford University Press.

———. 2004. *Desert Patriarchy: Gender Dynamics in the Chihuahua Valley.* Tucson: University of Arizona Press.

———. 2006. "Waata Polygyny on the Decline." Paper presented at the EPSCoR/NSF Symposium on Faculty/Student Ethnographic Research, Lyndon State College, August.

———. 2006. "Abbas Raptus: Exploring Factors Contributing to the Sexual Abuse of Females in Rural Mormon Fundamentalist Communities." *Forum on Public Policy: A Journal of the Oxford Round Table* 1:1–20.

———. 2008a. "Mormon Women in the 21st Century: A Critical Analysis of O'Dea's Work." In *Revisiting Thomas F. O'Dea's* The Mormons: *Contemporary Perspectives,* edited by Cardell K. Jacobson, John P. Hoffman, and Tim B. Heaton, Salt Lake City: University of Utah Press, 136–170.

———. 2008b. *Evaluating the Effects of Polygamy on Women and Children.* New York: Edwin Mellen Press.

———. 2011a. "History, Culture, and Variability of Mormon Schismatic Groups." In *Modern Polygamy in the United States: Historical, Cultural, and Legal Issues Surrounding the Raid on the FLDS in Texas,* edited by Cardell Jacobson. New York: Oxford University Press, 101–124.

———. 2011b. "The Many Faces of Polygamy: An Analysis of the Variability in Modern Mormon Fundamentalism in the Intermountain West." In *Modern Polygamy in the United States: Historical, Cultural, and Legal Issues Surrounding the Raid on the FLDS in Texas,* edited by Cardell Jacobson. New York: Oxford University Press, 163–184.

Bennion, Lowell. 1983. *I Believe.* Salt Lake City: Deseret Books.

Benokraitis, Nijole. 2009. *Families and Marriages: Changes, Choices, and Constraints.* Upper Saddle River, NJ: Prentice Hall.

Bentley, Paul. 2011. "Warren Jeffs Sentenced to Life Plus 20 Years." *Mail Online*, London, August 9.

Bingham, R. D., and R. W. Potts. 1993. "Homosexuality: An LDS Perspective." *Association of Mormon Counselors and Psychotherapists (AMCAP)* 19(1):1–16.

Bistline, Benjamin. 2004. *The Polygamists: A History of Colorado City, Arizona.* [Scottsdale, AZ]: Agreka Books.

———. 2004. *Colorado City Polygamists: An Inside Look for the Outsider.* [Scottsdale, AZ]: Agreka Books.

Black, Courtney, and Maxine Hanks. 2000. "Mormon Women Must Be Heard." *Boston Globe,* October 7:1.

Blackwood, E. 1993. "Breaking the Mirror: The Construction of Lesbianism and the Anthropological Discourse on Homosexuality." In *Culture and Human Sexuality: A Reader,* edited by David N. Suggs and Andrew W. Miracle. CA: Brooks/Cole, 328-40.

Blake, Adriana. 1996. *Women Can Win the Marriage Lottery: Share Your Man with Another Wife.* n.p.: Orange County University Press.

Bledsoe, Carolyn H., Susana Lerner, and Jane I. Guyer, eds. 2000. *Fertility and the Male Life-Cycle in the Era of Fertility Decline.* New York: Oxford University Press.

Blumenthal, Ralph. 2008. "Appeals Court Rules against Texas in Polygamy Case." *New York Times,* May 22.

Bonvillain, Nancy. 2001. *Native Nations.* Upper Saddle River, NJ: Prentice Hall.

Borger, Julian. 2005. "Hellfire and Sexual Coercion." *The Guardian,* June 30.

Bourdieu, Pierre. 1992. *Invitation to a Reflexive Sociology.* Chicago: University of Chicago Press.

Bowden, Vicy, and Cindy Greenberg. 2009. *Children and Their Families.* Baltimore, MD: Lippincott/Williams & Wilkins.

Bradley, Martha. 1990. "The Women of Fundamentalism: Short Creek, 1953." *Dialogue: A Journal of Mormon Thought* 23(2):15–37.

Bramham, Daphne. 2008. *The Secret Lives of Saints: Child Brides and Lost Boys in a Polygamous Mormon Sect.* [Toronto]: Random House Canada.

———. 2011. "Closing Arguments Begin in Bountiful Polygamy Case." *Vancouver Sun,* March 28.

Burton, Greg. 1998. "Incest Prominent Feature of Kingston Polygamists." *Salt Lake Tribune,* August 2.

Cairncross, J. 1974. *After Polygamy Was Made a Sin: The Social History of Christian Polygamy.* London: Routledge and Kegan Paul.

Campbell, Angela. 2005. "How Have Policy Approaches to Polygamy Responded to Women's Experiences and Rights?" In *Polygamy in Canada: Legal and So-*

cial *Implications for Women and Children: A Collection of Policy Research Reports,* edited by Angela Campbell et al., 3–63. Ottawa: Status of Women Canada. Available at http://www.vancouversun.com/pdf/polygamy_021209 .pdf.

Campbell, Angela, et al. 2005. *Polygamy in Canada: Legal and Social Implications for Women and Children: A Collection of Policy Research Reports.* Ottawa: Status of Women Canada. Available at http://www.vancouversun.com/pdf/ polygamy_021209.pdf.

Cannon, George Q. 1867. *Journal of Discourses 11:338,* March 3. Liverpool: LDS Church.

———. 1872. *Journal of Discourses* 13:202. Liverpool: LDS Church.

———. 1879. A George Q. Cannon "discourse." Compiled by Joseph A. Cannon on Oct. 2, also found in Gustive O. Larson's *Federal Government Efforts to "Americanize" Utah Before Admission to Statehood.* Huntington Library, 1971, and at www.georgeqcannon.com/GQC_Docs.htm.

Cannon, Janet (Janet Bennion). 1989–1994. Ethnographic research journals. In author's possession.

———. 1992. "My Sister, My Wife: An Examination of Sororal Polygyny in a Contemporary Mormon Fundamentalist Commune." *Syzygy: Journal of Alternative Religion and Culture* 1(4):315–322.

Cantera, Kevin. 2001. "Child Rape Charges Filed." *Salt Lake Tribune,* November 20.

Carneiro, Robert. 1980. "The Circumscription Theory: Challenge and Response." *American Behavioral Scientist* 31:497–511.

Carrier, J. M. 1980. "Homosexual Behavior in Cross Cultural Perspective." In *Homosexual Behavior: A Modern Reappraisal,* edited by J. Marmor, 100–122. New York: Basic Books.

CBC News. 2003. "The Canadian Home of Polygamy." January 15. Available at www.rickross.com/reference/polygamy/polygamy99.

———. 2006. "Bust-Up in Bountiful." *The Fifth Estate,* January 25. Available at www.cbc.ca/fifth/bustupinbountiful.

Chamberlain, Linda. 2002. "Domestic Violence: A Primary Care Issue for Rural Women." Available at http://www.ruralwomyn.net/primary_care.html.

Chodorow, Nancy. 1978. *The Reproduction of Mothering: Psychoanalysis and the Sociology of Gender.* Berkeley: University of California Press.

Civil Suit. 2003. "Law Suit [sic] Against Owen Allred and the Apostolic United Brethren," November 8. www.polygamybooks.com.

Clyde, William. 2004. "Guidelines for Practical Polygamy." Available at modern polygamy.org, accessed March 20, 2008.

CNN. 2004. "Man Sentenced for Marrying His 15-Year-Old Cousin." CNN, January 26.

Compton, Todd. 1997. *In Sacred Loneliness: The Plural Wives of Joseph Smith.* Salt Lake: Signature Book. Also see website "The Four Major Periods of Mormon Polygamy," at http://www.signaturebookslibrary.org/essays/mormonpolygamy .htm.

Cook, Rebecca, and Lisa M. Kelly. 2006. *Polygyny and Canada's Obligations under International Human Rights Law.* Family, Children, and Youth Section Research Report. [Toronto]: Department of Justice of Canada. Available at http://www.justice.gc.ca/eng/dept-min/pub/poly/poly.pdf.

Cooper, Rex. 1990. *Promises Made to Fathers.* Salt Lake City: University of Utah Press.

Corchadeo, Alredo. 2008. "Polygamists from Texas Unwelcome in Mexico Mormon Community." *Dallas Morning News,* May 8.

Cornwall, Marie. 1994. "The Institutional Role of Women." In *Contemporary Mormonism: Social Science Perspectives,* edited by M. Cornwall, Tim Heaton, and Lawrence Young et al. Chicago: University of Illinois Press, 239–264.

Costello, Barbara. 2009. "Against Relativism: A Harm-Based Conception of Deviance." In Patricia A. Adler and Peter Adler, *Constructions of Deviance: Social Power, Context, and Interaction,* [Belmont, CA]: Cengage Learning, 46–52.

Cragun, Ryan, and Michael Nielsen. 2011. "Social Scientific Perspectives on the FLDS Raid and the Corresponding Media Coverage." In *Modern Polygamy in the United States: Historical, Cultural, and Legal Issues,* edited by Cardell Jacobson. New York: Oxford University Press, 209–236.

Crawford, Amanda. 2008. "Mom's Case Revisits Child-Bigamy Issue." *Arizona Republic,* February 24.

CTV. 2005. "Women of Bountiful Defend Polygamous Lifestyle." April 21. Available at http://www.ctv.ca/CTVNews/TopStories/20050421/bountiful_women _050420/.

Darger, Joe, and Alina, Vicki, and Valerie Darger. 2011. *Love Times Three: Our True Story of a Polygamous Marriage.* New York: HarperOne.

Davis, Adrienne. 2010. "Regulating Polygamy: Intimacy, Default Rules, and Bargaining for Equality." *Columbia Law Review* 110(8):1955–1986.

Daynes, Kathryn. 2001. *More Wives Than One.* Urbana-Champaign: University of Illinois Press.

———. 2011. "Differing Polygamous Patterns: 19th-Century LDS and Twenty-First-Century FLDS Marriage Systems." In *Modern Polygamy in the United States: Historical, Cultural, and Legal Issues,* edited by Cardell Jacobson. New York: Oxford University Press, 125–150.

Deibert, Ken. 2008. Press statement found in "Most Reports of Child Abuse in Polygamist Community Not Sexual," *Arizona Republic,* April 11.

Dethman, Leigh, and Lucinda Dillon-Kinkead. 2005. "Polygamist Owen Allred Dies." *Deseret Morning News,* February 16.

Diamond, Jared. 1999. *Guns, Germs, and Steel: The Fates of Human Societies.* New York: W. W. Norton.

Dixon-Spear, Patricia. 2009. *We Want for Our Sisters What We Want for Ourselves: African American Women Who Practice Polygyny by Consent.* Baltimore: Black Classic Press.

Dobner, Jennifer. 2010. "'Sister Wives' Family Investigated for Bigamy." *MSNBC,* September 29. Available at http://today.msnbc.msn.com/id/39418047/ns/today-entertainment/t/sister-wives-family-investigated-bigamy.

Dobson, James. 1991. *Straight Talk to Men and Their Wives.* Dallas: World Publishing.

———. 2004. "An Open Letter to South Africans on Same-Sex Marriage." *Christians for Truth* website, November. Available at http://www.cft.org.za/articles/dobson_gay_marriage_sa.htm.

Dougherty, John. 2003. "Bound by Fear: Polygamy in Arizona." *Phoenix New Times,* May 13.

———. 2005. "Forbidden Fruit." *Phoenix New Times,* December 29.

Driggs, Ken. 2001. "'This Will Someday be the Head and Not the Tail of the Church': A History of the Mormon Fundamentalists at Short Creek." *Journal of Church and State,* January 1, 49–80.

———. 2005. "Imprisonment, Defiance, and Division: A History of Mormon Fundamentalism in the 1940s and 1950s." *Dialogue* 38(1):65–95.

———. 2011. "Twenty Years of Observations about the Fundamentalist Polygamists." In *Modern Polygamy in the United States: Historical, Cultural, and Legal Issues,* edited by Cardell Jacobson. New York: Oxford University Press, 77–100.

Drummond, Susan. 2009. "Polygamy's Inscrutable Secular Mischief." *Comparative Research in Law and Political Economy* (5)1–69.

Duncan, Emily. 2008. "The Positive Effects of Legalizing Polygamy: 'Love Is a Many Splendored Thing.'" *Duke Journal of Gender Law and Policy* 15:315.

Ebershoff, David. 2008. *The 19th Wife: A Novel.* New York: Random House.

El Alami, Dawoud Sudqi, and Doreen Hinchcliffe. 1996. *Islamic Marriage and Divorce Laws of the Arab World.* London: Kluwer Law International.

Ellison, John, and Chris Bartkowski. 1995. "Children Were Being Beaten." In *Armageddon in Waco,* edited by Stuart Wright. Chicago: University of Chicago Press, 120–121.

Evans-Pritchard, E. E. 1940. *The Nuer.* Oxford: Clarendon Press.

Fahrenthold, David. 2008. "An Unusual Prosecution of a Way of Life." *Washington Post,* April 27.

Fanon, Frantz. 2008. *Black Skin, White Masks.* New York: Grove Press.

Firmage, Ed. 2006. "Polygamy, Monogamy and Monotheism: The One and the Many." Entry on the blog *One Utah, Pending Approval,* May 26. Available at http://oneutah.org/utah-politics/pox-letter-iii/.

First Presidency (LDS). 1990a. "Is Your Church Membership in Danger?" In author's possession.

———. 1990b. "Profile of Splinter Group Members or Others with Troublesome Ideologies." In author's possession.

4TheFamily.us. 2008. Interview with Anne Wilde, Principle Voices Founder and Plural Wife. Available at http://www.4thefamily.us/Anne_Wilde_Interview.

Fox, Robin. 1993. *Reproduction and Succession.* New Brunswick, NJ: Transaction Publishers.

Fratini, Mary Elizabeth. 2004. "Professor and Students Study Polygyny in Africa." *Vermont Woman,* September. Available at www.vermontwomen/articles/0904/polygyny.

Frazier, Deborah. 2005. "Woman Shares Polygamy Tale." *Rocky Mountain News,* November 30.

Fremd, Mike. 2006. "Key Witness Testifies in Polygamist Warren Jeffs Hearing." *ABC News,* November 21.

Friedl, Erika. 1989. *The Women of Deh Koh: Lives in an Iranian Village.* Washington, DC: Smithsonian Institution.

Gage-Brandon, Anastasia J. 1992. "The Polygyny-Divorce Relationship: A Case Study of Nigeria." *Journal of Marriage and the Family* 54 (2): 282–292.

Garza, Jennifer. 2007. "Living in Polygamy." *Sacramento Bee,* October 7.

Gay, Judith. 1986. "Mummies and Babies." In *The Many Faces of Homosexuality: Anthropology Approaches to Homosexual Behavior,* edited by Evelyn Blackwood. New York: Harrington Park Press, 97–116.

Gluckman, Max. 1955. *Custom and Conflict in Africa.* New York: Free Press.

Goodwyn, Wade, Howard Berkes, and Amy Walters. 2005. "Warren Jeffs and the FLDS." *NPR,* May 3.

Gordon, Sarah. 2001. *The Mormon Question: Polygamy and Constitutional Conflict in Nineteenth Century America.* Chapel Hill: University of North Carolina Press.

Gray, Christen. 2001. "Got One Wife? Have Another." *The Tech,* May 17. Available at http://tech.mit.edu/V121/N37/col37gray.37c.html.

Grossman, Joanna, and L. Friedman. 2010. "'Sister Wives': Will Reality Show

Stars Face Prosecution for Polygamy in Utah?" *FindLaw,* October 4. Available at http://writ.news.findlaw.com/grossman/20101004.html.

Guttmacher Institute. 2006. "U.S. Teenage Pregnancy Statistics." www.guttmacher .org/pubs/2006/09/12, accessed November 2007.

Hage, Per, and Frank Harary. 1991. *Exchange in Oceania: A Graph Theoretic Analysis.* Oxford: Clarendon Press.

Hales, Brian. 2006. *Modern Polygamy and Mormon Fundamentalism: The Generations After the Manifesto.* Salt Lake City: Greg Kofford Books.

———. 2008a. "The Apostolic United Brethren." Available at http://www .mormonfundamentalism.com/ChartLinks/AUB.htm.

———. 2008b. "Owen Allred." Available at http://www.mormonfundamentalism .com/ChartLinks/OwenAllred.htm.

Hall, Katy. 2010. "'Sister Wives': TLC's Polygamist Family Asks Us to 'Rethink Marriage.'" *Huffington Post,* September 23. Available at http://www.huffington post.com/katy-hall/sister-wives-tlcs-polygam_b_736551.html.

Hancock, Kaziah. 1987. *Prisons of the Mind.* Salt Lake City: Deseret Blossom Publishing.

Hanks, Maxine. 1992. *Women and Authority: Re-emerging Mormon Feminism.* Salt Lake City: Signature Books.

Harmon, Dave. 1997. "Celibacy." *Liberated Christians* website. Available at http:// www.libchrist.com/bible/celibacy.html.

Hassouneh-Phillips, Dena. 2001. "Polygamy and Wife Abuse: A Qualitative Study of Muslim Women in America." *Health Care for Women International* 22(8):735–748.

Hayyat, Eman. 2011. "Cousin Marriages of the Middle East." Student presentation, Lyndon State College, Spring.

Heaton, Tim, K. L. Goodman, and T. B. Holman. 1994. "In Search of a Peculiar People: Are Mormon Families Really Different?" In *Contemporary Mormonism: Social Science Perspectives,* edited by M. Cornwall, Tim Heaton, and Lawrence Young. 87–117. Urbana: University of Illinois Press.

Heaton, Tim, and Cardell Jacobson. 2011. "Demographic, Social, and Economic Characteristics of a Polygamist Community." In *Modern Polygamy in the United States: Historical, Cultural, and Legal Issues,* edited by Cardell Jacobson. New York: Oxford University Press, 151–162.

Hendrix, Lewellyn, and Willie Pearson. 1995. "Spousal Interdependence, Female Power, and Divorce: A Cross Cultural Examination." *Journal of Comparative Family Studies,* 26:217–232.

Henkel, Mark. 2011. TruthBearer.org, accessed May 2011.

Hinckley, Gordon B. 1995. "The Family: A Proclamation to the World." A message to the General Relief Society in Salt Lake City, Utah. Available at http://lds.org/library/display/0,4945,161-1-11-1,00.html.

House, Dawn. 1998. "Prosecuting Polygamy Is No Easy Matter." *Salt Lake Tribune,* June 28. Available at http://www.geocities.ws/heartland/meadows/1247/pol-2.htm.

Hubbard, Ruth. 1990. *The Politics of Women's Biology.* New Brunswick, NJ: Rutgers University Press.

Hummel, Debbie. 2003. "Woman Sues Polygamist Clan for Abuse, Seeks $110 Million." *Associated Press,* August 28.

Hunt, Dave, and Ed Decker. 1980. *The God Makers.* Videocassette. Produced by R. J. M. Productions. Jeremiah Films, Inc.

Jankowiak, William. 2008. Interview with the author, August.

Jankowiak, William, and E. Allen. 1995. "The Balance of Duty and Desire in an American Polygamous Community." In William Jankowiak, *Romantic Passion: A Universal Experience?* New York: Columbia University Press, 166–186.

Jankowiak, William, and Monique Diderich. 2000. "Sibling Solidarity in a Polygamous Community in the USA." *Evolution & Human Behavior* 21(2):125–139.

Janofsky, Michael. 2003. "Young Brides Stir New Outcry on Utah Polygamy." *New York Times,* February 27.

Jessop, Carolyn, and Laura Palmer. 2007. *Escape.* New York: Broadway Books.

Jessop, Flora. 2009. *Church of Lies.* San Francisco: Jossey-Bass.

Johns, Becky. 1996. "The Manti Mormons: The Rise of the Latest Mormon Church." *Sunstone,* June, 30–36.

Joseph, Elizabeth. 1997. "Polygamy—the Ultimate Feminist Lifestyle." *Islam for Today,* May. Available at www.islamfortoday.com/polygamy3, accessed March 2007.

Josephson, Steven. 2002. "Does Polygyny Reduce Fertility?" *American Journal of Human Biology* 14(2):222–232.

Judd, Daniel K. 1999. *Religion, Mental Health and the Latter-day Saints.* Provo, UT: Brigham Young University.

Kanazawa, S., and M. Still. 1999. "Why Monogamy?" *Social Forces* 78(1):25–50.

Kaye, Randi. 2008. "Pentagon Paid $1.7 Million to Firms of Polygamy Bosses." CNN, April 17.

Keller, James. 2006. "Canada Should Legalize Polygamy: Study." *CTV News,* January 13.

———. 2011. "Teen Pregnancies Not Due to Polygamy: Lawyer." *CBC News,* February 9.

Kenworthy, Tom. 1998. "Spotlight on Utah Polygamy; Teenager's Escape from Sect Revives Scrutiny of Practice." *Washington Post,* August 9.

Kilbride, Phil. 1994. *Plural Marriage for Our Times: A Reinvented Option?* Westport, CT: Bergin and Garvey.

———. 1996. "African Polygyny: Family Values and Contemporary Changes." In *Applying Cultural Anthropology: An Introductory Reader,* edited by Aaron Podolefsky and Peter J. Brown. 6th ed. Boston: McGraw-Hill, 201–208.

Kimmel Michael. 2008. *The Gendered Society.* New York: Oxford University Press.

Kingston, Elden. 1947. "Perfecting Meditations." Mimeographed sheet in author's possession.

Kinsey, Alfred C., Wardell Baxter Pomeroy, and Clyde E. Martin. [1948] 1998. *Sexual Behavior in the Human Male.* Philadelphia: W. B. Saunders; reprint, Bloomington: Indiana University Press.

Kitahara, Michio. 1976. "Polygamy: Insufficient Father-Son Contact and Son's Masculine Identity." *Archives of Sexual Behavior* 5(3): 201–209.

Kocherga, Angela. 2005. "American Polygamist Living across the Border." *San Antonio Press,* February 22.

Krakauer, Jon. 2004. *Under the Banner of Heaven.* New York: Random House.

———. 2006. *Banking on Heaven: Polygamy in the Heartland of the American West.* DVD. Over the Moon Productions.

Kraut, Ogden. 1983. *Polygamy in the Bible.* Salt Lake City: Pioneer Press.

———. 1989. *The Fundamentalist Mormon.* Salt Lake City: Pioneer Press.

Krauthammer, Charles. 2006. "As Gay Marriage Gains Acceptance, Polygamy Meets Resistance." Editorial, *Seattle Times,* March 20, 1.

Kurtz, Stanley. 2006. "*Big Love* from the Set." *National Review Online,* March 13. Available at http://www.nationalreview.com/kurtz/kurtz200603130805.asp.

Laytner, Ron. 2008. "Polygamy Town USA." *Edit International.* Available at http://editinternational.com/read.php?id=48220e16294c6.

LeBaron, Ervil. 1955. *Priesthood Expounded,* 2:42, a pamphlet published by the Church of the Firstborn of the Fulness of Times.

LeBaron, Verlan. 1981. *The LeBaron Story.* El Paso: Keels and Co.

Lee, Felicia. 2006. "*Big Love*: Real Polygamists Look at HBO Polygamists and Find Sex." *New York Times,* March 28.

Leis, Nancy. 1974. "Women in Groups." In *Woman, Culture, and Society,* edited by Michele Rosaldo and Louise Lamphere. Stanford, CA: Stanford University Press, 232–254.

Leong, Melissa. 2006. "Legalize Polygamy: Study. Ottawa Paid for Report That Says Charter Might Negate Criminal Ban." *National Post,* January 13. Available at http://www.canada.com/nationalpost/story.html?id=8451dc17-5b5f-4ea4-a05f-71f7c758662a&k=52900.

LeVay S. 1991. "A Difference in Hypothalamic Structure between Heterosexual and Homosexual Men." *Science* 253(5023):1034–1037.

"Lisa, Martin, and Karen." 2010. Blog profile located on *polygamylovescompany. org*, January 23, 2010 and *pilegesh.blogspot.com*, November 15, 2011.

Llewellyn, John. 2000. "State Is Afraid to Go after Polygamy's Kingpins." *Salt Lake Tribune*, June 4.

———. 2004. *Polygamy under Attack*. Salt Lake City: Agreka Books.

———. 2006. *Polygamy's Rape of Rachael Strong*. Salt Lake City: Agreka Press.

———. 2010. "What John Learned about Polygamists." Available at http://agreka .com/John_Llewellyn_Utah_Polygamy_Expert.

Logue, Larry. 1985. "Tabernacles for Waiting Spirits: Monogamous and Polygamous Fertility in a Mormon Town." *Journal of Family History* 10(1):60–74.

Macintosh, George K., Ludmila B. Herbst, and Tom Dickson. 2009. "Opening Statement of the Amicus Addressing Breach." No. 2-097767, Vancouver Registry, November 1. Available at http://www.vancouversun.com/pdf/ amicus_opening%20.pdf.

Madhavan, S. 2002. "Best of Friends and Worst of Enemies: Competition and Collaboration in Polygyny." *Ethnology* 41(1): 69–84.

Majeed, Debra. 2010. "The Ethics of Sisterhood: African American Muslim Women and Polygyny." Paper presented at the conference "Polygamy, Polygyny, and Polyamory," Brandeis University, Waltham, Massachusetts, November 7.

Maillu, D. 1988. *Our Kind of Polygamy*. Nairobi: Beacon Press.

Malaysian Insider. 2009. "More Wives = Less Adultery and Prostitution?" *Malaysian Insider* November 19. Available at http://www.themalaysianinsider.com/ litee/malaysia/article/More-wives-less-adultery-and-prostitution/.

Martin, Wednesday. 2009. "Co-Wife Conflict: Why It's Easy to Hate the 'Other Woman.'" *Psychology Today*, December 1.

McConkie, Bruce R. 1961. *How to Start a Cult or Cultism as Practiced by the So-Called Church of the Firstborn*. Salt Lake City, self-published.

———. 1991. *Mormon Doctrine*. Salt Lake City: Bookcraft. [Encyclopedic work originally written in 1958; not an official publication of the LDS Church.]

McDonough, Ted. 2004. "Lost Boys Found." *Salt Lake City Weekly*, September 23.

Mencken, H. L. 1918. *In Defense of Women*. Chicago: Philip Goodman, 1922.

Melloy, Kilian. 2008. "Sex Abuse Suit Filed against Mormons, Scouts." *Edge* (San Francisco), February 25. Available at http://www.edgesanfrancisco.com/ index.php?ch=news&sc=glbt&sc2=news&sc3=&id=70753.

Merton, Robert. 1968. *Social Theory and Social Structure*. New York: Free Press.

Mikels, Ted. 1976. *Alex Joseph and His Wives.* DVD. Directed by Ted V. Mikels. Distributed by Ted V. Mikels.

Montana's News Station. 2008. "Pinesdale Resident Disturbed by Recent Events in Texas." *Montana's News Station,* April 22.

MS. 1847. *The Latter-day Saints' Millennial Star.* December 15 issue, 9:23.

Money, John, and Anke Ehrhardt. 1996. *Man & Woman, Boy & Girl: Gender Identity from Conception to Maturity.* Northvale, NJ: Jason Aronson. Originally published Baltimore: Johns Hopkins University Press, 1972.

Moore-Emmett,. Andrea. 2004. *God's Brothel: The Extortion of Sex for Salvation in Contemporary Mormon and Christian Fundamentalist Polygamy.* San Francisco, CA: Pince-nez Press.

Murdock, George Peter. 1967. "Ethnographic Atlas." *Ethnology* 6:109–236.

Murray, Jennifer. 2011. "Bonnie Says: Sisterwives' Kody Brown Is a Fame Whore! He Loved Going Public on Show Premiere!" HollywoodLife.com, March 14.

Musisi, Nakanike. 1991. "Women, Elite Polygyny, and Buganda State Formation." *Signs* 16(41):757–777.

Musser, Joseph. 1944. *Celestial or Plural Marriage.* Salt Lake City: Truth Publishing Company.

———. 1948. *The Inalienable Rights of Women.* Salt Lake City: Truth Publishing Company.

Musser, Joseph, and L. Broadbent. 1934. *Supplement to the New and Everlasting Covenant of Marriage.* Pamphlet. Salt Lake City: Truth Publishing Company.

Myerhoff, Barbara. 1978. *Number Our Days.* New York: Simon and Schuster.

Myers, Wade, and Steve Brasington. 2002. "A Father Marries His Daughters: A Case of Incestuous Polygamy." *Journal of Forensic Science* 47(5):1112–1116.

Nadel, S. F. 1952. *Witchcraft in Four African Societies.* London: Penguin Books.

Nakamura, David. "Obama Backs Bill to Repeal Defense of Marriage Act." *Washington Post,* July 19.

National Coalition for Child Protection Reform. 2008. *In Search of Middle Ground: Toward Better Solutions to the Texas Child Welfare Crisis.* Alexandria, Va.: National Coalition for Child Protection Reform. Available at http://www.nccpr.org/reports/texasreport2.pdf.

Netting, Robert. 1969. "Women's Weapons: The Politics of Domesticity among the Kofyar." *American Anthropology* 71:1037–1046.

Newell, L., and V. Avery. 1994. *Mormon Enigma: Emma Hale Smith.* Urbana: University of Illinois Press.

Oaks, Dallin H. 1995. "Same-Gender Attraction." *Ensign* (October): 7–14.

O'Dea, Thomas. 1957. *The Mormons.* Chicago: University of Chicago Press.

Ozorak, E. W. 1996. "The Power But Not the Glory: How Women Empower

Themselves through Religion." *Journal for the Scientific Study of Religion* 35(1):17–29.

Parker, Seymour. 1976. "The Precultural Basis of the Incest Taboo: Toward a Biosocial Theory." *American Anthropologist* 78 (2):285–305.

Perkins, Nancy 2003. "Plural Wives Defend Lifestyle." *Deseret News,* August 23.

Phillips, Harry, and Joseph Diaz. 2007. "Polygamists Practice Big Love in Arizona." *ABC News,* Augist 14.

Polygamy.com. 2009a. "Men Are Designed to Chase Skirts." December 6. Available at http://www.polygamy.com/index.php/commentary/men-are-designed -to-chase-skirts/.

Polygamy.com. 2009b. "Straight Woman in a Polygamous Marriage." December 26. Available at http://www.polygamy.com/index.php/commentary/the-straight -woman-in-a-polygamous-marriage/.

Pomfret, John. 2006. "Polygamists Fight to Be Seen as Part of Mainstream Society." *Washington Post,* November 21, A1.

Ponder, Kent. 2003. "Mormon Women, Prozac and Therapy." Available at http://packham.n4m.org/prozac.htm.

Posner, Richard. 1992. *Sex and Reason.* Cambridge, MA: Harvard University Press.

Pratt, Parley P. 1854. "Rules of Conduct." *The Seer.* London: Franklin D. Richards Press.

Preston, Cheryl. 2004. "Women in Traditional Religions: Refusing to Let Patriarchy Separate Us From the Source of Our Liberation." Paper presented at the conference "Perspectives: LDS Women in the Twentieth Century," Joseph Fielding Smith Institute for Church History, Provo, Utah, March 20.

Progressive Family Values Conference. 2007. Conference held at Yale, April 21. See description at http://www.feministe.us./blog/archieves/2007.

Pro-Polygamy.com. 2005. "Polygamy Poll Results Caused by Moral Relativism and Media Bias." May 17. Available at http://www.pro-polygamy.com/articles .php?news=0032.

Quinn, D. Michael. 1992. "Mormon Women Have Had the Priesthood since 1843." In *Women and Authority: Re-Emerging Mormon Feminism,* edited by Maxine Hanks. Salt Lake City: Signature Books, 23–48.

———. 1993. "Plural Marriage and Mormon Fundamentalism." In *Fundamentalisms and Society,* edited by Martin Marty and R. Scott Appleby. Chicago: University of Chicago Press, 240–266.

———. 1996. *Same-Sex Dynamics among 19th-Century Americans: A Mormon Example.* Chicago: University of Illinois Press.

Radke, Andrea. 2004. "The Place of Mormon Women: Perceptions, Prozac, Polygamy, Priesthood, Patriarchy, and Peace." *FAIR: Defending Mormonism.* Available at http://www.fairlds.org/FAIR_Conferences/2004_Place_of_Mormon _Women.html.

Rappaport, Roy A. 1971 "Nature, Culture, and Ecological Anthropology." In *Man, Culture and Society,* 2nd edition, edited by H. L. Shapiro. Oxford: Oxford University Press, 237–267.

Renteln, Alison D. 2004. *The Cultural Defense.* New York: Oxford University Press.

Reuters. 2007. "Polygamy Is No Joke, Man Discovers." Reuters, April 10. Available at http://uk.reuters.com/article/2007/04/11/oukoe-uk-saudi-idUKL1029458820 070411.

Richards, Stephen. 1932. Sermon delivered at April 1932 LDS general conference, also quoted in the *Salt Lake Tribune,* April 10, 1932.

Ritzer, George. 2007. *Sociological Theory.* New York: McGraw-Hill Higher Education, 251–257.

Roberts, Michelle. 2008. "DNA Samples Taken from Polygamist Children in Texas." *Burlington Free Press,* April 22, 3A.

———. 2009. "Jessop Convicted of Sexual Assault." *Deseret News,* November 5.

Rower, Alyssa. 2004. "The Legality of Polygamy: Using the Due Process Clause of the Fourteenth Amendment." *Family Law Quarterly* 38(3):711–728.

Saitoti, Tepilit. 1988. *The Worlds of a Maasai Warrior.* Berkeley: University of California Press.

Salt Lake City Tribune. 2008. "FLDS Women Speak." Available at www.youtube .com/watch?v=cDDXY5KHMqA.

Sanday, Peggy. 1982. *Female Power and Male Dominance.* Cambridge: Cambridge University Press.

Scharnberg, K., and Manya A. Brachear. 2006. "Polygamy (Utah's Open Little Secret)." *Chicago Tribune,* September 24.

Scheper-Hughes, Nancy. 2000. "Ire in Ireland." *Ethnography* 1(1): 117–140.

Schmidt, Susan Ray. 2006. *His Favorite Wife: Trapped in Polygamy.* Twin Falls, ID: Kassidy Lane. [Memoirs of Verlon LeBaron's wife, Irene Spencer.]

Scott, Anne Firor. 1986. "Mormon Women, Other Women: Pardoxes and Challenges." *Journal of Mormon History* 13(1): 3–20.

Shepherd, G., and G. Shepherd. 2011. "Learning the Wrong Lessons." In *Modern Polygamy in the United States: Historical, Cultural, and Legal Issues,* edited by Cardell Jacobson. New York: Oxford University Press, 237–258.

Singh, R. D., and M. J. Morey. 1987. "The Value of Work-at-Home and Contributions of Wives' Household Service in Polygynous Families." *Economic Development and Cultural Change* 35(4):743–765.

Singular, Stephen. 2008. *When Men Become Gods: Mormon Polygamist Warren Jeffs, His Cult of Fear, and the Women Who Fought Back.* New York: St. Martin's Press.

Sloan, Carrie. 2011. "Sister Wives TLC True Story—'I Married My Younger Sister's Husband.'" *MyDaily.com,* October 18.

Slocom, Sally. 1975. "Woman the Gatherer: Male Bias in Anthropology." In *Toward an Anthropology of Women,* edited by Rayna R. Reiter. New York: Monthly Review Press, 36–50.

Smith, Dorothy. 1992. "Sociology from Women's Experience: A Reaffirmation." *Sociological Theory* 10(1):88–98.

Smith, George Albert. 1856. "George Albert Smith, April 6, 1856." In *Journal of Discourses* 3:291. Liverpool: LDS Church.

Smith, Jordan. 2005. "Quotations of the Prophet Warren Jeffs." *The Austin Chronicle,* July 29, accessible at http://austinchronicle.com/news/2005-07-29/281917/.

Smith, Joseph. 1831. *The Joseph Smith Revelations Text and Commentary.* www.utlm.org/onlineresources/indianpolygamyrevelation.

Smith, Joseph Fielding. [1838] 2006. *Teachings of the Prophet Joseph Smith.* Compiled and edited by Joseph Fielding Smith. Salt Lake City: Deseret Books.

Smith, Linda. 2011. "Child Protection Law and the FLDS Raid in Texas." In *Modern Polygamy in the United States: Historical, Cultural, and Legal Issues,* edited by Cardell Jacobson. New York: Oxford University Press, 301–330.

Soloman, Dorothy Allred. 2004. *Daughter of the Saints: Growing up in Polygamy.* New York: W. W. Norton.

Song, Sarah. 2007. *Justice, Gender and the Politics of Multiculturalism.* Cambridge: Cambridge University Press.

———. 2010. "Should the US Decriminalize Polygamy? Considerations from the Mormon Case." Paper presented at the conference "Polygamy, Polygyny, and Polyamory," Brandeis University, Waltham, Massachusetts, November 7.

Soukup, Elise. 2008. "Into the Future: Mormons Prepare to Name a New Prophet, and Confront the Challenges Ahead." *Newsweek,* January 7.

Spangler, Jerry. 1988. "Judge Bars Adoption Attempt by Polygamists." *Deseret News,* December 6. Available at http://www.deseretnews.com/article/25971/judge-bars-adoption-attempt-by-polygamists.html.

Spencer, Orson. 1847. *Letters of Orson Spencer* in reply to the Rev. William Crowel, Liverpool, Nov. 30, located at archives of Brigham Young University.

Stacey, Judith, and Tey Meadow. 2009. *Politics & Society.* Sage Publications.

Stack, Carol. 1974. *All Our Kin: Strategies for Survival in a Black Community.* Harper and Row.

Starr, Michael. 2011. "'Sister Wives' File Lawsuit for Right to Polygamy." *New York Post,* July 12. Available at http://www.nypost.com/.

"Steady." 2010. "Once upon a Time." *Sisterwives* website, December 21. Available at http://sisterwives.yuku.com/topic/3542/Once-Upon-a-Time#.TpN8IN7iGU8.

Strange, Hannah. 2008. "400 Children Seized from Polygamy Sect in Texas after Claims of Abuse." *Sunday Times,* April 8. Available at www.timesonline.co.uk/tol/news/world/us_and_americas/article3706191.ece.

Strassberg, Maura. 2010. "Why the U.S. Should Not Decriminalize Polygamy, but Should Not Criminalize Polyamory." Paper presented at the conference "Polygamy, Polygyny, and Polyamory," Brandeis University, Waltham, Massachusetts, November 7.

Stumbo, Bella. 1988. "No Tidy Stereotype; Polygamists: Tale of Two Families." *L.A. Times,* May 13, Part 1, p. 1.

Telegraph. 2011. "Polygamist under Police Investigation after Appearing on Reality TV Show." *Telegraph,* October 11.

Texas Attorney General. 2008. Press release, Monday, July 28, from office of Attorney General Greg Abbott, oag.state.tx.us.

Thornhill, Randy, and Craig Palmer. 2000. *A Natural History of Rape.* Cambridge, MA: MIT Press.

Thornton, Arland. 2011. "The International Fight against Barbarism." In *Modern Polygamy in the United States: Historical, Cultural, and Legal Issues,* edited by Cardell Jacobson. New York: Oxford University Press, 259–300.

Tierney, John. 2006. "Who's Afraid of Polygamy?" *New York Times,* March 11.

Tiger, Lionel. 1969. *Men in Groups.* New York: Transaction Publishers.

———. 2001. "Rogue Males." *The Guardian,* October 2.

Tracy, Kathleen. 2001. *The Secret Story of Polygamy.* Naperville, IL: Sourcebooks.

20/20. 1997. "Man and Wives: A Look at Polygamous Marriages in the U.S." Episode of 20/20, ABC, aired October 17.

Turley, Jonathan. 2004. "Polygamy Laws Expose Our Hypocrisy." *USA Today,* October 4.

UNICEF. 2001. "A League Table of Teenage Births in Rich Nations," retrieved July 7, 2006.

Unitarian Universalists for Polyamory Awareness (UUPA). 2011. http://www.uupa.org.

U.S. Census. 2010. "Families and Living Arrangements," *U.S. Census Bureau,* at http://www.census.gov/population.

Utah Census. 2000. "Census Report." *American Association for Single People,* accessible at hhtp://www.unmarriedamerica.org/CensusHouseholds/States/Utpress.html.

Utah Code, 2003. Ann. 76-7-101(1).

UUPA. 2011. Unitarian Universalists for Polyamory Awareness' website, www.uupa.org/polyprinciples, p. 1.

Van Wagoner, Richard. 1986. *Mormon Polygamy: A History.* Salt Lake City: Signature Books.

Wagner, Dennis. 2008. "Family Defends Polygamy, Calls It a Culture of Love." *Arizona Republic,* June 1.

Wall, Elissa, and Lisa Pulitzer. 2008. *Stolen Innocence: My Story of Growing Up in a Polygamous Sect, Becoming a Teenage Bride, and Breaking Free of Warren Jeffs.* New York: William Morrow.

Walsh, Rebecca. 2008. "Feminists Waffle in FLDS Case." *Salt Lake Tribune,* May 25.

Weber, Max. 1949. *The Methodology of the Social Sciences.* Wilmington, IL: Free Press.

———. 1958. *Essays in Sociology.* New York: Oxford University Press.

Weinriter, Kelsey. 1994. "John Singer." In *Utah History Encyclopedia,* edited by Allan Kent Powell. Salt Lake City: University of Utah Press.

West, Brian. 2008. "Former FLDS Member Is Sharing Her Insights on the Sect." *Deseret News,* April 28.

Western, Carole. 2007. *The Power of Polygamy.* Hiram, GA: Wyndham House.

Weston, Kathy. 1997. *Families We Choose.* New York: Columbia University Press.

Whedon, Sarah. 2010. "Media Representations of Polygamous Fundamentalist Mormon Women." Paper presented at the conference "Polygamy, Polygyny, and Polyamory," Brandeis University, Waltham, Massachusetts, November 7.

White, Douglas R., and M. L. Burton. 1988. "Causes of Polygamy: Ecology, Economy, Kinship, and Warfare." *American Anthropologist* 90(4):871–887.

Widstoe, John. 1939. *Improvement Era,* March, 161. [Religious inhouse magazine published by LDS Church.]

Wilde, Anne, et al. 2010. *Principle Voices,* a pro-polygamy organization; census, 2010, accessible at http://principlevoices.org.

Williams, Florence. 1997. "A House, 10 Wives: Polygamy in Suburbia." *New York Times,* July 6.

Winslow, Ben. 2008. "Polygamy Prosecutions Spark Lively Debate at University of Utah." *Deseret News,* October 23.

Witte, John. 2004. *Religion and the American Constitutional Experiment: Essential Rights and Liberties.* Boulder, CO: Westview Press, also quoted on page 1 of http://www.zenit.org/article-17436?l=enlish.

Wolfson, Hannah. 1999. "Polygamy without Book of Mormon." *Phoenix Republic,* July 19.

Wynne-Jones, Jonathan. 2008. "Multiple Wives Will Mean Multiple Benefits." London *Telegraph,* February 3.

Young, Brigham. 1852. First sermon typed by George Watt on April 9, later published in 1854 in *Journal of Discourses* 4:51. Liverpool: LDS Church.

————. 1856. *Journal of Discourses* 4:53–54. Liverpool: LDS Church.

————. 1864. *Journal of Discourses* 10:329, June. Liverpool: LDS Church.

————. 1867a. *Journal of Discourses* 11:326, February. Liverpool: LDS Church.

————. 1867b. *Journal of Discourses* 12:103, November. Liverpool: LDS Church.

————. 1869. *Journal of Discourses* 13:61 and 197. Liverpool: LDS Church.

Young, Kimball. 1954. "Sex Roles in Polygamous Mormon Families." In *Readings in Psychology,* edited by Theodore Newcomb and Eugene Hartley. New York: Holt, 373–393.

Zeitzen, Miriam K. *Polygamy: A Cross-Cultural Analysis.* Oxford: Berg Publishers.

Zoll, Rachel. 2002. "Clergy Abuse Cases Seen Wider in Scope." *Boston Globe,* February 11.

Index